FIGHTING WORDS AND IMAGES

Fighting Words and Images

Representing War across the Disciplines

EDITED BY ELENA V. BARABAN,
STEPHAN JAEGER, AND ADAM MULLER

UNIVERSITY OF TORONTO PRESS
Toronto Buffalo London

ISBN 978-1-4426-4123-5 (cloth)

Printed on acid-free, 100% post-consumer recycled paper with
vegetable-based inks.

Library and Archives Canada Cataloguing in Publication

Fighting words and images : representing war across the disciplines /
edited by Elena V. Baraban, Stephan Jaeger, and Adam Muller.

Includes bibliographical references and index.
ISBN 978-1-4426-4123-5

1. War and society. 2. War in mass media. 3. War in literature.
I. Baraban, Elena V. (Elena Viktorovna), 1969– II. Jaeger, Stephan, 1970–
III. Muller, Adam, 1968–

HM554.F53 2012   303.6'6   C2011-908165-2

University of Toronto Press acknowledges the financial assistance to its
publishing program of the Canada Council for the Arts and the Ontario
Arts Council.

 Canada Council   Conseil des Arts   ONTARIO ARTS COUNCIL
for the Arts   du Canada   CONSEIL DES ARTS DE L'ONTARIO

University of Toronto Press acknowledges the financial support of the
Government of Canada through the Canada Book Fund for its publishing
activities.

Contents

Illustrations

Acknowledgments

We gratefully acknowledge the support of the many individuals and groups who assisted us in bringing this project to fruition. This publication was made possible through the financial support of the Social Sciences and Humanities Research Council of Canada, the Dean of the Faculty of Arts, the Department of English, Film and Theatre, the Department of German and Slavic Studies, the Centre for Defence and Security Studies, and the Arts Endowment Fund at the University of Manitoba.

Our project originated in the activities of the University of Manitoba Institute for the Humanities (UMIH) research cluster 'Representations of War' (2006–8). We particularly wish to thank Jila Ghomeshi, the UMIH's Director during this period, as well as the Institute's administrative assistant, Natalie Johnson, for their help with organizing the many engaging discussion sessions that served as the foundation for the present volume. Thanks are also due to the research cluster's members: James Chlup, Monique Dumontet, Emily Muller, Rob Shaver, Myroslav Shkandrij, Michael Stack, Lasha Tchantouridzé, and Andrew Woolford.

We are also grateful to Richard Ratzlaff, our editor at the University of Toronto Press, and to the press's two external readers, whose constructive criticisms of our work motivated responses that made this collection stronger. Many individuals commented upon portions of earlier drafts of this project, and we would like to express our appreciation of very helpful suggestions and comments by Lisa Alexandrin, Alyson Brickey, Heather Dreger-Allen, Cheryl Dueck, John-Paul Himka, Emily Muller, Struan Sinclair, Myroslav Shkandrij, Rodney Symington, George Toles, and Andrew Woolford. Our special thanks go to Sergei Oushakine, who suggested the present title for the volume.

Above all, we wish to thank our contributors for their hard work, patience, and continuing belief in the merits of this collection. It has been a pleasure, as well as a privilege, to work alongside them.

FIGHTING WORDS AND IMAGES

Introduction: Representing War across the Disciplines

ELENA V. BARABAN, STEPHAN JAEGER, AND
ADAM MULLER

The Vicissitudes of War

Julius van der Merwe fraudulently enlisted with the South African Air
Force (SAAF) at the age of fourteen. From July 1942 until the end of
the Second World War, he operated the tail guns of a B-26 Marauder.[1]
Part of the Desert Air Force and later the Balkan Air Force, both under
British command, the SAAF and van der Merwe along with it fought
in North Africa, Italy, and Yugoslavia. Upon cessation of hostilities, van
der Merwe stayed in northern Italy in order to assist with troop demobilization, the grunt work of getting tens of thousands of men and their
equipment returned to the various parts of the world from whence
they came. As part of this work he travelled to southern Austria to help
clean up one of the subcamps of the Nazi concentration camp in Mau-
thausen, some time since cleared of the living and the dead but still
bearing traces of past horrors in the form of soiled clothing and bloodstained meat hooks. In 1945, at the age of seventeen, van der Merwe
returned to South Africa to complete an education, start a family, and
get on with his life.

Over the course of his post-bellum existence van der Merwe spoke
about the war many times. When his children were young he regaled
them with stories of the possibilities war presented to young men for
prolonging their childhood and for having fun, such as the madcap
scheme to use wild desert camels for target practice or the adventure
of getting lost on leave in Cairo's crowded Khan el-Khalili market. As
his children grew older van der Merwe's stories became more socially
complex. Cairo's streets were revealed to be lined with noisy nightclubs
and darkly alluring women; Tripoli was presented teeming with dis-

solute English officers and indigenous petty criminals. Van der Merwe also began airing grievances against the much better-equipped American troops he fought alongside, whose arrogance and later claims to have 'won the war' by themselves did little to endear them to their former allies. All the while, though, van der Merwe stressed his sense of the justness of his struggle, the bravery of his companions, and the positive significance of his own contributions to the Allied success.

As time passed the tenor of van der Merwe's narratives became darker and more pessimistic. Recollections of the destruction the Allied forces brought to the places they also liberated intruded into the sense of just purposefulness he had prized in the stories of his middle age. He now conceived of war as a perversion of natural human impulses, a monstrosity accompanied by pain and suffering. Only now did van der Merwe speak of what had happened to the Italian village washerwomen with whom he and his friends used to flirt. One day he returned to a village that had recently been occupied by his squadron to pick up his forgotten gear and saw his former clothes cleaners being held down on stools, their heads in the process of being shaved – the standard European folk-punishment for collaboration. In aiding the Allies they were perceived by their fellow villagers as betraying Mussolini's Italy. Tearfully recalling the morbid spectacle of the glistening scalps arrayed before his adolescent eyes, van der Merwe experienced guilt at his realization that he was viewed as an enemy by the very people he thought he was liberating.

Van der Merwe's story highlights several aspects of the representation of war. It suggests the ways in which, as time passes, our measure of war changes and different aspects of martial conduct assume greater and lesser personal, social, political, and moral salience. It also suggests that memory remains a shifting and sometimes unstable foundation of war consciousness and its associated representations.[2] Indeed, the fact that van der Merwe recalled different parts of his own war story at different times of his life reveals how sensitive war narratives are to audience concerns. His war stories altered over time in response to the way he measured his children's competence as morally attuned listeners: as adults they were simply better equipped to understand the nature of the atrocities he described. Aside from these rather private concerns, however, the evolution of van der Merwe's recollections also reveals the influence of prevailing cultural discourses of warfare on personal storytelling. Against the changing backdrop of the vision of war expressed in North American news media, cinema, literature, and painting from the late 1960s to the present day,[3] van der Merwe's sense of the meaning of his own experiences evolved to a point at which he came to understand himself as both a victim of circumstance and the reluctant victimizer of others – a far cry from headier days and nobler self-characterizations. Over time he began to view war as humankind's pre-eminent *force majeure*, a political instrument of last resort and something to be feared.

The example of van der Merwe shows how fundamentally fluid are our ways of making sense of war. It underscores the deep contingency of war representations, their vulnerability to subsequent modification – enlargement, reduction, or reformulation – in response to changes in the storyteller's outlook as well as wider shifts in his culture's values and historical self-understanding. These alterations leave traces on all depictions of war, and to a great extent influence their later circulation and critical reception. In turn, the public response to war representations, the celebration or vilification of particular works, both speaks for and assists in mobilizing popular responses to war, thereby participating in establishing war's 'meaning' as well as the scope of its moral and political oversight. Comprehending war thus requires a nuanced understanding of war representations, their production and reception, the modes of their circulation, and, wherever relevant, the causes and effects of their canonization or more general perseverance.

War experiences encompass those of combat soldiers and non-combatants, the victors and the vanquished, the stories of those who died as well as of those who survived. The enormous variety and complexity of these experiences and perspectives ensures that the experience of no individual or group can adequately represent war in its entirety. Furthermore, the emergence of new technologies of war has given rise to novel ways of experiencing military conflict. In turn, the appearance of new representational techniques has influenced the ways in which war experience can be communicated. This predicament leads to the peculiar status of war representations in culture: constantly evolving and by nature never perfect, they evoke different or even contrasting responses from those involved in their production and reception.

The goal of this collection of essays is to enhance its readers' awareness of the multitude, variety, and interconnectedness of representations of war while at the same time articulating a set of theoretically attuned responses to the nature, origins, structure, and dynamics of those representations.[4] These are not modest objectives, for it is not always easy to approach the work of making sense of war full of critical concern for what gets lost in the struggle to translate its diverse experiences into words and images. The title of this collection – *Fighting Words and Images* – gestures towards the intensity of this struggle. If not approached critically, war representations may become viewed as 'authentic' or 'accurate.'[5] A selection of such representations eventually forms a 'habitual' war discourse as is the case, for example, with the United States' discourse of the Second World War described in Marianna Torgovnick's *The War Complex: World War II in Our Time.*[6] Consequently, failure to consider moral and political underpinnings of war representations risks leaving us unaware of the sedimentation of interests underlying war representations' propagandistic use for the purposes of preparing for, conducting, and justifying war.[7] At the same time, since words and images persistently fail their users, the phrase 'fighting words and images' also alludes to the insufficiencies and epistemological ruptures in representations charged with the task of making sense of war.

The Urgency and Challenges of Understanding War Representations

The need to understand the connection between war and its representation has been highlighted by the profusion of ideologically and thematically conflicting depictions of recent military conflicts, including the wars in Iraq and Afghanistan, the so-called War on Terror lacking clearly defined conceptual and strategic boundaries, and an increasing number of globalized yet simultaneously local wars in places such as the Democratic Republic of Congo. Even as in these and other conflicts combatants continue to make use of 'Western' military hardware and human resources, for most North Americans and Europeans the contexts in which people go to war with one another appear abstract, phenomenologically and geographically remote. Not having witnessed war directly,[8] most Westerners come to understand and respond to these recent conflicts through their representation in journalism, politics, and Internet blogs, as well as in works of art, literature, and cinema.

Adding to the sense of urgency of studying war representations is the fact that past wars have also shaped, and in their ongoing representations continue to shape, the identities of nations, communities, and individuals. Indeed, 'fighting' continues post-bellum in, for instance, disagreements between representatives of different generations or members of different cultures over competing and contradictory interpretations of wars.[9] Often the impact of these representations on communities and individuals is highly problematic. For example, the commemoration of the seventieth anniversary of the beginning of the

Second World War in Gdansk on 1 September 2009 shows how distinct interpretations of war are deeply ensconced in the collective memories of different nations where they are used to bolster sometimes radically different historical and moral truth claims.[10]

To identify just one such representational crux, for most Poles, Latvians, Estonians, and Lithuanians, the Molotov-Ribbentrop Pact between the Third Reich and the Soviet Union, signed one week before the start of the Second World War and thus perceived as its immediate cause, is an anathema: it initiated a reign of terror, mass deportations, slavery, and murder. Most Germans today also acknowledge the devastating impact of the Pact and, consequently, view the commemoration of the war's beginning as affording the chance for further reconciliation with the nation's past.[11] By contrast, Soviet historical approaches, which are today being revived by Russian historians and politicians, justified the Pact in terms of Russia's pragmatic requirements at the time, namely, the need to delay the onset of war with a better prepared Nazi Germany or to prevent the formation of an 'anti-Soviet alliance' between the West and Germany.[12] The present Russian leadership continuously points out that throughout the 1930s the West ignored Soviet appeals for an anti-Hitler coalition. Instead, a number of European states, including Poland, Britain, France, Lithuania, Estonia, and Latvia, signed non-aggression pacts with Hitler.[13] All of these serve, in the view of Russian politicians, as justification for the Soviet decision to sign the Molotov-Ribbentrop Pact.

Critical consideration of the political leaders' attempts to mobilize specific representations of this pact at moments of transnational commemoration of the beginning of the Second World War yields insight not just into the nature of the ideological investments in those representations. An examination of the nature of and a public's response to these representations' political underpinnings can significantly contribute to our knowledge of people and the imagined communities binding them together.[14] Given ongoing attempts to diminish current geopolitical instability by employing military force, and considering the significant impact of past wars upon the present of various nations, and upon the ways nations imagine themselves and their neighbours to be, it proves necessary to raise awareness of war representations' functions, the challenges they present for their producers and consumers, and the ways in which they have been approached in scholarship, politics, religion, and the arts.

The assumption that war and its representations are conceptually and pragmatically linked has inspired many academic studies (including those previously written by the contributors to this volume). However, rather than consider these representations from standpoints framed by the norms of enquiry specific to such single disciplines as History or Politics, this collection recognizes the necessity of studying war representations by scholars working at the interstices of literature, film, fine arts, anthropology, and psychology. Moreover, each chapter in this collection incorporates methods and insights derived from multiple academic formations and intellectual traditions, revealing in its own logic the explanatory power of interdisciplinary analysis.[15] No more does one individual experience of war speak for all war than does one academic discipline (or even congeries of disciplines) monopolize the tools for making sense of war representations. By choosing not to limit its analysis of war representations temporally or geographically, by including instead essays that span from Classical Antiquity to the present day and discuss a wide variety of regions and cultures, this collection emphasizes the necessity of engaging with war representations on as many different fronts as possible.

This then is our cumulative point: the analysis of war requires the analysis of its representation; its interdisciplinary analysis must increasingly include work by scholars in the humanities and social sciences, that is, the disciplines currently under-represented within war studies; and it is the role of collections such as this one to link insights gleaned from the analysis of war representations so as to suggest new directions for research. The contributors to this collection reflect on the possibilities and limitations inherent in the various media that represent war: historiography, sermons, literature (poetry, memoirs, and prose), painting, advertising posters, photography, architecture and war memorials, film, television broadcasts and media coverage, eyewitness accounts, as well as to a lesser extent philosophical, legal, disciplinary, and theological discourses. Although the categories of voice, perspective, identity, and aftermath foregrounded in this study are salient to the analysis of representations having nothing to do with war, the stakes in war representations are of a radically different order. In an age of 'global' violence and clashing 'civilizations,' what we perceive war to be influences judgments the consequences of which may be massively destructive.

Conflict and Agency in War Representations

Any attempt to conceive of war without taking representational factors into consideration is quickly exhausted. For example, the German sociological Research Group for Exploration of the Causes of War[16] proposes the definition of war as a mass conflict in which force is used by two or more sides of a conflict, one of which at least must contain regular government forces. Furthermore, according to this definition each side involved in a war must possess some kind of central organization, and therefore a measure of control over the fighting being carried out in its name.[17] While this kind of an approach has its pragmatic value in so far as it is conducive to the elaborate identifying, cataloguing, sorting, and relating of wars, its emphasis on war's coherence leaves no room for consideration of war's many ambiguities, contradictions, occlusions, and paradoxes.

For instance, in addition to the difficulty of classifying the continuing armed conflicts in Chechnya, it has been a challenge to define the start of the so-called second Chechen war (1999–). Some sources state that it began with the invasion of Dagestan by the Chechnya-based Islamic International Brigade and Shamil Basaev's Islamist militia in early August 1999. Other sources assert that the war started in September 1999 with the terrorist bombings of several apartment blocks in the Russian cities of Buynaksk, Moscow, and Volgodonsk. 1 October 1999, the date when federal troops first entered Chechnya, is also considered a possible start date. Rather than being a formality, or a matter of narrowly historical or temporal consequence, the issue of when the war began gives rise to questions of moral precedence that are indexed to questions of agency. Perhaps the most trenchant of these remains 'Who is the perpetrator in this conflict?'[18]

Another example of how hard it is sometimes to decide where war ends and peace begins is an instance of military occupation following the end of armed hostilities. As Brad Prager demonstrates in the third chapter of this collection, twilight zones such as military occupation blur war's conceptual and legal boundaries, thus complicating its representation and rendering judgments of its basic features difficult, if not totally impossible. Those who attempt the depiction of occupation are confronted with the difficult task of providing form and order to a sequence of spatio-temporal moments that actively contest their representation. Like all large-scale and multidimensional phenomena, including genocides such as the Holocaust, wars are marked by what Primo Levi recognizes as substantial moral and epistemological 'grey zones'[19] that serve to thwart a variety of representational impulses.

As even a cursory look at the history of philosophy shows, the concept of 'war' is inherently diachronic. Philosophers, for their part, have defined war in many different ways: as war of all against all, or man against man;[20] as conflict between states,[21] or between sovereign nation states; or more abstractly as a violent clash between opposing forces or principles.[22] In the second half of the nineteenth century and the first of the twentieth, war became generally recognized as part of what Jay Winter terms in this collection the 'unfolding saga of nationalism.' The post-1945 period, however, has been increasingly dominated by transnational or internal conflict, by organized violence 'within states and between non-state agents and territorial states,' which have obliged further reflection on war's nature and limits through the introduction of terms such as 'freedom fighter'[23] into war's lexicon.

Since the end of the Second World War it has become more difficult to identify the parties in wars. Wars have often been fragmented, becoming more local (such as, for example, the sub-national civil wars in Sudan and Yemen) and at the same time in certain respects transnational and global (as in, for example, certain forms of Islamic Jihad).[24] Because the concept of war as conflict between sovereign nation states has collapsed under the weight of its exceptions, the question arises whether a conflict still counts as war when its antagonists cannot be defined on the same level, as entities of the same political or organizational type, or else as moral equals. An alliance of nation states in conflict with members of an extremist religious group, or a conflict between a state and guerilla groups ensconced in it, destroys potentially clear boundaries serving to guarantee the integrity of the war concept. Russia's military involvement in Chechnya, for example, is organized around a radically underdetermined concept of war. Indeed, so thin was this concept that, as Serguei Oushakine's essay in chapter 8 of this volume asserts, Russian veterans of the Chechen war were denied official and public recognition as combatants, and therefore adequate compensation and respect for their many sacrifices.

The above example is also important in substantiating the point that questions of agency (including questions of blame and responsibility) are practically inseparable from the distinct qualities of a war's representation. Indeed, local and international descriptions of the Chechen war's antagonists have noticeably changed over time. In the 1990s, during the first Chechen war (1994–6) and at the start of the second (1999–), the international community often referred to Chechen guerrillas in favourable terms as fighters for their motherland's independence. However, after the 1 September 2004 terrorist attack on a secondary school in Beslan, the most vicious of all terrorist attacks by Chechens since the start of the conflict,[25] more and more Western commentators began describing the 'rebels' as 'terrorists.'

In an attempt to equip the reader with analytical tools well suited to exploring different dimensions of war representations, this collection includes several chapters specifically focused on the complexities associated with examining agency in war. This concern is especially pronounced in the contribution by Lilie Chouliaraki (chapter 5). With reference to a 2003 BBC TV broadcast from the Iraq War, she shows how the audience's perception of the figures she terms the 'sufferer,' the 'persecutor' (the 'bomber'), and the 'benefactor' are manipulated to forestall overidentification with (and therefore empathy for) the sufferer. Both Chouliaraki's and Oushakine's analyses make clear how the rhetoric of war representations is adjusted to facilitate specific identifications of war's agents, and they alert audiences to the need for more critical circumspection when confronted with the moral, political, psychological, and aesthetic underpinnings of such narratives.

The Narrative and Ideological Content of War Representations

The linguistic and narrative turns of the last forty years have given rise to increasing levels of academic discussion about the rhetorical and narrative dimensions of war representations, including not merely fictional texts and war propaganda but also non-fictional genres such as historiography and journalism, as well as work in other media such as film, painting, or photography. In one way or another, all the chapters of this collection reflect upon the languages of war and the patterns they inscribe in war representations. Several of the collection's contributions focus specifically on the function of tropes, tone, point of view, and narrative distance in representations of war.

Many case studies of war literature explore the rhetorical strategies employed by poets and other writers to capture the experience of war. The literary techniques used for this purpose must be evaluated in relation to particular literary traditions, to individual writers and poets, and to an artwork's time and place of creation (for instance during, after, or in anticipation of war). Kate McLoughlin's essay (chapter 2) considers the rhetorical strategies used by writers and poets to express war's horrors indirectly. These strategies create ominous gaps, silences, or interruptions that ultimately may speak louder than words, thereby proving more emotionally powerful than detailed analysis of what might have transpired on the battlefield. Appropriate and even desirable in literature, these rhetorical approaches are hardly acceptable for scholars of history or anyone else responsible for 'shortening the distance' between the reader and war while maintaining the illusion of authenticity and objectivity. As Stephan Jaeger argues in chapter 4, since its eyewitnesses are the only ones having had actual experiences of war, representations produced by anybody else need to deploy specific rhetorical and narratological techniques in order to simulate these experiences. The suffering of civilians can invite the use of a personal and more intimate voice that the historian simulates in order to evoke, for example, the 'atmosphere' of the allied bombings of German cities during the Second World War.

Explicitly comparative in its methodology, Helena Goscilo's essay (chapter 6) adds significantly to the collection's consideration of the relationship between war representations and rhetorical means that ultimately serve to wrap war experience in culture-specific morally and politically acceptable terms. Elaborating on the work of Hayden White, Goscilo shows how the representation of war is closely connected to the mythology of cultural and national identity, as is the case, for example, in Poland's self-presentation as the martyred nation in the Second World War. In her essay on Soviet films about the Battle of Stalingrad, Elena Baraban (chapter 10) further explores the ways in which governments establish their war aims' legitimacy through the production of wartime and post-war propaganda that serves as a powerful means of shaping distinct group identities. Historicizing the study of Soviet Stalingrad films, Baraban demonstrates how individual films, while generally supporting the state-sanctioned mythology of the Soviet people's unprecedented heroism during the Second World War, have created war memory strategies specific to their narrower historical contexts.

The consistency of shared responses to war based on historically stable collective identities is also explored by Jennifer James (chapter 7) in her rhetorical and intertextual analysis of Martin Luther King's speeches against the Vietnam War. By shaping group identities (such as the identity of African Americans inspired by the tradition of the black jeremiad), the languages of war can create justifications for or against present and future wars. Complementing each other in their methodology, focus, their choice of media, and the variety of their culturally or historically specific material, the above essays thus serve to emphasize one of this collection's key theoretical points, namely, that the language of war representations is ultimately linked to moral, ideological, and political discursive patterns.

Space in War Representations

War cannot be conceived of as confined just to its physical battlefields or military campaign sites. Its impact, and therefore some noteworthy aspects of its experience and character, can be felt far away from the military action, as we may detect in the Canadian and American populations during either world war, or in Germany's civilian population during the First World War. None of these populations experienced the war directly on their soil.[26] Consequently, the communication of war space, for contemporaries and for subsequent generations, requires an imaginary appropriation that can only be acquired through letters, stories, or images. This consideration of space as one more crucial axis for examining war representations is evident, for instance, in David Lubin's essay (chapter 11), which analyses the proliferation of images of monstrosity in the United States following the First World War. This conflict affected the American collective psyche much more strongly after the cessation of hostilities, when the horror most Americans did not experience first-hand returned home in the bodies as well as in the painful memories of wounded and disfigured veterans.

The impact of war on the iconography and organization of cultural space is of course quite different when war hits one's homeland. The devastation of spaces then frequently becomes a metaphor for ruined lives and cultures, as well as beliefs and values.[27] The indelibility of war's ruins may be recognized in the tendency of war to somehow persist in the minds of people who remember or are nostalgic for places substantially altered by conflict, or who are haunted by images of ruin. Such traces of destruction are the subject of Simon Baker's essay (chapter 12), which examines photographs of towns in post–First World War France that had become uninhabitable through the conflict.

Spatial concerns also inform explorations of war's aftermaths of a different order, those focusing not so much on ruined identities and landscapes as on the reshaping of post-war spaces through the erection of memorials commemorating victories or mourning defeats. The way in which urban spaces are interspersed with such monuments contributes to public discourse surrounding particular wars and thereby speaks for what is deemed significant in them for specific groups of people. As James Chlup argues in chapter 9, the ancient Romans placed the Arch of Titus in a central area of their capital city in order to express their view of the Roman-Jewish War as 'the definitive conflict in Roman history.' Such an example helps to demonstrate how the language of war and questions of political power, as well as of social identity, remain intertwined.

Scholarly Context and Structure of the Collection

Most studies dealing with the representation of war have focused on a specific period or culture[28] while attending to interests and categories that define the relation between a particular academic discipline and war.[29] Since the early days of the Cold War, the primary academic discipline responsible for the interdisciplinary study of war has been war studies, which owes much to the attempts by scholars like Michael Howard to enlarge the frame and enhance the reputation of military history by systematically placing it in conversation with work drawn particularly from political economy, anthropology, sociology, and philosophy.[30] In the past few decades, the interdisciplinary research paradigm of war studies has gradually expanded to include contributions by scholars in law, international relations, political science, and psychology. However, most war studies programs are organized around course modules devoted overwhelmingly to matters of political history and military strategy, and remain only peripherally concerned with war's representation.[31]

The growth of interdisciplinary research on war in fields with deeper investments in representations per se, such as cultural studies and communications studies, clearly indicates the need for further expansion of the war studies framework to include substantial engagement with the methods and issues more typical of the humanities and social sciences.[32] In important respects this need has already been acknowledged. Several book series such as Columbia University Press's Critical War Studies (edited by Tarak Barkawi and Shane Brighton) and Cornell University Press's Crises in Word Politics (edited by Tarak Barkawi and Brendan Simms) offer monographs rich in interdisciplinary conceptual and methodological synthesis. Barkawi's own research on orientalism in strategic thinking[33] is furthermore part of a vanguard of scholarship complicating some of the moral and political orthodoxies long-present in strategic studies and international relations circles, and it serves to place those in these disciplines engaging with his work in a much wider discursive network devoted to the analysis of war.

By including art historians, a classicist, language and literature scholars, a cultural/military historian, a communications scholar, and an anthropologist, all of whom read, commented on, and contributed to one another's work during the course of the manuscript's preparation, this collection moves beyond documenting war discourses ubiquitous in different cultures and across historical periods.[34] It examines how social, linguistic, aesthetic, moral, political, and other conventions interact with specific representational contents drawn from a variety of historical periods, locations, and disciplines. This arrangement of methods and concerns creates an interplay between the collection's different chapters, which allows consideration of numerous representational issues from distinct vantage points.[35] The reader is encouraged to understand each article not as a free-standing text but rather as a node in a much wider and more heterogeneous interdisciplinary network. Case studies presented here – such as Iraq War TV coverage or films about Stalingrad – only indicate the starting point for deeper theoretical reflection on the nature and implications of war representations. They provide the reader with the analytical tools required to analyse and reflect upon many different kinds of war representations. By this means, the collection aims to contribute to the growing field of interdisciplinary war studies, and to document some of the many ways in which more narrowly traditional approaches to war (found, for example, in political science, strategic studies, or military history) may be supplemented.

All of this collection's chapters revolve around a core framework of concerns designated by its four section headings: 'Silences,' 'Perspectives,' 'Identities,' and 'Aftermaths.' Each section is introduced by a brief explanation of its conceptual locus and of the analytical and theoretical links existing between its three component chapters. The first section – comprising chapters by Winter, McLoughlin, and Prager – considers silence in commemorations and memories of war as a multifaceted phenomenon whose complexity resists comprehensive articulation at nearly every turn. 'Perspectives' – consisting of essays by Jaeger, Chouliaraki, and Goscilo – concentrates on the ways in which 'realistic' war representations strive to disguise their perspectivity, their limited outlook or otherwise manipulative character, so as to influence the reader or viewer. The three chapters in 'Identities' – written by James, Oushakine, and Chlup – consider the processes whereby identities become mobilized in war's different representations (including commemorative rites and monuments) intended to promote social solidarity and civic virtue. The final section, 'Aftermaths' – containing essays by Baraban, Lubin, and Baker – assesses how, individually and collectively, post-war trauma and memories of war shape culture and works of art, and how the latter with its disregard of borders can stimulate an exploration of the human psyche in the aftermath of war.[36]

The interdisciplinarity and explanatory reach of each approach presented in this volume allows the reader to take multiple paths through the book. These options end up complicating attempts at ordering the wars discussed here according to any simple clustering by discipline, media, or chronology.[37] However, all of the multiple connections between the volume's chapters provide insights into the specific discursive or cultural conditions affecting the production and reception of representations of war.

NOTES

1 This summary is based on a series of interviews with Julius van der Merwe (not his real name) undertaken between November 2005 and July 2006 in Winnipeg, Canada.
2 On remembrance practices, see the essays constituting the collection *War and Remembrance in the Twentieth Century*, ed. Jay Winter and Emmanuel Sivan (Cambridge: Cambridge University Press, 1999).
3 Van der Merwe's emigration from South Africa to Canada in the late 1970s placed him squarely within a North American cultural context and shaped his outlook on war accordingly.
4 This volume uses the concept of 'representation' instead of 'narrative' because the latter is clearly linked to a temporal recounting of real or fictive events in form of a story (or as a meta-narrative), whereas the former allows for the inclusion of other genres and media such as photography, posters, or painting that emphasize presence and explicitly anti-narrative effects.
5 Maintaining a critical concern in studying war representations is additionally complicated by the fact that they are not always the explicit articulation of war experience, but, as Jay Winter argues in his contribution here, are also the silences constitutive of mourning and war's commemoration.
6 Marianna Torgovnick argues that the American collective memory of the Second World War has been extremely selective in its focus on aspects and episodes of the conflict, which have become incorporated into what Torgovnick calls wartime consciousness in the United States. This consciousness in turn has served as the foundation for interpreting and dealing with the events of 9/11. See Torgovnick, *The War Complex: World War II in Our Time* (Chicago: University of Chicago Press, 2005).

7 See, for example, the website of Rod Oakland, 'Fighting Words and Images: The Use of Leaflets in the Propaganda War in Vietnam 1945 to 1975,' http://www.btinternet.com/~rod.oakland/vietnam.htm (accessed 14 November 2010).

8 Even if war events are witnessed or experienced directly, as in the example of van der Merwe above, there remains the need to reflect upon the ways in which this experience is transfigured by diverse representational languages. For more on the constructed and discursive character of experience, see Joan W. Scott, 'The Evidence of Experience,' *Critical Inquiry* 17, no. 4 (1991): 773–97.

9 See, for example, the historiographical debates still raging over the representation of the Second World War in Japanese textbooks, or over German wartime suffering, the latter of which is touched on by Stephan Jaeger in his contribution to this collection.

10 For some context on the international debate between Poland, Russia, and Germany, see, for example, Michael Schwirtz, 'In a Visit, Putin Tries to Ease Rifts with Poland,' *The New York Times*, 1 September 2009, http://www.nytimes.com/2009/09/02/world/europe/02russia.html (accessed 14 November 2010).

11 David Crossland, 'The World from Berlin. "Putin Found the Right Words in Gdansk,"' *Spiegel Online International*, 2 September 2009, http://www.spiegel.de/international/europe/0,1518,646547,00.html (accessed 14 November 2010).

12 See the BBC News story 'Pact that set the scene for war,' 21 August 2009, http://news.bbc.co.uk/go/pr/fr/-/2/hi/europe/8212451.stm (accessed 14 November 2010).

13 On European diplomacy of the period, see Carlile A. Macartney and Alan. W. Palmer, *Independent Eastern Europe* (New York: St Martins Press, 1966); John Hiden, *Germany and Europe 1919–1939* (London: Longman, 1993); David Kaiser, *Economic Diplomacy and the Origin of the Second World War: Germany, Britain, France and Eastern Europe, 1930–1939* (Princeton, NJ: Princeton University Press, 1980).

14 See also Helena Goscilo's essay in this collection.

15 'Interdisciplinary' here means any academic-intellectual practice that seeks to overcome the interests vested within disciplines as they are constituted institutionally, and which serve to reinforce practitioners' sense of the exclusivity of their tools – the various discourses and schemes deployed in the generation of interpretive results; cf. Joe Moran, *Interdisciplinarity* (London: Routledge, 2002), 14.

16 *Arbeitsgemeinschaft Kriegsursachenforschung* (AKUF).

17 http://www.sozialwiss.uni-hamburg.de/publish/Ipw/Akuf/kriege_
    aktuell.htm#Def (accessed 14 November 2010). See also the 'Correlates of
    War' project at the University of Michigan that archived and analysed all
    wars worldwide between 1816 and 1997, http://www.correlatesofwar.org/
    (accessed 14 November 2010).

18 Moreover, politically the military confrontation in question is not easily
    identifiable either, since the official Russian media avoids using the term
    'war' in regard to the situation in Chechnya, preferring instead the term
    'counter-terrorist operation' or 'military actions on the territory of the
    Chechen Autonomous Republic,' thus denying the Islamic guerrillas the
    status of a political entity capable of declaring war.

19 For more on the moral ambiguities of the Holocaust, and particularly the
    consequences of these ambiguities for our capacity for moral judgment,
    see Primo Levi, *The Drowned and the Saved* (New York: Vintage, 1989). On
    the one hand, since 1968, discussions and representations of the Holocaust
    have been closely linked, as Jay Winter points out in his article in this vol-
    ume. On the other hand, notwithstanding their many points of ontological,
    ideological, and pragmatic convergence, war is not genocide nor are the
    (well-documented) representational peculiarities of the latter coextensive
    with those of the former. Minimally, war notionally ends in victory or
    defeat while genocide ends in the extermination of what a metaphysician
    might term a 'human kind.' Their moral and practical consequences are
    thus (again minimally) logically distinct.

20 Thomas Hobbes, *De Cive: The English Version entitled in the first edition
    'Philosophical Rudiments Concerning Government and Society'* [1642; 1651], ed.
    Howard Warrender (Oxford Clarendon Press, 1983), 34. For a history of the
    concept of *bellum omnium contra omnes*, see Otto Kimminich, 'Krieg,' in *His-
    torisches Wörterbuch der Philosophie*, ed. Joachim Ritter, vol. 4 (Darmstadt:
    Wissenschaftliche Buchgesellschaft, 1976), 1233.

21 'War is not [...] a relation between man and man, but between State and
    State, in which private individuals are enemies only by accident, not as
    men, nor even as citizens, but as soldiers; not as members of the fatherland
    but as its defenders,' Jean-Jacques Rousseau, *Social Contract* [1762], in *The
    Collected Writings of Rousseau*, ed. Roger D. Masters and Christopher Kelly,
    trans. J.R. Bush, R.D. Masters, and C. Kelly (Hanover, NH: University
    Press of New England, 1994), 135–6.

22 See, for example, Heraclitus in Charles H. Kahn's *The Art and Thought
    of Heraclitus: an Edition of the Fragments with Translation and Commentary*
    (Cambridge: Cambridge University Press, 1979), 67. For an overview of the
    concept of war in philosophical and intellectual history, see also Wilhelm

Janssen, 'Krieg,' in *Geschichtliche Grundbegriffe: Historisches Lexikon zur politisch-sozialen Sprache in Deutschland*, ed. Otto Brunner, Werner Conze, and Reinhart Koselleck, vol. 3 (Stuttgart: Klett-Cotta, 1982), 567–615.

23 According to the *OED*, the first contemporary usage of the term 'freedom fighter' dates back to 1941. This usage became standardized during antico-lonial resistance struggles of the 1950s and early 1960s.

24 Dieter Langewiesche, 'Zum Wandel von Krieg und Kriegslegitimation in der Neuzeit,' *Journal of Modern European History* 2 (2004): 5–6. See also the chapter by Winter in this volume.

25 1 September is the start of the academic year in the former Soviet Union. This day's festive celebrations traditionally attract many more people to schools than a regular school day. The terrorists took hostage 1128 children and adults. The treatment of the hostages was characterized by extreme cruelty. On 3 September 2004, during the storming of the school by Rus-sian Special Forces, 329 people (including 159 children) died.

26 However, the logistical demands of the military struggle (fuel, material, troop replacements, etc.), of combat itself (bullets, food, etc.), fundraising, espionage, and propaganda, were all importantly if not exclusively expe-rienced 'at home,' outside the traditional space of war and in ways that produced fundamental changes in the lives of affected populations.

27 See also Adam Piette, 'War Zones,' in the *Cambridge Companion to British and American War Writing*, ed. Kate McLoughlin (Cambridge: Cambridge University Press, 2009), 38–46.

28 See, for example, Evelyn Cobley, *Representing War: Form and Ideology in First World War Narratives* (Toronto: University of Toronto Press, 1996); Jay Winter, *Remembering War: The Great War between Memory and History in the Twentieth Century* (New Haven, CT: Yale University Press, 2006); Michael Paris, ed., *Repicturing the Second World War: Representations in Film and Television* (Basingstoke: Palgrave Macmillan, 2007); and Noël Valis, ed., *Teaching Representations of the Spanish Civil War* (New York: The Modern Language Association of America, 2007).

29 See, for instance, Angela Smith, ed., *Gender and Warfare in the Twentieth Century: Textual Representations* (Manchester: Manchester University Press, 2004); Michèle Martin, *Images at War: Illustrated Periodicals and Constructed Nations* (Toronto: University of Toronto Press, 2006); Brian Foss, *War Paint: Art, War, State and Identity in Britain 1939–1945* (New Haven, CT: Yale Uni-versity Press, 2007); Erin Steuter and Deborah Wills, *At War with Metaphor: Media, Propaganda, and Racism in the War on Terror* (Lanham: Rowman & Littlefield, 2008); Paul Cooke and Marc Silberman, ed., *Screening War: Perspectives on German Suffering* (Rochester, NY: Camden House, 2010). For

the development of media and technology in relation to the representation of war, see Manuel Köppen, *Das Entsetzen des Beobachters: Krieg und Medien im 19. und 20. Jahrhundert* (Heidelberg: Winter, 2005). For more on the relation of war and literature, see *Krieg und Literatur / War and Literature: International Yearbook on War and Anti-War Literature*, ed. Erich Maria Remarque-Friedenszentrum (Göttingen: V & R Unipress/Universitätsverlag Osnabrück, 1989–); for studies of cultural representations of war, see the *Journal of War & Culture Studies*, 2007–.

30   According to Brian Reid, the three main early influences on Howard's thought and writing were the British military historian and strategist Liddell Hart, the French sociologist Raymond Aron, and the German cultural and military historian Hans Delbrück. Howard also received academic training in philosophy. See Reid, 'Michael Howard and the Evolution of Modern War Studies,' *Journal of Military History* 73, no. 3 (2009): 877.

31   See the *Handbook of War Studies*, ed. Manus Midlarsky (Winchester, MA: Unwin Hyman, 1989). To date there have been three editions of this well-regarded survey of the field available, all of which are overtly realist and exhibit a near-total indifference to war's representation.

32   An example of a richly interdisciplinary work on war representations is the recent special issue *War* of *PMLA* which assembles a wide array of war studies, introduced by the concept of 'perpetual war.' See Srinivas Aravamudan, 'Introduction: Perpetual War,' *PMLA* 125, no. 5 (2009): 1505–14. In terms of the issues raised by this volume, the *PMLA* article 'War and Representation' by Fredric Jameson is particularly valuable (1532–47). See also James Dawes, *The Language of War: Literature and Culture in the U.S. from the Civil War through World War II* (Cambridge, MA: Harvard University Press, 2002), as well as the series *Zeichen des Krieges in Literatur, Film und den Medien*, ed. Christer Petersen (Kiel: Ludwig, 2004–), which focuses on the semiotics of war in literature, film, and media.

33   See Tarak Barkawi's publications: with Mark Laffey, 'The Postcolonial Moment in Security Studies,' *Review of International Studies* 32, no. 4 (2006): 329–52; 'Culture and Combat in the Colonies: The Indian Army in the Second World War,' *Journal of Contemporary History* 41, no. 2 (2006): 325–55; *Globalization and War* (Lanham: Rowman and Littlefield, 2005).

34   The *Cambridge Companion to British and American War Writing*, ed. Kate McLoughlin, conceptualizes war writing in several theoretical survey chapters before it classifies the poetics of war writing over the course of its thirteen chapters sorted according to time period and war.

35   Given the terms and diverse results of this interplay, it seems likely that no

one discipline, theory, or ideology may be said to possess a primacy in its understanding of war or its representation.

36 See also Judith Butler's *Frames of War: When Is Life Grievable?* (London: Verso, 2009) for an analysis of the development of frameworks within which loss in the twenty-first-century 'War on Terror' may be mourned.

37 Wars discussed span history from the Jugurthine War in the second century BCE to the current wars in Iraq, Chechnya, and Afghanistan.

Silences

The three chapters gathered together in this section address the silences arising from, and complicating, the representation of war. Each of them considers silence not so much as an absence as it does as a technique for indirectly evoking war, a large and multifaceted phenomenon whose complexity resists comprehensive articulation at nearly every turn. Jay Winter, Kate McLoughlin, and Brad Prager all work to show how silences about war may be deployed to animate an understanding of war's representational elusiveness. Each author, however, locates this elusiveness in different representational domains: Winter in commemorations of war organized around the construction of public memory; McLoughlin in the rhetoric of war representations; and Prager in the attempts of representations to capture the moral and phenomenological complexities of life under military occupation, a time during which the boundary distinguishing war from peace remains problematically indistinct.

In his contribution entitled 'Representations of War and the Social Construction of Silence,' Jay Winter responds to critics who are committed to the view not only that war's many horrors resist representational totalization, but that war representations distort our understanding of war by allowing room for their creators to specify the terms of the metonymies linking actual war to its signification. Since these terms must inevitably be ideologically charged given representers' 'objective social locations' – their values, ideological commitments, biases, and so forth – the conclusion is often drawn that such interests serve finally to undermine war representations' referential integrity.

In rejecting this argument, Winter draws on a wide range of material pertaining to different wars and cultures as they figure in public, politi-

cal, and academic discourses. He explores the rules and commemorative practices societies use to govern the expression of the 'unsayable,'
that which lies beyond the reach of relatively more standard representational techniques but which nevertheless remains morally or politically pressing. Silence, Winter argues, at least when it is deployed in
war representations in a way that is 'focused, directed, and purposeful,'
should be considered not in terms of the properties it lacks but rather in
terms of those it possesses, most notably its power to disrupt representational conventions. A jolt of this kind, he concludes, often occasions
further public reflection and discussion of the cause of the disruption
and its consequences. This conversation, which typically arises with
the passage of time as the need for silence following a conflict becomes
less certain, and as new interests contest the public space reserved for
collective memories, may require modifications to the boundaries of
war's commemorative discourses. It can quite literally change the public's understanding of war.

In her contribution 'Not Writing about War,' Kate McLoughlin closely examines the various rhetorical techniques available to writers who
wish to write about war without attempting its direct representation.
There are several reasons typically given to justify such indirection,
ranging from worries attached to 'combat gnosticism' (the view that
the intensity and privacy of the combat experience render it unrepresentable) to concern for the moral costs to misappropriating or else failing adequately to capture the war experiences of others. Many who
have written on war conceive of their subject in terms similar to those
of Theodor Adorno, that is, as an 'extremity that eludes the concept,' a
signifier lacking a signified. In the absence of this signified war must
be understood as inimical to signification. For proponents of this view,
war can only be lived and experienced in a way always-already epis-
temically and representationally undercut by such necessarily finite and
imperfect human faculties as attention, memory, sight, and rationality.

Over the course of her analysis of a diversity of fictional and poetic
texts, McLoughlin reveals the ways in which writers confronted with
the challenges of depicting war succeed in reconciling three ostensibly
incompatible imperatives: to treat war simultaneously as something
which cannot be, should not be, and yet must be represented. The key
to this reconciliation according to McLoughlin is the writers' use of rhetorical techniques not merely to articulate silence but, via the instrument of that articulation, to create meaning by imbuing silence with
significance. The writers she discusses opt for such techniques as privi-

leging the indexical over the iconic (i.e., the description of war's effects over its causes), parapolemics (emphasis on the margins of war experience), paralipsis (evocation through denial), and periphrasis (association). Together these tropes make up the toolbox of the war writer, constituting a mode of rhetorically engaging with war that McLoughlin labels 'apophatic.' Apophasis is the term applied to the technique of mentioning something by not mentioning it, a notion closely linked to Kant's concept of the sublime. For Kant, what defeats reason can nevertheless also stimulate the imagination, thereby serving to place the incomprehensible within conceptual reach.

Consideration of the conceptual instability of war lies at the heart of Brad Prager's contribution to this collection. 'Occupation as the Face of War: Concealing Violence in the Diary *A Woman in Berlin'* centres on attempts by writers to depict military occupation, a liminal time between war and peace during which many of the certainties characteristic of each state of affairs either clash or are suspended. Of particular concern to Prager is the tendency of this suspension to generate linguistic and traumatic silences, an estrangement of words from their users resulting from the violence against civilians that is ubiquitous during an occupation. With reference to the events described in a Second World War diary by a German woman repeatedly raped by occupying Russian troops, which he reads against Heinrich von Kleist's earlier Napoleonic War novella 'Die Marquise von O...' ('The Marquise of O...'), Prager reveals the deep contingency inherent in our understanding of war, whose concept includes a centre but no precisely determinable margins. Like rape itself, war possesses content in search of a form, something marked in both the diary and the novella by dashes and ellipses. These punctuation marks announce (by obscuring) the unsayable. Prager links these silences to a more general culture of silence surrounding the discussion of wartime and occupation rape in Germany, and explores the reciprocal relationship between this discussion and the ongoing (and highly charged) conversation concerning the moral and historical standing of Second World War German suffering.

Prager concludes that war's nebulousness is aptly captured by texts like the Berlin woman's diary. They also reveal the intensity of their authors' representational struggles. Such efforts affirm the value of texts such as the diary, whose periodic inarticulacy speaks for a troubling set of conceptual and other boundary problems. The acknowledgment of these problems, along with emphasis on the various strategies employed by artists to overcome them, constitute the two primary links between these three contributions. Together they demonstrate a shared understanding both of the difficulties inherent in the representation of war and of the reasons typically adduced to justify them.

Although for many artists and critics the challenges of representing war are insurmountable, and war for them remains unrepresentable and therefore silence its natural idiom, the three essays grouped in this section each rejects elements of this perspective. All three contributors acknowledge the silences contained in war representations but advocate different responses to the question of how these silences may be aestheticized, selectively and constructively, in order to permit artists to 'speak' meaningfully about war.

1 Representations of War and the Social Construction of Silence

JAY WINTER

The wrenching experience of war has occasioned commemorative practices of many kinds all over the world. Every one of them is framed by representations of war. Some are heroic, some filled with tragedy, some triumphalist, some angry, some resigned. Every one of them is incomplete, in that the visceral experience of combat, what Tolstoy called 'the actual killing,' the smell of it, the taste of it, is irreproduceable. This stark and unavoidable fact means that all commemoration is metaphoric, or metonymic, or in some sense at a considerable remove from the subject – war – and its bloody remains. Many scholars have interpreted, therefore, representations of war as lies, distortions, sanitized versions of an intolerable reality. In short, according to this point of view, representations of war are always ideological, in the sense of embodying a kind of biopolitics, a valuation of the bodies of the dead so that at some future date the bodies of the living can be remobilized for war.

This argument, in my view, is both incomplete and unpersuasive. The primary reason is that forgetting the ugliness of war is only one option in war commemoration. That option has been evident, to be sure, in many kinds of verbal and material tributes to the dead. But other forms of commemoration do not engage in self-serving euphemisms or acts of remembering the dismembered bodies of the dead. It is too simple to see commemoration as a form of forgetting; memories are too hard to suppress, and bitterness runs its course whatever the ideological needs of the current regime in power.

To make room for a multivocal interpretation of representations of war, I propose to move beyond the old divide between forgetting – the business of those in power – and remembering – the business of those in mourning. For reasons made apparent below, we need to add a third dimension to the landscape of war representations. That dimension is silence. This essay explores the utility of silence as a ubiquitous and powerful constitutive element in representations of war.

Below the Surface

The distinguished anthropologist Marc Augé tells us that 'memory is framed by forgetting in the same way as the contours of the shoreline are framed by the sea.'[1] This elegant formulation of the embrace of memory and forgetting draws upon a long tradition of philosophical and literary reflection. It is time, though, to go beyond it in the effort to transcend the now saturated field of memory studies dominated by scholarship that adopts this binary approach. For the topographical metaphor employed here is clearly incomplete – we need to see the landscape of the shoreline in all three dimensions. Doing so enables us to observe a vertical dimension to the creation and erosion of the shoreline that is dynamic, unstable, and at times intrusive. I speak of those deposits below the surface of the water that emerge with the tides or with other environmental changes. In the framework of how we think about memory and forgetting, these hidden shapes cannot simply be ignored because they are concealed at some moments and revealed at others. They must be examined as part of the cartography of recollection and remembrance, which always frames representations of war.

Silences: Liturgical, Political, Essentialist

Silences come in many forms. Nevertheless, it may be useful to cite a musical example to explore this domain. The composer John Cage said all that needs to be said about the performative nature of silence. It exists in the world, and is defined by the world according to certain arbitrary but powerfully reinforced conventions. Those who first heard his composition 4'33" in 1952 were stupefied by silence. What Cage did was to invite concert-goers to come together facing a pianist who sits at a piano and does not touch the keyboard for four minutes and thirty-three seconds precisely. What Cage showed them, much to their discomfort, was that silence is 'the presence of ambient and unintentional noise rather than the complete absence of sound.'[2] In this essay I want to draw attention to focused, directed, and purposeful silence, not conceived of as the absence of sound, but as the absence of conventional verbal exchanges. Such silences have marked representations of war throughout history. In other words, silences are spaces either beyond words or conventionally delimited as left out of what we talk about. Topographically, they are there whether or not they come to the surface; and their re-emergence into our line of sight can occasion a reiteration of the interdiction on talking about them or the end of the interdiction itself.

Critically, therefore, I cannot accept the commonplace view that silence is the space of forgetting and speech the realm of remembrance. Instead, I offer the following definition of silence. Silence, I hold, is a socially constructed space in which and about which subjects and words normally used in everyday life are not spoken. The circle around this space is described by groups of people who at one point deem it appropriate that there is a difference between the sayable and the unsayable, or the spoken and the unspoken, and that such a distinction can and should be maintained and observed over time. Such people codify and enforce norms that reinforce the injunction against breaking into the inner space of the circle of silence. The norms formed in this way are internalized by individuals, who learn what private reflections are in part by thinking about the limits of the sayable in public.

The reasons for this set of cultural practices are multiple, but in the context of war and violence, the primary, though not the only, impulses underlying the social construction of silence are three. In a nutshell, silences emerge in three different arenas: the liturgical, the political, and the proprietary or essentialist realms.

In the first place, silence is always part of the framing of public understandings of war and violence since these touch on the sacred and on eternal themes of loss, mourning, sacrifice, and redemption. I term these uses of silence as liturgical silences. They are clearly linked to fundamental moral problems, described in reflections on theodicy or the conundrum as to why, if God is all good, evil exists in the world. Such liturgical silences are essential parts of mourning practices in many religious traditions, since not speaking enables those experiencing loss to engage with their grief in their own time and in their own ways. For example, the Hebrew prayer for the dead, the Kaddish, does not mention the word 'death' or 'dying' or 'grief' or 'bereavement,' all conditions or states of mind associated with the seven days of mourning passed together by families in mourning. The prayer is silent over the critical reality this practice marks. Mourning practices always touch on such matters, since they perform the fragility of life and the limitations of our own understandings of our mortal existence.

The second impulse behind the social construction of silence address-
es problems of social conflict more directly. Here silence is chosen in
order to suspend or truncate open conflict over the meaning and/or
justification of violence, either domestic or transnational. The hope here
is that the passage of time can lower the temperature of disputes about
these events, or even heal the wounds they cause. I term these practices
as yielding political or strategic silences.

One example may suffice to illustrate this usage and stand for a
host of other instances directly relevant to the representation of war,
civil war, and transnational violence. In the late 1970s, the forty-year
reign of Franco's dictatorship in Spain came to an end peacefully. In
short order, a socialist government came to power and proceeded to
refashion the country as a dynamic and stable member of the new
European order. The price of that transition was the postponement or
adjournment *sine die* – that is, permanently – of any formal and public enquiry into atrocities committed during and after the civil war of
1936–9. Spain's new democracy chose peace over justice, order over the
open investigation of the abundant evidence on atrocities that – like
the underwater sandbars to which we referred above – was present but
invisible. Not seeing what everyone saw and not saying what everyone
knew became a strategy accepted by everyone at the time to ensure the
success of a peaceful transition to democratic rule.[3] Such accords are
matters of negotiation and thus suffer from all the faults of political
compromise. With time, their hold over the parties begins to loosen, a
new generation comes to power, and though silence is still ordained at
the national level as wise and necessary, people start talking, looking,
digging, writing, and inevitably accusing. And how could it be otherwise when the scale of accusations is monumental? Here we can see
that silence, like memory and forgetting, has a life history, and – when
new pressures or circumstances emerge – it can be transformed into its
opposite in very rapid order.

Such transformative moments are well known. Heidegger's silence
about Nazi crimes, and his complicity in them, echoed similar lacunae
in many German discursive fields after 1945. Paul Celan's poetry rup-
tured them. More recently, silence about war and violence ends when
victims are invited to come forward and are given a forum ensuring
that what they say will be heard. This is evidently the case in South
Africa and other countries where numerous 'truth commissions' were
established for this purpose.[4]

The third impulse behind strategies of silence arises from considerations of privilege. That is, who has the right to speak about the violent past? One nearly universal answer to this question privileges one group of people who pass through an experience and thereby assume the right to speak about it over or against others who were not there, and who therefore cannot know and judge. Only those who had been there, so this argument goes, can claim the authority of direct experience required to speak about these matters. This is what I term as essentialist silences.

There are many examples of such silences. Soldiers frequently speak about their war experiences only to other soldiers.[5] In other cases, soldiers express a kind of sexist rejection of the very capacity of women to enter and understand this masculine realm. Others take an essentialist line when defining experience as internal and ineffable. When I addressed a conference on the First World War at the Royal Military College, Sandhurst, some forty years ago, one of the participants, Charles Carrington, who was a noted author and survivor of the Great War, urged me to choose another profession. The reason: 'You will never know the war; only we who were there can know what it was like.' This advice, spoken with avuncular kindness, I acknowledged, ignored, but never forgot.

Other such strictures are more acerbic. Time and again, patriots ask how anyone can criticize soldiers and the choices they make under fire if they haven't been there. And when the fighting is still unfolding, what right civilians have to criticize what they do. Then there is the charge that moral issues are too easily framed by those who had the moral luck to avoid extreme or violent situations. And even among those who endured suffering, there are distinctions drawn between those who knew the worst and those who luckily never reached such a point. Primo Levi said that even survivors like him did not know the worst; that knowledge was restricted only to those at the bottom of the world he inhabited in Auschwitz, the Musselmen, those who had already become the living dead.[6]

Furthermore, others pose the question as to how we judge those who survived the war and kept secrets about their past. Pure and simple condemnation is the easy way out for people who live comfortable lives. Shoshana Felman took this tack in considering the puzzle that her colleague and great literary critic Paul de Man had written anti-Semitic prose in a Belgian newspaper in 1940. This unsavoury fact came to light only after de Man's death in 1982. How do we interpret his behaviour? Felman sees his scrupulous scholarship as distinct from his earlier behaviour, and she goes further in suggesting his silence about his own past was a profound philosophical reflection on the terrible difficulty of all moral judgment, including judging those who as young men and women fell into the trap of the fascist temptation.[7] While not sharing this conclusion, I feel Felman's argument does offer a telling riposte to what E.P. Thompson termed the 'enormous condescension of posterity,'[8] or the tendency to look down upon those stuck in predicaments we ourselves might not have resolved in any morally superior manner.

The problem with this approach to silence is its characteristic essentialism. Few any longer subscribe to the romantic definition of experience as ingested, visceral, and objectively present in the lives and minds of only some individuals. According to this view, experience is theirs and theirs alone. In contradistinction, some, though not all, experiences are more fruitfully defined as a set of events whose character changes when there are changes – through age, migration, illness, marriage, religious conversion, and so on – in the subject position of the person or group that had shared those events.[9] Students of memory in the cognitive and neurosciences no longer view their subject as fixed, as in a computer's hard drive, but more as dynamic and unstable, as in a collage. The work of Elizabeth Loftus has deepened our understanding of implanted memories, ones suggested to individuals by outsiders and sometimes by clinicians in therapeutic relationships. The danger of such interventions is evident.[10] If memory changes radically over time, then we must abandon the notion that not only memory but the right to speak about memory is the property of only a chosen few who recall the experience of what John Calvin termed 'election.'[11] Relegating the rest of us to silence must be seen as a strategy of control, of cutting off debate, of *ad hominem* assertions of a kind unworthy of serious reflection.

Who has the right to speak is a thorny question. War stories are never uncontested, and over time, they change as the people who frame them grow old, move on, and pass away. When the victims of violence have the sanction to speak out, as in a court of law or truth commission, then they become the authors not only of their stories, but also of their lives. Not speaking can entail accepting someone else's story about what happened to you. Or, it may be an assertion of dignity by those who, like rape victims, suffer through indignity. The central point is that the entitlement to speak about war and violence is in no sense universal. Some have the right; others do not. The difference between the two categories is a matter of social and cultural codes, which can and do change over time.

Silence and War

If we accept that the question of how to represent war and the penumbra of violence surrounding it both antedates the Holocaust and has continued long since, we can also escape from an exclusively Eurocentric approach to this matter. Since the Second World War, the institutions of war have fragmented. That is to say that, unlike in the years before 1945, now much public attention is fixed less on international than on transnational or internal conflict. We focus more than ever before on organized violence within states and between non-state agents and territorial states. This is in part because the post-1945 period was one dominated by wars of national liberation or ethnic conflict, leaving in their wake fundamental social, ethnic, and political cleavages, which in turn have bred armed conflicts of many different kinds. The genocide in Rwanda and the ongoing massacres – some say genocide – in Darfur are two African examples of the terrible plight of people caught in these post-colonial wars. Crimes committed in Bosnia during the Yugoslav civil war, in Colombia, in Lebanon, in Sri Lanka, in Kashmir, in Afghanistan, and in Iraq arise from what may be termed the post-national and post-colonial setting of armed conflict. Clearly, as war evolves, the representations of war we construct and the stories we tell about it evolve in turn. Today the collage of organized violence and the suffering it entails is much more complex, even dizzying in its shifting character. The tale of war can no longer be told primarily or exclusively within the unfolding saga of nationalism and the achievement of self-determination and national dignity.

When thinking about contemporary warfare, it is essential to take a step back from our current preoccupations. The Westphalian system of conflicts between states that we tend to take for granted as the natural order of things was nothing of the kind. It was not universal and not timeless. African warfare developed its own character outside of a European system of states. And efforts by colonial powers to keep their hold on colonies struggling for independence usually took on the kind of fragmentary character we mistake as unprecedented. Nothing could be further from the case. Still, the catastrophe of the two world wars has left its imprint on what Samuel Hynes terms our 'war in the head,' our shared assumptions about what war is.[12]

As war changes, so – in an indirect and incomplete manner – do representations of war. The de-centring of the experience of war and violence may make it less useful to apply the categories of memory and forgetting, which frequently assume that the story is determined by a top-down approach to political power configured in a national state. This is the landscape of Orwell's *1984*, a dystopia set in London during the Second World War, and of Camus's *The Plague*, set in Algiers in the same time period. Shifting our attention away from the hegemonic state or police apparatus to a broader social landscape may help reconfigure our understanding of subtler processes of the framing of debate through the construction of silence. This shift could also help us chart the life cycle of silence, in such a way as to show how different memory agents use different means to puncture the balloon of silence and put words in its place. Attention to silence and silencing also helps us turn the tense of our discussion from the passive to the active. Elsewhere I have called for greater rigour in the use of the terms 'memory' and 'forgetting,' such as to point to the person or group remembering or forgetting whenever possible.[13]

Unfortunately, the terms 'collective memory' and 'national memory' are parts of everyday speech, and as such lose any concrete meaning they may once have had. If we turn our discussion towards silence and silencing, there is usually someone not speaking and frequently someone making sure that those who break the rules know the consequences of doing so. Those individuals the historian Carol Gluck has termed 'memory activists' are also those who break silences and change the boundaries between what can and cannot be said. Social agency is the domain of the social construction of silence. On this point, I side with Michel de Certeau as against Michel Foucault in asserting that not all cultural practices can be collapsed into discourse.[14] Silence is one such practice with a life history of its own.

Commemorative Silences

Commemoration is the collective representation of a shared view of a past worth recalling. As such, it is performative; it selects elements of a narrative and necessarily suppresses other sides of the story. All commemorative moments convey representations of war and the loss of life in war, and silences are embedded in the choreography of commemoration.

Problems arise when military disasters or war crimes become the centrepiece of conversations about war. But even when representing a 'happier' facet of war – victory, liberation, or just plain survival – there are difficulties in what to say and what not to say. The key problems arise when wars become democratic. Before the early nineteenth century, nobles or mercenaries waged wars out of a sense of personal honour or for more mercenary reasons. Only the great or the powerful were immortalized in stone or on canvas. But by the twentieth century, war had become everyone's business. The extension of casualty lists to the thousands, then to millions, made commemoration much more difficult. The question arose as to how to glorify those who die in war without glorifying war itself.

One way to do so is to ensure that the names of everyone – and not only the generals – are listed and honoured. And yet even this format does not solve all the problems of remembering war in the modern age. In French, a war memorial is a memorial to the dead – *un monument aux morts*; in English, it is the more equivocal 'war memorial.' Which part of war does it commemorate? The justice of its outbreak? The justice of its outcome? The honourable treatment it gave to enemy prisoners or the wounded? No one knows the answer to these questions, and all commemorators start with the same puzzle: what do we leave out?

Consider but two examples of the problem. The war memorial in New College, Oxford, commemorates all those members of the College who died in the Great War. The question arose, what about German former students who died for the Kaiser? Do they get on the list of the fallen? In this College, the answer is yes; in others the answer is no. A second problem is more recent. In 2006 the British Ministry of Defence said that all those shot for cowardice in the 1914–18 war would be pardoned. This decision opened the door to the addition of these 343 names to war memorials commemorating those who died in that war. To date (2009) it is not at all clear what individual towns and villages will do when asked by a family to put recently pardoned great, great Uncle Harry's name on the town war memorial. These local authorities may choose silence on the issue; but this is hardly surprising since every decision to commemorate is a decision to simplify and clarify a message by leaving out substantial parts of the story surrounding it.[15]

Breaking Silences

All representations of war reflect or convey silences about parts of the story the moral character of which was contested both at the time of the conflict and in its aftermath. In the case of Nazi Germany, while there is a consensus regarding the immoral character of the German regime and the crimes it committed, there was and still is disagreement regarding the ways in which Germans should deal with this immoral past. The German army was up to its neck in the blood of atrocities on the Eastern Front of the Second World War; that historians have proven beyond doubt, but many Germans remained reluctant to admit these facts until two generations had passed.[16]

Silences about war break down when time passes and needs change. As in personal loss, groups of people need time in order to face collective loss or disaster. We have already noted that in many cultures, the initial stage of mourning demands silence. Thereafter men and women may be so busy rehabilitating themselves after a war or a violent conflict that they do not have the time, energy, or will to speak about what happened. At such moments, they may be tempted to absorb and disseminate heroic stories at the heart of their representations of war without much factual basis.

The post-1945 period in Western Europe is a good example. Pieter Lagrou has documented the construction of the myth of national resistance in Belgium, the Netherlands, and France. This heroic tapestry hid a much darker story, one whose re-emergence Henry Rousso has sketched in the case of France.[17] By the 1970s, it was possible to face some of the unpalatable history of the Second World War. Political and economic stability created the conditions for examining some of the hidden facets of the recent past.

What happens to societies happens to veterans of conflicts too. Young ex-soldiers grow old and tend to go over the ground of their youth. Grandchildren ask questions in ways grandparents may feel able at this stage of their lives to answer more fully and sometimes more honestly than they had done in the past. This is evident in the case of the young Israeli soldiers of 1948 interviewed fifty-five years later by Ben Ze'ev.[18] In their old age, they tended to speak of their war experiences differently from the ways they had done in the past. Their youthful certainty about their morality and the justness of their cause had faded.

Generational change may work in other ways too. Benjamin Stora describes how the Harkis (Muslim Algerians who fought on the French side during the Algerian War) kept silent both about 'their' war and about the shabby treatment they received after they came to France in the mid-1960s. Their children felt no such compunction, and by demanding their rights they helped draw aside the veil of silence on the war in Algeria as a whole. Such generational elements are among the many facets of the construction and deconstruction of silences about the Algerian war and about the violent suppression of Algerian demonstrations in Paris in October 1961, which has been the subject of considerable scholarship in recent years.[19]

Sometimes outsiders do the research that changes the way insiders talk about the past. Insiders risk being labelled as outcasts for 'dwelling' too much on the 'negative' history of their country; outsiders have more freedom and less social pressure to confirm self-serving narratives about the past. Doing research on Vichy France in the 1960s and 1970s was a risky matter; there were (and are) too many sensitivities to respect and too many secrets to hide. Young scholars and archivists risked their careers if they started actively snooping around. An American historian faced none of these problems. Robert Paxton wrote his *Vichy France* (1972) on the basis of German archives while important parts of French archives were still closed. Paxton's thesis, which has stood the test of time, was that Vichy policy, including its harsh measures against Jews, was first and foremost a French matter and not a German diktat.[20] Collaboration was thus not primarily an attempt to defend the country against an occupier, but a consciously worked-out vision of a 'better' future, one purged of communists, trade unionists, and Jews.

New academic fashions can also induce discussion of silenced issues. Oral history emerged as a sub-discipline when feminists and subaltern scholars insisted on bringing women's voices and the voices of subject people into the study of the past. Sticking to conventional archives would ensure that they would never be heard. In this way, women have entered the narrative of war, which is no longer gendered to highlight heroic masculinity to the exclusion of half the human race.

Representations of wars of decolonization change over time as well. The official silence in Indonesia regarding the violence that Indonesian 'freedom fighters' inflicted on their fellow villagers during the 1945–9 war of independence against the Netherlands was not easily maintained in the face of sustained research and publications by younger historians and anthropologists using life histories and oral sources. The Indonesian war produced long-lasting silences on the Dutch side as well. The ugliness of the end of colonial rule has never been easy to face. These evasions, silences, and outright lies could not be sustained in light of new research on war told from the soldiers' – and not the politicians' or generals' – point of view.[21]

Even though academic research can draw public attention to silenced past events, of much greater effect are 'memory agents' using trade publications, magazines, television, film, and the Internet to broadcast their historical narratives. Film-makers, journalists, television series producers and fiction writers can reach a much wider public, and can make a difference in broader currents of opinion about what can and cannot be said about the past. Marcel Ophuls's 1969 documentary *Le chagrin et la pitié* (*The Sorrow and the Pity*) dealt with French life under Nazi occupation, focusing on the town of Clermont-Ferrand and emphasizing the active collaboration of many French men and women with the Germans. The film was criticized by some historians as largely distorted and as replacing the myth of a nation of resisters with another one – that of a nation of collaborators. Nevertheless, through skilful interviewing techniques, Ophuls effectively broke the silence regarding French collaboration under Nazi occupation and helped open a debate in France over this subject, a debate which is still alive today.[22] The Italian film-maker Gillo Pontecorvo's 1966 *La Battaglia di Algeri* (*The Battle of Algiers*) produced considerable political controversy in France, and although banned from film theatres in France for five years, it helped to draw public attention to the Algerian war and to stimulate further discussion of dark subjects such as torture. The Senegalese director Ousmane Sembene's 1987 film, *Camp Thiaroye*, contributed to the initial breaking of the silence in Senegal and in France around the French brutal repression of an African soldiers' revolt in December 1944, a subject hidden from sight (and speech) for decades.[23]

The most obvious political change that can alter the boundaries of silence is a departure of a leader, and/or a change of regime. There is dispute among Soviet historians as to whether Stalin's purges constituted a war against his own people. My own view is that this was indeed the case. Nikita Khrushchev's speech at the Twentieth Congress of the Communist Party in 1956, three years after Stalin's death in which he criticized actions taken by the deceased leader, is a prominent example as to how and when silences collapse. Even though knowledge of his speech was confined initially to the forum of party members, Khrushchev had accomplished something no one had dared to do while Stalin was still alive. His euphemism for mass murder and for the war Stalin and his henchmen waged against the Soviet people – the cult of personality – fooled no one. Six years later, in 1962, the publication of Solzhenitsyn's *One Day in the Life of Ivan Denisovitch* broadcast the message in a story devastating in that it is simply the story of a good day; readers had little difficulty imagining what a bad day – or thirty years of bad days – was like.

The death or departure of a dictator does not always end the silence surrounding crimes committed under his rule. Indonesian historians and journalists may treat Suharto's role in the Indonesian revolution in a more critical light now that he has gone, but there is still much that cannot be said, at least in public, about many facets of his rule.[24] The same is true for the succession of rulers who have come to power in Ankara. The role of a long-defunct regime – that of the Ottoman Empire – in the Armenian genocide of 1915 still today cannot be discussed in public in Turkey; continuing such an embargo on speech is both absurd and an obstacle to Turkey's wish to join the European Union. Donald Bloxham and Taner Akcam have shown how Turkish fears of national dismemberment, based on some elements of reality in 1915, have become frozen into legally imposed silence.[25] The silence-breakers are still working at their task, and at their best, as in the work of Akcam and Peter Belakian,[26] they describe a future in which Turks and Armenians must and will speak to each other openly about their common past.

The May 1968 student revolt helped break a number of silences. Here was a generation's protest against a certain type of society and therefore, implicitly, of a certain vision of its history. The students challenged a society that had taken refuge behind the 'myth of the resistance' promoted, indeed embodied, by the then president Charles de Gaulle.[27] When he resigned, the obstacles to breaking the silence of the Vichy years shrank considerably.

Social movements can throw a searchlight on the past and uncover corners hitherto darkened by consent or conspiracy. In Germany and Austria in 1968, the student revolt had many targets including the war in Vietnam. But at its core, these protestors pointed an accusing finger at their parents' generation, not just with respect to their materialism but with respect to what they had done or had not done during the Third Reich.[28] In Vienna, a group of young medical students and doctors exposed the experiments on Jewish children conducted in the Nazi period by Dr Heinrich Gross in the Spiegelgrund Children's Hospital in Vienna. He never went to jail, hiding behind his reputation as a scientist and his advanced age, but his exposure was characteristic of the accusatory nature of inter-generational conflict in 1968 and after.[29] After 1968, both discussions and representations of the Second World War were inextricably braided together with ideas about and representations of the Holocaust.

Morally ambiguous chapters in the history of Israel time and again have become tied up in silences embedded deeply in the ways Israelis represent the series of wars they have fought since the 1940s. Ariel

Sharon was deemed by an Israeli judicial commission to be indirectly responsible for war crimes committed at the Sabra and Shatila refugee camps in 1982 during the Israeli invasion of Lebanon. Asher Kaufman[30] has shown that the focus on his culpability drew attention away from many other morally dubious episodes in that campaign while ultimately not preventing Sharon's re-emergence, twenty years later, as a man of peace and prime minister of his country. On the contrary: everyone knew about Sharon and the events of Sabra and Shatila, but no one talked about it.

Shameful incidents in a country's history can quickly recede into silence: the current eclipse of discussions of the crimes committed by American and Allied forces in Iraq is another case in point. Before Obama's election, these stories were widely circulated; thereafter, they faded away. No country to my knowledge is immune from the tendency to turn away as rapidly as possible from its inglorious recent past.

Conclusion

My central argument is that representations of war in language, material culture, and commemorative practices always embrace silences. These silences are constructed and maintained in many ways. First, morally ambiguous chapters of a country's account of its wars cannot be faced easily, and which country does not have them? This is recognized by small groups, by larger populations, and by societies as a whole. The risk is that talking about the past presents the danger of a breakdown of the legitimacy or the authority of a regime. In one respect, silence then is the insurance policy people take to protect the given order, even at the cost of the truth. This is the motor force behind what I term political silences in representations of war.

Secondly, over time such veils of silence fray, tear, disintegrate, or are torn apart. Memory activists – artists, poets, novelists, museum curators, historians, and others – are critical players in this process, and they work against the backdrop of the movement of time and the inevitable passage of generations. New technologies of the archiving and retrieval of survivors' accounts of war help dispel some silences, though not all. The braiding together of representations of the Second World War with representations of the Holocaust was partly due to the availability from the 1970s of cheap and efficient audio and video cassette recorders. Holocaust testimonies are now part of the archive of war. When the Imperial War Museum opened its wing dealing with the Holocaust, it presented many of the voices and faces of the survivors. By doing so, the museum recognized a wider change in representations of war within British society and beyond that has enabled people to see genocide as part of war. This very popular wing of the museum disseminates this view to a substantial population of visitors who see the Holocaust literally on top of representations of the two world wars. In this new use of space, the museum successfully broke its silence (alongside other silences) on the Holocaust. And just above the Holocaust wing is a new floor devoted to representations of later war crimes and genocide throughout the world. The new spatial organization of the Imperial War Museum speaks volumes about changing representations of war.

The evolution of the Imperial War Museum's representations of war is a story of changing scholarship, museology, and public attitudes. Here the political dimension of silence-breaking was by and large absent. No politician said that this design must be adopted, or that design scrapped. In many other countries, political pressures are more evident. When historians designed a display at the Smithsonian Museum in Washington on the dropping of the atomic bomb, veterans irate at the emphasis on Japanese suffering successfully forced changes in the way the subject was treated.[31]

No one should adopt a superior tone when confronting political pressures on those charged with representing wars in the developing world. All nations have skeletons in their own closets that resemble those hidden elsewhere. Still, a rough rule of thumb is that the process of democratization entails an ending of socially accepted silences about what happened in wartime, be it in Europe or beyond. The gradual democratization process in Senegal beginning in 1974 and accelerating with the resignation of Léopold Sédar Senghor in 1980 allowed playwrights and film-makers to criticize neocolonial relations with France and re-evaluate the French presence in this African country before and after independence.[32] The Spanish transition from Franco's dictatorship to a constitutional monarchy shows, though, that some silences may linger long after the new institutions of a democratic state have been established. Democracies have their silences too, and they are perhaps more insidious because they appear to be enforced without visible coercion.

We are fortunate in that there are people in a position to violate codes of silence in a way denied to or rejected by the rest of us. Madmen, actors, comedians, holy men, poets, and troubadours frequently occupy liminal positions within society, and sometimes manage to say the unsayable and live to tell the tale again. They renew, so to speak, our poetic licence, and help us, perhaps force us, to hear the silences built into the language we use to describe the past. Even under the most horrifying conditions, some individuals who perform language still have the courage and the conviction to speak out, and by doing so, point to what everyone else knows but is not saying.[33] This is as true in the case of civil wars or domestic repression as it is of international conflict. The writing of Alexander Solzhenitsyn and Anna Akhmatova are instances of this kind of silence-breaking, which bears on our theme even though their words dealt with a war waged by a dictator against his own people.[34] Unsanitized representations of conventional warfare in poetry, prose, and the visual arts are similar in character, helping to strip away the veil hiding the ugliness of the landscape of battle and the bodies strewn over it.

In sum, there are many reasons why we must study silences when we study representations of war. I have tried to show that silence has liturgical and essentialist functions, as much as political ones, and that while the political domain is ubiquitous in this field, we should also note that the subject of war and violence always touches the sphere of the sacred,[35] and in that sphere there are always silences. I have noted that many veterans of wars insist that only those who 'know' through direct experience can speak about war, but also that this claim is filled with contradictions and flaws. I have insisted that there are agents of silencing intent on keeping the lid on certain topics or words, just as there are memory agents equally dedicated to blowing the lid off. We need to recognize as well the socially sanctioned role of liminal figures, like writers, comedians, actors, who live in a special space accorded to risky speech, who can offend and provoke by saying things that everyone knows about war but no one dares to say in public. In sum, we all live our lives surrounded by a cloud of socially produced silence, a cloud which can be opaque or vanish in a flash.

Silence is not one but many things, and all occupy and frame the landscape of remembrance. When we represent war, we select, we distort, we speak some words and swallow others. This is inevitable, given the protean character of war and the painful legacies it leaves in its wake. The French writer Maurice Blanchot summed up this point with uncharacteristic Gallic directness: 'To be silent is still to speak,' he wrote in 1952.[36] And to speak of silence as a social phenomenon is to speak of the myriad ways in which representations of war are framed by silence. We all observe silences, and thereby tend to deal with moral ambiguities, to live with and through contradictions, by at one and the same time both remembering *and* forgetting truths about our violent past.

NOTES

1 Marc Augé, *Les formes de l'oubli* (Paris: Payot & Rivages, 1998), 4.
2 Branden W. Joseph, 'John Cage and the Architecture of Silence,' *October* 81 (Summer, 1997): 80–104.
3 Mary Vincent, 'Breaking the Silence? Memory and Oblivion since the Spanish Civil War,' in *Shadows of War: A Social History of Silence in the Twentieth Century*, ed. Efrat Ben-Ze'ev, Ruth Ginio, and Jay Winter (Cambridge: Cambridge University Press, 2010), ch. 3.
4 Louis Bethlehem, 'Now That All Is Said and Done: Reflections on the Truth and Reconciliation Commission in South Africa,' in *Shadows of War*, ed. Ben-Ze'ev, Ginio, and Winter, ch. 8.
5 Efrat Ben Ze'ev has studied an annual reunion of the members of a unit in the Israeli army of 1948; these events continue to this day. See Efrat Ben Ze'ev, 'Imposed Silences and Self-Censorship: *Palmach* soldiers remember 1948,' in *Shadows of War*, ed. Ben-Ze'ev, Ginio, and Winter, ch. 10.
6 Primo Levi, *Survival in Auschwitz* (New York: Basic Books, 2002), 90.
7 Shoshana Felman, 'Paul de Man's Silence,' *Critical Inquiry* 15 (1989): 704–44.
8 E.P. Thompson, *The Making of the English Working Class* (London: Victor Gollancz, 1963), 18.
9 Joan W. Scott, 'The Evidence of Experience,' *Critical Inquiry* 17 (1991): 773–97.
10 Daniel Schacter, *The Seven Sins of Memory* (Cambridge, MA: Harvard University Press, 1999), 20–3; Elizabeth Loftus, *Eyewitness Testimony* (Cambridge, MA: Harvard University Press, 1979); Veronica Nourkova, Daniel M. Bernstein, and Elizabeth Loftus, 'Biography Becomes Autobiography: Distorting the Subjective Past,' *American Journal of Psychology* 117 (2004): 65–80.
11 Jay Winter, *Remembering War: The Great War between History and Memory in the Twentieth Century* (New Haven, CT: Yale University Press, 2006), ch. 1.
12 Samuel Hynes, *The Soldiers' Tale* (New York: Penguin, 2000).
13 Jay Winter and Emmanuel Sivan, eds., *War and Remembrance in the Twentieth Century* (Cambridge: Cambridge University Press, 1999), ch. 1.
14 For a fuller discussion, see Winter, *Remembering War*, ch. 1.
15 On Oxford and Cambridge war memorials, see Jay M. Winter, *The Great War and the British People*, 2nd ed. (Basingstoke: Palgrave Macmillan, 2000), ch. 3. On the question of posthumous pardons, see Andrew MacKinlay, 'The Pardons Campaign,' *Western Front Association Bulletin* 39 (1994): 28–9.

16 Omer Bartov, *Germany's War and the Holocaust: Disputed Histories* (Ithaca, NY: Cornell University Press, 2003).

17 Pieter Lagrou, *The Legacy of Nazi Occupation: Patriotic Memory and National Recovery in Western Europe, 1945–1965* (Cambridge: Cambridge University Press, 2000); Henry Rousso, *The Vichy Syndrome: History and Memory in France since 1944*, trans. A. Goldhammer (Cambridge, MA: Harvard University Press, 1994), 10.

18 Ben Ze'ev, 'Imposed Silences.'

19 Benjamin Stora, *La gangrène et l'oubli: La mémoire de la guerre d'Algérie* (Paris: La Découverte, 1991), 261–5; Raphaëlle Branche and Jim House, 'Silences on State Violence during the Algerian War of Independence: France and Algeria, 1962–2007,' in *Shadows of War*, ed. Ben-Ze'ev, Ginio, and Winter, ch. 6.

20 John F. Sweets, 'Hold That Pendulum! Redefining Fascism, Collaborationism and Resistance in France,' *French Historical Studies* 15 (1988): 745.

21 Stef Scagliola, 'The Silences and Myths of a "Dirty War": Coming to Terms with the Dutch-Indonesian Decolonization War (1945–1949),' *European Review of History* 14 (2007): 249–51.

22 Another influential film was Louis Malle's *Lacombe Lucien* (1984), a fictional recreation of the last months of the occupation in southern France. Malle tells the story of a seventeen-year-old boy who works for the Gestapo after being turned away by the maquis. He is not so much immoral as amoral, an innocent fascinated by violence who could just as easily have been a Resistance hero.

23 Ruth Ginio, 'African Silences: Negotiating the Story of France's Colonial Soldiers, 1914–2009,' in *Shadows of War*, ed. Ben-Ze'ev, Ginio, and Winter, ch. 7.

24 Ginio, 'African Silences.'

25 *Taner Akçam*, 'Facing History: Denial and the Turkish National Security Concept,' in *Shadows of War*, ed. Ben-Ze'ev, Ginio, and Winter, ch. 9; Donald Bloxham, *The Great Game of Genocide: Imperialism, Nationalism, and the Destruction of the Ottoman Armenians* (Oxford: Oxford University Press, 2005).

26 Peter Belakian, *The Black Dog of Fate* (New York: Basic Books, 1997).

27 Rousso, *The Vichy Syndrome*, 98–9.

28 Michael A. Schmidtke, 'Cultural Revolution or Cultural Shock? Student Radicalism and 1968 in Germany,' *South Central Review* 14, no. 4 (2000): 77–89.

29 Thanks are due to Helmut Konrad, of the University of Graz, who has drawn this story to my attention.

30 Asher Kaufman, 'Forgetting the Lebanon War? On Silence, Denial and Selective Remembrance of the "First" Lebanon War,' in *Shadows of War: A*

Social History of Silence in the Twentieth Century, ed. Ben Ze'ev, Ginio, and Winter (Cambridge: Cambridge University Press, 2010), ch. 11.

31 On historical controversy and museums, see Margaret Macmillan, *The Uses and Abuses of History* (Toronto: Penguin Books, 2009).

32 Ginio, 'African Silences.'

33 The literature here is vast; for an aperitif, see Mary Douglas, *Purity and Danger: An Analysis of Concepts of Pollution and Taboo* (New York: Praeger, 1966); Victor Turner, *The Anthropology of Performance* (New York: PAJ Publications, 1986); Jan Kott, *Shakespeare Our Contemporary*, trans. B. Taborski (New York: Norton, 1974).

34 Alexander Solzhenitsyn, *The Gulag Archipelago*, 3 vols. (Boulder, CO: Westview Press, 1995), 69; Robin Kemball, 'Anna Akhmatova's "Requiem, 1935–1940,"' *Russian Review* 33 (1974): 303–12.

35 On the uses of the term 'the sacred,' there is a vast literature. For a start, see Thomas A. Idinopulos and Edward A. Yonan, eds., *The Sacred and Its Scholars: Comparative Methodologies for the Study of Primary Religious Data* (Leiden: E.J. Brill, 1996).

36 Maurice Blanchot, *The Writing of the Disaster*, trans. Ann Smock (Lincoln: University of Nebraska Press, 1986), 11.

2 Not Writing about War

KATE MCLOUGHLIN

Introduction: War Cannot and Should Not Be Written About

The reasons not to write about war are myriad and compelling. They fall into two overlapping categories: war cannot be written about and war should not be written about. For a start, war cannot be written about because the logistical difficulties of doing so are insuperable (the sheer scale of armed conflict is prohibitive). This makes a synoptic view practically and politically problematic to obtain. Then there is a premium on first-hand experience (or 'combat gnosticism')[1] that undermines the validity of non-combatant representations. Combatant representations are themselves suspect as they may lack the necessary distance and detachment; censorship and self-censorship are in force. The sensibilities and proprieties of various periods (on the part of writer, publisher, and reader) limit graphic description. The psychophysiological ability to articulate is vitiated by stress. Telling is also inhibited by the fear that no one will (properly) listen or by the sense that it is psychologically appropriate not to dwell on atrocity but to move on. Above all, the incommensurability of armed conflict lies in its capacity to inflict trauma on both a mass and a personal scale: parents, children, and spouses die as national boundaries are reconfigured and peoples decimated. The depth and breadth of the pain, loss, and horror constitute what Theodor Adorno in *Negative Dialectics* (1966) calls 'the extremity that eludes the concept.'[2] In a 2008 essay, 'Variations on the Right to Remain Silent,' Anne Carson posits an order of unsayable experience, giving as examples the voices heard by Joan of Arc, the scream that Francis Bacon sensed inside Velázquez's *Portrait of Pope Innocent X* and wished to paint, and the word 'moly' – an instance of what Homer called 'the language of the gods' with no equivalent in any mortal tongue. Carson terms these phenomena 'untranslatable': attempting to verbalize them results only in a 'catastrophizing of communication.'[3] Armed conflict is of this order of experience: it can be known but, arguably, not put into words.

It is also debatable whether it should be put into words. The ethical risks inherent in writing about war include voyeurism, sadism, bias, exploitation of others' suffering, invasion of privacy, and accommodation of atrocity. But at the same time, other considerations point to the absolute necessity of representing conflict: to act as a form of protest; to warn against future wars and even to prevent them; to keep an accurate record; to memorialize the dead; to give meaning to mass loss; to function as catharsis or therapy; to reduce the gap in understanding between combatant and non-combatant (particularly so that the former may be reintegrated into the community upon homecoming).

What arises is a complex situation in which war simultaneously cannot be, should not be, and must be represented. Not surprisingly, a common response to these contradictory imperatives has been to greet them with silence. Silence in the face of war is powerful, not least when experienced as the ritual refraining-from-sound observed in many parts of the world on martial anniversaries. The London *Times* reported on what, in 1920, was only the second time the two-minute Great Silence had been kept on Armistice Day in Britain: 'Time and space were obliterated, and the thoughts of men and women encircled the world ... The tension was almost too great. When seconds seemed to halt people held their breath lest they should be heard in the stillness.'[4] But silence as a representation of war, as opposed to a memorial response to it, is problematic. How can it be staged as a textual event? As the *Times* piece eloquently illustrates, silence requires words to record and even interpret it. 'When the words in the city are full of savagery and lies, nothing speaks louder than the unwritten poem,' George Steiner writes[5] – but how can such unwritten poems actually be heard? Again, Maurice Blanchot asserts that 'not writing is among the effects of writing'[6] – but how can such an effect be registered and known?

Paradoxical as it may seem, there do exist a number of strategies for not writing about war, and, more paradoxical still, they are deployed in the very process of writing about it. Such strategies, worked out in literature over centuries, range from topoi to subject matter, pushing linguistic resources to their limits in the project of *not* telling. To point out this phenomenon is not new. In particular, since the Second World

War, theorists of representation of the Holocaust have debated the possibility and advisability of silence;[7] two early but still influential essays by Steiner – 'The Retreat from the Word' (1961) and 'Silence and the Poet' (1966) – are quoted in this chapter to illuminate the view that silence in the face of atrocity is not only possible and imperative but takes on a kind of luminous significance. But it is not sufficient simply to note the tactics of indirection; this chapter also attempts to theorize them. In this attempt, Immanuel Kant's account of the sublime is helpful in that it suggests, stage by stage, how a reader's capacity to make aesthetic judgments can successfully intervene even when a subject seems ungraspable.

This chapter now looks at avoidance strategies in action in four texts, chosen because they indicate if not a non-writing tradition (no intertextual influence is asserted), then at least the possibility of a common practice. The texts are Charles Wolfe's 'The Burial of Sir John Moore after Corunna' (written ca 1814), Wilfred Owen's 'Anthem for Doomed Youth' (1917), Dylan Thomas's 'A Refusal to Mourn the Death, by Fire, of a Child in London' (1944), and Ernest Hemingway's 'On the Quai at Smyrna' (ca 1926–7). The last is a useful prose counterpoint to demonstrate that exploiting obliquity is not the sole prerogative of verse. Some generic variety in the works discussed is further evidence of what the tactics of indirection *can* do in the complex project of representing war.

A Strangely Hurried Burial

Wolfe's poem on the burial of the Scottish general Sir John Moore (1761–1809), commander of the British Army during the Peninsular War from 1808 to 1809, contains only a couple of oblique references to the military encounter in which he died. The battle took place on 16 January 1809, at A Coruña, north-west Spain, as, under pressure from French forces headed by Marshal Soult, Moore led the British in retreat to the coast, intending to sail for home. Though Moore was killed, the battle was a British victory and the majority of his troops were able to embark safely (albeit still in retreat).[8] Describing Moore's interment from the point of view of a member or members (the first person plural is used) of the burial party, the poem remarks that the general is laid down 'From the field of his fame fresh and gory.'[9] This allusion to the recentness and bloodiness of Moore's injuries scarcely does justice to the historical event: according to a contemporary report, an enemy cannon-shot threw him from his horse and 'carried away his left shoulder and part of the collar-bone, leaving the arm hanging by the flesh.'[10] Nonethe-less, the cursory reference is an example of what, after the semiotics of C.S. Peirce, may be termed an 'indexical' account of war. What is being described is not battle itself but the physical signs of battle's effects: in Peircean semiotics, the gore on Moore's dead body signifies war in the same way that smoke signifies fire.[11] Privileging the indexical over the iconic, Wolfe is effectively constructing a text with a battle-shaped hole at its heart.[12]

The depiction of the injured or dead body is part of a distinct subgen-re of war writing: a concentration on the 'outskirts' of armed conflict (at least when combat is located as the central experience). Circumventing what Walt Whitman called 'the red business' of actual fighting,[13] this subgenre deals in such phenomena as eve-of-battle scenes, preparation, waiting and recovery, aftermath. It may aptly be termed 'parapolem-ics':[14] the discourse of the temporal and spatial borders of war (it is traditionally the field to which those without combat experience, par-ticularly women, are confined). With the word 'distant' – 'the distant and random gun / That the foe was sullenly firing' – Wolfe matches the parapolemical subject matter of his poem with its mise-en-scène.

Within the poem, there are further distancing effects. Wolfe deploys euphemism, favouring words with pleasant or positive connotations over harsher or more offensive terms that would more precisely desig-nate what is intended.[15] In instances of the rhetorical downsizing device of meiosis (allied to litotes), Moore's grave becomes a 'bed,' the earth his head will lie on becomes a 'smoothed down ... pillow,' and death becomes 'sleep.' Euphemisms – as in this case – are often also clichés. According to Carson, 'we resort to cliché because it's easier than try-ing to make up something new. Implicit in it is the question, Don't we already know what we think about this? Don't we have a formula we use for this?'[16] The deployment of cliché and euphemism – widespread in war writing – 'throws white paint'[17] over its subject, hiding it from view rather than illuminating it.

Further strategies are used to distance the poem from war. The pre-dominant structural unit is negative. Wolfe concentrates not on what did occur or what was present, but on what did not or was not: 'Not a drum was heard,' 'not a funeral note,' 'Not a soldier discharged his farewell shot,' 'No useless coffin enclosed his breast,' 'Not in sheet or in shroud we wound him,' 'Few and short were the prayers,' 'not a word of sorrow,' 'We carved not a line, and we raised not a stone.' But the reality of Moore's interment was rather different. From the field of fighting outside the town, six soldiers carried him in a blanket – slowly, so as not to cause him pain by jostling his wounds – to his lodgings in Corunna, where he died some hours later, aware of the British victory.[18] In *A Narrative of the Campaign of the British Army in Spain*, the dedication of which is dated 4 July 1809, James Carrick Moore wrote of his elder brother's death: 'From a sentiment of veneration that has been felt in every age, the corpse of a man who has excited admiration cannot be neglected as common clay. This impression leads mankind sometimes to treat an inanimate body with peculiar respect; and even to bestow upon it unfelt honours.'[19] Rather than 'hurrying' his corpse out for burial, Moore's military colleagues deliberated over how to inter it with more than usual honour. James Carrick Moore continues his account:

> When Colonel Anderson informed them, that he had heard the General repeatedly declare, 'that, if he was killed in battle, he wished to be buried where he had fallen!' General Hope and Colonel Graham immediately acceded to this suggestion: and it was determined that the body should be interred on the rampart of the Citadel of Corunna.
>
> At twelve o'clock at night the remains of Sir John Moore were accordingly carried to the Citadel … and deposited in Colonel Graham's quarters.
>
> A grave was dug by a party of the 9th Regiment, the Aides-de-Camp attending by turns. No coffin could be procured, and the body was never undressed, but wrapt up by the Officers of his Staff in a military cloak and blankets.
>
> Towards eight o'clock in the morning some firing was heard. It was then resolved to finish the interment, lest a serious attack should be made; on which the Officers would be ordered away, and not suffered to pay the last duties to their General.
>
> The officers of his family bore the body to the grave; the funeral service was read by the Chaplain, and the corpse was covered with earth.[20]

Now, an account of Moore's death very similar to this appeared in the Edinburgh *Annual Register* for 1808 (published on 21 July 1810) in a 'History of Europe' written by Robert Southey.[21] It follows James Carrick Moore's version, with the addition of a single salient detail. This was that the interment was 'hastened' when the enemy firing was heard.[22] It was the *Register*'s version, read to him by a fellow student at Trinity College, Dublin, that would inspire Wolfe to compose his verses.[23] Far from believing that 'not a funeral note' and 'not a word of sorrow' were heard, Wolfe would have been aware that Moore had received the full rites of burial, including the funeral service read by the Chaplain and the 'last duties' of his fellow officers. No coffin or shroud was available, but the funeral ritual was not hastened halfway through ('But half of our heavy task was done') and the interment did not take place 'darkly at dead of night ... / By the struggling moonbeam's misty light / And the lanthorn dimly burning' but early in the morning. The final couplet 'We carved not a line, and we raised not a stone, / But we left him alone with his glory' is an ironic written testament to non-writing (the literary monument cancels out the lack of lapidary monument), but it also ignores significant subsequent memorializing of which Wolfe would also presumably have been aware: a vote of thanks proposed to Moore in the House of Lords on 25 January 1809;[24] James Carrick Moore's *A Narrative of the Campaign of the British Army in Spain*, published in July 1809, with twenty pages of eulogies to his brother;[25] a monument erected by the Spanish at Corunna over Moore's grave, later made permanent by the British; the marking of the precise spot where he fell; the erection in 1809 of a public monument in St Paul's Cathedral, London, on the orders of the British government (the placing of a statue, paid for by public subscription, in the central square of Moore's hometown, Glasgow, came later, in 1819).[26] Indeed, the final stanza itself, with its reference to the field of his 'fame,' confusingly suggests that Moore's conduct in his last battle was instantly renowned. What, then, motivated Wolfe to claim the opposite of these things, to insist – ten negatives in the poem – on the absence or lack of due obsequies?

Likely, his motivation was his recognition of the power of indirection. The device Wolfe uses is a species of paralipsis (also known as cataphasis): the rhetorical trope of stating and drawing attention to something in the very act of appearing to pass it over. The trick of this trope depends upon the power of the absent referent: conjuring up what is not there by naming it *in absentia*. Every element listed in Wolfe's lines is felt as something missing and therefore summoned into virtual being. Hence the rudimentary burial evokes the respect due to the great warrior, the lack of ceremony evokes the famous victory (and, in passing, Wolfe comments on the vanity of all earthly glory). Aided by a balladic form more suited to bruiting martial exploits than elegizing, the poem points beyond its ostensible subject matter of a modest burial to trace the contours of a bloody battle. In the manner of a military feint, Wolfe exposes war by drawing attention elsewhere.

An Anthem That Is Not an Anthem

A century later, another poem was written about what was not available by way of obsequies to those killed in armed conflict. Wilfred Owen had served at the front in the First World War for some eighteen months before he was posted, suffering from shell shock, to Craiglockhart War Hospital outside Edinburgh, where, with some help from Siegfried Sassoon, he composed 'Anthem for Doomed Youth.'[27] 'Anthem' opens with what seems like a rhetorical question – 'What passing-bells for these who die as cattle?'[28] – but an immediate reply demonstrates that this is no empty enquiry:[29] '– Only the monstrous anger of the guns.' In his first draft, Owen followed this with 'Let the majestic insults of their mouths / Be as the priest-words of their burials.'[30] As Dominic Hibberd points out, this could be interpreted as 'a statement in support of the British war effort': 'the only possible response to the slaughter (of British troops) is that "our" guns should hurl angry "insults" at the enemy.'[31] But the original wording makes a further suggestion: that interment is a possibility. In no subsequent draft did Owen make the mistake of mentioning 'burials': disinterment and lack of interment were the norm in the trenches of France and Belgium during the First World War, where corpses were routinely used to prop up dugouts, form parapets, and line trenches, and where half the British dead left no identifiable body.[32] Later versions of the poem concentrated on the absent or the insufficient, moving from the inappropriate replacements of the battlefield in the octave to the pathetic stand-ins of the home front in the sestet. Words such as 'only' (repeated) and 'save' emphasize the inadequacy of the substitutes. The rattle of the rifles and the wailing shells and calling bugles make a cacophonous contrast with prayers (the pleonasm of 'orisons' and 'prayers' makes this a doubly felt lack), bells, and voices of mourning. The 'glimmers of goodbyes' in boys' eyes and the 'pallor of girls' brows' are small consolation for candles and palls. Instead of flowers, there is but 'the tenderness of patient minds' and the fall of dusk must do for the respectful closing of curtains. There is one jarring element in the series of negatives: 'No mockeries now for them.' Inconsistent with the structure of gap-and-unsatisfactory-substitute, this suggests that the dead are now (happily) beyond insult (a suggestion in line with Hibberd's reading of the first draft of the poem). The antithesis to the overall thesis that the dead are let down or dishonoured by the missing obsequies, the line opens the way for synthesis but there is none. A rogue entry in the catalogue of absences, 'No mockeries now for them' permanently perforates the poem's fabric.

Like Wolfe, then, Owen exploits the power of both parapolemics and paralipsis. The trope of the inadequate substitute extends even to the poem's title. It was Sassoon who suggested 'Anthem' (initially 'for Dead Youth'), but Owen declared it 'just what I meant it to be.'[33] Yet, just as the rifles' rattles are no orisons and the pallor of girls' brows no palls, the 'Anthem' is no anthem, at least in the OED definition of 'a song, as of praise or gladness.' Reproachful and sorrowing rather than praiseful or glad, Owen's sonnet is a dirge, a non-anthem or anti-anthem for bodies missing anyway: a hole where an anthem should be. Steiner, writing on efforts in modern art to access what is anterior to language or outside it, notes the proliferation of titles that are 'often … ironic mystification[s]' and a tendency within the works to 'seek to establish reference only to themselves.'[34] In its own (mis-)naming, Owen's 'Anthem' turns inwards – away from the war – only to collapse in on itself by failing to fulfil its own self-description.

Mourning Postponed

Dylan Thomas's 'A Refusal to Mourn the Death, by Fire, of a Child in London' works this trick in reverse. In attempting to give a child's death in the London Blitz due deference and meaning, Thomas arguably shows a willingness to mourn. But the poem is, again, constructed on negativity. The first thirteen lines out of twenty-four – from 'Never until the mankind making' to 'the child's death'[35] – are an extended statement of what the speaker will not do and when he will not do it. These lines are rich in periphrasis or *circumlocutio* ('salt seed' for tears, the multiple-epithet-bearing darkness), bypassing the bombardment to the point of baffling readers. 'On the poem *A Refusal to Mourn* Mr. Holbrook grumbles that it is not clear why the poet says he won't say things,' wrote William Empson waspishly. 'The poem is about the German bombing of London, and the poet erected not writing propaganda into a point of honour. There is no great credit in not understanding this.'[36] Like euphemism and cliché, periphrasis and abstraction throw white paint at their intended subjects, redirecting the discourse from the apparent matter in hand.

But the first thirteen lines of 'A Refusal to Mourn' go further than abstraction. Thomas sets a number of conditions that must be fulfilled before he will mourn. To paraphrase, before grieving can take place, the darkness must signal the last day, the sea must be still, and the speaker himself must have returned in death to the elements, his atoms re-entering the promised land that is the drop of water and the holy place that is the ear of corn. To satisfy such conditions is obviously impossible, not least because the speaker's own death would prevent his mourning anyway. The stipulation of insuperable requirements is the rhetorical device known as adynaton or *impossibilia*. In Virgil's first Eclogue, for example, Tityrus extravagantly claims that deer will graze in the air and the sea will deposit fish naked on the shore before the future Emperor Augustus's face fades from people's memories.[37] These outcomes being impossible, the poet neatly figures a fame in perpetuity. In Thomas's case, the insuperable criteria serve to postpone mourning indefinitely.

Therefore also in play in the poem is the rhetorical figure of *praeteritio*. Though this term can be used loosely to describe the strategy of drawing attention to something by professing to omit it (the function of paralipsis mentioned above), it more strictly refers to a temporal act of passing over. *Praeteritio* says, 'I will speak of this, but not yet' – in Thomas's case, the claim is 'I will mourn, but not yet.' Deferring the expression of grief, 'A Refusal to Mourn' is an elegiac rain check.

A twenty-four-line postponement of mourning may seem a counterintuitive way to mark the London Blitz. Yet, arguably, Thomas is not so much ignoring or diminishing the catastrophe as drawing back from it. George Steiner writes: 'language does have its frontiers … it borders on three other modes of statement – light, music, and silence,' and when the poet enters the last of these, 'the word borders not on radiance or music, but on night.'[38] In its apocalyptic and sacred-sounding imagery, 'A Refusal to Mourn' borders light and silence/darkness, invoking 'the last light breaking' and the stillness of the sea. But, while Steiner is concerned with the evocation of the ineffable 'transcendent presence in the fabric of the world,'[39] the unsayable in Thomas's case is the pain and loss inflicted by a bombing campaign of the Second World War. In what amounts to a 'private notation'[40] of abstract images, combined with the metonymy of the death of a single child ('After the first death, there is no other'), Thomas conveys the scale of the trauma even as he deliberately refuses to acknowledge it.

A Non-Story

If Thomas's circumlocutions obscure through their richness, the opposite is true of Hemingway's unclassifiable 'On the Quai at Smyrna.' For Steiner, the Hemingway style is a 'thin medium,' but he also calls it 'a powerful lyric, shorthand.'[41] 'On the Quai at Smyrna' was first published as 'Introduction by the Author' in the 1930 Scribner's edition of *In Our Time*, but it is likely to have been written around 1926–7,[42] when Hemingway was still in the process of honing his pared-down declarative sentences. But even when the author's application of his favourite 'iceberg principle,' his journalistic apprenticeship on the *Kansas City Star* and the *Toronto Daily Star*,[43] the plain speaking that was in the stylistic air, and the wish to reproduce the clipped discourse of a British officer are taken into consideration, 'On the Quai at Smyrna' still constitutes a notably oblique account of an incident in the Graeco-Turkish War of 1922.

Like the poems already considered, this piece of prose is distinctive for the gaps in its information (incidentally demonstrating that the tactics of indirection go beyond poetic obliquity). With no prior knowledge, the reader may wonder who exactly is speaking; who 'they' are who are screaming; who the women with the dead babies are and why the babies are dead; who or what has to be cleared off the pier; what is meant by 'it wasn't at all like an earthquake or that sort of thing because they never knew about the Turk'; who ordered whom 'not to come in to take off any more.'[44] It is possible to read critical explanations that furnish enough historical details to make all these puzzles clear,[45] but to supplement Hemingway's text in this way is arguably to miss the point of the speaker's failure to be forthcoming. Horror has been witnessed – 'That was the only time in my life I got so I dreamed about things' – and is simultaneously being tentatively revisited and strenuously avoided. In the words of Cathy Caruth, 'the historical power of the trauma is not just that the experience is repeated after its forgetting, but that it is only in and through its inherent forgetting that it is first experienced at all.'[46] The traumatized voice of 'On the Quai' attempts to approach the atrocity, but various lacunae make this a lacerated narrative. The beginning *in media res* denies the reader the sense-making assistance of a context.[47] The 'welter of antecedentless pronouns'[48] makes it difficult to identify the voice(s) of the piece. The references to information that is presumed already to be known to the interlocutor ('You remember when they ordered us not to come in to take off any more?' 'You remember the harbor')[49] but that is not in the public domain and so is unavailable to the reader creates confusion. Irony adds to the sense that the piece's *prima facie* meaning is not reliable, and the inclusion of 'non-stories' induces perplexity.

The irony in 'On the Quai' consists of straight semantic reversals. 'Great friends we were,' 'plenty of nice things floating around in it,' 'nice chaps,' and 'a most pleasant business' all signify the opposite of their ostensible meanings. The 'non-stories' are three. The narrator relates that a Turkish officer complained to him 'because one of our sailors had been most insulting to him' and pointed out as the offender a 'most inoffensive chap'[50]:

> I called him over and said, 'And just in case you should have spoken to any Turkish officers.'
> 'I haven't spoken to any of them, sir.'
> 'I'm quite sure of it,' I said, 'but you'd best go on board ship and not come ashore again for the rest of the day.'
> Then I told the Turk that the man was being sent on board ship and would be most severely dealt with. Oh most rigorously. He felt topping about it. Great friends we were.[51]

Taking up about a quarter of the short piece, this is an account that is at least second-hand of an incident that most likely did not take place, followed by a 'punishment' that was not a punishment. In the course of the description of these non-events is an odd non-utterance: 'And just in case you should have spoken to any Turkish officers.'[52] This, an incomplete sentence desperate for a main clause, recapitulates in miniature the elliptical quality of the whole account. The second 'non-story' concerns the death of an old woman on the pier. The narrator relates: 'Just then she died and went absolutely stiff. Her legs drew up and she drew up from the waist and went quite rigid.'[53] Performing what Caruth calls the 'determined repetition' of trauma,[54] the narrator reveals that he has articulated this experience before – to a doctor who told him he 'was lying' and that what he described 'was impossible.' The doctor's scepticism is stated twice by the narrator, as though his failure to be believed is itself traumatic. The reader is left pondering the ontological status of an event said to be a medical impossibility. The third 'non-story' in the piece concerns an attempt by the narrator to bring his ship in close to the pier and shell the Turkish quarter of the town. Though not stated explicitly, it is apparent that this manoeuvre was aborted. The event is placed in the realm of the hypothetical: 'It would have been a hell of a mess.'[55]

'On the Quai at Smyrna' adds ironies, ellipses, and omissions; ontologically problematic incidents and unwarranted assumptions; lack of context and orphaned pronouns to the avoidance strategies already illustrated in this chapter: indexical signs, parapolemics, euphemism, cliché, meiosis/litotes, paralipsis, rhetorical questions, self-referentiality, abstraction, negativity, periphrasis, adynaton, *praeteritio*, lacunae, inconsistencies, contradictions, and repetition. To these can be added the explicit acknowledgment (as opposed to the implication) that war cannot be – and is not being – written about. The four texts under discussion do not yield an example, but an instance can be adduced from the *Iliad*. 'How can I picture it all? It would take a god to tell the tale,' despairs Homer,[56] inaugurating a tradition of linguistic disclaimers ('words fail me,' 'this was indescribable,' 'I cannot tell of this') in war writing that is still ongoing. The rhetorical term for the linguistic disclaimer – adynaton – has already been mentioned in this chapter. Ἀδύνατον is a cognate of ἀδυναμία (adynamia): want of strength or lack of dynamism (the Latin version, *impossibilia*, also contains the etymological suggestion of powerlessness). Though strictly applied to the stating of unfulfillable conditions – as observed in the long opening sentence of Thomas's 'A Refusal to Mourn' – adynaton has also been defined in rhetorical handbooks as the expression of 'the impossibility of addressing oneself adequately to the topic.'[57] The mother of all avoidance tropes, adynaton, not-writes about war by making not-writing its very subject.

Sublime Appreciation

But what is happening when a writer states – or implies by means of one or more of the avoidance strategies described in this chapter – that he or she cannot or will not write about war? The thesis of this chapter so far has been that not writing about war is a means of representing war in relief, like a photographic negative or a sculptor's mould. The techniques described adumbrate catastrophe without articulating it, and therefore it is when the fact of adumbration is acknowledged – by means of adynaton in its disclamatory mode – that not writing about war becomes writing about war at its most powerful. But is it possible to be more specific about the source of this power?

Such specificity as is possible involves an appreciation of the workings of another literary concept of ancient standing: the sublime (long integrated into theories of representing the Holocaust).[58] In his 'Analytic of the Sublime,' contained in his *Critique of the Power of Judgment* (1790), Kant writes: 'What is properly sublime cannot be contained in any sensible form, but concerns only ideas of reason, which, though no presentation adequate to them is possible, are provoked and called to mind precisely by this inadequacy, which does allow of sensible presentation.'[59] To expand this: the sublime brings with itself 'the idea of its infinity' and induces in the beholder a feeling of 'displeasure' at the inability of his or her imagination to apprehend it.[60] But the failure of the imagination in turn 'makes intuitable the superiority of the rational vocation of our cognitive faculty' and this, in turn, evokes a feeling of 'pleasure.'[61] In a complex power play between the faculties, the Kantian sublime renders the despair of imaginative failure the precondition of joyful aesthetic judgment.

Strategies of not writing about war resonate at various junctures with Kant's 'Analytic' (and it is worth noting that Kant himself stated that war could be sublime).[62] Kant notes that presentation of the ineffable 'can never be anything other than a merely negative presentation,'[63] a remark endorsed by Jean-François Lyotard in his own observation that 'the inadequacy of ... images is a negative sign of the immense power of ideas.'[64] For Lyotard, this is the germ of minimalism and the avant-garde:[65] in war writing, radical or otherwise, the phenomenon, as this chapter has noted, is widespread. When Homer despairs of picturing the scene of war at the outset of one of the greatest pieces of war representation in Western literature, the reader must pause to revise preconceptions and recalibrate his or her apprehension of what the poet is trying to describe. Similarly, when a reader senses that a writer is skirting around an atrocity, he or she is likely to envisage horrors exceeding anything that straightforward description could invoke. In this sense, not writing about war is hyperbolic, opening up limitless scope for the application of aesthetic judgment. Gotthold Ephraim Lessing, writing on the *Iliad* in *Laocoön: An Essay upon the Limits of Painting and Poetry* (1766), noticed precisely this effect: 'When, for instance, the gods who take different sides in the Trojan war come at last to actual blows, the contest goes on in the poem unseen [21.385]. This invisibility leaves the imagination free play to enlarge the scene at will, and picture the gods and their movements on a scale far grander than the measure of common humanity.'[66]

For Jacques Derrida, 'the feeling of the colossal [a Kantian word] ... is the experience of an inadequation of presentation to itself, or rather, since every presentation is adequate to itself, of an inadequation of the presenter to the presented of presentation.'[67] As these remarks suggest, the successful execution of the rhetorical devices of not writing about war necessitates a curious disempowerment (the 'harsh modesty' recommended by Steiner in the face of what cannot be understood).[68] The deployment of these confessions of inadequacy corresponds to the point, identified by Kant, during which the 'momentary inhibition of the vital powers' in the face of the sublime occurs.[69] Writing specifically on the Holocaust, Michael Bernard-Donals and Richard Glejzer describe this 'sublime moment' as that 'in which the witness knows that she is seeing, but can't say what it is, and yet must say what it is.'[70] Instances of self-effacement, withdrawal, mortification, defeat, each use of an avoidance device lets off an authorial distress flare signalling a linguistic state of emergency.

But an instant later comes Kant's 'vital outpouring':[71] the point at which the reason apprehends what is beyond the limits of the imagination. In this sense, each event of non-writing is also a cause for celebration, marking the moment when representative possibilities are released and aesthetic judgment is given free rein. Hence, the tropes figure the beginning, as well as the end, of communication, which makes their presence in successful war representations more comprehensible. Indeed, 'success' is twofold, since the ensuing depiction comprises both all that the writer can convey and all that the reader can apprehend.

Now, placing this emphasis on the role of the sublime in war writing necessitates a comment on 'combat gnosticism.' The phrase was coined by James Campbell in a 1999 article where he defined it as 'the belief that combat represents a qualitatively separate order of experience that is difficult if not impossible to communicate to any who have not undergone an identical experience.'[72] Treating war as sublime or ineffable, Campbell would argue, perpetuates this ideology in critical discourse and has a correspondingly deleterious effect on the war literature canon. In fact, the four authors discussed in this chapter are associated with a high degree of combat *a*gnosticism: the Reverend Charles Wolfe had no military experience, let alone in the Peninsular War; Wilfred Owen was an active combatant but wrote 'Anthem for Doomed Youth' away from the front in Craiglockhart; Dylan Thomas was exempted from military service on medical grounds and wrote 'A Refusal to Mourn' in Wales; Hemingway would not have witnessed comparable refugee scenes in his capacity as a volunteer ambulance driver in Italy during the First World War – he travelled to Anatolia in 1922 for the *Toronto Daily Star* but arrived after the burning of Smyrna and never visited the town. The gnosis, or insight, of the texts derives from imagination, rather than from experience.

This chapter has noted a dizzying variety of strategies to avoid writing directly about conflict – ways, as it were, of throwing white paint at the red business – all of which do not so much communicate war as initiate the reader into the mysteries of imagining it. It is therefore possible to posit an 'apophatic' mode of war writing: the mode of conveying combat through negation. Cleverly, representation in this mode contrives to obey the simultaneous and contradictory imperatives to write and not to write about conflict. Its product is nevertheless limitless in pain and horror, being nothing less than the wars of the mind. As Steiner remarks of Stéphane Mallarmé: he 'made of words acts not primarily of *communication* but of *initiation* into a private mystery.'[73]

NOTES

I am grateful to the volume's editors and to Brad Prager for kindly reading this chapter in draft and making helpful suggestions.

1 See James Campbell, 'Combat Gnosticism: The Ideology of First World War Poetry Criticism,' *New Literary History* 30 (1999): 203–15.

2 Theodor W. Adorno, *Negative Dialectics*, trans. E.B. Ashton (London: Routledge & Kegan Paul, 1973), 365.

3 Anne Carson, 'Variations on the Right to Remain Silent,' *A Public Space* 7 (2008): 181. Available at http://www.apublicspace.org/ (accessed 21 May 2009). I am grateful to Elizabeth Reeder for drawing my attention to this essay.

4 Anonymous, 'In the Abbey. The Warrior Laid to Rest,' *The Times*, 12 November 1920, supplement, ii.

5 Steiner, *Language and Silence: Essays 1958–1966* (Harmondsworth: Penguin, 1969), 76.

6 Maurice Blanchot, *The Writing of the Disaster*, trans. A. Smock (Lincoln: University of Nebraska Press, 1986), 11.

7 See, for example, Saul Friedlander, ed., *Probing the Limits of Representation: Nazism and the 'Final Solution'* (Cambridge, MA: Harvard University Press, 1992); Berel Lang, ed., *Writing and the Holocaust* (New York: Holmes & Meier, 1988) and *Act and Idea in the Nazi Genocide* (Chicago: University of Chicago Press, 1990); and Michael Rothberg, *Traumatic Realism* (Minneapolis: University of Minnesota Press, 2000).

8 Charles Esdaile, *The Peninsular War: A New History* (London: Penguin, 2003), 141–55.

9 Charles Wolfe, 'The Burial of Sir John Moore after Corunna,' in *The Oxford Book of War Poetry*, ed. Jon Stallworthy (Oxford: Oxford University Press, 1984), 83–4. Subsequent references to the poem are to this edition.

10 James Carrick Moore, *A Narrative of the Campaign of the British Army in Spain: Commanded by his Excellency Sir John Moore ... Authenticated by Official Papers and Original Letters* (London: J. Johnson, 1809), 359. Moore quotes a letter from a Captain H. Hardinge.

11 Charles S. Peirce, from 'On the Algebra of Logic: A Contribution to the Philosophy of Notation,' in *The Essential Peirce: Selected Philosophical Writings. Volume 1 (1867–1893)*, ed. Nathan Hauser and Christian Kloesel (Bloomington: Indiana University Press, 1992), 226–8.

12 The gore is also an example of synecdoche (another method of depiction that works by omitting data), but not all synecdoche is indexical.

13 Walt Whitman, 'First O Songs for a Prelude,' in *Complete Poetry and Collected Prose*, ed. Justin Kaplan (New York, NY: Library of America, 1982), 417.

14 See Kate McLoughlin, 'War in Print Journalism,' in *The Cambridge Companion to War Writing*, ed. K. McLoughlin (Cambridge: Cambridge University Press, 2009), 49.

15 See OED.

16 Carson, 'Variations on the Right to Remain Silent,' 178.

17 Ibid., 178.

18 Moore, *A Narrative of the Campaign of the British Army*, 358–65. Moore quotes letters from Captain Hardinge and a Colonel P. Anderson.

19 Ibid., 366.

20 Ibid., 366–7.

21 See Harold A. Small, *The Field of his Fame: A Ramble in the Curious History of Charles Wolfe's Poem 'The Burial of Sir John Moore'* (Berkeley and Los Angeles: University of California Press, 1953), 1; and *New Letters of Robert Southey*, ed. Kenneth Curry (New York: Cambridge University Press, 1965), 515. There is no evidence to corroborate the hypothesis that Southey read James Carrick Moore, but the resemblances between the accounts are remarkable.

22 'Chapter 23,' *Edinburgh Annual Register* 1 (January 1808): 458–9.

23 C. Litton Falkiner, 'Introductory Memoir,' in *The Burial of Sir John Moore and Other Poems* by Charles Wolfe (London: Sidgwick & Jackson, 1909), xxv–xxvi.

24 Hansard HL Deb 25 January 1809, vol. 12 cc133–8, 'Vote of Thanks - Battle of Corunna,' http://hansard.millbanksystems.com/lords/1809/jan/25/vote-of-thanks-battle-of-corunna (accessed 5 May 2009).

25 Ibid., 368–88.

26 John Sweetman, 'Moore, Sir John (1761–1809),' *Oxford Dictionary of National Biography* (Oxford University Press, September 2004; online ed., May 2008), http://www.oxforddnb.com/view/article/19132 (accessed 21 May 2009).

27 Jon Stallworthy, *Wilfred Owen* (London: Oxford University Press and Chatto & Windus, 1974), 188.

28 Wilfred Owen, *The Complete Poems and Fragments. Volume I: The Poems*, ed. Jon Stallworthy (London: Chatto & Windus, The Hogarth Press, Oxford University Press, 1983), 99–100. Subsequent references to the poem are to this edition.

29 A source given by Jon Stallworthy for 'Anthem for Doomed Youth' suggests that the question may in fact be in the manner of a response, prompted by the anonymous Prefatory Note to *Poems of Today: an Anthology* (1916), of which Owen possessed the December 1916 reprint: 'This book has been compiled in order that boys and girls, already perhaps familiar with the great classics of the English speech, may also know something of the newer poetry of their own day [...] there is no arbitrary isolation of one theme from another; they mingle and interpenetrate throughout, to the music of Pan's flute, and of Love's viol, and the bugle-call of Endeavour, and the passing-bells of Death' (Owen, *The Complete Poems and Fragments. Volume I*, 99n)

30 Wilfred Owen, *The Complete Poems and Fragments. Volume II: The Manuscripts of the Poems and the Fragments*, ed. Jon Stallworthy (London: Chatto & Windus, The Hogarth Press, Oxford University Press, 1983), 250.

31 Dominic Hibberd, *Owen the Poet* (Basingstoke: Macmillan, 1986), 110.

32 Trudi Tate, *Modernism, History and the First World War* (Manchester: Manchester University Press, 1998), 65–6.

33 Wilfred Owen, *Collected Letters*, ed. Harold Owen and John Bell (Oxford: Oxford University Press, 1967), 496.

34 Steiner, *Language and Silence*, 42.

35 Dylan Thomas, *Collected Poems 1834–1952* (London: J.M. Dent, 1952), 101. Subsequent references to the poem are to this edition.

36 William Empson, 'Dylan Thomas,' *Essays in Criticism* 13, no. 2 (1963): 205.

37 Virgil, Eclogue I: 59–60, 63.

38 Steiner, *Language and Silence*, 60, 69.

39 Ibid., 60.

40 Ibid., 48.

41 Ibid., 51.

42 Michael Reynolds, 'Hemingway's *In Our Time*: the Biography of a Book,' in *Modern American Short Story Sequences: Composite Fictions and Fictive Communities*, ed. J. Gerald Kennedy (Cambridge: Cambridge University Press, 1995), 44–5.

43 'Use short first paragraphs. Use vigorous English. Be positive, not negative,' ran the *Kansas City Star's* style sheet, quoted in Ronald Weber, *Hemingway's Art of Non-Fiction* (Basingstoke: Macmillan, 1990), 6.

44 Ernest Hemingway, *In Our Time* (New York: Scribner, 2003), 11–12. Subsequent references to the piece are to this edition.

45 For example, Matthew Stewart's excellent 'It Was All a Pleasant Business: The Historical Context of "On the Quai at Smyrna,"' *The Hemingway Review* 23, no. 1 (2003): 58.

46 Cathy Caruth, *Unclaimed Experience: Trauma, Narrative, and History* (Baltimore: Johns Hopkins University Press 1996), 17.

47 Stewart, 'It Was All A Pleasant Business,' 59.

48 Ibid., 59.

49 Hemingway, *In Our Time*, 11; 12.

50 Ibid., 12.

51 Ibid.

52 Ibid., 11.

53 Ibid., 12.

54 Caruth, *Unclaimed Experience*, 63.

55 Hemingway, *In Our Time*, 12.

56 Book 12, ll. 176–7; Homer, *The Iliad*, trans. E.V. Rieu (Harmondsworth: Penguin, 1950), 225.

57 Brian Vickers, *In Defence of Rhetoric* (Oxford: Oxford University Press, 1988), 491.

58 It is acknowledged that warfare in general does not share all the features of the Holocaust, but theories of the sublime in relation to the Shoah illuminate those aspects of conflict that seem ungraspable. There is not space in this chapter to do justice to these theories, but for further discussion of the sublime in relation to the Holocaust, see Michael Bernard-Donals and Richard Glejzer, *Between Witness and Testimony: The Holocaust and the Limits of Representation* (Albany: State University of New York Press, 2001); David Carroll, 'Foreword,' *Heidegger and 'the jews,'* by Jean-François Lyotard (Minneapolis: University of Minnesota Press, 1990), vii–xix; Sidra DeKoven Ezrahi, '"The Grave in the Air": Unbound Metaphors in Post-Holocaust Poetry,' in *Probing the Limits of Representation*, ed. Friedlander, 259–76; Shoshana Felman and Dori Laub, *Testimony: Crises of Witnessing in Literature, Psychoanalysis, and History* (New York and London: Routledge, 1992); John Felstiner, 'Translating Paul Celan's "Todesfuge": Rhythm and Repetition as Metaphor,' in *Probing the Limits of Representation*, ed. Friedlander, 240–58; Saul Friedlander, 'Introduction,' *Probing the Limits of Representation*, ed. Friedlander, 1–21; Peter Haidu, 'The Dialectics of Unspeakability: Language, Silence, and the Narratives of Desubjectification,' in *Probing the Limits of Representation*, ed. Friedlander, 277–99; Geoffrey Hartman, 'The Book of the Destruction,' in *Probing the Limits of Representation*, ed. Fried-

lander, 318–34; Dominick LaCapra, *History and Memory After Auschwitz* (Ithaca, NY: Cornell University Press, 1998) and *Writing History, Writing Trauma* (Baltimore: Johns Hopkins University Press, 2003); Berel Lang, 'The Representation of Limits,' in *Probing the Limits of Representation*, ed. Friedlander, 300–17; Lawrence Langer, *Holocaust Testimonies: The Ruins of Memory* (New Haven, CT: Yale University Press, 1991); Michael Rothberg, *Traumatic Realism*; Thomas Trezise, 'Unspeakable,' *Yale Journal of Criticism* 14, no. 1 (2001), 39–66; and Hayden White, 'Historical Emplotment and the Problem of Truth,' in *Probing the Limits of Representation*, ed. Friedlander, 37–53.

59 Immanuel Kant, *Critique of the Power of Judgment*, ed. Paul Guyer, trans. P. Guyer and E. Matthews, *The Cambridge Edition of the Works of Immanuel Kant* (Cambridge: Cambridge University Press, 2000), 5:129.

60 Ibid., 138.

61 Ibid., 141.

62 Kant's precise remark is: 'Even war, if it is conducted with order and reverence for the rights of civilians, has something sublime about it.' Ibid., 146.

63 Ibid., 156.

64 Jean-François Lyotard, *Lessons on the Analytic of the Sublime*, trans. E. Rottenberg (Stanford, CA: Stanford University Press, 1994), 98.

65 Ibid., 98.

66 Gotthold Ephraim Lessing, *Laocoön: An Essay Upon the Limits of Painting and Poetry*, trans. Ellen Frothingham (Boston: Roberts Brothers, 1880), 78. The *Iliad* reference in square brackets is given by Lessing.

67 Jacques Derrida, *The Truth in Painting*, trans. G. Bennington and I. McLeod (Chicago: University of Chicago Press, 1987), 132.

68 Steiner, *Language and Silence*, 55.

69 Kant, 'Analytic of the Sublime,' 128–9.

70 Bernard-Donals and Glejzer, *Between Witness and Testimony*, 20.

71 Kant, 'Analytic of the Sublime,' 128–9.

72 Campbell, 'Combat Gnosticism,' 203.

73 Steiner, *Language and Silence*, 48.

3 Occupation as the Face of War: Concealing Violence in the Diary *A Woman in Berlin*

BRAD PRAGER

Representations of war are determined not only by the ages in which they appear, but also by the boundaries understood to define war. The idea, for example, that it is not battle but war itself that leaves behind scars presumes that war has both a beginning and an end, or that we can differentiate between the event and its traces. War is, however, an extended process, one that can hardly be isolated or made wholly distinct from peace. The vagueness of the concept suggests that much remains unknown about its limits. For this reason, detailed depictions of occupation are of central importance; in that their object is neither war nor peace, they reveal how the disorder of war is linked to its orderly opposite, and how each one permeates the other. The published diary *A Woman in Berlin: Eight Weeks in the Conquered City* (*Eine Frau in Berlin. Tagebuchaufzeichnungen vom 20. April bis 22. Juni 1945*) is among such depictions. As argued below, a reading of the diary sheds light on the poorly defined boundaries that separate occupation from war, and war from the continuities of quotidian life. In writing about occupation, the trauma of war – that about which it is too horrible to speak, and about which one must remain silent – can be seen and understood alongside its very ordinariness. The formal options concerning whether and how one represents war and its accompanying violence as a traumatic occlusion bespeak the complexities that encumber the ordering of its unruly boundaries.

In order to understand the politics of the diary's representation of war – to understand the formal analysis that follows – it is necessary to see the history of its reception in a new light. The diary's authenticity has been the subject of much debate. Its author long withheld her identity and published simply under the name Anonyma. The German text was first issued in an English translation in 1954 and then later in German, in 1959. While some scholars in the decades that followed mention the diary as a particularly personal account of the occupation of Berlin by the Russians during the last days of the Second World War, the text received greater attention when it was republished in 2003 following the death of the woman now named as the diarist.[1] It was acclaimed by some as having originated authentically in its wartime milieu, its author an unmediated voice speaking from beneath the rubble. However, the work's lucid tone, fluid prose, thoughtful metaphors, and apparent literary conceits led critics to suggest that it might have been composed at a later, calmer time, or that it had been so significantly altered after the fact that it was of little value as a document of the occupation.

The terms that defined the debate surrounding the diary's value as an authentic work of wartime witnessing are well known: Laurel Cohen-Pfister summarizes that 'the central question played out in the culture sections of major newspapers in the fall of 2003 was to what degree the published text corresponds to the text penned in 1945, and to what degree its editor, Kurt W. Marek – a "master of successful docu-fiction" – embellished the original to make it appeal more to a public market.'[2] Among those leading the charge was the journalist Jens Bisky, who approached the problem from a disciplinary perspective, asking whether the work should be viewed through a historical or a literary lens. Bisky noted that the book was worthless as a contemporaneous historical document, and raised the question of whether this unknown woman was simply a literary construction. He demanded to know what in the work was documentarily substantiated.[3] Hans Magnus Enzensberger, who had a hand in publishing the diary, defended its authenticity, and many rushed to proclaim their support both for him and the text. The literary editor Walter Kempowski declared the material authentic based on an examination of source material,[4] and both Enzensberger as well as the historian Antony Beevor iterated that verdict.[5] The issue concerned whether the work should be seen as a diary or an embellished memoir, and whether it would in the latter case have less value than an unadulterated text. Although the question is important, the book also offers other types of truths about the relationship between the rapes committed by occupying Russians and the acts of aggression generally ascribed to the passions loosed by war.

Not only did the book's provenance vex its reception, but so did specific aspects of its content. The diary contains a number of accounts of rapes by Russian soldiers, and Cohen-Pfister notes: 'the controversy over authenticity and the author's identity are reminders of the social and political constraints related to the rape of German women in 1945 and rape in general.' She adds, 'Analysts point to the difficulty still surrounding an open discussion of rape, as well as ideological conflicts in some circles for implicating the Red Army.'[6] Along exactly these lines the terms of the 2003 debate rehearsed issues surrounding how the public reacts to rape victims. Readers' sympathies – both then and now – are traditionally mitigated by the tendency to shame victims. Even the term 'victim' stigmatizes inappropriately, which is among the reasons women are often discouraged from avowing the event.

Along these lines, Enzensberger's dispute with Bisky also included the accusation that it was crass to reveal – or to insist upon revealing – the name of a woman who had been raped and who expressed a wish to remain unnamed. Enzensberger argued that this type of public inquisition of a rape victim, even a deceased one, was unjust and that readers should on this basis draw conclusions about Bisky's ethics.[7] However, the presumed diarist's name, Marta Hillers, is now a matter of record. She was a journalist who spoke Russian and who evidently experienced what she wrote about in these diaries, or at least something similar. The book tells the story of eight weeks that followed Hitler's birthday, 20 April 1945, through to 22 June of that year. Hillers struggled to survive in those weeks while being sexually assaulted repeatedly by occupying Russians. Her survival, which entailed submitting to the will of Russian soldiers, made her wonder whether she was collaborating, and thus her status as a victim of the war – one who had been ideologically aligned with its perpetrators – intersects with her complicated and at times unsayable status as a victim of rape. The story is thus more than merely a testimony about rape, it is a narrative of emotions, survival, and even working conditions once 'war rolls into Berlin,' to borrow a phrase from the diary's first page.[8]

Bracketing out questions concerning the authenticity of the original document and precisely when it was written is obviously problematic for historians. At the same time, however, the language and narrative of *A Woman in Berlin* also invite other modes of interpretation. Despite its status as a 'document,' the work also has literary qualities and could be read with attention to its narrative means of expression. It should be emphasized that looking at the diary's language, or discussing it as one might discuss well-crafted fiction, is not the same as challenging its veracity. My aim here is much more to consider how the diarist in her writing figures the boundaries between war and occupation, and between war and peace, in order to demonstrate how these various terms are interwoven.

The very first words of the diary's initial entry already call for exegesis. War did not roll into Berlin on 20 April 1945. The bombing of Berlin began in 1940, and violence against the Jewish community came to a boil in 1938 if not earlier. In these and other respects many in the city had long since seen the face of war. The diarist's assertion that war rolled into the city is more about her personal relationship to violence, or the fact that it now directly confronted her. War at that point became something different: it was an occupation, but it was also an assault. One may then ask what this ambiguity – the shifting and confusion associated with these varied terms – tells us about the blurring of boundaries in war, as well as the rhetorical differences that aim to dissociate war from related acts of violence. The encroachment of tanks and Russians upon the diarist's city had a transformative effect: war was already there, yet suddenly it manifested itself anew. Her assertion only draws our attention to the illusory lines that separate violence and 'the theatre of war' from the appearance of normalcy associated with the home front.

A Woman in Berlin is hardly the first depiction in German letters of raping Russians, nor is it the first to draw attention to war's unruliness. Heinrich von Kleist's novella 'The Marquise of O...,' which was written during the Napoleonic Wars and published in 1808, sheds light on the matter because it shows how a literary text may self-consciously write around the act of rape. Kleist, whose writings are replete with expressive ambiguities, and who has for good reasons been taken as an object of deconstructive scrutiny, based his story 'on a true event' ('Nach einer wahren Begebenheit').[9] This may, however, be simply an element of Kleist's irony insofar as once readers have finished with the author's many reversals, they can take allusions to the truth only lightly. What really happened, as in Kleist's 'The Duel' (1811), 'The Earthquake in Chile' (1807/10), and elsewhere, can hardly be known. As I will show, the structure and substance of Kleist's tale, owing in particular to its reliance on absences, ambiguities, and misapprehensions, productively inform a reading of *A Woman in Berlin*. Even a glance at the two titles, 'The Marquise of O...' and *A Woman in Berlin*, suggests an obvious parallel: the social standing of the protagonist, whether as a member of the nobility or an ordinary German, is tied to a place, which implies that it may be that very standing – the woman's social coordinates – to which the author or editor means to draw our attention.[10] In both titles the woman, manipulated and transformed by a wartime situation such as invasion or occupation, is objectified, defined in collective terms, and potentially divested of her standing as an individual.

The prehistory of Kleist's tale has been tied to a passage in Michel de Montaigne's 'On Drunkenness' (1588), which concerns a woman of chaste repute who is taken in her sleep by an intoxicated servant.[11] Upon realizing she is carrying a child, the woman publicly offers to marry her unidentified rapist, if only he would admit to the act. The man comes forward, they are joined, and Montaigne informs us that the two still today live together as man and wife. This is, in some respects, the plot of 'The Marquise of O...,' although it is more the heat of war than drunkenness that brings about the crime at the centre of the subsequent version. Kleist's story deals with a widowed Marquise who publishes an advertisement explaining that she finds herself in a certain situation, and that she would like the father to come forward and is prepared to marry him. The story of how she got into this situation is then told: upon the storming of her father's Italian citadel by Russian troops, the Marquise had fallen into the hands of ill-intentioned soldiers whereupon she was subjected to 'the most degrading mistreatment' ('die schändlichsten Mißhandlungen').[12] She was then apparently spared an impending rape by a valiant Russian officer, one who 'diverted the lascivious dogs from their prey,' but it seems that her saviour may then have raped her himself.[13] Of this occurrence we cannot be certain because Kleist famously conceals the details of the sexual assault, if there is one, beneath a dash in his text. The description of the event itself is missing, and the Marquise can recall nothing about it, having fallen completely unconscious. After that night the family is given word that Count F., the Marquise's noble saviour, has died in battle. Contrary to reports, however, he then reappears and declares his love. The family does not readily agree that the Marquise should marry, and the Count is sent away. When the Marquise subsequently discovers she is pregnant, her father casts her out of the house and she then publishes the advertisement with which the tale began. After one attempt to assign paternity to another man – a hunter named Leopardo – the family determines that little can be determined. The Russian Count eventually returns and avows responsibility for what he has done. It is agreed that the two may marry, but, because of the strange circumstances, they may only marry under the condition that he take on none of the husband's conjugal rights and all of the responsibilities.

The Count agrees and moves in close by. Eventually he wins over the family's trust, and this story, like Montaigne's, has a happy ending.

This abridged account does not pretend to capture the subtlety and complexity of the novella. Its many layers of unknowabilty, however, bespeak the point. Kleist's literary work about war converges with *A Woman in Berlin* in that it provides provocative insights into the apparently unsayable acts around which the diary is constructed. Although 'The Marquise of O...' is no war diary, the author himself was a prisoner of war not long before the tale was published. Kleist's imprisonment as a spy was the result of wartime confusion: at the end of January 1807, he was arrested while heading west through French occupied territory. He was imprisoned in France, first at the Fortress Joux, where he was held until 11 April, and then at Châlons-sur-Marne, where he had the opportunity to write.[14] The disorder may have inflected the author's work, and Herbert Kraft concludes that Kleist depicted the confusion of war in 'The Marquise of O...,' which – according to Kraft – he worked on during his captivity.[15]

The tale's events have been tied to the period of the Second Coalition, and possibly more specifically to 1799, when the Austrians and Russians succeeded in driving back the French.[16] This interpretation has been disputed, but it may not be crucial to all readings insofar as the story can be understood to take war itself as its subject. This altered state – the state of war – accounts for the behaviour of the Count, who acts much like the drunk in Montaigne's homily. It was the heat of battle and the Count was flustered, perhaps as a result of the fact that beyond the bounds of war he is a decent man. The family's ostensible forgiveness of him seems rooted in their knowledge that the world is an imperfect place and that everyone makes mistakes. However, because this is a tale by Kleist, who perpetually undermines his own statements and with whom most critics associate the trope of moral contingency, these excuses are not to be taken at face value. Writing of Kleist but citing Robert Musil's playful inversion of von Clausewitz's most famous motto, Herbert Kraft notes: '"War is the continuation of peace by other means." For force, which otherwise remains half hidden, rises to the surface.'[17] Whether it has to do with power, force, or the inequities typically associated with gendered property relations, the violence enacted upon the Marquise is an expression of a general state of affairs. War is, for Kleist, rarely the exception to the rules.

That for which the story is best known, and the literary gesture by which it is tied to *A Woman in Berlin*, is what it elects not to articulate.

Kleist's dash (the *Gedankenstrich*), which may or may not elide the tale's rape insofar as we are unsure about precisely what has happened, is not the only dash in the author's oeuvre, nor is it even the only dash in this story, but it is the one most often cited.[18] If it is treated as representing the moment of a rape, or if we take for granted that at that point the gallant Russian who liberates the protagonist from her aggressors himself takes liberties,[19] then the dash represents a rupture, or something the author means to self-consciously suppress. Noting the abundance of speculation around this simple line, Michel Chaouli asserts that too much has been read into it. He suggests instead that its ambiguities should be taken as a figure for literature itself. In that it signals a failure in the narrative, it is also the author's calling card; it is the line that tells us that this is a story by Kleist, and that we are bound to read in a hermeneutic circle (or in an endless 'O'). As a void onto which much is projected, it illustrates the process by which readers construct meaning.[20] Close reading reveals that the Marquise might be understood to have willingly given herself to the Count, or, despite evidence that suggests otherwise, a scene of father-daughter affection in the text may be meant to allude to the Marquise's own father as the one responsible for her pregnancy. These are only two among a number of possible readings.[21] Analysing the story without reference to these ambiguities – saying that we know for certain what is hidden beneath the dash – surrenders all that is literary, that is, open to interpretation, about the text.[22] And yet that which is concealed can also be understood in terms of what is specific to the representation of rape, the details of which frequently remain unspoken, and war, which often remains ill defined. Kleist's gesture is literary and rife with poetic ambiguities, but it also conceals something quite particular to the extent that its use reflects an overlap between a textual device and the ambiguous ground upon which its unspoken object rests.

Whether it is interpreted as a contemporaneous historical document or as an intimately told narrative about rape, *A Woman in Berlin* also at key moments relies on dashes and ellipses. These are ambiguous figures about which certain knowledge, not to mention the firm foundation of a narrator's moral certitude, is lacking. Symptomatic of this lack is the compulsion on the part of the diary's author to ask herself whether or not she is a victim. Although we surely understand her reasons, the diarist feels ashamed for playing a part akin to that of a prostitute, exchanging sex for security and necessities. In this way, her dashes also conceal an indeterminacy closely connected with the contingencies of wartime writing – of writing during an occupation where daily life both does and does not persist. If we accept that the dash denotes an uncertainty about how precisely the diarist sees her situation, then we are in the position of treating this historical document as literature; our attention is drawn to how we find ourselves projecting onto a veritable blank spot in the text, as we had in the case of 'The Marquise of O...'

When the Russian soldiers rape the diarist for the first time, there is little ambiguity about what has transpired. Simultaneously, however, the dash in her text amounts to an apophasis – a reference to something by denying that it will be referenced – insofar as it has the effect of focusing our attention all the more on the omitted details. The diarist describes the scene:

> The door above is ajar and lets in a little light. One man stands there keep-ing watch, while the other tears my underclothes, forcing his way –
> I grope around on the floor with my left hand until I find my key ring. I hold it tight. I use my right hand to defend myself. It's no use. He's sim-ply torn off my garter, ripping it in two. When I struggle to come up, the second one throws himself on me as well, forcing me back on the ground with his fists and knees.[23]

Her dash, unlike Kleist's, conceals little. But knowing what happens is not the same as knowing what it means. What has happened here is evident; the event was not blotted out by the interference of psychic trauma. The author may have concluded that readers need not be told. However, the dash also indicates an avowal that certain aspects of this type of transgression typically remain unspoken. The rules of propri-ety and perhaps those of publication dictate that certain words are not supposed to be written. Similarly, when an occupying Russian asks the diarist's permission to have sex with her, prior to the scene above, the break in the text either signifies that he cannot say directly what it is he expects, or, what is more likely, owing to her discomfort or shame, she cannot write it. The diarist narrates: 'One young man, small and yellow and reeking of alcohol, gets me involved in a conversation. He wants to coax me off into the courtyard, shows me two watches on his hairy arm, he'll give one to me if I ...'[24] As they are depicted in the diary, her fellow Germans likewise fail to refer to rape in definite terms, and their ques-tions end in ellipses. She explains: 'The standard question' [die stere-otype Frage] they ask is, 'how often did they ...?' [Wie oft haben die ...?].[25]

That something is concealed by these deferrals does not suggest genuine ambiguity as regards the facts of the matter. There is little question as to the essential truths behind *A Woman in Berlin*. The Russians raped large numbers of women, apparently far more than did the Allied troops. Historian Elizabeth Heinemann explains that Germans moving westward, away from the Russian armies, brought news of widespread slaughter and rape, which 'confirmed other Germans' worst fears about the Red Army.' She adds: 'Estimates of the numbers of rapes at the hands of Soviet soldiers range widely, from the tens of thousands to 2 million. Whatever the precise numbers, rape was a common experience for women in eastern parts of the old Reich, and fear of rape was universal.'[26] Antony Beevor writes: 'Berliners remember that, because all the windows had been blown in, you could hear the screams every night. Estimates from the two main Berlin hospitals ranged from 95 000 to 130 000 rape victims. One doctor deduced that out of approximately 100 000 women raped in Berlin, some 10 000 died as a result, mostly from suicide.'[27] Similarly, Atina Grossmann notes: 'The numbers reported for these rapes vary wildly, from as few as 20 000 to almost 1 million or even 2 million altogether, as the Red Army pounded westward. A conservative estimate might be about 110 000 women raped, many more than once, of whom up to 10 000 died in the aftermath; others suggest that perhaps one out of every three of about 1.5 million women in Berlin fell victim to Soviet rapes.'[28]

For an explanation of why this happened more frequently under the Russian occupation than under the Allies, some return to stereotypes of Russian soldiers' greater misogyny and the preponderance of alcohol (which recalls the theme of Montaigne's story).[29] Rape was against the Russians' rules of war, but it occurred nonetheless. Employing yet another euphemism, the diarist reports that 'apparently Stalin has declared that "this kind of thing" (*sowas*) is not to happen. But it happens anyway.'[30] Giles MacDonogh notes: 'It was rumored that the severity of the rapine was caused by the fact that the Russians had sent in units made of criminals – such as the Nazis had used at the time of the Warsaw uprising – but this was later revealed to have been untrue. Rapists were threatened with gruesome punishments, but the prospect of satisfying their lust proved stronger than the fear of chastisement.'[31] Accounts suggest that forces of the Russian occupation frequently considered the conquered women to be among the spoils of war. Beevor makes this point more than once, noting: 'By the time the Red Army reached Berlin [subsequent to the Wehrmacht's invasion of the Soviet Union], its soldiers tended to regard German women more as a casual right of conquest than a target of hate.'[32] He adds: 'The definition of rape had been blurred into sexual coercion. A gun or physical violence became unnecessary when women faced starvation.'[33] Beevor concludes that this led to a 'stage in the evolution of rape in Germany in 1945,' characterized by 'a strange form of cohabitation in which many Soviet officers settled in with German "occupation wives" who replaced the Soviet "campaign wife."'[34]

The phrase 'a strange form of cohabitation' – yet another unspecific expression, only slightly less indefinite than 'this kind of thing' – echoes the obscuring language found throughout *A Woman in Berlin*. Some of the diarist's entries underscore this sense of strangeness. Owing to the matter-of-factness associated with the Russians' ostensible carte blanche and with the starkness of the power dynamics, the diarist is compelled to re-evaluate the part she plays. When she takes up with a Major as a matter of self-protection – when she enters into 'a strange form of cohabitation' with him – she is compelled to avow the unusualness of her situation, that it is she who is the criminal rather than the rapist. Though readers would most certainly identify all that transpires in these situations as rape, the diarist is forced to question the extent to which she is engaging in prostitution. Although many of her reflections are typical of rape victims who wonder whether they were themselves at fault, her considerations are also symptomatic of the state of occupation. Life during an occupation continues, but the violence and the severely proprietary relationships associated with war infiltrate that life. She reflects:

> *This is a new situation.* By no means could it be said that the major is raping me. One cold word and he'd probably go his way and never come back. So I am placing myself at his service of my own accord ... I can actually talk with the major. Which still isn't an answer to the question of whether I should now call myself a whore, since I am essentially living off my body, trading it for something to eat.
>
> On the other hand, writing this makes me wonder why I'm being so moralistic and acting as if prostitution were so much beneath my dignity.[35]

In passages such as these, the diarist, finding herself in 'a new situation,' wonders why rape does not seem to her like the wholesale transgression of a boundary. She asks: 'What does it mean – rape? When I said the word for the first time aloud ... it sent shivers down my spine. Now I can think it and write it with an untrembling hand, say it out loud to get used to hearing it said. It sounds like the absolute worst, the end of everything – but it's not.'[36] Reading this passage, one may conjecture that its author has been traumatized by the experience and, because the trauma is ongoing, she is not yet capable of coming to terms with it. More likely, however, is that this type of reflection is evidence of the purgatorial limbo associated with occupation, which is simultaneously war *and* the continuity of daily life; it is not a scar that war has left behind, but rather a quotidian space from which violent conflict cannot be disentangled. Along these lines, Heinemann notes: 'Women's immediate reactions to rape varied widely. Some women seem to have experienced rape as one problem among many: it was a horrible episode, but so were many other events of the winter and spring of 1945.'[37] The assertion that it was not as apocalyptic as she would have imagined may be taken as evidence of how an occupation becomes a symptom or mode of the overall confusion of war; not the end of everything but its continuation. None of this is to suggest that being coerced into prostitution is anything less than abuse and may even be torture, but rather that the forced performance of such a role in a time of occupation casts light on the warlike power relations made manifest in other spheres.

Similar to its dashes and ellipses, the diary also contains references to the multiplicity of terms adopted to name the rapes. The author notes that 'an official expression has been invented to describe the whole business of raping: "forced intercourse" (*Zwangsverkehr*).'[38] She then adds facetiously: 'maybe they ought to include that phrase next time they print up the soldiers' phrase book.'[39] Similarly, when Gerd, a lover of hers from before the war, returns at the diary's end, having stolen away from his anti-aircraft unit, he reads through her diaries and tells her he doesn't understand the use of the word *Schändung*. The word means rape, but it also means 'defilement' and is less commonly used than *Vergewaltigung*. Not only is the word a circumlocution, but it has been abbreviated in the diary. Gerd asks what 'Schdg' is supposed to mean, and the diarist explains: 'I had to laugh: "Schändung," of course – rape. He looked at me as if I were out of my mind, but said nothing more.'[40] Her laughter alludes to an inability to speak directly about certain subjects, and the misunderstanding between Gerd and the diarist is a function of the new distance that has emerged between them. Cohen-Pfister notes: 'Discussion of rapes reveals emotions not associated with other facets of German wartime suffering, such as the air war or expulsion. The common use of terms like *Schändung* (despoilment) and *Erniedrigung* (degradation) even in current journalistic discourse illuminates the stigma attached to rape victims, despite the horror, shock, or pity that the rapes elicit.'[41] Grossmann makes a similar point: 'In both official affidavits and more private accounts, women mobilized a wide range of direct and indirect vocabulary – *Schändung* (violation), *Vergewaltigung* (rape), *Übergriff* (encroachment), *Überfall* (attack) – to denote the "it" (*es*) that had been endured.'[42]

In the entry of 16 May the diarist explains that she helped a Russian First Lieutenant take a tour of the city's banks. After he asks her some personal questions and about her education, he switches from Russian and begins to speak with her in French. She recounts: 'suddenly he says in French, very quietly and without looking at me: "Dites-moi, est-ce qu'on vous a fait du mal?" I'm taken aback, stammer in reply, "Mais non, pas du tout." Then I correct myself. "Oui, monsieur, enfin, vous comprenez."'[43] Asserting that he 'understands' is of course a way of suggesting that this is something about which one ought not speak. The fact that he elects to enquire euphemistically ('have you been harmed?'), and that he introduces the topic in a language native to neither of them, redoubles the enquiry's indirectness. Also telling is that at first she cannot say for certain whether she has been harmed – her initial answer is 'no.' She continues: 'After our first exchange in French, we grow quiet again. The man is clearly uncomfortable, unsure. All of a sudden he blurts out, staring ahead of him: "Oui, je comprends. Mais je vous prie, Mademoiselle, n'y pensez plus. Il faut oublier. Tout." He looks for the right words, speaks earnestly and forcefully. I answer, "C'est la guerre. N'en parlons plus." And we don't speak any more about it.'[44] This is war, or, as the sentiment is more frequently expressed, 'war is war,' and on the basis of this tautological rationale not another word need be said. The generality of the concept 'war' conceals a multiplicity of sins. About its unruliness one need not be specific, and the term's very lack of specificity serves, still more than the dash, to efface its violence.

Much has been written about the taboo on open discussion of the rapes, on the shame that silenced many German women, and on taboo-breaking interventions such as Helke Sander's documentary film on the subject *BeFreier und BeFreite* (1992). The ambiguity surrounding the treatment of rape, reflected in the concealments of the dash, in part informed the reception of the book. It was, in other words, not only the debate about Jörg Friedrich, W.G. Sebald, and Günter Grass, and the contemporaneous 'proliferation of narrative texts which reconstruct[ed] an account of the past, authenticating German wartime suffering and victimization,'[45] which determined how this wartime story was reread when it appeared in 2003, but also the discourse on rape as connected to the liberation in 1945.

Despite some small amount of debate as to the diarist's precise wartime activities, and about the fact that she wrote journalism that enthusiastically supported the Nazi Party, readers of the diary have been slow to accuse its author of being a perpetrator.[46] As Gertrud Koch points out, reflexively sympathizing with post-war Germans is a thorny issue; sympathizing with German victims is complex because 'the majority of Germans, who surely yearned for an end to the war, did not wish for it in the form of military defeat.'[47] Grossmann likewise takes up this point when she writes critically about Sander's film *BeFreier und BeFreite*. She notes that the mass rape of German women became a part of the Germans' self-understanding as victims rather than as agents of National Socialism and war. She then feels the need to clarify her conclusion:

> Let me be clear: I am not suggesting that raped German women were not victims (as long as we are stuck with this somewhat insufficient vocabulary); there must be no doubt that they were. The problem is that Sander's eagerness to integrate German women into the international transhistorical sisterhood of victims of male violence leads to a problematic historical slippage and displacement in which German women seem to become the victims primarily of National Socialism and the war, rather than of the failure of National Socialism, and defeat in the war.[48]

Grossmann's assessment recalls dilemmas associated with identifying German victims of National Socialism. As Grossmann is aware, however, some of this matters only insofar as one seeks to assess blame rather than to reach an understanding of the interrelated experiences of war and occupation – conditions by which the diarist was doubtless victimized.

The diarist entitles the entry of Friday 27 April 'Day of catastrophe, wild turmoil.'[49] Subsequent to the first incident, discussed above, which is likely the 'catastrophe' to which she is referring, the diarist is raped again by a soldier named Petka, who takes the time to make himself at home. With this man, who is 'wide as a wardrobe,' she describes her state of mind as only half present, and adds that this half no longer resists.[50] She then looks back at a thought she had in the hours that followed:

> I remember the strange vision I had this morning, something like a daydream, while I was trying in vain to fall asleep after Petka left. It was as if I

were flat on my bed and seeing myself lying there when a luminous white being rose from my body, a kind of angel, but without wings, that floated high into the air. Even now as I'm writing this I can still feel that sense of rising up and floating. Of course, it's just a fantasy, a pipe dream, a means of escape – my true self simply leaving my body behind.[51]

Here, in this figurative passage, the diarist imagines another perspective, one from which she is no longer the subject of a traumatizing assault, but instead views the act from a vantage point from which the whole may finally be understood. It is a futural vision, a projection onto a time of peace; a vision that is quite understandably utopian. To be sure, she wishes to be elsewhere physically, yet in her longing there is also the desire to be free of feelings of both anxiety and complicity.

The image of the angel appears more than once in Kleist's 'The Marquise of O...' Upon accepting that her daughter has not been deceiving her parents about the identity of the child's father, the Marquise's mother pronounces her daughter more pure than an angel. Still more significant, however, are the uses of the term 'angel' and 'devil' when it comes to the identity of the Count: When he first arrives to save the Marquise, we are told that he seemed to her 'to be an angel from heaven.'[52] This is, of course, highly ironic because the observation refers to the very moment when the Count is about to rape her (or so we infer). Typically for Kleist, the claim that he is an angel is meant to foreshadow that his behaviour will soon turn diabolical, and also to bespeak the Marquise's erotic desire for her saviour, a desire that in one reading turns her into a willing sexual partner. The image of the angel then recurs at the tale's end when the Count asks his bride to explain why she fled from him, 'as if from the devil,' upon his initial confession that he was her child's true father.[53] She provides him with the explanation that 'he would not have seemed to be a devil then, had he not seemed to be an angel when he first appeared.'[54] Kleist here toys with both the protagonist's perception of the rapist and with ours; images of angels and devils signal an uncertainty about who the aggressor is – a man who appeared renewed and forgiven once the drunken madness of war became part of the past. However, in *A Woman in Berlin*, the angel appears as a symptom of the diarist's uncertainty as to whom she has become. The vision has little to do with the rapist, but instead with the diarist's self-understanding. Her personal account depicts her as both an angel and a prostitute. She assumes the moral contingency and madness associated with war as her own.

Part of the final entry of *A Woman in Berlin* speaks to this same anxiety about whom or what she has become. The diarist writes:

Yesterday I experienced something comic: a cart stopped outside our house, with an old horse in front, nothing but skin and bones. Four-year-old Lutz Lehmann came walking up holding his mother's hand, stopped beside the cart, and asked, in a dreamy voice "*Mutti*, can we eat the horse?"
God knows what we'll all end up eating, I think I'm far from any life-threatening extreme, but I don't really know how far. I only know that I want to survive – against all sense and reason, just like an animal.[55]

Consuming the horse would be a transgression against norms, and becoming an animal is a greater expression of that blurring of boundaries. Her anxiety about crossing from human behaviour into animality is a function of the confusion symptomatic of the occupation, as well as the blurring of the lines that separate German perpetrators from German victims. The diarist has to contend with the person that this particular war, and this occupation – a curious zone more on the side of war than that of peace – has made her. The human she once was may not reappear, and her lover's reluctance to return to how things were – Gerd's estrangement from her upon his homecoming – intimates the difficulties that will accompany a return to normal life.

If war is only peace by other means, as both this diary and other chronicles of occupation suggest, then where does war end and peace begin? The outpouring of id [*es*] that Freud would describe as part and parcel of war – and that which Grossmann refers to as the 'it' [*es*] that so many women endured – resembles a state of drunken confusion insofar as we do not expect warriors to behave normally and we tolerate their outpourings of aggression and madness. What is most striking about *A Woman in Berlin* is that it sounds as though the diarist herself is seeking forgiveness. These disparities are gendered: Kleist (who knew what he was doing, which is to say his tale is ironic) depicts a count who is forgiven, domesticated, and even apparently improved by having raped a woman in wartime. The diarist, however, feels understandably damaged by what has happened, even if it is all 'after the war has ended,' and even if we are only speaking of the scars and traces war leaves behind. Reflecting on the work in literary terms is not to suggest that the diary is less than history, nor is it a pronouncement on the book's authenticity, but is instead meant as a consideration of the limits of war and occupation as ill-defined terms. Such ambiguities may be less symptoms of the omnipresence of traumatic silences than they are statements about the nebulousness of war. Although dashes or ellipses can express uncertainty about events, they can also indicate uncertainty about how to categorize those events. As a consequence of the disorder of war and its signs *A Woman in Berlin* lacks fixed referents; its author wants to differentiate war from non-war, but cannot always find appropriate terms. In this way, however, her writing about war, rape, and occupation, akin to so much that is generally termed literary, serves to recast the limits that define them.

NOTES

1 Max Färberböck's feature film, *Anonyma – Eine Frau in Berlin*, which was shot in 2007 and released in Germany in 2008, is an adaptation of the diary.
2 Laurel Cohen-Pfister, 'Rape, War, and Outrage: Changing Perceptions on German Victimhood in the Period of Post-Unification,' in *Victims and Perpetrators: 1933–1945: (Re)Presenting the Past in Post-Unification Culture*, ed. Laurel Cohen-Pfister and Dagmar Wienroder-Skinner (Berlin: Walter de Gruyter, 2006), 328–9. The comment about 'docufiction' is drawn from Gustav Seibt, 'Schaulust vor dem Schrecken: Was für die Identifizierung der Anonyma spricht,' *Süddeutsche Zeitung*, 27 September 2003, 44.
3 See Jens Bisky, 'Wenn Jungen Weltgeschichte spielen, haben Mädchen stumme Rollen,' *Süddeutsche Zeitung*, 24 September 2003, 16.
4 See 'Anonyma-Tagebücher "Authentisch,"' in *Der Spiegel*, 19 January 2004, 135.
5 See Hans Magnus Enzensberger and Antony Beevor, 'A Woman in Berlin,' *New York Times Book Review*, 25 September 2005, letters page, 6.
6 Cohen-Pfister, 'Rape, War, and Outrage,' 329.
7 On Enzensberger's reproach of Bisky, see '*Eine Frau in Berlin*: Hans Magnus Enzensberger zu Vorwürfen,' *Frankfurter Allgemeine Zeitung*, 26 September 2003, 35; and Dirk Knipphals, 'Viel Getöse um ein Tagebuch: Wie authentisch ist das Buch *Eine Frau in Berlin*? Hans Magnus Enzensberger reagiert auf Fragen mit Empörung,' *taz, die tageszeitung*, 28 January 2004, Kultur, 18.
8 Anonymous, *A Woman in Berlin: Eight Weeks in the Conquered City – A Diary*, trans. P. Boehm (New York: Metropolitan Books, 2005), 1. This is a translation of Anonyma, *Eine Frau in Berlin: Tagebuchaufzeichnungen vom 20. April bis 22. Juni 1945* (Frankfurt a.M: Eichborn, 2003), 9. For the English-language passages in this chapter Boehm's translation has been used.

9 Heinrich von Kleist, *Sämtliche Werke*, ed. Roland Reuß and Peter Staengle (Basel, Frankfurt am Main: Stroemfeld / Roter Stern, 1989), vol II/2 ('Die Marquise von O...'), 7. Translations of Kleist's text are my own.

10 On the title of 'Die Marquise von O...' Sabine Doering notes: 'Während andere Erzählungen Kleists ein Ereignis in den Titel stellen (Das Erdbeben in Chili, Die Verlobung in St. Domingo), wird hier (wie bei Michael Kohlhaas) eine Person hervorgehoben. Deren Kennzeichnung mit dem Adelsprädikat ('Marquise') statt mit dem Vornamen ('Julietta') weist bereits auf die Möglichkeit eines gesellschaftlichen Konfliktes voraus.' See Sabine Doering, *Heinrich von Kleist 'Die Marquise von O...' Erläuterungen und Dokumente* (Stuttgart: Reclam, 1993), 5.

11 Ibid., 37.

12 Kleist, 'Die Marquise von O...,' 10.

13 Ibid., 11.

14 See Herbert Kraft, *Kleist: Leben und Werk* (Münster: Aschendorff, 2007), 107–8.

15 Ibid., 108. Katherine R. Goodman contests this conclusion in 'Swan Song of Prussia? Kleist's "Marquise von O...,"' *Deutsche Vierteljahrsschrift für Literaturwissenschaft und Geistesgeschichte* 82 (2008): 563n42. Joachim Maass dates Kleist's work on the story to his time in Königsberg in 1806. See Joachim Maass, *Kleist: Die Geschichte seines Lebens* (Bern: Scherz, 1977), 140.

16 See Doering, *Heinrich von Kleist*, 9. Goodman, 'Swan Song of Prussia,' 559n19, contests this conclusion as well.

17 Kraft, *Kleist*, 109. The German reads: 'Der Krieg ist "die Fortsetzung des Friedens mit stärkeren Mitteln." Dann wird die Gewalt offensichtlich, sonst bleibt sie halb verborgen.' Kraft is citing Robert Musil, *Gesammelte Werke*, ed. Adolf Frisé (Hamburg: Reinbeck, 1981), 2nd ed., vol. 2, 521 (from *Der Mann ohne Eigenschaften*). Elisabeth Krimmer, 'The Gender of Terror: War as (Im)Moral Institution in Kleist's *Hermannschlacht* and *Penthesilea*,' *German Quarterly* 81 (2008): 66–7, similarly observes that although Kleist's plays 'paint a vivid portrait of the terror of war, they also show that war is not the 'Other' of civil society, but integrated into its very core. In Kleist's texts, wars are all but inevitable because society is itself the continuation of war by other means.'

18 For an account of the dashes in Kleist, see László F. Földényi, *Heinrich von Kleist: Im Netz der Wörter*, trans. from the Hungarian by A. Doma (Munich: Matthes & Seitz, 1999), 154–60.

19 I am here referring to the English-language title of Helke Sander's film about the mass rapes, *BeFreier und BeFreite* (1992), which is *Liberators take Liberties*.

20 See Michel Chaouli, 'Irresistible Rape: The Lure of Closure in "The Marquise of O...,"' *Yale Journal of Criticism* 17 (2004): esp. 64.
21 Ibid., 63.
22 On the specifically deconstructive use of the term 'literature' here, see
Chaouli, 'Irresistible Rape,' esp. 67.
23 *A Woman in Berlin*, 53; *Eine Frau in Berlin*, 62–3.
24 *A Woman in Berlin*, 48. The dash in the German text is converted to an ellip-
sis in Boehm's English translation. See *Eine Frau in Berlin*, 57.
25 *A Woman in Berlin* 163; *Eine Frau in Berlin*, 181.
26 Elizabeth Heinemann, 'The Hour of the Woman: Memories of Germany's
"Crisis Years' and West German National Identity," *American Historical
Review* 101 (1996): 364.
27 Antony Beevor, *The Fall of Berlin 1945* (New York: Penguin, 2002), 410.
28 Atina Grossmann, *Jews, Germans, and Allies. Close Encounters in Occupied
Germany* (Princeton: Princeton UP, 2007), 49.
29 Catherine Merridale cites alcohol as an important enabling factor in the
rapes. See *Ivan's War: Life and Death in the Red Army, 1939–1945* (New York:
Metropolitan Books, 2006), 313. Merridale uses *Eine Frau in Berlin* among
her sources.
30 *A Woman in Berlin*, 52. The term *sowas* appears as one word in the German
text. See *Eine Frau in Berlin*, 62.
31 Giles MacDonogh, *After the Reich: The Brutal History of the Allied Occupation*
(New York: Basic Books, 2007), 98. He uses the term 'rapine,' which generally means 'plunder.'
32 Beevor, *The Fall of Berlin*, 32.
33 Ibid., 414.
34 Ibid. Beevor explains more about the rapes on 409–12. This and other of his
observations treat *Eine Frau in Berlin* as a source of historical testimony.
35 *A Woman in Berlin*, 115–16; *Eine Frau in Berlin*, 130–1. Italics B.P.
36 *A Woman in Berlin*, 63; *Eine Frau in Berlin*, 73.
37 Heinemann, 'The Hour of the Woman,' 365.
38 *A Woman in Berlin*, 215; *Eine Frau in Berlin*, 235.
39 Ibid.
40 *A Woman in Berlin*, 260; *Eine Frau in Berlin*, 281.
41 Cohen-Pfister, 'Rape, War, and Outrage,' 319. Götz Aly, to whom Cohen-
Pfister refers, writes: 'Es überrascht auch nicht, wenn diejenigen, die die
Tage der Erniedrigung, der Schändung physisch überlebten, später über
ihre Traumatisierung schweigen.' See Götz Aly, 'Ein Fall für Historiker:
Offene Fragen um das Buch *Eine Frau in Berlin*,' *Süddeutsche Zeitung*, 18
October 2003, 15.

42 Grossmann, *Jews, Germans, and Allies*, 53.

43 *A Woman in Berlin*, 186. *Eine Frau in Berlin*, 206.

44 *A Woman in Berlin*, 186, 187. *Eine Frau in Berlin*, 206.

45 See Laurel Cohen-Pfister, 'The Suffering of the Perpetrators: Unleashing Collective Memory in German Literature of the Twenty-First Century,' *Forum for Modern Language Studies* 41 (2005): 125.

46 As Götz Aly points out: 'Anders als Enzensberger in einem Interview vermutete, handelt es sich nicht um eine Autorin, die in großer innerer Distanz zum NS-Staat womöglich "in einem Modejournal überwintert" hatte. Marta H. war bestimmt keine hundertfünfzigprozentige Parteigängerin der Nazis, aber sie gehörte zu den in vielen Ich-AGs tätigen Kleinpropagandisten des Hitler-Staates. In ihrer Arbeit als Journalistin präparierte sie die deutsche Jugend für den Krieg' (Aly, 'Ein Fall für Historiker,' 15).

47 See Gertrud Koch, 'Blood, Sperm, and Tears,' *October* 72 (1995): 33. Koch also draws on Kleist's writing about war, especially on *Penthisilea*. See 38–40.

48 Atina Grossmann, 'A Question of Silence: The Rape of German Women by Occupation Soldiers,' *October* 72 (1995): 49.

49 *A Woman in Berlin*, 44; *Eine Frau in Berlin*, 53.

50 *A Woman in Berlin*, 57, *Eine Frau in Berlin*, 68. Boehm translates the diarist's phrase 'breit wie ein Schrank' as 'broad as a bear.'

51 *A Woman in Berlin*, 61; *Eine Frau in Berlin*, 71.

52 Kleist, 'Die Marquise von O...,' 11.

53 Ibid., 102.

54 Ibid.

55 *A Woman in Berlin*, 261; *Eine Frau in Berlin*, 282–3.

Perspectives

Though relevant to any representation, perspective is a particularly important theoretical issue in war representations. At first glance this is readily apparent, since every struggle, military or otherwise, involves at least two antagonists, and representations of conflict usually emphasize the concerns of only one of them. At the same time, there are numerous journalistic and academic accounts of war that aim for a bird's-eye view. For example, a historian sifting through historical sources must deal with many different perspectives, all in some way unreliable since they are written from limited – and often during times of war strategically manipulated – standpoints. The important point is not that war produces an infinite number of perspectives and realities, but rather that many war representations explicitly adhering to a realistic explanatory paradigm – that is, they do not intentionally surpass such realism through parody, irony, surrealism, or some other antirealist mode – disguise their perspectivity, their limited or manipulative character, and move the reader or viewer to believe in the 'truth' or accuracy of the account in question.

This 'disguised mode,' which makes the study of perspective so vital to a robust understanding of realistic war representations, is explored in each of the three chapters that constitute this section. Each chapter deals with a different genre: historiography that aims to represent an accurate picture of the past (Stephan Jaeger); television journalism that tries to capture war experiences in real time (Lilie Chouliaraki); and cinema and other cultural representations responsible for articulating 'official' war histories (Helena Goscilo). All three refer or allude to a historical or ongoing war and real people, even if some of the representations under analysis are fictional. The three chapters also dissect the notion that the representations in question here depict war – its atrocities, sublimity, suffering, or thrill – as such, which means these representations all remain linked to the notions of historical accuracy, objectivity, and authenticity. The three contributors reveal how war representations deliberately construct authenticity effects and disguise their perspectival nature behind a mask of objectivity. In this way they unearth the function of perspective in war representations and expose war representers' manifold investments in perspective within their works.

With reference to both the Seven Years' War (1756–63) and the Second World War, Stephan Jaeger's essay 'Historiographical Simulations of War' discloses how various of historiography's rhetorical strategies can work together to *simulate* collective and individual historical experiences of war. Historiography usually seeks to provide a vantage point from which different perspectives can be synthesized, and to objectify war history as much as possible. Jaeger explains how the traditional historiographical narrative perspective, developed in nineteenth-century historiography and known as the bird's-eye view, emphasizes the value of cognitive analysis and attempts to analyse and objectify the ideological and affective sides of war's representation. But, he argues, in war representations the bird's-eye view is constantly tested because of the specific epistemological, ideological, and emotional challenges that confront anyone representing war. Jaeger goes on to consider historical accounts of the bombardment and air war over Germany during the Second World War. He concentrates on the representation of the atmosphere surrounding individual and collective war experiences, which are all marked by the idea that one needs eyewitness experience in order to be able to understand combat experience and the suffering of civilians. Jaeger then shows how historiography – as a secondary hybrid text operating between the real and the imagined – can sustain the aesthetic illusion of the 'real' while affirming pragmatic truth claims. Understanding how such an illusion is performed allows the scholar of war representations also to reflect upon the ideological subtexts and the self-reflexive potential of war historiography in general.

Like Jaeger, Lilie Chouliaraki, the author of 'The Aestheticization of Suffering on Television,' uses a framework grounded in spectator or reader-response aesthetics as well as theories of narrative distance to show how war representations attempt to mimic authenticity and create proximity effects. Chouliaraki argues that apparently 'transparent'

real-time TV news footage is in fact as manipulative as any other kind
of war representation. To support her contention, Chouliaraki offers
detailed analysis of a specific BBC News broadcast covering the early
'shock and awe' phase of the Iraq War in 2003. The footage she considers
details aspects of the night-time bombing of Baghdad. She avoids the
now-standard criticism of this footage that the narrative accompanying
it does not rise to the level of objective journalism, and instead shows
how the mechanisms of televised war representation – even in public
television that purports to offer 'objective' journalism – always involves
the taking of sides, a kind of partisanship which creates perspectives
that work to undermine claims to representational authenticity.

Unlike war propaganda, journalistic broadcasting claims to resist
any simple identification of the 'good' and 'bad' sides in war in favour
of more objective reporting. Yet, by diagramming the complex interaction of broadcast images, editing, camera movements, and voice-over
narration, Chouliaraki is able to explain how the phantasmagoric spectacle of Baghdad's destruction literally overwhelms audiences' capacity to empathize with and therefore pity those under bombardment,
causing coalition troops to become seen as benefactors and not merely
combatants. The most significant result of this reorientation is a 'sublime regime of pity' within which audiences are strategically directed
away from the mortal and material consequences of destruction given
to them by the BBC in a hyperaestheticized form. The spectacle of distant suffering, she argues, gives rise to pity that is not directed towards
the actual sufferers of the bombardment but instead towards the horror
of suffering itself.

The third chapter of this section is Helena Goscilo's essay entitled
'Slotting War Narratives into Culture's Ready-Made.' In this paper
Goscilo extends the preceding discussions of historiography and
television journalism to encompass concerns with the perspectives on
offer in fictional representations of war, particularly those available in
feature films. Unlike Jaeger and Chouliaraki, who offer close readings
of the war representations of primary concern to them, Goscilo opts for
a comparative and intertextual approach that allows her – via juxtaposition – to analyse 'ready-made' (and essentialized) identities present
in a wide variety of Russian, Polish, English, and American war texts.
Although the basic language and stereotyping techniques of propaganda are universal – as seen for example in the same techniques being
used to demonize the enemy in war propaganda – Goscilo concludes
that war representations cannot avoid becoming rhetorically marked

by much narrower national perspectives on war's political value and cultural significance.

So, for example, Goscilo shows how Russia has repeatedly projected onto its war representations a national identity organized around representations of superhuman feats of heroism and self-sacrifice, not only in order to affirm (and at times rework) the legitimacy of pre-existing values and national-cultural self-understandings, but as a kind of warning to its enemy Others (especially the nations making up the industrialized West). The national marking may at times be gendered, and so it can be seen to have special significance for the representation of women, especially victims of war-related atrocities such as rape. Women, she explains, serve an 'abstract, tropological function as nation,' and national metanarratives tend to privilege (sacralize) the suffering of the male body.

In summary, then, historiography cannot penetrate the minds of participants of war or those who experience its effects, even though it can construct and simulate the individual and collective perspectives that sustain the textual impression of authenticity. Media – here real-time television – pretends authenticity and objectivity, but its close analysis reveals how viewers' sympathies may be steered in the production of specific perspectives. Cultural ready-mades in literature, cinema, propaganda posters, and other cultural representations seem at first glance subject to a kind of universalized representational code, but a second glance reveals how they react to and evoke specific national as well as gendered perspectives that skew all representations of war. Each of the three chapters in this section thus invite their readers to understand the nature and function of perspective in war representations, the perspectives in question usually concealed by (intradiegetic and extradiegetic) claims to authenticity, objectivity, universality, and realism.

4 Historiographical Simulations of War

STEPHAN JAEGER

Challenges of Representing War in Historiography

The numerous narrative techniques available to represent war and violence must allow for the expression of an immense range of perspectives. It spans from the survey perspective of the historian to the personal experiences of participants in the war such as soldiers or civilians, from first-hand experiences to considering the impact on future generations. Representations oscillate between distance and proximity, between critical summary or analysis and personal experience. For historiography in its narrower meaning as historical writing within the scholarly field of history, representing war seems particularly difficult since historiography is traditionally seen as a secondary narrative discourse, one in which personal experience is overshadowed by the critical synthesis of the historian who creates an argument out of all of the available historical sources available.[1] In contrast, fictional representations and primary war narratives such as diaries or autobiographies have the flexibility of creating their own worlds. In this respect, they seem better suited to expressing personal experiences, traumas, or fragmented memories.

War narrative in historiography does not necessarily differentiate from other fields of history, but it does produce several representational effects that are specifically more intense. One such specificity concerns the prevalence of chance and chaos in war that any representation must deal with, though various sides or agents often assume they are in control of war's representation. Then war, like every act of violence, also challenges any explicit language as its effects – such as trauma, horror, and pain – cannot sufficiently be expressed and easily shared with other people.[2] Another specificity concerns the constant need for perspective: no one participant in war has a complete overview of war. Consequently, primary narratives as the historian's main sources are unreliable since they are written from a limited and often manipulated or biased perspective.

One could argue that it is precisely the historian's task to bring order into the chaos, to create critical tools for the analysis of personal pain or trauma, to provide a vantage point from which different perspectives can be synthesized, and to objectify war history as much as it is possible within the discursive nature of history. The representational difficulties confronting the historian occur on the levels of ideology (the evaluation of events, especially regarding right or wrong, good or bad), of cognition (the interpretation or analysis of events), and of affect (the aesthetic or emotional experience).[3] The traditional historiographical narrative perspective, developed in nineteenth-century historiography and known as the bird's-eye view, emphasizes the value of cognitive analysis and attempts to analyse and objectify the ideological and affective sides of representation. But this perspective is constantly tested because of the specific epistemological, ideological, and emotional challenges that confront anyone representing war.

A particular challenge occurs when the historian intends to capture something of the atmosphere of the individual and collective war experiences. In other words, the historiographer who surpasses the level of factuality (the reporting of facts and events) must represent the perspectives and reactions of the historical actors – as individuals or as a collective – to the events around them. Yet, is that possible? Can scholarly historiography represent experience, which seems to convey historical authenticity?

From the perspective of Hayden White, the linguistic turn, and postmodernism, the answer is no. They have demonstrated the constructed and poetic nature of historical narrative. White's greatest narratological achievement has been to show the necessary emplotment strategies of historiography.[4] According to White, events are not real because they occurred in the past but only because they were remembered and narrated.[5] On the one hand, the historical narrative is shaped by forms and tropes. On the other hand, historical narrative is shaped by the ideology, moral convictions, knowledge, and background of the historian, as well as of the subjects providing the historian's sources. Any view and any representation of the past are perspectival depending on their discursive formations. There is no absolute historical truth. The category of experience – as Joan Scott has precisely argued – cannot be fully based on individual agency since subjects' experiences are constructed within its discursive rules and desires.[6] Even the most critical historiographical narrative can only maintain the truth claim that it represents the past in the best possible way, but the past itself is gone. It only exists in an infinite number of possible representations. One conclusion from the insights of the linguistic turn could be that historiography and historical experience are simply incompatible, that experience is historiographically unrepresentable.

Yet in this chapter I defend the thesis that historiography – despite its narrative structure and its discursive character – can *simulate* the historical experience of war. There is no need to reverse the insights of the linguistic turn, but White in particular misses the point that history is not simply another narrative form of fiction, but possesses a drive to simulate, and not merely represent, what it takes to be as 'real.' This notion of the 'real' constitutes the importance of historical experience; indeed, it is even more important in today's public historical discourse that is focused on historical events and experiences. Historiography can pretend presences of war events or war atmosphere to its readers,[7] while the war historian (and his or her readers) is nevertheless always aware of the constructive nature of this simulated presence. I will demonstrate this – after a theoretical discussion of the concepts of historical experience and simulation – with reference to three case studies: Johann Wilhelm von Archenholz's *History of the Seven Years' War* (1793), Frederick Taylor's *Dresden* (2005), and Jörg Friedrich's *The Fire* (2002).

Historical Experience

The Dutch philosopher and historical theorist Frank Ankersmit sees the connection between historical experience and the sublime as a solution for the representational challenges posed by the linguistic turn. It enables the representation of the 'real.' The whole concept of history is based on the assumption that there is a past that is unattainable but somehow desired. Since the language-based historical narrative – replaced by the term 'historical representation' in Ankersmit's work – fails to represent historical experience, Ankersmit, inspired by Aristotle, argues that historical experience is based on touch.[8] The haptic feeling creates a way of blurring subject (for Ankersmit, the subjective historian) and object (the past); they connect and change through the sense of touch. The object has no existence outside the experience, and the subject is being formed while it explores the object, much as fingers adjust their articulation while they explore the form of a vase.[9] Ankersmit contends with Wilhelm von Humboldt and Johan Huizinga that the subject gains an intuitive feeling of the past, an *Ahnung*. But whereas the vase exists as a material object in the present, which allows the subject to touch it and encounter a material trace of the past, Ankersmit expands the idea of touch metaphorically. For him, any piece of history such as a phrase or an old image can create an authentic and true experience that unites subject and historical object in one experience.[10] As Ankersmit writes, 'The object of historical experience is given to us prior to conscious reflection by the historian.'[11] Consequently, for Ankersmit, historical experience is beyond truth or falsehood; it is organized around the unique, unrepeatable interaction between subject and object and does not depend on any interaction with an objective, verifiable reality.[12]

Ankersmit develops his experience theory with strong allusions to the Romantic models of imagination, mainly in literature and paintings. The question that remains unanswered in his work is whether or not historiography, despite its inclination towards abstraction and historical synthesis, and despite its status as a language-based narrative, can simulate such an experience at all. Ankersmit takes any historiography[13] out of the experience equation.[14] Instead of leaving the historiographical narrative behind, as it tries to establish truth claims where there are none, I will argue that the concepts of experience and simulation can be combined in historiography to go beyond what Ankersmit proposes, so that historiography can pretend constructed presences.

Historiographical Simulation of War

Unlike Ankersmit's vase, the bombing of Dresden or the events of D-Day exist only in representations or performances. For a moment, from the historiographical perspective, it seems easy to accept not just the linguistic turn but also Jean Baudrillard's postmodern thesis about the disappearance of the real or authentic in today's media age.[15] But Baudrillard's concept of simulation, which questions the reality status of war and its ideological reasons, seems to negate history as such.[16] The postmodern understanding of simulation implies that external things and facts are not in the foreground of the semiotic process but that the process of simulation itself replaces external reality.[17]

What Baudrillard's concept of simulation does not consider is the at least imagined existence of the real as seen in Ankersmit above. To understand the relation between the real and historiography we must consider the pragmatic notion of historiographical narrative. Following Hayden White and others, there can be no doubt that the form of historiographical writing is not fundamentally different from that of fictional writing.[18] But in most cases the relation between text and reality in each genre is different: historiographic and fiction writing generate different kinds of pragmatic truth claims. Lubomír Doležel explains these differences as follows: 'Historical discourse has to be truth-functional in order to construct possible worlds that serve as *models* of the past. While fictional poiesis constructs a possible world that did not exist prior to the act of writing, historical noesis uses writing to construct models of the past that exists (existed) prior to the act of writing.'[19] A historiographical narrative does not claim to reconstruct a factual world that existed in the past, but to denote a past world that used to exist in one form or another.

Docudramas on the Second World War or on life in the ancient world are popular in contemporary society precisely because they reconstruct or simulate a world of the past.[20] The viewer is given a privileged perspective from which to at least watch past events unfold, though without forgetting that scenes – such as the ones detailing the bombing of Dresden in *Das Drama von Dresden* [*The Drama of Dresden*][21] – are restaged and not authentic. Today's history didactics goes even further, as for example when the Imperial War Museum in London stages the Blitz experience through a reconstruction of an air raid shelter and a blitzed street in 1940. The installation relies on the reproduction or imitation of sounds, sights, and smells, as well as on somatic sensations such when the shelter seems to vibrate after a bombing. In the Imperial War Museum the experience of the Blitz or of the trenches in the First World War supplements a representation of war that emphasizes a more documentary and educational approach with text panels, historical objects, and photographs. In contrast, the installation of the historical event in a preserved section of a London underground air raid shelter in Winston Churchill's Britain at War Experience dominates the exhibition. As the highlight of the museum, visitors enter through a steel door into a space that is set up as a bombed-out London street where searchlights criss-cross the night sky and the air is filled with the violent sounds of screaming shells passing by overhead, anti-aircraft gunfire, sirens, and exploding bombs. The light, noise, smell, and shaking of the whole space adds to the experience. The museum presents itself on its website with the slogan 'See it, feel it, breathe it – the adventure of war torn London.'[22] History has become in part an event culture that uses the idea of simulating the past.[23] And war seems to be particularly appealing for this historical event culture since it puts people in an unimaginable situation, without any overview of what is going on.

To explain the *simulation* of the past, it is necessary to take a brief look at the concept's history. It is either aesthetic or semiotic.[24] In the history of rhetoric – deriving from the Latin word *simulatio* – simulation refers to the deception of the recipient. A speaker pretends to agree with an opponent; a speaker simulates a mask before showing his or her real intentions.[25] Francis Bacon sees simulation as one way in which humans can hide and veil themselves: simulation for him occurs 'when a man industriously and expressly feigns and pretends what he is not.'[26] Here, simulation is still closely connected to a concept of mimetic truth that can be regarded as the mimetic side of simulation.[27] Whereas Baudrillard maintains that the act of simulation has been increasingly disconnected from the simulated 'original,'[28] one can argue that strategic war games try to simulate actual battles or computer simulations simulate, for example, an air attack.[29] The idea is always to pretend to be as close to reality in the simulation as is possible, often, for instance in military training, to prepare for reality.

Consequently, simulation's mimetic side remains critical for war historiography, even in today's digital media age. To simulate means to create an illusion of a presence. A reader of a text can be temporarily overpowered by media[30] and forget that the text being read is about a virtual reality.[31] The reader imagines the historical scene and suspends all reflective judgments. The German Enlightenment thinker Gotthold Ephraim Lessing describes this aesthetic illusion in *Laokoon* as follows: the poet attempts to deceive his reader in the way that he believes to perceive 'true' sensations at this particular moment of deception.[32]

This aesthetic illusion can function not just in poetry but also in historiography. A reader of historiographical texts can be drawn into the reality of the world created by the historiographical representation before realizing its illusory status and remembering that the past is gone. To achieve such an effect a historiographical prose text must become more scenic – representing constructed presences as a drama – and less analytic or descriptive. The representation of the events' happening, not their critical analysis, can create an aesthetic illusion.

At this point in my argument, Doležel's pragmatic differentiation of historical and fictional worlds needs to be refined, since Doležel cannot explain which world is represented through historiographical narratives that simulate the past and use their poietic capacity to recreate a constructed historical reality. A historiographical text that simulates a specific historical air raid in the Second World War from the perspective of German civilians or that simulates how Prussian soldiers as a collective might have experienced a specific battle in the Seven Years' War creates neither a fictional world nor a historical world. If it follows its disciplinary rules, it tries to be accurate and denotes a past reality that is external to the historiographical representation. Therefore, what is represented is not fictional. But it is neither purely historical, since the actual poietic simulation process produces a reality of the text itself. An air raid happened in the past. This past exists – unspoken and in infinite primary representations – before the historian represents it. Then what kind of world does a historiographical simulation of war produce? The argument in this chapter is that it develops a textual world which is not fictional, but is often created by means resembling those of fictional narration and its poietic capacity. The simulated textual world refers to a 'real' or historical world of the past. As a secondary hybrid text operating between the real and imagined it creates the aesthetic illusion of the real while maintaining a pragmatic truth claim. This truth claim differentiates the textual world from fiction, since it is generated by a historiographical text following the rules of its discipline.

I will now go on to develop different categories of historiographical simulations of war: the collective experience of combatants and civilians; individual war experiences; and the simulation of the contingencies and of the course of war. In order to clarify these distinctions I have chosen canonical examples from the eighteenth and the twenty-first centuries – Johann Wilhelm von Archenholz's *History of the Seven Years' War* (1793), Frederick Taylor's *Dresden, Tuesday, February 13, 1945* (2005), and Jörg Friedrich's *The Fire* (2002). On the one hand, German historiography developed the narrative means to express history as a singular and unique story only relatively recently, in the late eighteenth century. The old system of rhetoric was transformed into a modern aesthetics, emphasizing questions of perspective and textual representation. On the other hand, the memory boom in recent years, particularly in regard to the representation of the Second World War, has challenged modes of overarching historiographical narrative that synthesizes historical sources in retrospect, allowing instead for a multiplicity of perspectives that must stand for themselves in historiography. The air war serves as my example of where narrative requires the narration of historical experience. The use of examples from the eighteenth and the twenty-first centuries also supports the idea that historiographical war narratives – despite methodological developments in the discipline of history – must respond to some stable set of representational challenges that have remained basically unchanged over the course of more than two hundred years.

Simulating the Collective Military War Experience

Johann Wilhelm von Archenholz's *History of the Seven Years' War* (1793)[33] is a prime example of how around 1790 the branch of German historiography concerned with military and political history developed the representational means to create historical unity at the national or universal level. This unity was not found in history itself, on the story level, but rather in the act of historical writing, at the level of discourse.[34] Archenholz simulates collective experiences of war as well as the contingent and teleological course of war. This can be seen by analysing different representations of the Battle of Torgau between the Prussian army of Frederick the Great and the Austrian army, led by Field Marshall Daun, on 3 November 1760. Archenholz's main sources are the military history of the Seven Years' War by the Prussian colonel G.F. Tempelhof[35] and Frederick's own historical account of the war.[36]

One key event during the battle is the Prussian attack against the Austrian army in the afternoon of that day. Frederick followed his strategic plan strictly, according to which the Prussians attacked the Austrian army at its two wings at the same time, on the one side led by Frederick and on the other by General Ziethen. Frederick ignored the fact that most of his cavalry and artillery were still behind him, which led to a massacre of Prussian soldiers by the Austrian artillery. How do the three representations deal with this presumably disastrous event for the Prussians? Frederick – creating some distance between himself as a historical person and a historian by using the third-person singular to talk about himself – gives a chronological account that reports the event in a factual tone,[37] before he reflects on its causes. The Prussian king regards war and history as something that can be planned and executed according to rational calculations. Only the phlegm of one of his commanders, he claims, led to the failed operation and massacre. If the commander of the cavalry, the Prince of Holstein, had not been that slow or had General Ziethen arrived earlier, Frederick would have won the battle according to his plan.[38] In Frederick's account, the course of events is usually altered through human mistakes, usually by his officers, and certainly not by the Prussian king himself. Contingencies do not exist; there is only bad execution.[39] Frederick's perspective is presented mostly from a bird's-eye view from which the narrator follows the events. Tempelhof, like Frederick, reports the events chronologically and in great detail.[40] Tempelhof clearly employs a perspective of zero focalization, knowing the events before and after, whereas Frederick's narration seems more like external focalization, following the events of the battle.

Archenholz represents the deadly massacre of Prussian soldiers via the Austrian cannons differently than his predecessors: 'Daun received the Prussians with a heavy cannonade, which had never been experienced on the planet Earth since the invention of gunpowder. Four hundred cannons were set up in batteries, and their abysses of fire, as if directed toward one focal point, spread continuous death and destruction. It was an image of hell, which seemed to open itself to receive its prey.'[41] Archenholz employs a metaphorical language unlike Tempelhof's, which relies on precise naming of the different regiments and quantitative expressions. Only at the very beginning of his narrative of the event does Archenholz employ an external perspective. Afterwards he represents the events from an internal perspective through the eyes of the brave and dying grenadiers who look at the four hundred cannons and perceive them as 'abysses of fire.' Each individual soldier feels that the cannons aim at one spot, directly at him. The sentence contains some factual knowledge – the figure of four hundred cannons – which the individual soldier or even the Prussian command could not have had at the time. Simultaneously, the text creates a particular perspective: that of the individual observer, the 'focal point,' which is the vanishing point of the cannons. The next sentence intensifies this inner perspective: the 'image of hell, which seemed to open itself to receive its prey' also relates to the fact that Archenholz participated and was wounded in the battle.[42]

By incorporating different perspectives, varying the distance between narration and events in his narrative, as well as by extensive use of metaphors that evoke the horrors of war, Archenholz is capable of representing the chaos of war without giving up one critical standard of historiography, without inventing an internal perspective or the thoughts of the soldiers. He simulates their war experience on a collective level. On the one hand, this allows the reader to have an aesthetic experience of the battle at Torgau, as in this example, or of life during the Seven Years' War in general. On the other hand, the aesthetic illusion will not last for the reader, as the narrative continues with quotations from the Prussian king and the historian-narrator's general evaluation of the horror of the bombardment that go beyond the aesthetic illusion of one horrific scene. So there is no doubt that the simulated perspective has been constructed by the historian-narrator Archenholz.

Simulating the Contingencies and the Course of War

Simulating war in all its unrepresentable chaos and lack of a master perspective goes beyond just simulating the experience of soldiers on the battlefield. Archenholz is able – unlike Frederick or Tempelhof – to accept the incomprehensible and contingent aspects of war and history. He does not search for definite historical answers in every incident.[43] For example, Archenholz acknowledges that the Prussian king might make mistakes or that a little incident could change the whole trajectory of the war. Another look at Archenholz's representation of the Battle of Torgau illustrates this. First, Archenholz celebrates the historic greatness and uniqueness of the battle, which is described as one of the most horrific war experiences in human history.[44] He marks the bravery of the Prussians, so that from the beginning the reader knows that they will eventually win the battle. Archenholz's narrative is then shaped by dramatic turns both positive and catastrophic, mostly from the Prussian perspective. These turns are always dramatized and rhetorically highlighted, in particular as a battle between quantitative and qualitative necessities. The feeling of a guaranteed victory at Torgau constantly shifts from one side to the other. Based on their inferior numbers in the larger war, Prussia is likely to lose. The Prussian army is always on the brink of complete destruction. Its defeat may be delayed or accelerated by contingent events, but nevertheless seems inevitable. Archenholz pits the superior Prussian values and skills – Fredericks's genius, Prussian bravery, virtue, tactics, charisma, honour, etc.[45] – against this inevitability. These constant turns become part of an overall narrative structure that points towards the Prussians' necessary victory and survival. Archenholz's representation allows the reader to be drawn into this development because of the increased proximity to the historical events. The reader can experience the aesthetic illusion of the Prussian force and the continuous imminent danger to this force. Archenholz can simulate the contingencies and chaos of war, as well as create a story of the eventual Prussian triumph. His reader is torn between the aesthetic illusion of these developments and a more reflective distance from which it is possible to differentiate between the simulated textual world and the past historical world.

Simulating Individual War Experience

My second and third examples of the historiographical simulation of war concern the air or bombing war over Germany during the Second World War. Unlike in German late-eighteenth-century historiography, the philosophical background has disappeared from war historiography in the twenty-first century. There is no simulation of the course of history via war. A deeper philosophical meaning cannot exist in the chaos of modern technological war, or in regard to its atrocities. At the same time, the blurring of military and civilian targets in warfare, which Archenholz's history already indicated, raises questions of morality such as whether the war or specific actions in war are right or wrong. As in Archenholz, the impression of chaos and the unattainable overall perspective prevail, and both texts employ techniques to simulate this in textual performances.

At first glance, the British historian Frederick Taylor does not simulate war in *Dresden, Tuesday, February 13, 1945*.[46] He establishes the context of the air war as well as that of Dresden's history and role during the Second World War. The historian-narrator Taylor represents past events with the gesture of full knowledge of what is to come in much the same way as can be seen in Tempelhof's descriptive bird's-eye history of the Seven Years' War. His text is a report of known past events. Since Taylor writes a popular history for a wider audience, his work is a less critical scholarly historiography in so far as he narrates more than he critically analyses, from above, synthesizing different sources and voices.

The simulation of war experience plays a decisive role in Taylor's war narrative, in particular in the chapters that represent the bombings that took place on 13 and 14 February 1945. Taylor represents an abstracted form of individual historical experience, which allows the reader the same perspective as if he or she were on the ground with those being bombed. As in Archenholz's history, a constant shift of perspective and distance between narration and events is decisive in the creation of this textual effect. I will analyse one passage in detail to show how Taylor represents the chaos in the firestorm of Dresden:

Some Dresdners who escaped from the inner city survived, like Hans Schröter, by finding islands of space – air pockets. For most, though, unless they managed to get out of the city altogether, there were only two sure refuges: the green spaces of the Grosser Garten and, north of this, the terraces and water meadows beside the Elbe.

Often it was only a few hundred yards, but with a firestorm raging, narrow streets blocked by collapsed buildings, and many familiar landmarks obliterated, the journey was often epically, sometimes fatally, tortuous and slow. Berthold Meyer had begun by escaping from a burning building in the Blochmannstrasse, around a third of a mile from the Elbe as the crow flies.

Clutching a briefcase packed with his most important possessions – he had already been bombed out of his home in Bremen earlier in the war – and with his free hand holding a plank in front of him to protect himself from burning debris, the twenty-one-year-old had not gotten far when he lost his way and was tempted to give up, to sink into deoxygenated oblivion.[47]

The first thing to notice about this passage is that the text focalizes from above. The reader becomes familiar with situation and terrain. Then in the second paragraph the perspective becomes narrower. A general statement concerning how close the 'sure refuges' are introduces the reader to the challenge faced by every individual who tried to escape the firestorm. Then the narrator introduces a specific historical person, Berthold Meyer. It becomes possible for the reader – as an effect of the aesthetic illusion – to watch Meyer move, alongside the narration, to see what he carries and how he almost passes out, only interrupted by the phrase in hyphens that points to Meyer's bombing experience earlier in the war. The text has moved from zero focalization to a kind of external focalization; the reader sees the scene, nothing else. Taylor does not enter the mind of Berthold Meyer; instead Meyer's own narrative is allowed to speak.[48] Meyer describes his further journey to the river before the narrative jumps to a different but comparable scene concerning somebody else who narrowly escaped the firestorm.

The shifting of focalization, the emphasis on individual voices that represent a more general experience, and the constant variation of the distance between narration and historical event bring the reader closer to the experience of war without the historian-narrator having to relinquish his control of the overall perspective. The narration works like a camera that zooms in and out from its object. To a certain extent,

the historian can suspend his evaluative responsibility – on the ideological and the cognitive levels – and hide behind the eye of a camera
that is moving through different experiences and variable distances.
Consequently, the reader is drawn into the scene and participates for
a moment in the illusionary historical experience of the air war. This is
especially true of the existential moments of chaos during and between
the air raids. In these, memories and individual stories take over the
war historian's synthetic control over the events narrated. Taylor – in
his role as historian – decides on these voices as examples for the night
of the firestorm, but after this his authority is strongly reduced. The
reader could question the accounts provided, but the historian does not
help in that respect; the accounts stand for themselves. Consequently,
the reader is more likely to be drawn into the aesthetic illusion of the
past's presence instead of analysing the text critically.

Taylor creates a collage of fragmented voices belonging to historical eyewitnesses whose statements are transformed into a third-person
narration and occur at different stages of Dresden's war history. The
fragmenting of eyewitness accounts[49] – very common in many recent
war documentary films – intensifies the textual effect so that the reader
takes the narrative less as an isolated eyewitness account than as the
simulation of individual war experience in the chaos of war that cannot
be told from one perspective alone.

Simulating the Collective Civilian War Experience

Jörg Friedrich's book *Der Brand* (*The Fire*)[50] was highly debated in the
international press in regard to a series of moral and ideological questions to which it gave rise. Any bombing representation that assumes
a third-person view distinct from the social actors – and attributes a
'voice-of-God' knowledge to this voice – shifts almost inevitably to a
moral perspective.[51] In this analysis, however, it is important to note
that Friedrich uses an extremely innovative approach to bring the experience of the air war close to the reader. I will focus on the chapter 'We'
to show how Friedrich simulates the collective war experience of Germans, with a particular emphasis on the perspective of civilians.

Friedrich is very aware that the air war relies on perception and
experience. Therefore, the text offers multiple perspectives that help to
bring the mechanisms of war closer to the reader. To a certain extent,
his text is a montage of unreferenced quotations. Quotations are signalled through quotation marks, but they lack any reference. Here, the

challenge in a war narrative of how to depict the atmosphere during a campaign, when it is clearly influenced by propaganda and ideology, is dealt with extensively. Friedrich's representational solution is to play the propaganda voices against the voices of the people and see how they match or contrast.

In 'We,' the reader is presented with a journey through the experience of air-war propaganda. The historian's voice is partly suspended. Instead, in a manner resembling Taylor's scenic approach, the effects of propaganda are enacted. The historian begins the chapter by clearly demonstrating to what extent both British and German propaganda manipulated the numbers detailing the effects of the air war. As the chapter develops, the narrator increasingly enters into the collective psyche of German civilians. The following example demonstrates how Friedrich constructs a secondary, textual world in order to represent the atmosphere in Germany during the air war. He writes about German disillusionment with Nazi propaganda that claims the German citizenry must endure suffering in the air war as a needed sacrifice. He documents 'a seething hunger for revenge'[52] building amongst the German populace:

> Feelings of hatred rolled over the entire population. 'There is almost unanimous agreement among the national comrades in their demand that the British people be exterminated. Revenge against England cannot be strong enough.' Not even a Christian's duty muted this wish. Believers spit out biblical curses. 'The brood must be eradicated root and branch.' Fear of gas turned around into active voice; Göring wanted to respond to the bomber terror with gas. People either longed for reprisal or fell into despair; there was nothing in between, only a transition from one to the other. 'If we could strike back, we would have done it long ago, before the Cologne cathedral was destroyed, but we can't.'[53]

This paragraph demonstrates the representational effect of Friedrich's narrative in a nutshell. The text indicates 'the entire population' as the subject of the represented feelings. This is proven by an unreferenced quotation about the population's hatred for the British. The intensification of this hatred becomes evident through the next quotation with its biblical allusions, a source that is identified precisely as coming from the Federal Archives. However, it remains unclear who said this sentence. It could have been the Nazi propaganda machine, an independent newspaper, a correspondent reporting on the feelings of German civilians, or an individual person suffering through the bombings. Friedrich synthesizes many voices into one collective voice. The first, unreferenced quotation looks like Nazi propaganda; the 'unanimous agreement' about revenge against the British is unlikely to be proven empirically. One does not have to go further than Friedrich's own chapter to see that the public's hatred was often directed towards the Nazis and Berlin as well.[54] Friedrich's text simulates or re-enacts the process of perception during the war. The first quotation is perceived by the public. That historiographical construct increases the hatred and the feeling for revenge, which culminates in the biblical quotation. Then the text indicates Göring as the agent of a possible revenge, which demonstrates how the Nazi regime supported those feelings, before the text turns to the disillusioned people who stopped believing in Nazi propaganda. Friedrich's text does not provide a historical explanation for this shift from the German population's hatred of the enemy to resignation to their fate and anger with the regime. The voice of the historian does not interfere by explaining or questioning this statement in the text. Historical changes happen. On this textual level, the reader receives insight into the shifts in propaganda, the reaction to these shifts, and the resulting changes in behaviour by the collective public; more generally, with regard to the entire chapter, the reader is shown how the collective reaction to the air war moves the public towards complete resignation about the military capabilities of the Nazi regime. Both the temporary suspension of cause-and-effect explanations and the relinquishing of exact referencing demonstrate that in Friedrich's text historical experience supersedes the deductions from historiographical facts. Consequently, the war is represented to the reader through the constructed perspective of German civilians. Narratologically, Friedrich simultaneously achieves effects of proximity (via the reconstruction of the collective mind of the bombed citizenry) and distantiation (knowledge about the atmosphere and mechanisms of the war).

Non-fictional Simulations of War Experience

This chapter has shown that war historiography and simulating history and war experience on different levels is possible without giving up the pragmatic truth claim of scholarly historiography. There is no doubt that Archenholz, Taylor, and Friedrich refer to historical worlds, to text-external data and events, and that their general readers will accept the trustworthiness of their texts. Historiographical texts have the narrative and aesthetic means to create textual realities and textual worlds, and to influence the reader through the production of aesthetic illusions. Their means of doing so are similar to those employed in fiction-making, such as their variation of perspective and narrative distance. However, it is important to see where a historiographical narrative differs from fiction. It needs to construct collective and individual perspectives that represent the typical group or group member and put less emphasis on the thoughts of one specific individual. The aesthetic illusion can never be complete, not just because language cannot imitate a prior reality completely, but because by definition academic historiography creates secondary constructions of the past.

Historiography's specific relation to the real makes simulation an attractive concept. The representation of war in historiography cannot serve the same purpose as that in fictional feature films or poetry, which are able to express the inner thoughts of war participants or remain explicitly silent about them. Yet it can simulate collective reactions to war or overall developments of the war with a specific claim to reality that fiction does not have.

Finally, there is one limitation to the approaches analysed in this chapter. The more experience is simulated, the less able are some historians – such as Friedrich – to provide explicit analysis or criticism. In Friedrich's text, analysis is part of the war performance and so the reader has no possibility of dissecting a critical position. Consequently, though representing text-external reality, Friedrich's text is not able to reflect explicitly on the ideology in the voices of war that he utilizes. The reader recognizes the effectiveness of the propaganda, but if the German collective mind is manipulated, so might be the reader's. One can argue that in this case the narrative cannot maintain the balance between factuality/objectivity and experience. The reader has no insight into Friedrich's historical sources, and the historian's critical voice seems to be suspended. Then the simulation of war experience, the creation of textual worlds through historiographical writing, loses an important ingredient of modern scholarly historiography: the open narrator and the self-reflection of the methodology used in the representation. The concept of simulation, however, offers this reflective potential: since it is always aware of its secondary constructive nature, it can cite the past and reflect upon the gaps between the present and the past instead. Therefore the lack of explicit self-reflection in Friedrich's text only shows that any historiographical simulation of war experience must be careful not to give up its critical and reflective narrator. Otherwise, the reader, accepting the historiographical truth claim of the text, may fall into the same propagandistic traps as the historical subjects and thus fail to understand the mechanisms whereby he or she is being manipulated.

NOTES

1 For the traditional narratological distinction between historical and fictional narratives, see Gérard Genette, 'Fictional Narrative, Factual Narrative,' *Poetics Today* 11 (1990): 755–74; and Dorrit Cohn, *The Distinction of Fiction* (Baltimore: Johns Hopkins University Press, 1999), 109–31.

2 Cf. the chapters by Kate McLoughlin and Jay Winter in this volume. For the suspension of language in representing war, see also Antje Kapust, *Der Krieg und der Ausfall der Sprache* (Munich: Fink, 2004); and, for the precise discussion of the limitations of the relation between war, violence, and language, the introductory chapter of James Dawes, *The Language of War: Literature and Culture in the U.S. from the Civil War through World War II* (Cambridge, MA: Harvard University Press, 2002), 1–23.

3 Cf. Mark Salber Phillips, 'Distance and Historical Representation,' *History Workshop Journal* 57 (2004): 123–41.

4 See Hayden White, *Metahistory: The Historical Imagination in Nineteenth-Century Europe* (Baltimore: Johns Hopkins University Press, 1973), in particular 5–38; and Hayden White, 'Interpretation in History,' in *Tropics of Discourse: Essays in Literary Criticism* (Baltimore: Johns Hopkins University Press, 1978), 51–80. The discussion of whether White is too schematic in his different patterns of correlations – for the mode of emplotment he differentiates between romance, comedy, tragedy, and satire – is not relevant here.

5 Hayden White, 'The Value of Narrativity in the Representation of Reality,' in *The Content of the Form: Narrative Discourse and Historical Representation* (Baltimore: Johns Hopkins University Press, 1987), 20.

6 Joan W. Scott, 'The Evidence of Experience,' *Critical Inquiry* 17, no. 4 (1991): 773–97.

7 The concept of the 'reader,' as used in this book chapter, refers to the interaction between text and its general reader. It neither denotes an 'actual' reader in specific cultural discourses, nor an 'implied' reader who is specifically addressed by a text that presupposes its readers. Instead, the term 'reader' is used as a generalized concept of a reader's possibilities to react to historiographical texts, steered by their narrative and representational means.

8 Frank Ankersmit, *Sublime Historical Experience* (Stanford, CA: Stanford University Press, 2005), 248f.

9 Ibid., 249.

10 See also Hans Kellner's review of Ankersmit's *Sublime Historical Experience*. H. Kellner, 'Ankersmit's Proposal: Let's Keep in Touch,' *Clio* 36, no. 1 (2006): 95.

11 Ankersmit, *Sublime Historical Experience*, 121.

12 However, this shows Ankersmit's tendency to merely reproduce the typical foundational tendency that is part of the concept of 'experience.' Cf. Scott, 'The Evidence of Experience,' 788.

13 Ankersmit discusses some historiographical dimensions of very spatial approaches like Huizinga's or Jacob Burckhardt's.

14 Ankersmit maintains that historical experiences are traumatic, because any 'former identity is irrevocably lost forever and superseded by a new historical or cultural identity.' *Sublime Historical Experience*, 324. These identities cannot be reconciled.

15 Jean Baudrillard, *Simulacra and Simulation*, trans. S.F. Glaser (1981; Ann Arbor: University of Michigan Press, 1994).

16 Jean Baudrillard, *The Gulf War Did Not Take Place*, trans. P. Patton (1991; Bloomington: Indiana University Press, 1995), 29–32.

17 Bernard J. Dotzler, 'Simulation,' in *Ästhetische Grundbegriffe: Historisches Wörterbuch in sieben Bänden*, ed. Karlheinz Barck et al., vol. 5 (Stuttgart: Metzler, 2003), 509.

18 Cf. Stephan Jaeger, 'Erzählen im historiographischen Diskurs,' *Wirklichkeitserzählungen: Formen und Funktionen nichtliterarischen Erzählens*, ed. Christian Klein and Matías Martínez (Stuttgart: Metzler, 2009), 110–35. Though historiography and fiction use similar poetic and narrative devices, it is important to note that there are gradual differences in the form that are relevant for either discourse, such as the need to construct collective voices in historiography (see below).

19 Lubomír Doležel, 'Fictional and Historical Narrative: Meeting the Postmodern Challenge,' in *Narratologies: New Perspectives on Narrative Analysis*, ed. David Herman (Columbus: Ohio State University Press, 1999), 262.

20 For the popularity of history as such, see, for example, Kevin Williams, 'Flattened Vision from Timeless Machines: History in the Mass Media,' in *Reconstructing the Past: History in the Mass Media 1890–2005*, ed. Siân Nicholas, Tom O'Malley, and K. Williams (London: Routledge, 2008), 7–28. For Germany and the Second World War, see Helmut Schmitz, 'Introduction: The Return of Wartime Suffering in Contemporary German Memory Culture, Literature and Film,' in *A Nation of Victims? Representations of*

German Wartime Suffering from 1945 to the Present, ed. Schmitz (Amsterdam: Rodopi, 2007), 1–30.

21 *Das Drama von Dresden*, dir. Sebastian Dehnhardt, Warner Home Video Germany, 2005.

22 http://www.britainatwar.co.uk/page1.html (accessed 23 July 2009).

23 For an example of the German context, especially in TV-event production, see Paul Cooke, 'Dresden (2006), Teamworx and *Titanic* (1997): German Wartime Suffering as Hollywood Disaster Movie,' *German Life and Letters* 61, no. 2 (2008): 279–94.

24 Dotzler, 'Simulation,' 524–5. Dotzler argues with reference to Baudrillard that simulation becomes semiotic instead of aesthetic, because of the dismissal of a possible differentiation between the real and the fictional or virtual.

25 Oliver Bettrich and Jutta Krautter, 'Simulatio,' in, *Historisches Wörterbuch der Rhetorik*, ed. Gert Ueding, vol. 8 (Tübingen: Niemeyer, 2007), 920.

26 Francis Bacon, 'Of Simulation and Dissimulation' (1625), quoted in Dotzler, 'Simulation,' 514.

27 Dotzler, 'Simulation,' 511–14.

28 Ibid., 514–25.

29 See Philipp von Hilgers, *Kriegsspiele: Eine Geschichte der Ausnahmezustände und Unberechenbarkeiten* (Munich: Fink, 2008). One can, of course, argue that today's video games have lost the reality component that the war games of a military command implicate.

30 Martin Andree, *Archäologie der Medienwirkung: Faszinationstypen von der Antike bis heute* (Munich: Fink, 2005), 11.

31 Martin Andree, 'Simulation und Präsenz: Mimesis, Illusion und der Tod des Signifikats am Beispiel zweier Tristantexte,' *Weimarer Beiträge* 52 (2006): 485.

32 Gotthold Ephraim Lessing: *Laokoon oder über die Grenzen der Malerei und Poesie*, in G.E. Lessing, *Werke in drei Bänden: Nach den Ausgaben letzter Hand*, 3rd ed., vol. 2 (Munich: Winkler, 1995), 97.

33 Johann Wilhelm von Archenholz, *Geschichte des Siebenjährigen Krieges in Deutschland von 1756–1763*, in *Aufklärung und Kriegserfahrung: Klassische Zeitzeugen zum Siebenjährigen Krieg*, ed. Johannes Kunisch (Frankfurt: Deutscher Klassiker Verlag, 1996), 9–513.

34 Cf. Stephan Jaeger, 'The Performative Birth of the German Nation out of War in German Eighteenth-Century Historiography: Johann Wilhelm von Archenholz' *History of the Seven Years' War,' Lumen* 27 (2009): 85–6.

35 Georg Friedrich v. Tempelhof, *Geschichte des Siebenjährigen Krieges in Deutschland*, 6 vols. (1783–1801; repr. Osnabrück: Biblio Verlag, 1977).

36 *Die Werke Friedrichs des Großen*, ed. Gustav Berthold Volz, trans. F. v. Oppeln-Bronikowski and T. v. Scheffer, vol. 3 and 4, *Geschichte des Siebenjährigen Krieges 1 and 2 (1788, Berlin: Hobbing, 1913).*

37 *Die Werke Friedrichs des Großen* 4: 69–74.

38 *Die Werke Friedrichs des Großen* 4: 71–2.

39 See Hilgers, *Kriegsspiele*, 43–71, for the development of war games that simulate battles but fail because they cannot transfer the strategic planning to the tactical operational battle. Strategists of the nineteenth century – Archenholz can serve as an early example here – begin to include coincidence and probability in their war simulations.

40 Tempelhof, *Geschichte des Siebenjährigen Krieges* 4: 296–311.

41 Archenholz, *Geschichte des Siebenjährigen Krieges*, 351, my translation.

42 Friedrich Ruof, *Johann Wilhelm von Archenholtz. Ein deutscher Schriftsteller zur Zeit der Französischen Revolution und Napoleons (1741 [sic] –1812)* (Berlin: Ebering, 1915), 7.

43 Reinhart Koselleck, 'Chance as Motivational Trace in Historical Writing,' in *Futures Past: On the Semantics of Historical Time*, trans. K. Tribe (1979; Cambridge, MA: MIT Press, 1985), 116–29.

44 Archenholz, *Geschichte des Siebenjährigen Krieges*, 349.

45 Jaeger, 'The Performative Birth of the German Nation,' 89–92.

46 Frederick Taylor, *Dresden: Tuesday, February 13, 1945* (New York: Perennial, 2005).

47 Ibid., 296–7.

48 The passage quoted above is followed by an extensive quotation by Meyer.

49 The fragmenting reflects the fact that people cannot fully verbalize their experiences in war as such – they can only provide accounts of their memories, which are often distorted by time and exposure to other narratives. Cf. Matthias Neutzner, 'Vom Anklagen zum Erinnern: Die Erzählung vom 13. Februar,' in *Das Rote Leuchten: Dresden und der Bombenkrieg*, ed. Oliver Reinhard and M. Neutzner (Dresden: SAXO'Phon, 2005), 138–9.

50 Jörg Friedrich, *The Fire: The Bombing of Germany, 1940-1945*, trans. A. Brown (New York: Columbia University Press, 2006); in the original, *Der Brand: Deutschland im Bombenkrieg 1940–1945* (Munich: Propyläen, 2002).

51 This becomes most evident in Friedrich's text. Although Friedrich constantly experiments with different perspectives and creates an innovative narrative, the historian's voice behind these perspectives guarantees historical knowledge and truth. Because of this truth claim, the book was perceived – in particular in the Anglo-American world – as a biased representation that made the Allied bombing campaign a war crime, or even suggestively led to the comparison between bombing terror and the Holo-

caust. See Stephan Jaeger, 'Infinite Closures: Narrative(s) of Bombing in Historiography and Literature on the Borderline between Fact and Fiction,' in *Bombs Away: Representing the Air War over Europe and Japan*, ed. Wilfried Wilms and William Rasch (Amsterdam: Rodopi, 2006), 68–71; for a reading that emphasizes a multiplicity of perspectives in Friedrich's text, see Daniel Fulda, 'Abschied von der Zentralperspektive: Der nicht nur literarische Geschichtsdiskurs im Nachwende-Deutschland für Jörg Friedrichs *Brand*,' in *Bombs Away*, 45–64.

52 Friedrich, *The Fire*, 427.
53 Ibid.
54 E.g., ibid., 421.

5 The Aestheticization of Suffering on Television

LILIE CHOULIARAKI

> A suffering child fills our heart with sadness, but we greet the news of a terrible battle with indifference.
>
> Luke Boltanski

The Mediation of War

The broadcast of Iraq War footage on Western televisions from March to April 2003 was a paradoxical event. It was the most transparent war footage ever but at the same time it was also condemned as the most manipulative. It was transparent in its first-time use of embedded journalists and in the concentration of an international pool of reporting journalists in Baghdad itself. It was manipulative in that this unprecedented proliferation of information and imagery intensified the processes of news regulation and censorship, opening the footage to criticism of a heavy bias in favour of the coalition troops. But, one might ask, haven't such processes always belonged to the propagandist apparatus of warfare? Indeed, to put it provocatively, aren't processes of regulation and bias already inherent in the very logic of broadcasting?

In this chapter, I address the question of bias by examining a single but illustrative example – the BBC's war footage of the bombardment of Baghdad during the early days of 'shock and awe.'[1] Despite its reputed impartiality, the BBC provoked controversy over the side it took during the war, specifically, its reports from the Baghdad front that played a considerable part in this controversy.[2] My intention is not to rush into taking sides in this news bias controversy but to examine the BBC example in a broader framework in order to understand how the taking of sides may occur in journalistic discourse. I argue that instead of appealing to the elusive ideal of objective journalism, it is perhaps more useful to consider television footage as a mechanism of representation that by definition involves the taking of sides.[3] The key question then becomes to find out how this mechanism of representation works: what semiotic and narrative resources the footage employs in order to represent the Iraq conflict, and what effect this construction has in legitimizing the pro- or anti-war side of the conflict.[4] The value of this analytical perspective lies in its capacity to evaluate the moral implications and political agendas of journalistic discourse not through an abstract norm of objectivity but through a concrete description of how war and suffering appear on our television screens.

To this end, the 'analytics of mediation' is a framework for the study of television as a mechanism of representation that construes war and suffering within specific 'regimes of pity,' that is, within specific semantic fields where emotions and dispositions to action vis-à-vis the suffering of others are evoked for the spectator.[5] The 'analytics of mediation' thus conceptualizes war footage as a semiotic accomplishment that combines camera work and voice-over in order to establish a degree of *proximity* between the spectator and the scene of suffering and to propose certain possibilities of *action* upon the suffering.[6] The assumption behind the 'analytics of mediation' is that choices over how suffering is portrayed – where, when, and who are the victims of the suffering – always entail specific ethical dispositions, independent of our own evaluative judgment on these dispositions as undesirable or desirable.[7]

My discussion of the Baghdad footage is organized around the three related categories that make up the 'analytics of mediation': (i) the *multimodality* of the footage (the moving image-verbal narrative combination on screen), and the impact of this semiotic combination on (ii) the *space-time* of suffering (how the footage represents the where and when of the bombing event) and on (iii) *agency* in suffering (who is represented to act upon whom and under what capacity in the scene of suffering).

My argument is that the semiotic choices of the footage construe the bombardment of Baghdad in a 'sublime' regime of pity whereby the phantasmagoria of the spectacle obliterates the humanitarian quality of suffering and the aesthetic of 'shock and awe' takes over other ethical and political considerations of the conduct of war – a construal of the war presented not only in a number of reports on the night-time air operations on Baghdad, but also in other significant aspects of war coverage.[8]

It is important not to consider the sublime to be a fixed and palpable presence on the television screen, that is to say, an empirical reality existing in the world 'out there.' As the concept of a 'regime of pity' suggests, the sublime is an analytical construct that offers a particular interpretation of how distant suffering appears on television and the possible effects it may have on the ethical dispositions and beliefs of Western spectators. In this sense, the sublime is neither the only perspective nor the most 'correct' one on the footage. It is, however, a particularly useful perspective on the study of journalistic discourse in that it makes possible the analysis of the footage from a critical, but not a prescriptive, perspective. Evidently, in choosing not to prescribe what is 'objective' footage, the analysis of the sublime does not abandon the normative perspective. Rather, it tactically sidelines such a perspective in order to analyse how norms of right and wrong are produced in the course of the footage itself and how such norms construe a certain version of the war as valid and legitimate for Western audiences at the expense of other norms of humanity and justice.

Pity and the Public Sphere

The regime of pity through which our sample footage represents the war takes part in a broader field of journalistic meanings that attempts to define the ethical and political content of the Iraq conflict across national-cultural contexts and in diverse institutions. In so doing, the footage plays a crucial role in identifying 'good' and 'bad' sides and, broadly, in legitimizing the causes and intended outcomes of the war. However, the taking of sides in public service broadcasting requires that the representation of the conflict and the attempt to engage the spectator take place within the boundaries of the public sphere.[9] This means that the footage cannot resort to common propaganda, openly expressing a pro- or anti-war position or explicitly stirring up emotions. Rather, the footage must appear to be impartial and must gain its legitimacy by offering objective information to the spectator.

In her reports from the front, Christiane Amanpour, CNN Senior International Correspondent, captures the tension between the perspectivalism inherent in the representation of the war and the necessity of maintaining an objective distance from it: 'The problem,' she says, 'is that the coalition troops want to be seen as benefactors not just as bombers.'[10] Amanpour's remark connects the legitimacy of the war with the media image of the troops either as benefactors, helping the suffering Iraqis, or as bombers, harming the already suffering Iraqis. In this manner, the notion of 'pity' is elevated to a key component of the representation of the Iraq War on television.

The notion of pity, in this context, does not refer to our supposedly natural sentiments of empathy and tender-heartedness towards the spectacle of human pain. Pity, rather, refers to a type of social relationship between the spectator and a distant sufferer, which raises the moral obligation for the spectator to respond to the sufferer's misfortune in public – even if, as Luc Boltanski says, this public response takes the minimal form of a conversation at home.[11] Pity here, far from a faculty of the spectator's soul, is a sociological category that is constituted in meaning. As the mechanism of representation that establishes a generalized concern for the suffering 'other,' pity is thus central to contemporary conceptions of Western sociality and indispensable for the constitution of modern democratic collectivities.[12] Pity, by this token, is also a key signifier in organizing the justification and legitimation strategies of political discourse, including the coalition's decision to overthrow the Saddam Hussein regime by means of a military invasion in Iraq.

The focus of the 'analytics of mediation' on the semiotic operations by which television engages the spectator in degrees of proximity and dispositions to action towards suffering stems precisely from the assumption that pity does not precede representation but is produced through representation in a range of public practices and discourses – through what Boltanski calls a 'politics of pity.' The concept of the politics of pity draws attention to the fact that, in order for the television spectator to take sides in the conflict, a mechanism of representation needs to be in place that focuses on the suffering of the Iraqi people and objectively reports on those who act upon this suffering.

The politics of pity is thus a set of historically shaped and culturally specific practices of the public presentation of suffering that can be traced back to the emergence of the modern public sphere in Europe and its Enlightenment ideal of universal moralism.[13] Mediated in public through textual conventions (such as literary language or painting) and public genres (such as the novel or the political manifesto), the idea of pity has shaped the Western collective imaginary by connecting the public figure of the citizen to the figure of a spectator who contemplates upon and feels for a distant sufferer.[14]

Today, appropriated and reconfigured by modern technologies of mediation such as television, the politics of pity still performs the crucial political function of presenting human misfortune in public with a view to arousing the emotion of the spectators as well as inviting their impartial deliberation on how to act upon the misfortune. The politics of pity is, in this contemporary context, the politics of narrating and portraying suffering on television and thereby producing discourse about how we are connected to the world, what matters to us, what joins us together, and how we are supposed to respond to the needs of the suffering. By the same token, however, the clinical narration of suffering – the establishment of a radical distance from the location of suffering or the refusal to humanize the sufferer – may indeed come to block an active relationship between spectator and sufferer, but this should not be regarded as a semiotic choice that lie outside the enactment of a politics of pity. The interruption of pity is a variation of this enactment and a moral claim in its own right.

Even though the making of a moral claim on the television spectator is a shared aim in the politics of pity as well as in war propaganda, there is a crucial difference. In propaganda, the taking of sides is explicit and the point of view from which the suffering is presented is often partisan, either sentimental or polemical.[15] In the politics of pity, there is no explicit perspective from which stories of suffering are narrated but instead suffering is surrounded by an aura of objectivity, of impartial observation. Thus the difference between propaganda and the politics of pity is also a difference in the nature of the public sphere that each mode of mediated communication appeals to. Propaganda presupposes the prior commitment of the spectator to a cause, an already constituted community of shared interests and views – a community, however, whose very homogeneity is often established through coercion or brainwashing. The politics of pity, in contrast, presupposes a public space where the spectator is a citizen with both affective sensibilities (moved by the suffering he or she witnesses) and cognitive capacities (reflecting impartially upon the spectacle of suffering), before exercising his or her right to make the decision on which side to take and what action to take.

Pity and the Aestheticization of Suffering

The Baghdad footage evokes this ideal of the public sphere insofar as it claims to represent the war in Iraq from a perspective of impartiality whilst simultaneously evoking pity for the misfortune of the Iraqi people.[16] But if the production of pity does not involve the explicit naming of the good and the bad, how does it operate? According to Boltanski, the production of pity involves a certain distribution of the spectator's emotions around the two key figures who ultimately organize the spectator's own orientation towards action upon suffering. The first is the figure who alleviates the suffering of the unfortunate and hence wins the spectator's heart and support, what Boltanski, in a telling terminological convergence with Amanpour, calls the 'benefactor.' The second is the figure who inflicts the suffering upon the unfortunate and thus provokes the spectator's indignation, what Boltanski calls the 'persecutor.'

Depending on the semiotic choices in various sequences, the Baghdad footage manages to construe the Iraq War through two different regimes of pity: a 'regime of care,' when beneficiary action organizes the spectacle of suffering around feelings of tender-heartedness for those who comfort the sufferer; and a 'regime of justice,' when violent action organizes the spectacle of suffering around feelings of indignation against those who are responsible for the misfortune of the sufferer. Each regime entails its own distributions of agency, such as benefactors offering food supplies or medical aid to Iraqis, or of persecutors, such as Saddam Hussein and his Republican Guards.

At the same time, each regime also entails its own measure of proximity and distance vis-à-vis the scene of suffering in order for the spectator to contemplate the misfortune of the sufferer from a perspective of (claimed) objectivity. For example, the choice of placing the spectator within the scene of action together with embedded journalists or keeping the spectator outside the scene of action by offering panoramic views of Baghdad creates two different observational perspectives. As we shall see, the perspective of 'detached' observation makes a distinct claim to impartiality as opposed to the 'involved' perspective, and it therefore construes a distinct type of public space within which the spectator makes decisions about the suffering he or she witnesses. In this way, even though regimes of pity involve normative views and incite a range of emotions in relation to the suffering, each regime of pity also manages to appear distanced from moralizing norms and can thus be claimed to be objective and representing a public issue.

A difficult question arises, however, when television footage attempts to represent an instance of warfare in which the figure that aspires to be seen as a benefactor, the coalition troops, now coincides with the persecutor, the bombers. Amanpour's dilemmatic formulation of the coalition troops simultaneously as 'benefactors' and as 'bombers' comes to capture the contradiction in terms inherent in the spectacle of Baghdad burning, insofar as this spectacle fuses both these figures into one and risks blocking the effective production of pity. How does the footage deal with this essentially political question of redistributing the potential for pity in the spectacle of a city blasted by 320 cruise missiles in one night by its own liberators?

My own response is that the footage of the Baghdad bombardment enacts a third possibility for the representation of suffering, which does not seek to mediate the emotional potential of the spectator through the figures of pity. Pity in this footage involves neither a celebration of the good, in the action of benefactors, nor a denunciation of evil, in the action of persecutors. As a consequence of the effacement of the figures of pity, the spectacle of Baghdad offers to the spectator a scene of action without enemies or victims. Rather, the emotional potential of the bombardment is intended to 'stay with' the spectator as the experience of a sensational performance.

The moralization of the spectator now takes place through a mechanism of 'sublimation,' the representation of suffering through an aesthetic register that discourages spectators from feeling for or denouncing the suffering and invites them to contemplate the horror of the spectacle, the shock and awe of the bombardment.[17] Sublimation's emphasis on the aesthetic elements of suffering raises the question of how the footage manages to articulate a moral argument and induce the taking of sides: what are the semiotic features of the sublime regime, and how do these features construe the scene of suffering both as an aesthetic experience and an objective space of reflection? What consequences does this aestheticization of suffering have upon the moralization of the spectator? How is the taking of sides ultimately induced in the footage?

I address these questions through the analytics of mediation, focusing on the *multimodal* semiotic properties of the update's text and on the *space-times* and *agency* options within the scene of suffering that this text construes. I conclude that the question of how television participates in the legitimation of the war becomes more amenable to political and ethical criticism when seen in the light of the semiotic aestheticization of suffering than when it is confined to the general denunciation of news bias and in the pursuit of an abstract objectivity.

The Baghdad Bombardment on BBC: The Politics of Pity

The Baghdad bombardments, one of the most visually arresting and emotionally compelling pieces of warfare on television, were broadcast live on *BBC World* at approximately 19.00 CET and were subsequently inserted as regular updates in the channel's 24-7 footage flow. The piece under study is the next-morning update of the 26 March night bombing, shown on 27 March 2003 at around 09.00 CET, in between visuals from the Battle of Basra and on-location reports from the port of Umm Qasr. The update was introduced by Nik Gowing, the BBC's main presenter, from Doha, Qatar. Gowing invited the spectator 'to reflect upon the scale of the operation' – tellingly, the word 'reflect' involves the contemplative attitude of both looking at a spectacle and thinking about it – and informed viewers about the types of weaponry used in the operation. 'What was the impact upon Baghdad?' he asks and rounds off his introduction by mentioning that 'this report by Rageh Omaar has been subject to scrutiny by the Iraqi authorities.' The circulation of war news thus appears to be subjected to regulative principles, which include not only the concerns of the coalition but also those of the Iraqi side. Such concerns evidently complicate the regulative regime in which the footage was edited and narrated; nevertheless, they do not remove the key question of how the footage takes sides between benefactors and bombers. They intensify it.[18] In order to see exactly how the taking of sides is subtly managed, I begin with the *multimodality* of the update before I move on to its *space-time* and *agency* properties.

Multimodality

The mode of presentation of the update is a moving image (the edited video of the previous night's footage) accompanied by a running voice-over that comments on the image broken up by occasional pauses to allow for the harsh sounds of the bombardment to take over – a powerful audio effect.

On the visual plane, the *point of view* of the filming is from afar and above with a steady camera, probably from a terrace of the Palestine Hotel, where foreign journalists stayed during the war. The camera captures Baghdad in its visual plenitude, tracking swiftly across the dimly lit cityscape at night. This introductory shot of the update is filmed 'seconds' before 'the attack began in earnest,' to use Rageh Omaar's words, so that images still have the tranquil spectacularity of a nocturnal city panorama – illuminated darkness without a sense of movement. As the air strikes begin, movement is introduced to the spectacle of the cityscape. Movement is visualized on-screen through camera tracks and zooms, the cameras seeking to capture the hectic 'explosions' of shapes and colours against the dark background of the cityscape. First, movement is an effect of the city building contours, which, once hit by missiles, become illuminated before they fade out of sight again, in smoke and fire. Second, movement is the effect of weapons fire: of the bomb explosions themselves, which appear as random orange-coloured flashes that temporarily amplify the sense of on-screen space, and of Iraqi anti-aircraft fire, which appears on-screen as a tiny round fluorescent whiteness that glows in the dark on its way towards the sky. Finally, movement is visualized as the vector of a blue blinking light on an ambulance vehicle, dashing over a Tigris bridge and being reflected in the river water. This pictorial composition, a panorama of shape and colour, is accompanied twice by the sound effects of rattles and blasts and a howling ambulance siren, all of which amplify the visual effect of unrelenting action taking place in this obscure cityscape. On the whole, the Baghdad bombing is a phantasmagoric spectacle of rare audio-visual power and immense intensity.

On the verbal plane, the on-screen spectacle is framed by a complex narrative that simultaneously achieves multiple functions. Adapting Chatman's three narrative categories, I would claim that Rageh Omaar's voice-over is a hybrid text that combines description with narration and exposition.[19] Whereas *description* is of the 'this-is-what-we-see' narrative type that uses language referentially to put words onto and illustrate visual action, *narration* introduces elements of storytelling proper, such as opening and closing conventions of the 'once-upon-a time' type; finally, *exposition* carries the evaluative element of the voice-over, implicitly articulating a moral stance vis-à-vis the visual text, such as 'isn't-this-horrific, extraordinary or sad?' But it is not exclusively the expository talk that frames the scene of suffering in moral discourse. It is, as we shall see, the combination of all three narrative types added to the power of the moving image that together determine the overall moralizing function of the footage. Let us now look more closely into selected instances, where the narrative types of the voice-over interact with the visual mode.

Narration both introduces and rounds off the voice-over. The opening frame, a long shot of the Baghdad cityscape before the attack, is accompanied by 'Baghdad was bracing itself for a ferocious night,' a sentence that not only construes the city of Baghdad as a human agent but also begins to build a climaxing plot, as it anticipates an ominous change in the visual stillness of the screen. The temporal circumstance – '... *But seconds later* it began in earnest' – is a marker of chronological (rather than causal) cohesion in the voice-over, which propels a narrative climax from the previous visual shot, by articulating the verbal contrast between before and after with the visual contrast between tranquillity and bombing hell. The closing sentence – 'And all *this is not the end*. The president of the US said that this is just the beginning ' – imitates a conventional ending to the 'story' but also acts as an ironic hint, intertextually referring to 'This is the end,' the song by The Doors that concludes one of the most memorable war movies of all times, *Apocalypse Now*.

In this way, a link is forged between television war footage and Hollywood dramaturgy, blurring the distinction between the historical world and the world of cinema. Narration then makes a sporadic but instrumental appearance in the voice-over in two ways. First, narration introduces drama, by climaxing and contrasting moments of the event of bombardment; second, it amplifies the appeal to the audience by alluding to and capitalizing upon popular genres of storytelling, a movie and a song. Both the drama and the allusion to cinematic experience, important as they are in triggering emotion, place the event in the grey area between the genre of fact and the genre of fiction.

Description works in the opposite direction, namely, by establishing a relationship of factual correspondence between visual and verbal text. This is obvious in the references: 'The *anti-aircraft gunner* desperately trying to …,' 'You'll see the *missiles* actually ripping into …', 'Beneath all of this, *emergency teams* raced …,' and finally, 'what looks like a *surface-to-air missile*. This was Iraq retaliating.' All these statements take the moving image to be the external reality that language refers to, singles out, and illustrates. The linguistic referents of these statements, highlighted in bold, may appear on-screen as vague shapes and random colours, but their naming endows them with physical appearance and function. Description, in this sense, works to create an indexical relationship between the nominal use of gunner, missile, or emergency teams and the pictorial composition of the glowing white light, the orange-coloured flash, or the blue blinking vector. At the same time, the references 'you see …,' 'we saw …,' 'take a closer look …,' and 'what looks like …' capitalize upon the semiotic function of the camera zoom to focus on detail and use the power of vision to validate the reality bond between the name and its external referent that each description forges. The narrative type of description is, in this sense, instrumental in establishing objectivity, the quality of broadcasting necessary to legitimize the television footage as a public sphere genre.

Finally, *exposition* works through both narration and description to provide a point of view, a value judgment on the spectacle we witness. In this respect, exposition signals a shift from description's 'look-at-this' mode of address to a 'this-is-what-it-means' mode of address that also carries the moralizing function of the update. An example of expository narrative follows the harsh rattling sounds of the bombardment, in the statement: 'Even this city that has been through so much has not experienced anything like this.' This statement not only humanizes Baghdad as a sufferer – this city 'has been through so much'– but it further stresses the intensity of its suffering – has 'not experienced anything like this.' In combination with the visuals of unrelenting bombing action, this statement is moralizing in that it seeks to evoke a sense of humanity that we all share and that is now challenged by the ferocity of the bombardment – notice the use of superlatives in 'even this,' 'so much,' 'anything like this.' Which politics of pity is played out in this particular combination of moral talk with objective description and dramatic narration? The update no doubt manages to evoke the idea of Baghdad as a sufferer and moreover to invite the spectator to relate with empathy to the ordinary Iraqi. Nevertheless, it does so ambivalently.

One indication of ambivalence is that the exhortation to think about the Iraqi sufferer does not stand on its own. It is linguistically subordinated, by use of the adversative 'but,' to the main clause 'the strikes appear to be carefully targetted' – itself an intertextual echo of Donald Rumsfeld's comment the previous evening on the 'high precision' weapons used in the strikes. But the key semiotic feature of ambivalence is the formulation 'This is what shock and awe looked like as it tore into Iraq's capital.' Inserted between pauses that foreground the bombing sound effects, this explicit reference to 'shock and awe' steers the emotional potential of the spectator away from empathy by performing two functions at once. On the one hand, it describes reality as it is. The use of the deictic '*this* is what shock and awe looked like' reinforces the indexical link between what we see on-screen and the official code name of the airborne operations in the early days of the war. On the other hand, it also invites the spectator to relate to this reality in a specific manner. The reference to 'shock and awe' stands not only literally for the name of the operations – the *locutionary* meaning of the wording – but also signifies, in a more metaphorical sense, an emotional orientation to the spectacle of the bombings itself: the *perlocutionary* meaning of the wording.[20] By capitalizing upon the meaning potential of 'shock and awe,' then, the voice-over manages to convey a balanced sense of description and exposition, fact and emotion. The dual meaning of this nominal clause, at once locutionary and perlocutionary, combined with the rare visual intensity of the action on-screen, strongly urges the spectator of the update to indulge in the bombardment as a spectacle, sidelining the sporadic and subordinate references to 'ordinary Iraqis' or to 'a city that has been through so much.'

Space-time

The presence of the camera in the city of Baghdad and the sheer visualization of warfare certainly bring the Western spectator closer to the scene of this suffering than ever before in any previous war coverage. The spectators not only hear, read about, or skim through snapshots of bombed buildings, but can actually witness the bombardment as a reality unfolding in front of their own eyes – although in the update the dimension of live broadcasting is obviously lost. It is the total visibility enabled by the on-location camera that has provided justification for the celebratory argument that this war footage was the most transparent ever.

However, the point of view of the camera is from afar and above, providing spectators with panoramic views of the city. Despite the total visibility that this point of view offers, or precisely because of this, spectators of the update are simultaneously kept resolutely outside the scene of action. They are onlookers, watching the action from a safe distance. One consequence of the combination between distance and total visibility is 'detached' observation, a witness position that turns the reality of the war into a *tableau vivant*. In a similar vein to Rageh Omaar's verbal allusion to *Apocalypse Now*, the war panorama on our television screens bears an eerie resemblance to the opening frame of *Blade Runner*, itself a night cityscape regularly punctuated by orange flashes. Indeed, the quality of proximity that this detached observation provides to the spectator is cinematic. This is not so much the proximity to a lived space populated by people but more to a screen animated by alternating colours, shapes, and sounds. Another consequence of the steady camera is that the update does not alternate between different points of views and is therefore unable to shift the position of the spectator from detached to 'involved' observation, by moving through the streets of Baghdad, into the home of an ordinary Iraqi, into hospitals or indeed the city morgues (as for example Al-Jazeera was able to do).

The temporality of the update, narrated in time past – 'was bracing,' 'it began,' 'looked like' – reinforces the emotional distance that cinematic proximity imposes upon the scene of suffering. This is the temporality of an already finalized event, which opens up the possibility for analytical engagement with it: '*This is what* shock and awe looked like ...' There are further instances in the voice-over suggesting that we are now analysing the details of the military operation: '*Look carefully and you'll see* the missile ...,' '*In the distance what looks like* surface-to-air missiles ...,' '*This is* Iraq *retaliating* ...' There is, in these statements, an orientation towards the impartial contemplation of the scene of suffering as a terrain for the study of the logistics of war rather than as a political or moral fact.

Agency

In this section, I examine mainly the two agency categories in the update, the sufferer and the persecutor (or the 'bomber'), but I also briefly mention the benefactor, who makes a passing appearance in the scene of suffering. The sufferer of the bombing is represented largely in non-human terms. Specifically, the sufferer is verbalized as 'compounds' and 'buildings,' that is, as the physical but non-living targets of coalition fire; naturally, such targets are also visualized by camera zooms upon concrete blasts and explosions in the night cityscape. The sufferer is also verbalized as a diffused entity, in formulations such as 'Baghdad,' 'this city,' and 'Iraq's capital.' These formulations may act to humanize the city (as we saw in 'even this city that has been through so much ...'), but they also collectivize the sufferer and, in this way, work to subtract from the intensity that singular and personalized cases of suffering bear. Whereas a city can only feel in a metaphorical way, the physical and psychological pain of a single human being is a strong point of identification for the spectator, as the idea behind the politics of pity suggests. In this respect, the collective verbalization of the sufferer parallels the visual effect of the long shot as they both offer a 'panorama' of the city at the cost of failing to evoke any proximity – geographical or emotional –between the spectator and the sufferer. But the construal of the non-human sufferer is not only passive, 'a building' or 'Iraq's capital.' It is also active. The sufferer appears in the rather ambivalent but nonetheless active position of the retaliator, in the collective wordings of 'anti-aircraft gunners' or 'fluorescent tracers.' At the same time, the use of adverbials, either of manner, '*desperately* trying ...,' or of location, '*in the distance* what looks like ...' or '*beneath* all of this ...,' convey a sense of asymmetry in the warfare and signal the incapacity of the Iraqi side to properly retaliate or to act effectively as a benefactor for the suffering Iraqis – in the single reference to 'emergency teams.' The vague gesture of sympathy for such powerlessness has, however, no recipient. Indeed, the only reference to the sufferer as human lies in the sentence 'the ordinary Iraqis living near these targets,' which is simply verbal. Unlike the references to 'anti-aircraft gunners' or 'emergency teams,' which are simultaneously spectacularly visualized, the 'ordinary Iraqi' is a significant visual absence in the footage of the bombardment of Baghdad.

The persecutor of the Iraqi sufferer is represented in non-human terms, too. This happens through verbal references such as 'the plane' and 'the strikes.' The former, 'the plane,' remains non-visualized, but the latter, 'the strikes,' obviously the main topic of the update, occupies the pictorial mass of the screen throughout the report. In so doing, it performs the same semiotic function as the collective naming of the sufferer. 'The strikes' diffuses the figure of the persecutor and, in so doing, it avoids evoking the emotional potential of the spectator to take a denunciatory attitude towards the bombardment. However, this does not necessarily mean that the spectators of the update would not feel indignation or empathy vis-à-vis what they witness; this would be a naïve assumption as the spectators' reflexivity amounts to much more than the television text itself imagines or expects of them. What the diffusion of the persecutor points to, however, is that the representation of suffering in this piece of the footage systematically steers away from emotional engagement with the figures of pity and proposes to the spectator a different approach to the element of suffering.

Sublime Warfare

The regime of pity constituted through the semiotic features of the update is characterized by a hybrid multimodal text that invests the panorama of air war with factual description, dramatic narration, and moralizing exposition. This combination, whilst authenticating the event of bombardment as an objective reality, ultimately invites the spectator to study the event as a spectacle. This occurs within a space-time of cinematic proximity and analytical temporality, which is devoid of human agency but full of the spectacularity of striking action.

In short, the update construes suffering within a sublime regime of pity. The sublime is, in this context, a regime of representation traditionally inscribed into the aesthetic register and historically associated with the representation of suffering in the public genre of painting – as Boltanski's extended reference to Baudelaire's 'The painter of modern life' testifies.[21] The complex and multidisciplinary use of the term 'sublime' granted, I here take it to refer to a specific regime of pity that constitutes distant suffering less through emotions towards the sufferer and primarily through aesthetic appreciation derived from the horror of suffering itself. Such aesthetic pleasure comes about in a double movement: 'an initial movement of horror, which would be confused with fear if the spectator was not ... personally sheltered from danger ... is transformed by a second movement which appropriates and thereby appreciates and enhances what an ordinary perception would have rejected.'[22]

How can we semiotically differentiate between the two movements that bring about aesthetic pleasure in the update? The 'initial movement of horror' is clearly evoked in the visualization of the strikes, that is, the camera zooms in on the explosions and the gunfire, and it is particularly intense in the sound effects of blasts and rattles; verbal choices of dramatic narration such as 'Baghdad was bracing itself for a ferocious night' and 'even this city ... has not experienced anything like this' further contribute to amplifying the horror effect of the images of warfare. However, the transformation of horror into pleasure, whereby the spectator comes to appreciate the horrific sight of suffering, must be mediated by the spectators' realization that they are 'personally sheltered from danger.' Evidently, this realization is already inherent in the condition of spectatorship itself, which rests on the technological mediation of suffering and hence on the clear separation of the zone of dangerous living (which is being watched) from the zone of safety (from which the spectator is watching).[23]

But the realization that the spectator is personally sheltered from danger is also achieved on-screen through the semiotic construal of space-time. As we saw, instead of an 'involved' perspective, the bombing spectacle is represented from afar and above, giving spectators an 'imperial' perspective from which to gaze on the scene of suffering and providing them with a commentary on what is happening. As a consequence of this spatio-temporal arrangement, the second movement in the construal of the sublime regime rests on the careful study of warfare, which ultimately opens up the possibility of 'appropriat[ing] ..., appreciat[ing] and enhanc[ing] what an ordinary perception would have rejected.' The process of enhancing ordinary perception is evident in the verbal choices of description – 'look carefully and you'll see …,' 'in the distance what looks like …,' 'this is Iraq retaliating' – that urge the spectator to stay with the spectacle and appreciate the detail of visual experience. Sublimation is finally rounded off by the use of expository talk, which makes an explicit gesture to *the shock and awe* manner of relating to the bombing event – 'this is what shock and awe looks like' – and which further intensifies this manner of relating by the use of superlative formulations: 'even this city … has not experienced anything like this.'

Sublimation and the Public Sphere

What are the consequences of the sublimation of warfare for the public sphere of television? First, obviously, the effacement of figures of pity produces the effect of impartiality. Without a benefactor or a bomber, the update does not appear to take sides in the Iraq conflict, and, in this way, it considerably strengthens its claim to represent the war with objectivity. Indeed, in the absence of figures of pity and, thus, free of the urgent obligation with which these figures engage the spectator in emotion and commitment, the sublime allows the spectator to engage with the scene of suffering through reflexive contemplation. Reflexive contemplation can be understood as an arrangement that turns this scene into a passive object of the spectator's gaze, and the spectator into a gazing subject aware of his or her own act of seeing, a 'meta-describer.'[24] Of crucial importance for the moralization of the spectator is the fact that this arrangement does not entail empathy or indignation, but emotion distantiated from its object.

The implication of non-obligation to the suffering object is this: the spectator is given the option of pondering upon the horror of war outside its specific historical context and vested interests. Although links to both empathy ('just think of those ordinary Iraqis …') and to denunciation ('the President of the US says that this is the beginning of a new phase of air war') are present in the update, they are too weak to carry through a sustained orientation either towards the benefactors or towards the bombers, towards, that is, the practical and ethical tensions that traverse historical action. As a consequence of this politics of pity, the BBC footage lives up to its role as a global news channel that disseminates information without bias and operates within the premises of legitimacy that the public sphere sets and the channel's logo itself upholds: 'Demand a Broader View.' However, television footage is also a mechanism of representation that, despite its claim to objectivity, inevitably involves the taking of sides. In placing the scene of suffering at centre stage, the footage of the Baghdad bombing throws into relief precisely this tension of the public sphere between reporting on the bombing as objective fact and an instance of suffering that demands a response.

This tension between fact and emotion, both of which are qualities of the spectator as a public figure, introduces the second consequence of the sublime regime of pity on the public sphere of television. This consequence is related to the danger, inherent in the sublimation of suffering, of refraining from any moral stance vis-à-vis the suffering it reports and thereby completely blocking the capacity of the spectator to feel pity for the sufferer. The relevant question, in this context, is how the spectacle of suffering can provoke the spectator's emotions if it does not, at the same time, portray any of the dynamics of beneficiary or persecutory action? The answer is that the sublime seeks to moralize the spectator by simply making suffering visible. Rather than resorting to easy sentimentalism or angry denunciation, the sublime enables the spectator's encounter with suffering on the minimum condition that the latter is put on view.

In spectacularizing suffering, then, the sublime seeks to create the public space of emotion and deliberation in the face of suffering not through political or moral argument but through aesthetic representation.[25] Indeed, doesn't the combination of cinematic visuals with verbal prompts such as '... we saw this building take a direct hit. Look carefully and you'll see ...' and 'this is what shock and awe looked like ...' cultivate precisely this aesthetic grasp of the world through which the sublime aspires to capture the essence of suffering? At the same time, the hybridity of the update, combining dramatic description with moralizing exposition, testifies to the function of the sublime to bring together a strong appreciation of sensual experience with a – weaker, to be sure – norm of right and wrong: 'think of the ordinary Iraqis,' 'even this city ... has never experienced anything like this.' The sublime regime then constitutes the public sphere of television through articulating aesthetic judgment together with the 'quasi-political requirement of common humanity.'[26] Common humanity is this universal principle that aspires to coordinate the spectator's encounter with the sufferer into the civic disposition of detached and analytical observation without rendering the encounter an explicit pro- or anti-war statement, hence its quasi-political character. The spectatorial public thus constituted is a public of reflexive contemplators who 'feel together' at the moment of witnessing the naked fact of destruction and death. As Jean-Marie Schaeffer puts it, 'the feeling of aesthetic pleasure is nothing other than the feeling of this *communicability of judgement*.'[27]

There are, nevertheless, two problems with the sublimation of suffering. To begin with, this is a regime of pity that does not dispose the spectator towards action. Unlike the regimes of 'care' or 'justice,' which enable the imaginary identification of the spectator with the figures for pity and therefore are action-oriented dispositions (even if this action is often only action at a distance), the regime of the sublime is founded upon the condition of inaction. This is because, in order to grasp the suffering, the spectator must do nothing but 'be subjected to the gaze' and to 'feel penetrated and possessed by the other.'[28] Secondly, because no regime of pity is able to bear the weight of representing the suffering of the war alone, the aesthetic register alternates and often fuses with other regimes of pity and their orientation to emotion and practical action. It is therefore the broader context of spectatorial dispositions within which the spectator as a reflexive contemplator is located that decides how the regime of the sublime participates in the taking of sides. In the course of the 24-7 footage flow, this update is immediately sequenced by a regime of care that foregrounds the role of the coalition forces as benefactors of the Iraqi population. After having introduced the update through the prompt to 'reflect upon' the scale of the air war, Nik Gowing speaks over the direct visual shift from the obscurity of the Baghdad hell to clear, bright morning pictures from the port of Umm Qasr. A convoy of military trucks filmed at street level, and therefore through an 'involved' visual perspective, is crossing the highway while Gowring observes that 'This port will be the crucial entry for any humanitarian supplies. There are already ships at sea with humanitarian supplies waiting to be brought in. These are live pictures …,' as the on-location reporter describes it.

Here there is a shift from a regime of representation, which suppressed the possibility of pity when Baghdad was being blasted to pieces, to a regime where the benefactor is reported to be fully active even before Umm Qasr itself was securely in coalition hands. Thanks to the strategic sequencing of the footage, however, the contemplative spectator can now sigh in relief as the coalition forces take care of the 'ordinary Iraqis.' It appears that the troops' dilemma of being seen as benefactors and not just bombers, in Amanpour's words, is continually constituted through the alternating regimes of pity that the footage involves and is provisionally resolved in the transition points between sequences and the shifts between regimes. The taking of sides in the BBC footage occurs not through campaigning and propaganda but through the aesthetic register and its relationship to other regimes of pity and at the 'edges' of the representation of the war.

Conclusion

In light of the foregoing analysis, I would suggest that the televisual sublimation of suffering constitutes a form of regulation of the public sphere that does not simply impact upon what we actually see or hear but, as Butler further claims, poses a deeper constraint upon 'what *"can"* be heard, read, seen, felt and known.'[29] It is this constraint on how it is at all possible to represent the war on television that is thrown into relief by the inscription of the suffering of Iraqi people in the aesthetic register. As we saw, this inscription endows the journalistic genre of the update with an important ethical and political function.

As part of a broader field of regimes of pity, the sublime helps to even out the unresolved or, more accurately, the unresolvable tension in the identity of the coalition forces as benefactors or bombers, by suppressing rather than producing pity for the suffering Iraqis. It proposes to the spectator neither the regime of care – and the emotional and practical option of empathizing with the civil population of Baghdad – nor the regime of justice and the option of denouncing the invasion and demanding another resolution to the crisis in Iraq. In this way, the sublime becomes instrumental in taking sides in the conflict not by regulating the actors on-screen but by rendering their identities irrelevant in the public sphere of television.

NOTES

This chapter is an abbreviated and edited version of an article by the same name published in *Visual Communication* 5, no. 3 (2006): 261–85. The generous permission by SAGE Publications Ltd to publish this version is gratefully acknowledged.

1 See Rageh Omaar's report, 26–7 March 2003. For an analysis of a similar footage extract (Omaar, 8 April 2003), but from the perspective of political communication and the question of political legitimacy in the media, see Lilie Chouliaraki, 'Spectacular Ethics: On the Television Footage of the

Iraq War,' *Journal of Language and Politics* 4, no. 1 (2005): 43–59, special issue entitled 'The Soft Power of War,' ed. Lilie Chouliaraki.

2 For a criticism of the BBC as pro-war, see, for example, John Pilger, *New Statesman*(December 2003).

3 John Corner, *Television Form and Public Address* (London: Edward Arnold, 1995); Norman Fairclough, *Media Discourse* (London: Edward Arnold, 1995); Roger Silverstone, *Why Study the Media* (London: Sage, 1999).

4 Sociological research on how the British television coverage of the Iraq issue influenced public opinion on the war shows that such coverage has indeed helped create a pro-war climate but, significantly, not as a consequence of 'crude forms of bias,' but 'as the product of news values which privileged certain assumptions and narratives over others.' Justin Lewis, 'Television, Public Opinion and the War in Iraq: The Case of Britain,' *International Journal of Public Opinion Research* 16, no. 3 (2004): 295–310.

5 For the Foucauldian term 'analytics,' see Bent Flyvbjerg, *Making Social Science Matter* (Cambridge: Cambridge University Press, 1999); Nikolas S. Rose, *Powers of Freedom: Reframing Political Thought* (London: Routledge, 1999); Clive Barnett, *Culture and Democracy: Media, Space and Representation* (Edinburgh: Edinburgh University Press 2003). For the 'analytics of mediation,' see Lilie Chouliaraki, 'Watching September 11: The Politics of Pity,' *Discourse & Society* 15, nos. 2–3 (2004): 185–98; Chouliaraki, 'Spectacular Ethics'; Lilie Chouliaraki, *The Spectatorship of Suffering* (London: Sage, 2006).

6 For semiotic analyses of suffering on the Israeli-Palestinian conflict, see Theo J. van Leeuwen and Adam Jaworski, 'The Discourses of War Photography: Photojournalistic Representations of the Palestinian-Israeli War,' *Journal of Language and Politics* 1, no. 2 (2002): 255–76. On the violent conflicts at the G8 Summit in Genoa, see David D. Perlmutter and Gretchen L. Wagner, 'The Anatomy of a Photojournalistic Icon: Marginalization of Dissent in the Selection and Framing of *A Death in Genoa*,' *Visual Communication* 3, no. 1 (2004): 91–108. For the language of mourning in public and, specifically, media discourse, see Judith Butler, *Precarious Life: The Powers of Death and Mourning* (London: Verso, 2003). On the language of mourning concerning the September 11 events, see James R. Martin, 'Mourning: How We Are Aligned,' *Discourse & Society* 15, nos. 2–3 (2004): 321–44.

7 Cf. Luc Boltanski, *Distant Suffering: Politics, Morality and the Media* (Cambridge: Cambridge University Press, 1999).

8 Lewis, 'Television, Public Opinion and the War in Iraq'; and Rod Brookes et al., *Embeds or In-Beds? Media Coverag of the 2003 Iraq War*. Report commissioned for the BBC, Cardiff School of Journalism, Cardiff 2003.

 9 For this and relevant notions of the public sphere, see Boltanski, *Distant Suffering*, 1–19; Butler, *Precarious Life*, 128–51; Roger Chartier, *The Cultural Origins of the French Revolution*, Durham, NC: Duke University Press, 1999), 20–37.

10 CNN, 29 March 2003.

11 Boltanski, *Distant Suffering*, 20.

12 For the connection between pity and citizenship see Boltanski, *Distant Suffering*, 20–34; and Hannah Arendt, *On Revolution* (1973; London: Penguin Books, 1990), 59–114). For the connection between private and public disposition, see John Durham Peters, *Speaking into the Air: A History of the Idea of Communication* (Chicago: Chicago University Press, 1999), 214–25; and for the connection between the communication of the private self and the public sphere of television, see Paddy Scannell, *Broadcast Talk* (London: Sage, 1991), 1–9.

13 For relevant discussions of iconography see Boltanski, *Distant Suffering*, 51–4; Theo J. van Leeuwen, 'Semiotics and Iconography,' in *Handbook of Visual Analysis*, ed. T.J. v. Leeuwen and C. Jewitt (London: Sage, 2001), 92; Keith Tester, *Compassion, Morality and the Media* (Milton Keynes: Open University Press, 2001), 92–103; Stanley Cohen, *States of Denial: Knowing about Atrocities and Suffering* (Cambridge: Polity Press, 2001), 168–95.

14 Arendt, *On Revolution*, 70.

15 For propaganda as strategic communication, see, for example, Brian McNair, *An Introduction to Political Communication* (London: Routledge, 2003), particularly his discussion of propaganda in the Gulf War (210–20).

16 It is beyond the scope of this article to approach the question of the public sphere in the context of global media, which the BBC World is part of. For the relationship between the public sphere and global television, see Daniel Dayan and Elihu Katz, *Media Events: The Live Broadcasting of History* (Cambridge, MA: Harvard University Press, 1994); John Tomlinson, *Globalisation and Culture* (London: Sage, 1999), 32–70; Ulf Hannerz, *Transnational Connections: Culture, People, Places* (London: Routledge, 1996), 112–24; and Roger Silverstone, 'Mediation and Communication,' in *The Sage Handbook of Sociological Analysis*, ed. Craig Calhoun, Chris Rojek, and Bryan S. Turner (London: Sage, 2005).

17 Boltanski, *Distant Suffering*, 115.

18 The multilateral pressure on the BBC to perform with objectivity, relevant as it is in the case of the Iraq War, transcends this particular coverage. Responding to a BBC Watch critical report on the channel's use of the term 'terrorist,' the channel argues that the BBC Producers' Guidelines increasingly need to be in line with an international rather than domestic

audience: 'Reporting terrorist violence is an area that particularly tests our international services. *Our credibility is severely undermined if international audiences detect a bias for or against any of those involved. Neutral language is the key*: even the word 'terrorist' can appear judgmental in parts of the world where there is no clear consensus about the legitimacy of militant political groups.' Richard Sambrook, letter to *BBC Watch*, December 2002, emphasis added.

19 Seymour Chatman, *Coming to Terms: The Rhetoric of Narrative in Fiction and Film* (Ithaca, NY: Cornell University Press, 1991).

20 See Roger Silverstone, 'Narrative Strategies in Television Science: A Case Study,' *Media, Culture & Society* 6 (1984): 377–410, for the Austin-based distinction of television meanings as 'locutionary acts,' that is, meanings that are 'a matter of sense and reference,' and as 'perlocutionary acts,' that is, meanings that are 'an attempt to convince, persuade or deter' (387).

21 Boltanski, *Distant Suffering*, 117.

22 Ibid., 121.

23 For this geopolitical topography of viewing relationships, see Paul Chilton, *Analysing Political Discourse: Theory and Practice* (London: Routledge, 2004); Chouliaraki, *The Spectatorship of Suffering* (London: Sage, 2006); Roger Silverstone, *Why Study the Media* (London: Sage, 1999);

24 Boltanski, *Distant Suffering*, 19.

25 Ibid., 128–9.

26 Ibid., 124.

27 Quoted in Boltanski, *Distant Suffering*, 125, emphasis added.

28 Boltanski, *Distant Suffering*, 128–9, drawing on Sartre.

29 Butler, *Precarious Life*, xx, emphasis in the original.

6 Slotting War Narratives into Culture's Ready-Made

HELENA GOSCILO

In war, truth is the first casualty.

Aeschylus

I am now certain that a film about Katyn cannot set a goal of discovering the whole truth about that event, since it is now a historical and political fact.

Andrzej Wajda

Patriotism is the willingness to kill and be killed for trivial reasons.

Bertrand Russell

Perspective

Friedrich Nietzsche's famous lapidary dictum 'There are no facts, only interpretations' summarizes his vastly influential assertion that if an objective reality exists, the perspectival nature of human cognition renders that reality inaccessible. War, according to Lev Tolstoy's *War and Peace* (1869), reveals that incapacity as deriving at least partly from the two extremes of proximity and remoteness: both Nikolai Rostov's complete submersion in the immediacy of battle and Napoleon's distant, hence more abstract, viewpoint hamper their powers of perception. The two radically contrasting subject/ive positions are equally disabling for, in the complex, chaotic circumstances of war no such vantage point exists: one cannot simultaneously sustain the bird's-eye and the worm's-eye view – in cinematic terms, the aerial and the low-angle shot or the panoramic shot and the close-up. Sisyphus therefore provides an apt metaphor for attempts to arrive at an objective, informed stance vis-à-vis war, though, as with Sisyphus, the very struggle to do so has inestimable existential (that is, moral) significance.

If Tolstoy and Nietzsche are correct, then by definition neither witness/participant reports nor inevitably mediated accounts by historians can fully and accurately 'capture' the events of war. Fundamentally undermined by cognitive limitations, participants' reports and memoirs are additionally vulnerable to the distorting effects of fear, the pressures of psychological mechanisms, and the vagaries of memory over time,[1] while historians' compulsion to structure events as plotted 'stories' (Hayden White's milestone argument) compromises the purported objectivity of their narratives:[2] 'Strictly speaking, it would seem impossible to write an account of anything without some "literature" leaking in,' for narration depends on 'the principles of sequence and unity and transition and causality.'[3] Moreover, as Paul Fussell has argued in several unflinching examinations of war, the perceived necessity not only of withholding from the public the gruesome physical details of violent death via wholesale bodily dismemberment, but also of concealing fatal errors in judgment by generals and decision makers that led to the decimation of entire platoons or civilians, sanitizes the image of war into a heroic enterprise fuelled by impassioned patriotism. As Fussell titles a chapter on the body in combat, 'The Real War Will Never Get in the Books.'[4] To complicate matters, one of the fundamental dilemmas is 'the collision between the events and the language available – or thought appropriate – to describe them … less a problem of "linguistics" than rhetoric.'[5] Whether produced synchronically or retrospectively, rhetoric at the service of national interests dominates the discourse of war in both verbal and visual genres. Furthermore, revisionist or contrary accounts unavoidably engage official interests, if only implicitly, as a point of departure or as a 'false consciousness' against which to wage a polemic.

The Imperative of National Mythology

These transformative factors, I believe, are exacerbated and perhaps subsumed by a weightier, psychologically internalized imperative – namely, to align a given war with the mythology of national identity.[6] At the most complex level, that mythology, which usually requires a 'masquerade of information,' strives to condense not so much verifiable facts or their simulacra as the 'truth' of collective desire, both state-imposed and sedimented in the populace's unconscious. It is no accident that, officially and personally, Russians bond in viewing the Second World War as the single unadulterated moment of heroic self-sacrifice in their history, for that is the master narrative of the Soviet collective subject, recuperated during Vladimir Putin's presidency and hailed by a sizable majority of contemporary Russians. Symptomatically, a new law recently proposed by Emergency Minister Sergei Shoigu would institute severe reprisals for anyone (Russians or foreign visitors) 'belittling the role of the Soviet Union in the anti-Hitler coalition' – a proposal reportedly endorsed by 60 per cent of the Russian citizens polled.[7] Regardless of their political affiliations, countless Russians regard the defeat of the Axis powers not as the triumph of the Allies' dogged endurance and strategic offensives, but as a Soviet/Russian victory. The sheer number of Soviet casualties (estimated at more than 26 million) and the inherited self-image of 'Europe's saviour' provide the rhetorical grounds for such a perspective.

Poland's self-presentation as the martyred nation, squeezed between Russia on its Eastern and Germany on its Western border (in A.O. Scott's vivid phrase, 'caught in the pincers of two toxic strains of European totalitarianism' during the Second World War),[8] likewise bred a wealth of martyrological texts during and after the three Partitions (1772–1918) effectively demolished Polish independence for more than a century. That self-image resurfaced during Stalinism in Polish posters, film, and literature, which highlighted the primacy of Polish honour (*polski honor*), a deep-rooted idealism that famously led Polish cavalry to attack German tanks during the Second World War. Reproduced in Andrzej Wajda's film *Lotna* (1959), that episode starkly illustrates the enduring tenacity of endemic traditions – specifically, that of 'noble self-immolation for the sake of the nation,'[9] which reigned supreme during Polish Romanticism in the messianic, visionary poetry and drama of Adam Mickiewicz (1798–1855), Juliusz Słowacki (1809–48), and Zygmunt Krasinski (1812–59). Released approximately half a century later, Wajda's *Katyń* (2007), which dramatizes the wholesale liquidation of the Polish officer corps (approximately fifteen thousand men) by Stalin's Red Army in the spring of 1940, underscores the officers' lofty stoicism, though in a less flamboyant mode than favoured by Wajda's earlier cinema.[10]

Since external military threat dictates jettisoning avant-garde, liberal, or dissenting tendencies so as to unite a given nation through hallowed traditions jeopardized by the enemy, narratives of war, particularly during the conflict, rely on values and mores that have withstood the test of time – that is to say, those that are by definition conservative. Exigency partly accounts for the wartime relegation of progressive agendas, such as gender parity, to subordinate status and deferment, as illustrated by the October Revolution of 1917 in Russia and the Second World War in Eastern Europe. Moreover, propaganda invariably packages women's military engagement and their replacement of enlisted men in industry and agriculture as a temporary anomaly necessitated by extraordinary (nation-threatening) circumstances, reassuring the populace that restoration of peace will automatically guarantee women's resumption of their 'natural' domestic/maternal roles. Thus in the early 1950s in Germany, women who had cooperated in the war effort experienced a reversal of their 'emancipation,' whereby 'traditional familial roles and gender relationships were reestablished and the majority of German women adapted without resistance.'[11] The same regressive tendencies, attesting to the 'impermanence of wartime transformations,'[12] quickly took hold in post-war Russia, Poland, and Great Britain through 'the rhetoric of gender that establishes postwar social assignments of men and women.'[13] Indeed, such genres as war posters reveal the extent to which those transformations are superficial, selectively presented, and subject to change dependent on fluctuations in official propaganda.[14]

The very function of war propaganda predicates, *mutatis mutandis*, certain ecumenical stereotypes within war rhetoric: 'Our' rectitude, bravery, and patriotism, by contrast with the enemy's craven, brutal aggressiveness; 'our' noble defense of sacrosanct values, versus 'their' numerically stronger military equipment but morally weaker fighting spirit; 'our' troops' defence of women and children, as opposed to 'their' defilement and murder of the defenceless, and so forth. Even specific symbols transcend national boundaries: For instance, St George as defender appears in British, Russian, and Polish war posters (see figure 6.1), while the demonization of the enemy as a hydra, dragon,[15] snake, ape, or insect reticulates in war graphics in America, Germany, and the Slavic countries (see figure 6.2). These are standard propaganda techniques, for centuries-old cultural representations of war have established an arsenal of generic conventions that serve as a convenient and easily recognizable starting point for any visual or verbal depiction of war.

Yet nation-specific features inevitably cut across such universal topoi. For instance, if the United States publicly conceives its heroic military role abroad as the white-Stetsoned cowboys' rescue of threatened, allegedly weaker nations (e.g., numerous John Wayne vehicles; and,

6.1 The British St George in the First World War, 1915. Personal Collection.

6.2 Anonymous, *The Great European War*, ca 1925. Russian National Library.

satirically, Joseph Heller's *Catch-22* [1961] and Stanley Kubrick's *Doctor Strangelove* [1964]), while the British self-image rests on the perceived uniqueness of its understated, stiff-upper-lipped courage (e.g., the W.E. Johns series of books for adolescents about the pilot Biggles; films such as Anthony Asquith's *We Dive at Dawn* [1943], Michael Anderson's *The Dam Busters* [1955], and Lewis Gilbert's *Reach for the Sky* [1956]),[16] Russia traditionally casts its narrative of military heroism as kenosis.[17] Rooted in medieval Orthodox texts and legends, that self-identity encompasses the concept of *imitatio Christi* – salvific suffering, reinforced by Russia's interpretation of the fall of Constantinople (1453),[18] the French defeat in the Napoleonic Wars (1812), and above all the casualty-heavy victory over the Axis powers in the Second World War (1945). That iconic identity ideally fulfils the prerequisite of the ubiquitous rhetoric rooted in the concept of a 'sacred war' posited by Fussell: 'A really successful war, a psychologically Good War, requires not merely the extirpation of a cruel enemy abroad. It requires as a corollary the apotheosis of the pure at heart at home.'[19] The religious associations inhering in apotheosis and emotional immaculacy partly explain Stalin's suspension of the Communist ban on all aspects of religion during the Second World War. Astute and pragmatic, he realized that long-standing spiritual values and rituals would provide psychological inspiration for the nation's defense against the Germans. Millions of Soviets died to save even greater millions from 'the scourge' of Nazism.

In contrast to such sweeping Slavic claims, Protestant England settled for secular stories, narrated in a measured tone, of British decency, common sense, and quiet resistance in the midst of relentless bombardment and deprivation. The popular British TV series *Foyle's War*, created by Anthony Horowitz in 2002, perfectly captures the understated nature of British self-projection regarding the Second World War. Indeed, one reviewer particularly praised its leading actor, Michael Kitchen, for 'his infinite capacity for sensitive understatement,'[20] while another commentator mused that 'understatement might almost be a theme of the series.'[21] Litotes not only as a rhetorical device but also as part of the British concept of fortitude could hardly contrast more sharply with the hyperbolic forms of courage overrunning Slavic and American images of war.

Kenotic Heroism and Depicted Death

Russia and the Soviet Union repeatedly have performed a balancing act in their projection of a messianic national identity that showcases superhuman feats of self-sacrificing heroism for the sake of the Western world. This self-presentation, originating in medievalism and buttressed by Russia's geographical straddling of East and West, calls for a paradoxical synthesis of classic epic-warrior topoi (the military) on the one hand, and stoic, self-abnegating passivity or acceptance modelled on 'the paradigm of the Cross' (the religious)[22] on the other. During state parades, that conflation eloquently manifests itself in the Second World War veterans' proud display of their war medals as stigmata to be revered. Illustrative verbal and visual genres in which this double-discourse subjectivity frames or underpins the narrative include epic (*byliny*) and narrative poems, folktales, novels, journalism, commemorative speeches, songs, film, graphic art, and such pseudo-philosophical tracts as Daniil Andreev's *Roza mira* (*The Rose of the World*, 1970s).

Tellingly, the Polish American historian-sociologist Jan Gross, reacting to the scandalous reception in Poland of *Strach* (*Fear*, 2006), his study of Polish anti-Semitism during the post-war years, noted, 'The memories of the war here [in Poland] are fixed, of people being victims and heroes.'[23] Poles prefer to criticize specialists in Holocaust studies for ignoring or downplaying the fact that not only Jews, but also Polish Catholics, perished in Hitler's camps rather than confronting the consequences of their own deep-rooted prejudices, the ramifications of which hardly accord with the victim/hero paradigm. Reluctance to accept their passive collusion in genocide (i.e., victims victimizing the supreme victim) at least partly explains Poles' indignant rejection of Jerzy Andrzejewski's novel *Wielki Tydzień* (*Holy Week*, 1945) and their lukewarm response to its adaptation (1995) by Wajda, Poland's premier 'veteran' director,[24] because both implicate Poles in the calamitous fate of Poland's Jews during the German occupation. The extent to which Slavs under siege acquiesced to the persecution of Jews remains a part of the Slavs' national Unsaid. In like fashion, for decades Poland and the Soviet Union repressed any revelations of their military forces' desertion in the midst of combat and their citizens' collaboration with the enemy on occupied territory, for such acts contravene official claims of a unanimous patriotism in which an 'honourable death' for the sake of the nation is infinitely preferable to personal survival – a notion that Heller's darkly hilarious *Catch-22* satirizes as both hypocritical and dangerous.

Deep-rooted national mythologies adapt and undergo modification according to both genre and gender conventions. For instance, death,

rape, and children's violent demise or suffering receive diverse treatment depending on the cultural medium. As Elżbieta Ostrowska has
argued, in Wajda's Second World War films, female characters' deaths,
unlike men's, occur off-screen,[25] possibly because of women's abstract,
tropological function as nation and the impulse to spotlight flesh-and-
blood men's readiness to perish for the patriotic cause. Yet the Second
World War Polish graphics regularly depict women in their allegorical
capacity of martyred Poland as tortured and crucified (see figure 6.3).
By contrast, Soviet directors had no hesitation about portraying the
heroic deaths of either gender, especially later in the war, often elevat-
ing the expiring patriot into an exemplar of transfiguration via devices
borrowed from religious rituals: lighting as halo or celestial space, solemn music, and the hushed tones of worshipful, mourning survivors.[26]
Salvation of the Motherland and its future generations, according to
these messages, was worth the ultimate sacrifice. Soviet Second World
War posters, however, rigorously avoided images of male vulnerability, which they displaced onto women and children, to emphasize their
defence by invincible, stalwart male warriors (see figure 6.4). Such dis-
crepancies partially stem from the political deployment of cultural genres. Daily displayed on walls, in windows, and in newspapers, posters
carried an immediate impact, agitating for ever-greater military efforts
and promising victory, whereas films, which took months or years to
produce, sustained hatred of the enemy while glorifying models of
uncompromising resistance. Mid-war American films also strove to
cushion audiences from the grim realities of war by muting representations of death. According to Thomas Doherty, 'The War Department,
the Office of War Information (OWI), and Hollywood's studio heads
colluded in keeping the devastations of combat from the home-front
screen – sometimes by outright fabrication, usually by expedient omission.'[27] Preferably filmed in long shot instead of close-up, American
deaths on screen were 'clean and quick.'[28]

Rape as Spoils of War

Susan Brownmiller's widely acclaimed study *Against Our Will: Men,
Women, and Rape* (1975) documents the immemorial twinning of war
and rape, noting, 'It has been argued that when killing is viewed not
only as permissible but heroic behavior sanctioned by one's government or cause, the distinction between taking a human life and other
forms of impermissible violence gets lost, and rape becomes an unfor-

Nie płacz Ojczyzno cierpieniem stroskana...
Krew twa płynąca to perły przyszłości ;
Zbita zsieczona wściekłością tyrana,
W podziw wprowadzasz wsze narodowości,
My u stóp tronu Jezusa na Niebie,
Błagamy Polsko o pomoc dla Ciebie

POLSKA

MOC I WIARA W CIERPIENIACH SIĘ RODZĄ

6.3 Władysław Krawiec, *Strength and Faith Are Born of Suffering*, 1942. Gendered allegory of suffering Poland, trapped between the 'pincers'/pistols of Germany and the Soviet Union. Stalinka website, http://images.library.pitt.edu/cgi-bin/i/image/image-idx?rgn1=ic_all;op2=And;rgn2=ic_all;q1=krawiec;size=20;c=stalinka;back=back1313243740;subview=detail;resnum=3;view=entry;lastview=thumbnail;cc=stalinka;entryid=x-gr000152;viewid=GR000152.TIF

tunate but inevitable by-product of the necessary game called war ... Among the ancient Greeks, rape was also socially acceptable behavior well within the rules of warfare, an act without stigma for warriors who viewed the women they conquered as legitimate booty, useful as wives, concubines, slave labor or battle-camp trophy.'[29]

Brownmiller proceeds to adduce culturally memorable instances of war rape – in *The Iliad*, in various paintings depicting the rape of the

Сын мой! Ты видишь долю мою...
Громи фашистов в святом бою!

6.4 Older and younger women, as well as children, plead for protection by their invincible males. Fedor Antonov, 1942. Russian National Library.

Sabine women, and in propaganda during the two world wars – charting the evolving significance of rape throughout the ages ('a simple rule of thumb is that the winning side is the side that does the raping').[30] For various understandable reasons, her purview excludes or sidelines such genres as graphics and film. Since pornography not only glorifies, but also according to many, conduces to rape, censorship laws and the cultural codes of various countries frown upon its visual (re)presentation as potentially pornographic. Until fairly recently, the very possibility that showing or describing rape, no matter how censoriously, could stimulate violent reactions generally discouraged rape as a topic of mainstream narratives, including those about the military.

Virtually absent from (or relegated to the periphery in) British, American, French, Polish, and Soviet[31] cinema for decades – owing to traditions of propriety or whitewashing – sexual violation by soldiers figured earlier in Italian film. For instance, Allied (Moroccan) soldiers' gang rape of an Italian mother and her virgin thirteen-year-old daughter inside a derelict church during the Second World War constitutes a key episode in Vittorio de Sica's 1961 adaptation of Alberto Moravia's novel *La Ciociara*, known in the United States as *Two Women*. A leading exponent of Italian neo-realism, which focused on the socially demeaned and economically dispossessed, the pro-Communist De Sica was working within the conventions of an aesthetic movement whose political agenda easily accommodated the barbaric despoliation of innocence – even by 'ours.' By contrast, since Hollywood's Production (Hays) Code, which oversaw 'morality' in domestic cinema from 1930 until 1968, censored any films containing explicit sex or sexual violence, approved American films of that era never feature rape.

Folkloric traditions, which by definition are accepting of elemental drives, likewise provided a visual aesthetic for Bulgarian director Metodi Adonov's *Kozijat Rog* (*Goat Horn*, 1972), which depicts the rape and murder of a female Bulgarian villager by the occupying Turkish marauders in medieval Bulgaria. For obvious reasons, war rhetoric customarily attributes rape to the enemy as part of its atavism. On the rare occasions that a text shows one of 'ours' committing the act, it is treated as heinous but anomalous, an exception that demands investigation, punishment, and condemnation by the majority, thereby certifying 'our' collective moral probity, as in Brian De Palma's *Casualties of War* (1989). Yet no less a figure than the 'inspirational leader and outstanding tactician' General George Patton records in his memoirs, *War As I Knew It* (1947), that during the Second World War North African campaign in Morocco in 1942 (cf. *Two Women*), he viewed rape as an inevitable concomitant of war, declaring '[I]n spite of my most diligent efforts, there would unquestionably [*sic*] be some raping [by American soldiers under my command].'[32] Though Russians prefer to ignore Soviet troops' violation of German females at the end of the Second World War, impartial sources estimate that Red Army troops raped approximately two million German women and girls.[33] According to some, they also raped Soviet women as they liberated them from Nazi camps.[34]

Unwillingness to portray wartime sexual violence explains why corpses of women appear in early Soviet Second World War posters, wherein their rape is implied and often abstracted into allegory (see figure 6.5). That restraint originates in official Soviet prohibitions against sexual explicitness (deemed typical of Western corruption) as well as in the awareness that rape intimates the inability of a given nation's manhood to defend its women, while the rhetoric of war propaganda invariably casts women and children as helpless victims requiring the protection of 'our' strong men from 'their' atrocities.

The Orphan as Child and Man

As sentimentalists Charles Dickens, Walt Disney, and Steven Spielberg realized, the comforting presumption of children's innocence and vulnerability invests their suffering with tremendous affective power. Exploiting their capacity to tug at the heartstrings of readers and viewers has been a standard literary, marketing, and propagandistic stratagem, one to which the Soviet (and other nations') graphic artists who designed Second World War posters frequently resorted. Whether held in their mothers' arms, lying dead beside their corpses, crying behind barbed wire, or gratefully hugging the Soviet soldiers who liberated them, children symbolized both helplessness and the nation's future – which had to be salvaged at all costs (see figure 6.6). The sight of children's death on screen, as for example in Fridrikh Ermler's *Ona zashchishchaet rodinu* (*She Defends the Motherland*, 1943) and Mark Donskoi's *Raduga* (*Rainbow*, 1944), or their sadistic torture (as in Lev Arnshtam's *Zoia*, 1944), was intended not only to justify any and all forms of revenge, but also to provoke audiences' outrage and hatred for the German invaders.[35]

Children, however, played a key role in another major scenario specific to Soviet literature and cinema under Nikita Khrushchev, which conveyed the psychological traumas and losses of the Second

За честь жены, за жизнь детей,   За наши нивы и луга—
За счастье родины своей,   Убей захватчика-врага!

6.5 The murdered and probably violated mother and her child. Leonid
Golovanov, 1942. Russian National Library.

СЛАВА ОСВОБОДИТЕЛЯМ УКРАИНЫ!
СМЕРТЬ НЕМЕЦКИМ ЗАХВАТЧИКАМ!

6.6 Dementii Shmarinov, *Glory to the Liberators of Ukraine! Death to the German Invaders*, 1943, with the historical monument in the background emphasizing a tradition of victory despite overwhelming odds. Russian National Library.

World War and the struggle to surmount them.[36] Sergei Bondarchuk's *Sud'ba cheloveka* (*Fate of a Man*, 1959), based on a 1957 story by Mikhail Sholokhov, and Marlen Khutsiev's *Dva Fedora* (*Two Fedors*, 1958) dramatize the creation of a surrogate homosocial family in the bonding of two 'wounded' males: an orphaned boy and a disillusioned, solitary war veteran, whom the Second World War robbed of family, home, and ideals. The pathos inhering in the arduous process of recovery through constructing the semblance of a family life that is constantly buffeted by memories of past happiness and security is intensified by the directors' clever casting of the child actors. In both cases the blond, wide-eyed, cherubic countenances of the little orphans – played by Pavel Boriskin and Nikolai Chursin, respectively – evoke associations with angels and celestial purity. The same visual aesthetic operates in Andrei Tarkovsky's debut full-length feature, *Ivanovo detstvo* (*My Name Is Ivan*, 1962), in which Tarkovsky opts not for the inconclusiveness of the two earlier films, but for a tragic finale. Orphaned early in the Second World War, the thin, delicate-looking, blond Ivan stirs surrogate paternal desires in all the Russian soldiers whom he aids through his precocious, adult capacity as a scout in the Soviet resistance (see figure 6.7). A quintessentially Russian kenotic figure, Ivan dies by hanging after interrogation by the Germans, who capture him and treat him as the adult that he prematurely is forced to become owing to the perverse circumstances of war.

Parallel Narratives, with Culturally Marked Differences

How national cultural traditions determine representations of war 'heroes' may be deduced from two narratives about real-life pilots: the British Douglas Bader (1910–82) and the Soviet Aleksei Meresiev (1916–2001).[37] With both legs amputated, they not only continued to fly but became adulated leaders, broke records in shooting down the enemy, and earned their respective countries' highest awards and decorations for bravery in the Second World War. Paul Brickhill, an Australian journalist and Second World War fighter pilot, wrote a sober, balanced biography of Bader (*Reach for the Sky*, 1956), which Lewis Gilbert adapted into an award-winning film with the same title (1956).[38] Both document Bader's remarkable resilience and stoic determination after his 1931 flying accident and his capture and imprisonment by the Germans in 1941; his repeated attempts to escape landed him in the high-security Colditz Castle. Yet neither work glosses over Bader's obsessiveness,

6.7 Andrei Tarkovsky, *Ivanovo detstvo* (*My Name Is Ivan*), 1962. Visible signs of a childhood warped by the traumas of war.

irascibility, and opinionated dogmatism – the 'warts' that provoked dislike and irritation within the RAF and without. Kenneth More's nuanced performance as Bader on screen likewise skilfully suggests the ace aviator's unlikable as well as admirable traits. Worshipped by countless younger pilots, Bader, however, did not permit his arrogance to assume hyperbolic forms of discourse, so alien to British self-expression: The notation in his logbook after the foolish accident that cost him both limbs epitomized quintessential British restraint and laconism ('Crashed slow-rolling near ground. Bad show'),[39] and Brickhill and the biopic share their subject's low-key style.

The cultural processing of Bader's case seems particularly modest by comparison with the Soviet Union's treatment of his Russian 'counterpart.' The aviator Meresiev's Second World War exploits as recounted by the Soviet journalist Boris Polevoi in *Povest' o nastoiashchem cheloveke* (*The Story of a Real Man*, 1946) formally established the author's credentials and consolidated Meresiev's reputation in the pantheon of patriotic heroes. Dramatizing the triumph of Soviet will over body and circumstance, Polevoi's ideology-saturated pseudo-novel became a classic of Socialist Realism, the film version by Aleksandr Stolper (1948) enjoying enormous popularity and the state's enthusiastic endorsement. Where Brickhill and Gilbert opted for moderation, both Polevoi and Stolper resorted to melodrama in limning Meresiev as an exceptionally courageous, committed fighter, therefore, paradoxically, 'typical' of Soviet citizens faced by seemingly insurmountable adversity.[40] Always the best combat aviator in his unit, the modest, cheerful Meresiev saves fellow pilots, perpetually smiles and jokes with his comrades, exudes merry energy and friendliness, and possesses 'a keen mind, a good memory, and a big heart.'[41] When the story's journalist/narrator contrasts his amazing achievements with those of an aviator who lost only one foot and piloted a non-fighter plane, Meresiev responds: 'But I am a Soviet airman.'[42] The insistence on Soviet superiority and exceptionalism gathers momentum toward the work's conclusion, when at the Nuremberg Tribunal the journalist hears Hermann Goering trot out a cliché about Russians that they had long welcomed as part of their self-conception: 'Soviet Russians ... have been and remain a riddle ... The Russians have always been a riddle to a foreigner. Napoleon, too, failed to understand them. We merely repeated Napoleon's mistake.' 'How,' the journalist muses, 'indeed, could the inventors of the wretched "theory" about the Germans being the "*Herrenvolk*" understand the soul and strength of a people reared in a socialist country?'[43] Enshrined as

the iconic ideal that 'set such a striking example of courage and fortitude in the struggle against the enemy who had encroached upon our
sacred [sic] Soviet soil,'[44] Meresiev as 'a son of his mighty and freedom-
loving people'[45] purportedly typifies Russianness remoulded into Sovi-
etness. The closing bombastic assertions supply the finishing touch to a
verbal monument exalting the Soviet Union's – not the Allies' – victory
over the Nazis.[46]

The Rule of Temporal Distance

What organizes Russians' beliefs regarding the various spirits in the
demonology within their folklore is 'the rule of spatial distance,'
whereby the more domestic the spirit (such as the household *domovoi*),
the more benign the activities imputed to it. Perspectives on war in
cultural production seem analogously influenced by the rule of temporal distance: with time, sobriety, scepticism, and repudiation surface
where patriotism, morale boosting, and myths of superhuman courage
formerly preponderated.[47] Thus Clint Eastwood's contemplative *Letters
from Iwo Jima* (2006) supplies a corrective to the naked propaganda of
the rousing John Wayne vehicle *The Sands of Iwo Jima* (dir. Allan Dwan,
1949). Yet Eastwood himself drew criticism from the independent film
director Spike Lee, who in 2008 faulted him for excluding black soldiers
from both *Flags of Our Fathers* and *Letters from Iwo Jima*.[48] Insistent on
setting the record straight, Lee polemically opens *Miracle at St Anna*
(2008), his version of African Americans' contribution to the war, with
a scene in which an elderly black watching on television *The Longest
Day*, another cheerleading John Wayne paean to American derring-do,
with an all-white cast, objects 'Pilgrim, we fought for this country too.'[49]
Later, a black sergeant contends, 'This is a white man's war. Negroes
got nothin' to do with it.'[50]

   Indeed, the majority of mainstream Hollywood portrayals of the
Second World War tend to include, at best, a token Jew and a token
Afro-American in an otherwise 'true-blue' white American' cast, with
Hispanics and Russians appearing in minor roles. The make-up of the
patrol in Tay Garnett's *Bataan* (1943) established the combat formula,[51]
comprising a Hollywood leading man as the tough commander, a Fili-
pino scout, a Hispanic Los Angeleno, a black trainee preacher from the
South, a Russian from Pennsylvania, and a Jewish engineer, in addition
to several ethnically 'unmarked' Americans. Synecdoches for a cross-
section of the American population – of various 'types,' ethnicities, and

geographical areas – the combatants reflect the OWI's determination to show the military as 'an army of citizen soldiers.'[52] Sooner motivated by the politics of race than scrupulous observance of historical accuracy, Lee's wholesale reinstatement of blacks in the struggle against the Axis powers nonetheless exposes and compensates for the racial tokenism that earlier characterized the genre. A similar change marks relatively recent films, such as Steven Spielberg's *Saving Private Ryan* (1998), which justify war and memorialize soldiers' self-sacrifice for the sake of future generations, yet, unlike earlier Hollywood offerings, dwell on the murderous chaos of combat instead of glossing over it.[53]

Parallel revisions have occurred in Russian cinema following the dissolution of the Soviet Union (1991). Until then, the overwhelming majority of the numerous celluloid Second World War narratives complied with official propaganda, in which the polarization of courageous, idealistic Soviets and merciless, inhumane Nazis ultimately reduced the world to a two-dimensional, Manichaean struggle of Good and Evil. Works such as Mikhail Chiaureli's *Padenie Berlina* (*The Fall of Berlin*, 1949) – a florid hymn to Stalin's spurious strategic genius and Soviets' extraterrestrial moral superiority and indomitable valour – arguably belong to the genre of fairy tale, with its distinctly delineated binaries. Home-front melodramas featuring female partisans or immaculately faithful, devoted women and their antipodes – promiscuous wives and 'good-time girls' – proliferate in films conceived around the wartime injunction of 'Wait for me.' Originally a poem by the writer and wartime journalist Konstantin Simonov that almost instantly bred songs and a film by the same title, this exhortation by a soldier to his sweetheart/spouse established a psychologically coercive link between a woman's fidelity and 'her man's' likelihood of surviving the war. This cause-and-effect continuum appears in Aleksandr Stolper's *Zhdi menia* (*Wait for Me*, 1943), which dogmatically contrasts the saintly Lisa with the sluttish Sonia. Even Mikhail Kalatozov's incomparably more complex Thaw-era *Letiat zhuravli* (*Cranes Are Flying*, 1957) through intercutting connects Veronika's betrayal of her lover, Boris, to his death at the front.[54] That betrayal entails marriage to his cousin Mark after the latter rapes her during a symbolically loaded bombardment that serves as an equivalent of Mark's 'attack' on a national scale and thus identifies him as the internal enemy.[55]

Although later films modified the black-and-white moralized dualism structuring the portrayal of 'them' versus 'us' and of women's sexuality, a genuinely fresh, non-partisan cinematic treatment of the

Second World War had to wait until the collapse of the Soviet Union. And here Aleksei German Jr's bleak, disconcerting debut film, *Poslednii poezd* (*The Last Train*, 2003), stands out for its complete avoidance of triumphant drumbeats at the 1943 turning point of the Second World War, during the unprecedented slaughter at Stalingrad, where on average a Soviet soldier survived twenty-four hours of combat. Like Eastwood, German takes the extraordinary step of eliminating hyperbolic heroics and presenting events from 'the enemy's' viewpoint – an unthinkable device during the war, and one chiefly enabled by the passage of time.[56]

'The Enemy Is Us': Disillusionment, Dementia, and Despair

Perhaps understandably, in light of the controversy that from the outset accompanied the Vietnam War (1959–75), the most memorable (and prize-winning) American films about it counter 'the rule of temporal distance.'[57] Released in the 1970s and 1980s, *Coming Home* (dir. Hal Ashby, 1978), *Deer Hunter* (dir. Michael Cimino, 1978), *Apocalypse Now* (dir. Francis Ford Coppola, 1979), *Full Metal Jacket* (1986, dir. Stanley Kubrick), and *Platoon* and *Born on the Fourth of July* (1986; 1989, dir. Oliver Stone) indicted the war as irrational, brutalizing, and futile. Ravaged veterans, soldiers psychologically mangled by their experiences, and insane commanders, such as Col. Kilgore in *Apocalypse Now* ('I love the smell of napalm in the morning') confirm the adage that 'war is hell.' War's defining traits are not patriotic fervour and courage, but savagery and mayhem, which leave an indelible mark on traumatized survivors and consequently on those to whom they return. Crippled not only physically but also psychologically, veterans cannot assimilate into a society that seems uncomprehending and indifferent, including the familial collective, from which their combat experience has alienated them (*Coming Home* and *Born on the Fourth of July*). The acknowledgment that war is a gory, devastating series of ill-judged, confused, suicidal confrontations with the enemy mandated by those remote from its everyday actuality increasingly has eroded the earlier glorification of war as a grand, heroic example of men's 'doing what a man's gotta do.' Thus *Platoon*, which regularly connects sex and violence through the phallic nature of weapons,[58] shows several American soldiers raping two young Vietnamese girls, and though their actions elicit the protagonist's disgusted protest, the rapes are a group activity, no longer an individual aberration. The same holds for the violation of a soldier by the men in his unit in *Full Metal Jacket*. With few exceptions, disillusionment and anti-war sentiments are the staples of the Vietnam War on celluloid.

Films about the Vietnam War raise the theoretical question of whether directors can portray on screen their country's military defeats in anything other than a dispiriting or grotesque light.[59] As Guy Westwell notes, 'the codes and conventions of the [American] war movie genre were found inadequate to the task of describing the experience of losing a war,'[60] hence the genre's recourse to metaphysics and myth.[61] Would Coppola, Kubrick, and Stone have adopted a different stance and aesthetic had America not suffered a humiliating defeat? By the late 1970s, public knowledge of the civilian bombings of North Vietnamese cities and the massacre at My Lai (1968), among other atrocities, had transformed the GI from the 'site of authentic, unquestionably honourable experience' into a symbol of America's fallibility and wrong-headedness.'[62] The macho jingoism of the 1960s John Wayne vehicle *The Green Berets* (dir. Ray Kellogg and John Wayne, 1968) was no longer tenable, having gradually ceded to self-criticism, soul-searching, and a profound sense of failure. Susan Jeffords has noted how the male body in these post-war films is vulnerable to multiple threats – 'to castration by Viet Cong men ... to infection by Vietnamese women, and to death at the hands of unseen enemies' in scenarios of 'confusion, disorientation, death, and helplessness.'[63] For a disaffected domestic audience, the sort of rousing heroic patriotism that infused numerous Second World War films now seemed part of a bygone innocent era that could never be reclaimed.

In this regard, the case of Russian cinema is particularly complicated because, as Tatiana Smorodinskaya has justly argued, whereas Russia during the 1990s welcomed efforts to examine Soviets' role in the Second World War critically, the resurgent patriotism of the 2000s has revived the rhetoric of empire.[64] For many today, anything less than positive images of Russians' role in the Second World War verges on Russophobe heresy. The glut of war films during the current decade has featured 'tough-guy heroes' in narratives typical of the adventure/action genre, aureoled in macho patriotism.[65] That the revival of bellicose nationalism on screen and in the media coincided with Putin's call to restore Russia's lost status as a superpower attests to the pragmatic orientation and psychological needs of all involved.

Conclusion

The controversies ignited by two Brian De Palma films about war rape by 'ours' suggest the multifaceted nature of the impediments to non-partisan cultural representations of war. *Casualties of War* dramatizes at leisurely, lip-licking pace the abduction, repeated rape, torture, and murder of a young Vietnamese woman seized by a group of bored and disillusioned American troops (a real-life incident reported in an article at the time) who are subsequently brought to trial and sentenced to prison terms for their crime. De Palma's low-budget *Redacted* (2007), billed as 'a fictional story inspired by true events' and the film that most distressed audiences at its first screening during the 2007 Venice Film Festival, likewise shows American soldiers in Iraq raping a teenage girl and slaughtering her family, with a finale comprising a montage of shocking real-life photographs of Iraqis, including women and children, killed or disfigured during the war. Since the film's title adverts to the mainstream media's sanitized reporting of war events, De Palma has made much of the decision by the film's distributor, Magnolia Pictures, to black out the faces of the dead or maimed Iraqis. Magnolia's president, Eamonn Bowles, bluntly admitted that the unedited photos were too graphic to run in mainstream newspapers or television reports.[66]

While De Palma's accusation that American media whitewash such atrocities is valid, even a cursory glance at his career reveals why some critics disparage both *Casualties of War* and *Redacted* as exploitative rather than fuelled by dedication to historical accuracy or moral responsibility. Several De Palma movies, and especially his Hitchcock-cloned *Dressed to Kill* (1980), reveal the director's fascination with sexual violence and scenes bordering on soft porn, which he seems to savour rather than deplore – a preoccupation that allies him with popular entertainment rather than pitting him against censored, conservative journalism. The dilemma, in other words, resides not in De Palma's support of the war, which he has condemned on more than one occasion, but in his seemingly uncontrollable, decades-long fascination with violence to and by women. Whatever De Palma's motives, the point is that lingering shots of visceral female nudity and rape, as well as sustained close-ups of torture, mutilation, dismemberment, and other forms of military violence, risk reproducing what they purport to represent and reprehend.[67] One could argue that *Redacted*'s 'harrowing exposé' may be compared, however paradoxically, to *The Green Berets* (1968), the flag-waving, lachrymose melodrama about the Vietnam War, starring and directed by the right-wing actor John Wayne, insofar as both films too blatantly reflect the directors' personal obsessions, colouring the presentation of events.[68] But, then, according to Nietzsche, such is the very nature of perception, and therefore *a fortiori* of cultural representation.

NOTES

1 To cite Annemarie Tröger's succinct contention, 'Memories are constantly being recreated; there is no "original" and therefore accurate memory.' A. Tröger, 'German Women's Memories of World War II,' in *Behind the Lines: Gender and the Two World Wars*, ed. Margaret Randolph Higonnet et al. (New Haven, CT: Yale University Press, 1987), 288. As Ken Burns's six-part documentary *War* (2007) makes clear, many soldiers intent on sparing family members back home anxiety write reassuring, anodyne letters masking their daily horrors, while others resent the ignorance of those on the home front, who cannot conceive of what fighting troops endure.

2 Hayden White, *Tropics of Discourse: Essays in Cultural Criticism* (Baltimore: Johns Hopkins University Press, 1978), 121. White rejected the notion of causality in history and famously argued that historians differ little from authors of fiction in the discourse they employ for their narratives.

3 Paul Fussell, *The Great War and Modern Memory* (London: Oxford University Press, 1975), 173.

4 Paul Fussell, *Wartime: Understanding and Behavior in the Second World War* (New York: Oxford University Press, 1989), 267–97. Other overlooked aspects of war documented by Fussell include soldiers (and officers) involuntarily urinating and excreting from terror, their slide into madness at witnessing numerous heads and limbs blown off and falling onto rotting corpses, along with other nightmares, ignored by media.

5 Fussell, *The Great War*, 169–70.

6 The military's elimination of individualism and the collective nature of battle abet the rhetoric of national cohesiveness.

7 Sergei Balashov, 'Outlawed Disgreement,' *Russia Profile*, 12 May 2009, http://www.russiaprofile.org/page/php?[ageod=Politics&articleid=a1 (accessed 12 May 2009).

8 Scott's metaphor adopts the visual image of pincers, which flourished in Slavic Second World War graphics, and, paradoxically, above all, in Soviet posters: for example, Aleksei Kokorekin's *Bei fashistskogo gada!* (1941), the Kukryniksy's *Kleshchi v kleshchi* (1941), Boris Efimov's *Sovetskie kleshchi nemetskikh kleshchei* (1942), Viktor Deni's *Dlia nemtsev strashnye veshchi: 'meshki' i 'kleshchi'!* (1944), and the Kukryniksy's *Tri goda voiny* (1944). A.O. Scott, 'Bearing Witness to Poland's Pain,' *New York Times*, 18 February 2009.

 9 See Christopher J. Caes, 'Catastrophic Spectacles: Historical Trauma and
   the Masculine Subject in *Lotna*,' in *The Cinema of Andrzej Wajda: The Art of
   Irony and Defiance*, ed. John Orr and Elzbieta Ostrowska (London: Wallflower Press, 2003), 122.
10 For decades the Soviets placed blame for the mass murder on the Nazis,
   vehemently denying Poles' allegations of their guilt. Only in 1990 did
   Mikhail Gorbachev officially acknowledge Soviet responsibility for the
   executions, and in 1991 Boris Yeltsin made public the documents containing the pertinent orders. See Anne Applebaum, 'A Movie that Matters.' *The
   New York Review of Books*, 14 February 2008, http://www.nybooks.com/
   articles/21012 (accessed 24 May 2008). The number of massacred officers
   varies according to who reports the event, the claimed figure ranging from
   fifteen to twenty thousand.
11 Tröger, 'German Women's Memories,' 294.
12 Margaret R. Higonnet and Patrice L.-R. Higgonet, 'The Double Helix,' in
   Behind the Lines, ed. M.R. Higgonet et al., 32.
13 'Introduction,' in *Behind the Line*, ed. Higgonet et al., 4.
14 For an analysis of gendered images in Soviet Second World War posters,
   see Susan Corbesero, 'Femininity (Con)scripted: Female Images in Soviet
   Wartime Poster Propaganda, 1941–1945,' *Aspasia*, Vol. 4 (2010): 103–20;
   Helena Goscilo, 'Graphic Womanhood,' in *Trumpet and Taboo*, ed. H.
   Goscilo and Yana Hashamova (forthcoming).
15 The dragon, which in Russian fairy tales is invariably the hero's arch-
   enemy, likewise troped late tsarist-period Russia's and the Soviet Union's
   real or perceived enemies. The image proliferated not only in war propaganda, but even in peacetime ideological 'warfare,' as, for example, in
   the design of the first Soviet stamp, issued in August 1921, 'The Liberated
   Proletarian,' which depicts a worker defeating a dragon as the symbol of
   capitalism. Evgeny Dobrenko, 'The Art of Social Navigation: The Cultural
   Topography of the Stalin Era,' in *The Landscape of Stalinism: The Art and Ideology of Soviet Space*, ed. E. Dobrenko and Eric Naiman (Seattle: University
   of Washington Press, 2003), 164.
16 The latter two derive from books by Paul Brickhill, himself a fighter pilot
   during the Second World War.
17 On kenosis, see George P. Fedotov, *The Russian Religious Mind (I): Kievan
   Christianity: The 10th to the 13th Centuries* (Belmont, MA: Nordland Pub.
   Co., 1975), 390–5.
18 The event led to the concept of Moscow as the Third Rome, articulated in
   a letter by the monk Filofei to the Moscow Prince Vasilii III in 1511, which
   arguably marked the birth of Russian messianism.

19 Paul Fussell, 'Writing in Wartime: The Uses of Innocence,' in *Thank God for the Atom Bomb and Other Essays* (New York: Summit Books, 1988), 53.

20 Sarah Crompton, *Daily Telegraph* (13 November 2002).

21 *Guardian*, 30 October 2002.

22 Susan Sontag. 'The Artist as Exemplary Sufferer,' in *Against Interpretation* (New York: Dell, 1966), 49–57.

23 Craig Whitlock, 'A Scholar's Legal Peril in Poland,' *Washington Post*, 18 January 2008, A14.

24 J. Orr and E. Ostrowska, eds., *The Cinema of Andrzej Wajda*, xviii. Several articles in this volume, the first significant Anglophone study of Wajda, investigate the director's 'continuing confrontations with Polish history' and his links with Romanticism (xix, 132–45).

25 See Elżbieta Ostrowska, 'Invisible Deaths: Women in Polish Cinema's Representations of World War II,' paper presented at the conference 'Women in War: World War II,' University of Pittsburgh, 30 November 2007.

26 Perhaps Lev Arnshtam's *Zoia* (1944), about the teenage female partisan tortured and hanged by the Nazis, wrings the most lachrymose empathy from viewers at the youthful protagonist's defiant and 'joyous' death.

27 Thomas Doherty, *Projections of War: Hollywood, American Culture, and World War II* (New York: Columbia University Press, 1993), 3.

28 Guy Westwell, *War Cinema: Hollywood on the Front Line* (London: Wallflower Press, 2006), 37.

29 Susan Brownmiller, *Against Our Will: Men, Women and Rape* (New York: Bantam, 1975), 24–5.

30 Ibid., 27.

31 Mikhail Kalatozov's *Cranes Are Flying* (*Letiat zhuravli*, 1957) stands out as an exception, for it implies, in terms that require unpacking because of the complex visual techniques Kalatozov employs, the rape of the female protagonist by her fiancé's brother, whom she subsequently marries. Through intercutting, Kalatozov directly links her betrayal, in the form of passive submission, to her fiancé's death at the front.

32 Brownmiller, *Against Our Will*, 72.

33 Antony Beevor, 'They raped every German female from eight to 80,' *Guardian* (1 May 2002), http://www.guardian.co.uk/books/2002/may/01/news.features11/print (accessed 10 April 2009).

34 Daniel Johnson, 'Red Army troops raped even Russian women as they freed them from camps,' *Telegraph* (25 January 2002), http://www.telegraph.co.uk/news/worldnews/europe/russia/1382565/Red-Army-troops-raped-even-Russian-women-as-they-freed-them-from-camps.html (accessed 10 April 2009).

35 For a discussion of the three films, see Denise J. Youngblood, *Russian War
Films: On the Cinema Front, 1914–2005* (Lawrence: University Press of Kansas, 2007), 60–7. The German director Josef Vilsmaier's inclusion of a painful scene in *Stalingrad* (1993) in which German soldiers obey their sadistic
commander's arbitrary order to execute the Russian boy Kolia says a great
deal for his efforts at even-handedness in the gruelling film. Vilsmaier's
grim tracking of the German army's disintegration as it confronts not only
the Russians' adamant refusal to surrender but also the rigours of the Russian winter (the film closes with the two remaining members of the unit
freezing to death) profits from a comparison with Jean-Jacques Annaud's
Enemy at the Gates (2001), an Americanized treatment of Stalingrad
reduced to a shoot-out, cowboy-style, between a Russian and a German
sharpshooter, as well as a love story. As one reviewer noted, the film is 'a
lurching mélange of the obvious and the implausible,' which Vilsmaier
scrupulously avoids. A.O.Scott, '*Enemy at the Gates*: World War II from a
Different Perspective,' *New York Times*, 16 March 2001.
36 Soviet cinema had an upbeat precedent for such a 'male union' in an entire
military unit's adoption of an orphaned boy: Vasilii Pronin's *Syn polka* (*The
Regiment's Son*, 1946).
37 The Soviet Union awarded Maresiev (the prototype of Polevoi's hero
Meresiev) not only the Golden Star of a Hero of the USSR, but also a
plethora of orders and medals, and made him a member of the Supreme
Soviet.
38 Paul Brickhill, *Reach for the Sky* (New York: Norton, 1954). Gilbert's film
won the BAFTA Award for Best British Film of 1956.
39 Laddie Lucas, *Flying Colours: The Epic Story of Douglas Bader* (London:
Hutchinson Publishing Group, 1981), 60.
40 Late Stalinism called for typicality in its heroes, who incarnated the Soviet
ethos but in no wise competed with the Supreme Hero, Stalin.
41 Boris Polevoi, *A Story about a Real Man*, trans. Joe Fineberg (Moscow: Foreign Languages Publishing House, 3rd ed., no date), 565.
42 Ibid.
43 Ibid., 570.
44 Ibid., 574.
45 Ibid., 575.
46 The son born to Maresiev and his faithful Olga bears the symbolic name of
Viktor.
47 Among the exceptions are frontline soldiers' frank, down-to-earth diaries,
such as those of the articulate Sledge, which both Fussell and Ken Burns's
documentary cite.

48 Richard Corliss, 'Spike Lee Goes to War,' *Time*, 6 October 2008, 77.

49 Ibid.

50 Ibid., 78.

51 See J. Basinger, 'The World War II Combat Film: Definition,' in *The War Film*, ed. Robert Eberwein (New Brunswick, NJ: Rutgers University Press, 2004), 30–52, especially 38–9 and 46–9.

52 Westwell, *War Cinema*, 35.

53 Westwell's commentary on the film astutely notes its tapping into 'the strong celebratory view of World War II' in the late 1990s, reassuring audiences who experienced guilt over the Vietnam War and softening the impact of America's 'reluctant commitments to, and limited success in, "humanitarian" foreign policy engagements in Somalia, Bosnia and Kosovo in the 1990s.' *War Cinema*, 89, 98.

54 The artistic excellence of *Cranes Are Flying* and its more humane approach to those who violate Soviet secular commandments does not negate the moralized gender bias against women.

55 The modernist stylization of the rape scene does not make it immediately apparent, especially to the average viewer, what actually takes place. A straightforward naturalistic treatment would not have passed censorship.

56 Similarly, whereas in the first two years of war it was impossible to depict Soviet vulnerability, the Red Army's costly 'victory' at Stalingrad lifted that prohibition.

57 They also provide a welcome antidote to the hawkish and macho-mawkish heroics of John Wayne (*The Green Berets*) and Sylvester Stallone (*First Blood*, 1982).

58 For an intelligent commentary on the continuity between weaponry and male sexuality, see Chapter 7 ('Bodies, Weapons') in Robert Eberwein, *Armed Forces: Masculinity and Sexuality in the American War Film* (New Brunswick, NJ: Rutgers University Press, 2007), 114–36.

59 Vilsmaier's chilly *Stalingrad* and the sheer dearth of German Second World War films suggest the difficulties of portraying one's own defeat in war movies, though antic comedies conceivably could tackle the phenomenon, risking accusations of bad taste.

60 Westwell, *War Cinema*, 57.

61 Ibid., 65.

62 Ibid., 64.

63 Susan Jeffords, *Hard Bodies: Hollywood Masculinity in the Reagan Era* (New Brunswick, NJ: Rutgers University Press, 1994), 119.

64 Tatiana Smorodinskaya, 'The Fathers' War through the Sons' Lens,' in *Cinepaternity: Fathers and Sons in Soviet and Post-Soviet Film*, ed. Helena

Goscilo and Yana Hashamova (Bloomington, IN: Indiana University Press, 2010), chapter 4.

65 Smorodinskaya, 'The Fathers' War,' 1. This holds true for Aleksandr Balabanov's film about the war in Chechnya, *Voina* (*War*, 2002), and Fedor Bondarchuk's *Deviataia rota* (*Ninth Regiment*, 2005), an über-patriotic validation of self-sacrifice for 'the nation' that elicited President Putin's enthusiasm and reportedly renewed his faith in the film industry.

66 Christine Kearney, 'Director De Palma disturbed over Iraq film edit,' *Reuters*, 19 October 2007, http://www.reuters.com/articlePrint?articleId+U SN1846489220071019 (accessed 25 January 2008).

67 It is worth comparing De Palma's approach with that of Jasmila Zbanic in *Grbavica* (*Esma's Secret/The Land of My Dreams*; Bosnia, 2006) about the ineradicable affects of rape on a woman violated and impregnated during the Bosnian War. While the act never appears on the screen, Zbanic skilfully traces its consequences for the victim, her daughter, and those around them.

68 This criticism could also be levelled at Vladimir Nevzorov's film about the first Chechen War, *Chistilishche* (*Purgatory*, 1997), steeped in racist nationalism and simplistic 'us' versus 'them' oppositions, as well as addicted to bloody scenes of torture, crippling, etc., that make up most of the film and seem to be its raison d'être. See Youngblood, *Russian War Films*, 211–13.

SECTION THREE

Identities

The three chapters that make up this section address questions of identity from perspectives rooted in the disciplines of literary studies, anthropology, and classics, which themselves are simultaneously inflected by ideas drawn from such other domains as history, philosophy, political studies, and sociology. Each considers not so much the frequently discussed ways in which our identities are subject to alteration under conditions of war, but rather the processes whereby identities become mobilized in war's many different representational contexts, including commemorative rites and monuments, in order to produce, respectively, political resistance (Jennifer James), social solidarity (Serguei Oushakine), and civic virtue (James Chlup). All three contributors underscore that what we take ourselves to be greatly depends on what we tell ourselves we are now, or else have been in the past. More particularly, they reveal how identitarian demands impinge on representations of war, sharpening their political edge and transforming depictions of human conflict and its aftermath into requests for 'recognition,' one of the core elements of moral respect.

Each contributor demonstrates the way in which specific modalities of talking about war, of representing it in sermons, oral testimony, commemorative occasions, and public monuments, presumes something about the nature of war's actors, just as it does about the nature of war itself. Consideration of war representations' construction of past and present social and martial imaginaries, along with the identities constitutive of them, reveals the moral and political stakes in these representations. For the way in which war comes to be represented – justified, honoured, or shown to be performed – profoundly informs the response of the publics required to act in its name: to seize on war as an instrument of liberation; to understand the sacrifices of its principals as deserving of compensation; and to see in its monumentalization the reflection of a shared (and understood as shared) historical and cultural consciousness.

In her contribution 'Blessed are the Warmakers: Martin Luther King, Vietnam, and the Black Prophetic Tradition,' Jennifer James examines the literary, political, and religious antecedents of Martin Luther King in order to explain the black community's response to the Vietnam War. She enquires into the causes of black Americans' hesitancy to denounce the Vietnam conflict in its early stages, and locates at its root what she calls a 'black prophetic tradition,' whose assumptions about war and pacifism continue to influence black Americans' moral and political self-understanding. James is especially concerned with what she calls 'languages of violence emerging from sites falling "outside" of the government proper and its official discourses.' These languages – born in and used to make sense of struggle – serve to consolidate particular group identities and admit novel forms of political and moral agency.

James concentrates on black American revolutionary jeremiads, documents traditionally devoted to cataloguing societies' ills and prophesying their immanent and divinely ordained destruction. She shows how Martin Luther King's pacifism clashes with this prophetic tradition in which collective violence is understood as a tool of justice. African Americans' historical experience of displacement and confinement left them finally unable to absorb Christ's pacifist message. The radical transformation of the status quo promised by various Black Power movements that championed the violent overcoming of American racism offered blacks an alternative route to social justice and undamaged self-realization.

The framing and reframing of violence in order to secure a politically viable identity figures prominently in Serguei Oushakine's contribution entitled 'Exchange of Sacrifices: Symbolizing an Unpopular War in Post-Soviet Russia.' In this essay, Oushakine considers attempts made by Russian veterans of the Chechen war to have their role as instruments of Russian foreign policy dignified by public and official acknowledgment of the sacrifices it required. This respect was markedly lacking in the war's wake, not merely due to its widespread unpopularity. Oushakine shows how confusion within the official Russian discourse on the war provided the public with no means to make adequate sense of returning veterans and their special needs and complaints. In response to this confusion, veterans became tasked with responsibility for creating a politically and socially viable collective identity, one which Oush-akine argues is derived from their discursive 'framing' of the war and its costs.

Particularly difficult for Chechen veterans was the absence of any legal framework capable of specifying (and securing) their rights and privileges. Given the additional lack of any significant anti-war movement in Russia sympathetic to their plight (notwithstanding the war's unpopularity), Russian soldiers returning to peacetime life found themselves critically short of financial benefits and public respect. In response, these soldiers opted to represent their military service, reframed as a heroic contribution to the welfare of the nation, as a sacrificial exchange. Since they have sacrificed something for Russia, they now view Russia as being in their debt. This emphasis on sacrifice as the moral essence of the demand for compensation results in a 'community of loss,' an imagined community bonded by real and imagined suffering to which veterans turn in order to understand (and cope with) their experiences of marginalization and despair.

Whereas Oushakine's contribution is concerned with a state's representational failures, its initial denial of the sacrifices of its soldiers and refusal to stitch them into the fabric of the national narrative, James Chlup analyses the public commemoration of war and the identities sustained through its official representation in monuments and works of history. In his essay entitled 'Identity and the Representation of War in Ancient Rome,' he is particularly interested in Roman historiography and monumental architecture from the first centuries BCE and CE. Chlup reads war historiography as an important instrument in the forging of Roman identity, contributing to Romans' own sense of their moral excellence and providing them with an opportunity to exemplify it in the performance of acts of war. He shows how even in peacetime, mediated by monuments such as the Arch of Titus, Roman military victories continued to shape and hybridize identities including the Roman-Jewish one, at the same time narrowing the gap between civilian and military life.

What is especially salient in Chlup's analysis is his documentation of the long-standing complicity between official discourses – those that speak for a state as it is imagined to be – and narratives of war. More particularly, Chlup shows how the identities circulating within officially sanctioned war representations speak for, and thereby serve to reinforce, the identities variously celebrated and denigrated by the state given the terms specific to its self-conception. For example, to the extent that Josephus was able to depict the First Jewish-Roman War in a way that confirmed Romans' sense of their own civic and martial excellence, he was at the same time articulating a conception of Roman identity as inherently virtuous. Similarly, by not representing Jews as captives following their defeat at Jerusalem and by making the Temple spoils visually accessible to all residents of and visitors to Rome, the Arch of Titus served to articulate the new terms of Jewish perseverance in the wake of a catastrophic defeat: not as an independent people but as Roman subjects, as newly minted Roman-Jews.

What all three contributions in this section thus explore is the way in which identities are put to use in representations of war. Some of these uses are offensive, as with the identities of the principled opponents to slavery and the Vietnam War emerging from within the black Jeremiads discussed by Jennifer James and going on to mobilize wider black American resistance to oppression; some uses are defensive, as with the identities constructed by Serguei Oushakine's Chechen veterans in their attempts to secure their post-war well-being; and, lastly, some are proscriptive, as with the deeply normative Roman and Jewish identities considered by James Chlup, which in the monument and histories he examines announce the 'official' Roman view of imperial belonging.

7 Blessed Are the Warmakers: Martin Luther King, Vietnam, and the Black Prophetic Tradition

JENNIFER C. JAMES

Pacifism and Prophecy

On 4 April 1967, at Riverside Church in New York City, Martin Luther King delivered his first public indictment of the Vietnam War. Standing before the Clergy and Laity Concerned about the Vietnam War, he praised fellow religious leaders for having the courage to 'move beyond the prophesying of smooth patriotism' to speak from the transcendent 'mandates of conscience.'[1] At the same time, he rebuked those in the civil rights movement who characterized his anti-war activism as a distraction from his primary mission: '[T]hough I often understand the source of their concern, I am nevertheless greatly saddened, for such questions mean that the inquirers have not really known me, my commitment or my calling.'[2]

Barely a week after Riverside, the national board of the National Association for the Advancement of Colored People (NAACP) crafted a resolution declaring that the kind of 'mix' King advocated would be 'a serious tactical mistake' for the Association.[3] King was hardly surprised. An astute student of history and a keen observer of the present, he had long recognized that bringing African Americans into the anti-war movement would prove difficult. Although Blacks had voiced opposition to every major U.S. war leading to Vietnam, they had never done so in great numbers; and in 1967 the war claimed broad, if diminishing, black support. As one measure of this support, African Americans continued to voluntarily enlist at a steady rate. They did so in part because a war 'against communism' held ideological appeal,[4] but also because military service was still viewed as a means to secure social and economic benefits some found otherwise elusive. Others felt that each new military foray presented a renewed test of black patriotism; supporting Vietnam, whether as soldier, sailor, or citizen, again offered the opportunity to demonstrate national allegiance. Certainly, African Americans from across the political spectrum understood that the mere hint of anti-U.S. sentiment during a Cold War conflict ensured political backlash. Given this environment, it would be logical, and maybe correct, to assume that King's greatest obstacles in converting black communities to the anti-war cause took the form of such worldly matters as ideology, social concerns, political strategies, or any host of dissuasive feelings his followers might have experienced (e.g., apathy, ambivalence, confusion, fear).

King addressed these more pragmatic considerations in the subsequent speeches and sermons he tailored for black communities. But as 'a preacher by calling,'[5] he was troubled by the fact that many failed to make what he characterized as an 'almost facile connection'[6] between the primary belief system animating the core ethic of the civil rights movement – Christian non-violence[7] – and a principled stance against Vietnam. He had in fact spent the previous year persuading his own organization, the Southern Christian Leadership Conference (SCLC), of the moral imperative compelling him to speak before its leaders permitted him to go public with his view.[8]

Writing five years after the end of Vietnam, Cornel West lamented that the majority of 'black theologians remain[ed] uncritical of America's imperialist presence in Third World countries,' blaming the failure to adopt an encompassing 'social vision' that would tie black American socio-economic inequality to global capitalism and U.S. foreign policy.[9] He charged black clergy with the task of critiquing the United States' 'imperial ventures,' which might very well include imperial warfare, although West does not address war explicitly here.[10] It is therefore curious that students of the period have rarely, if ever, examined whether beliefs about war circulating within the 'Black Church' might have contributed to blacks' hesitance to denounce the Vietnam War during its early stages, or to protest other American conflicts in the enduring aftermath of a war that devastated many black communities. What interests me here, however, exceeds the specific instance of Vietnam. Rather, in exploring conceptualizations of war derived from Afro-Protestant theological discourse, I wish to suggest how these ideas have informed African Americans' political responses to war and pacifism in the past and might continue to do so in the present. Examining this relationship also gives insight into how languages of violence emerging from sites falling 'outside' of the government proper and its official discourses (in this case, the church and scripture, respectively) have the effect of naturalizing war while making peace alien; as such, they help to condition a citizenry to accept war as normal.

This enquiry first requires understanding how the defining mode of Afro-Protestant religious thought, the black prophetic tradition, developed within the U.S. context. Theologian Dwight Hopkins' succinct assessment summarizes scholarly consensus: 'The black church begins in slavery; thus slave religion provides the first source for a contemporary of black theology.'[11] Intimately related to the prophetic tradition in Judaism, black prophecy envisions the trials of the Jewish people in the Old Testament as parallels to the modern black historical experience in the West: dispersal, bondage, and the continuing struggle for a fully realized freedom. A deeply eschatological tradition, it is intended to inspire hope for deliverance in the hands of an angry God who will ultimately side with the oppressed. Thomas Wentworth Higginson, a white Northern abolitionist preacher chosen to command the first black unit raised for the Union Army, was among the first Americans to document black Christian spiritual practices in the United States. In memoirs published after the war, he devotes an entire chapter to transcribing black spirituals, issuing commentary on their content that, while sometimes dismissive, accurately represents conclusions contemporary scholars have drawn from slave narratives, sermons, and other antebellum source material. Most pointedly, Higginson notes the absence of the Gospels in the slaves' scripture: '[Revelation], with the books of Moses, constituted their Bible; all that lay between, even the narratives of the life of Jesus, they hardly cared to read or to hear.'[12] This is surely exaggeration – Higginson's own transcription of black spirituals in his memoir attest to the presence of Jesus in them – but slaves' attraction to Revelation over other parts of the New Testament makes sense in light of the theological and textual correspondences with the Hebrew Bible. Nearly three hundred of the verses in Revelation allude to the Hebrew Bible at least once, including references to apocalyptic images from the Old Testament.[13] While the ultimate eschatology of the Old and New differ – the Old Testament promised the restoration of Israel for the chosen Jewish people while the New Testament imagined a worldwide Christendom for all believers – both privilege a God who will save some and destroy others in preparation for a better world to come.

With that in mind, I will entertain three interrelated claims about the relationship between this religious tradition and African Americans' attitudes toward war: first, that blacks have developed a notion of 'just war' in light of their own historical experiences of oppression; second, that those experiences have made it correspondingly difficult to abandon collective violence as a tool of liberation and justice; and third, that the centrality of sacred warfare in the black prophetic tradition's mythologies has led to a tolerance of secular war, however unintentionally.

Slavery, Prophecy, and War

In 'Why I Am Opposed to the War in Vietnam,' a sermon delivered later that April before his own congregation at Ebenezer Baptist Church, King reiterated his dismay with those who questioned his transition into anti-war activism: 'To me the relationship of this ministry to the making of peace is so obvious that I sometimes marvel at those who ask me why I am speaking against the war ... Have they forgotten that my ministry is in obedience to the one who loved his enemies so fully that he died for them?'[14] The message is clear: *imitatio Christi*.

Yet it is important to note that King's pacifist readings of the Gospels had already rendered him an ideological minority within the U.S. Christian community. With the exception of the historic peace churches, such as the Quakers and Mennonites, few denominations had ever subscribed unilaterally to pacifism and had instead adopted variations of the 'just war doctrine' to evaluate the morality of individual wars. In 'A Christmas Sermon on Peace,' also given before Ebenezer in 1967, King endeavours to dismantle the 'just war' rationale. King argues that the notion of an 'unjust means to a just ends' is a *prima facie* contradiction perpetuated by world leaders seeking to rationalize slaughter: 'Hitler contended that everything he did in Germany was for peace ... Every time we drop our bombs in North Vietnam ... Johnson speaks eloquently about peace ... The means represents the ideal in the making ... peace is not a merely a distant goal we seek, but it is a means by which we arrive at that goal.'[15] Aware that he was speaking only one hundred years after slavery and a mere twenty after the Holocaust, King concedes that '[t]here may have been a time when war served as a negative good by preventing the spread and growth of an evil force.'[16] Now, he claims, 'the very destructive power of modern weapons of warfare has eliminated the possibility that war may any longer serve as a negative good.'[17]

To strengthen the religious aspects of his case, he appealed to African Americans' eschatological consciousness, offering clear pictures of a better time to come in which black deliverance and a peaceful world are mutually animating visions. For example, after praising the strength blacks managed to muster for the fight for civil rights in 'Why,' he recalls the Old Testament prophet Isaiah's reassurances to the Jewish people that although they were living through troubling times, peace would accompany their return from exile: 'With this faith, we'll sing it as we're getting ready to sing it now. Men will beat their swords into plowshares and their spears into pruning hooks. And nations will not rise up against nations, neither shall they study war anymore. And I don't know about you, I ain't gonna study war no more.'[18]

Well before Vietnam, black Americans had transformed the vision God revealed to Isaiah, 'neither shall they learn war any more' (Isa 2:4),[19] into the black spiritual King uses to conclude his sermon and lead his congregation into song:

I'm gonna lay down my sword and shield
Down by the riverside ...
I ain't gonna study war no more.[20]

Moving deftly from Isaiah to the idiom of the spiritual, King reminds his audience that they know Isaiah's words very well; they had believed in its message enough to craft it into a song celebrating peace. Perhaps this cultural cue was King's way of reclaiming anti-war sentiment as organically *black* when faced with many who, at this relatively early juncture, were apt to dismiss the anti-war movement and anti-imperialism as 'white' concerns.

Ushering in Isaiah to serve a pacifist agenda is nevertheless a theologically tricky move. While this spiritual originated in slavery, it was also sung during the civil rights movement, gaining further prominence when white musicians of the Left adopted it as an anti-war anthem. But 'Down by the Riverside' is not a radical call for disarmament. True to its biblical source, the laying down of 'sword and shield' will come only after God decides to deliver the Jewish people, an eschatological message that makes sense when considering its historical roots. Its words preach 'patience' rather than 'pacifism'; it is not, therefore, a corollary to Christ's message to 'turn the other cheek' when confronted with abuse (Mat 53:9). The meaning more closely approximates his counsel to remain steady within the chaos that will signal his return: 'And you will hear of wars and rumours of wars; see that you are not alarmed; for this must take place, but the end is not yet … all thus is but the beginning of the birth pangs' (Mat 24:6–8).

In the Old Testament especially, there are many wars and many rumours of wars. Noting that thirty-nine books of the Hebrew Bible mention war, the theologian Richard Hess argues that the ancients 'assumed' that war was 'a necessary part of the world.'[21] Within this context, the allusion to Isaiah in 'Down by the Riverside' may offer additional insight into black Christians' visions of war. It is in Isaiah that God affirms that all historical events – including wars – are his divine will. The Babylonian and Assyrian armies, for instance, are instruments God uses to punish the Jewish people for their betrayals. At the same time, prophets in the Hebrew Bible derive comfort from the belief that God will destroy those empires when he is prepared to redeliver his people. Hess argues that because the distinction between sacred and secular wars in the Old Testament are non-existent, the questions of the morality of war are absent from the text.[22] The graphic depictions of conflict in the Old Testament ensures that war is presented as terrifying, tragic, and violent, but never 'senseless,' as violence is habitually described in anti-war rhetoric. War is a potent and polyvalent sign, an essential *parole* in a divine *langue* – a trial for the chosen, a tool to punish the errant, an index of divine displeasure, a signal of God's imminent return.

The meaning of war in 'Down by the Riverside' could lie in any of the above; yet its futurist vision most powerfully evokes war as a sign of imminence and deliverance. The question of the spiritual's interpretation points to a larger problem attending theological interpretations of war. If war is part of 'God's language,' how do believers know, exactly, what is being said? Literary critic Harold Bloom has in fact suggested that the New Testament's recurrent theme, so to speak, is the misapprehension of portent. 'The weirdness of the entire New Testament,' he writes, 'is that everyone in it is utterly persuaded that Christ will soon return. Two thousand years later, he has not.'[23] Issues of temporality notwithstanding (what is 'soon'?), Bloom misses a crucial element of Christian prophecy here. The New Testament calls *all* of the faithful to participate: 'Even upon my slaves, both men and women … they will prophesy. And I will show portents in the heaven above and signs on the earth below, blood, and fire, and smoky mists' (Act 2:18). Prophesying is a radically democratizing act, replacing the restrictive realms of *logos* with an expansive interpretive praxis involving worldly signs.

Accordingly, this cosmic vigilance – the search for signs foretelling a new beginning – often belongs to the 'wretched of the earth,' those in greatest need of intervention.

Certainly, prophecy has appealed to African Americans precisely because it offers a source of empowerment and hope. This partly explains why abandoning the 'study' of war follows rather than precedes the peace Armageddon will bring. Until then, war must be studied carefully as a possible sign of God's return. Unsurprisingly, blacks read the Civil War in this manner, quickly accommodating its 'blood and fire' within a prophetic framework that had prepared them for a violent emancipation. In *The Souls of Black Folk*, W.E.B. Du Bois portrays this hopeful moment with great sensitivity to black prophetic consciousness. According to Du Bois, 'Negro religion' and the 'dream of Abolition' had become so 'indentified' that 'when Emancipation finally came, it seemed to the freedman a literal Coming of the Lord ... He stood dumb and motionless before the whirlwind: what had he to do with it? Was it not the Lord's doing, and marvellous in his eyes?'[24] Similarly, Higginson notes that many religious spirituals were already 'militant'[25] in sound, spirit, and imagery, and merely retooled to fit the specific context of the Civil War. In his words, they were 'readily available for camp purposes with very little strain on their symbolism.'[26] Far from a moral abomination, the war affirmed Christian slaves' existential faith in a just God.

It is easy to understand how blacks would evaluate an emancipatory war in prophetic terms. But an observation Higginson makes about how blacks viewed a war that had *not* altered most slaves' lives sheds light on how black prophecy might have broadened their acceptance of war. Noting the mix of the sacred and the secular in slaves' historical narratives, Higginson makes this claim: 'Most of the great events of the past, down to the period of the American Revolution, they instinctively attribute to Moses.'[27] To be sure, the American Revolution had long held a place of symbolic significance in African-American political discourse. From the moment it became clear that the North American colonies were poised to shed tyrannical rule, free and enslaved blacks began to weave the Revolutionary War and anti-imperialist discourses into arguments for their own independence. Afterwards, they remained profoundly invested in holding the new nation to its egalitarian ideals. Yet, there is little evidence to suggest that before the Civil War, blacks in the North or the South had widely envisioned the Revolution in *sacred* terms. If the early Republic was the fulfilment of white prophetic deliverance – the result of a 'holy' war – it would follow that God had intended his New World Canaan to include black bondage. Placed in this light, slaves' insertion of Moses into the Revolution is theologically revealing. Perhaps once blacks felt that they were on a path towards freedom, and therefore destined to share the fruits of a New Canaan, they felt it safe to incorporate the Revolution into black providential history, willing to share the Moses they had jealously guarded as their own.

While we may never know the reason for Moses' appearance here, it is clear that most slaves viewed the Revolutionary War as prophetic only *retrospectively*. The collapsing of the sacred and the secular has also facilitated a collapsing of space and time into an eschatological narrative that is at once retrospective, presentist, and futurist. We can thus see how black prophetic time might interfere with pacifist aims. If some black believers feel that the future pertinence of any given war might be revealed only after its occurrence, then what are the implications, even risks, of working actively for war's eradication in the present?

Black Christianity in 'Revolutionary Times'

In the year before King began to denounce the war in public forums, two radicalized civil rights groups, the Congress of Racial Equality (CORE) and the Student Non-Violent Coordinating Committee (SNCC), issued statements condemning the war.[28] By that time, both had abandoned King's arm of the movement for Black Power, and to King's great disappointment, had relinquished non-violence for the 'right of revolution.' Floyd McKissick, the head of CORE, stated his reason with clarity: 'We know [the white man] will kill us if he can ... The right of revolution is a constitutional right, condoned by the creation of the American Revolution itself.'[29]

For many on the black Left, the National Liberation Front and others engaged in anti-colonial struggles across Asia, Africa, and Latin America were exercising an identical right. King disagreed; while he had followed the decolonization movement with great attention and sympathy, his position on non-violence extended to victims of colonialism and imperialism. He could turn to the example of India, however isolated, to illustrate the effectiveness of a pacifist approach to imperialist domination.[30] He also viewed some African Americans' tendency to romanticize uprising as a destructive inclination that minimized the bloodshed at the same time it encouraged the violence erupting in ghettos across the United States.[31] His writing on Vietnam nonetheless reveals genuine ambivalence about oppressed subjects' recourse to violence under colonial rule, voicing his disapproval of anti-imperialist revolution in the mildest of terms, even characterizing it as a necessary stage of 'young nations.'[32] To some extent, King's attitude reflects his sense of moral proportion. He decries the United States as 'the greatest purveyor of violence in the world'[33] while detailing how French and U.S. imperialism created the conditions for the National Liberation Front to emerge. King also pushed blacks to see their own struggles as bound to those of other people of colour inhabiting the 'world house,' whether African villagers or Vietnamese peasants. In 'Why,' he celebrates Third World revolt: '[T]hese are revolutionary times. All over the globe men are revolting against old systems of exploitation and oppression, and out of the wounds of a frail world, new systems of justice and equality are being born. The shirtless and barefoot people of the land are rising up as never before ... They are saying, unconsciously, as we say in one of our freedom songs, "Ain't gonna let nobody turn me around!"'[34]

By no means did the statement 'all over the globe' refer solely to instances of non-violent social transformation. King even laments that the

> Western nations who had initiated so much of the revolutionary spirit of the modern world have now become the arch anti-revolutionaries ... America has strayed to the far country of racism and militarism. The home that all too many Americans left was solidly structured idealistically; its pillars were solidly grounded in the insights of our Judeo-Christian heritage. All men are made in the image of God. All men are bothers. All men are created equal. Every man is an heir to a legacy of dignity and worth. Every man has rights that are neither conferred by, nor derived from the State – they are God-given.[35]

In both of the passages quoted above, King's religious imagination works to subsume the bloody reality of revolution. In the first, he ends with a civil rights song that evokes Exodus: 'Ain't nobody gonna let nobody turn me around ... I'm marchin' to the promised [or freedom's] land.'[36] Global uprisings here become deliverance; the revolutionaries are 'unconsciously' Christians. In the second, he implicitly praises the American Revolution, criticizes the West for crushing people's revolutions, then attributes the Revolution to a Judaeo-Christian ethic while he invokes the language of the Constitution, whose authors had carefully crafted a secular interpretation of natural law for its authority. King's zigzagging conflation of actors, events, and ideologies could lead his listeners to a single conclusion – that all revolutions, American, civil rights, and those of the Third World, are the work of Christian ideals. In his final book, King does in fact attribute decolonization movements to their leaders' contact with Christianity in the West.[37] My point is this: if King himself had trouble cleanly rejecting violence as a tool of the oppressed, and thus sought refuge in the belief that some revolutions were, at least, inspired by a 'Judaeo-Christian' God, would his followers not experience similar trouble and, like King, turn to religious rationalizations?

Nonetheless, it would be an error to reduce King's attraction to black secular revolution to a personal test of his Christian faith or to a crisis borne solely from the exigencies of his historical moment. 'The Age of Revolution' had already given rise to a generation of nineteenth-century black religious thinkers drawn to the events, ideals, and actors of the American, Haitian, and French revolutions. The spectacular overturning of old social orders in the secular world led them to produce radical biblical exegeses that intertwined secular and sacred law to justify black rebellion. The result was a new African American rhetorical formation, the black revolutionary jeremiad, a discursive genre that left a lasting legacy on the prophetic tradition King inherited.

The Black Revolutionary Jeremiad

What I am distinguishing as the 'black revolutionary jeremiad' is part of a larger antebellum rhetorical tradition Wilson Jeremiah Moses has identified as the 'black jeremiad.' As Wilson notes, the jeremiad draws inspiration from three sources: the prophet Jeremiah, who castigates Israel and Judah for breaking their covenant with God; the Puritan Jeremiad, whose authors warned the Puritans that their errant ways were tempting God's wrath; and Thomas Jefferson's anxious prediction in *Notes on the State of Virginia* that a nation that was forfeiting its ideals to embrace slavery could only expect God to inflict misery upon it.[38] In sermons, speeches, and political tracts, black Christians, including prominent figures such as Sojourner Truth and Frederick Douglass, advised their oppressors that unless they altered their course they could expect to feel the full measure of God's displeasure. Moses maintains that authors of jeremiads harboured no 'real desire for a racial Armageddon … they were not prescriptions for revolution.'[39]

Given that most black jeremiads were produced after Haiti, and after a series of U.S. slave revolts led by Christian slave rebels, any such broad generalization warrants examination. For one, the absence of an explicit 'prescription' for revolution hardly precludes the presence of an underlying, very 'real desire.' Even more, authors of the revolutionary jeremiads quite consciously addressed blacks in overt efforts to incite liberational violence. They strengthened their appeals by working on their audiences' awareness of prophecy – exalting the model of God's righteous vengeance and casting black Christian rebels as soldiers divinely commissioned to spread God's wrath. Notably, this interpretation of Christian scripture entirely contradicts Paul's admonition that God alone had the authority to punish human error.[40] Circumventing the complex questions regarding human agency in the service of God gives these writers the theological loophole they need: their own desire for racial warfare is deemed God's will. Nevertheless, the most salient question here is not whether the writers of the revolutionary jeremiad actually encouraged uprising, but how these calls to arms imprinted black Christian attitudes about violence and warfare, including King's own.

In 1829 David Walker, a free black Boston abolitionist born to a slave father in North Carolina, published *Walker's Appeal, in Four Articles; Together with a Preamble, to the Coloured Citizens of the World, but in Particular, and Very Expressly, to Those of the United States of America.*[41] The *Appeal* stands as the most influential and incendiary revolutionary jeremiad in American letters, serving to inspire many of the black radicals of the 1960s and 70s who saw a viable alternative to Christian non-violence in Walker's words and embraced him as an early voice of black nationalist ideology. In the document that led to calls for his death, Walker levels a remorseless and erudite attack on white American slaveholders, dismissing them as mere 'pretenders to Christianity'[42] who have turned their backs on their faith for greed and avarice. In a prediction typical of the jeremiad, Walker warns them that if they fail to give blacks their freedom, they will reap what they have sown: 'O Americans! Americans!! I call God – I call angels – I call men, to witness, that your DESTRUCTION *is at hand*, and will be speedily consummated unless you REPENT.'[43] He also accuses them of making a mockery of the ideals contained in their founding documents, and thus warns them that they might reap what they have *written*: 'Do you understand your own language? ... "We hold these truths to be self evident – that ALL MEN ARE CREATED EQUAL!!" ... Hear your language further! "But when a long train of abuses and usurpation, pursuing invariably the same object, evinces a design to reduce them under absolute despotism, it is their *right*, it is their *duty*, to throw off such government.'"[44]

Walker has another purpose in recalling the words of the founding fathers: he uses the *Appeal* to symbolically bestow free and enslaved blacks with the citizenship the United States has denied them. He then sets about educating these new citizens about their rights under a Constitution they now share with their white countrymen and convincing them of their equality in the eyes of God. At the same time, Walker is determined to inspire black transnational identification, endeavouring to construct an *alternative* constitution for the 'coloured citizens of the world.' Walker implies that this black cosmopolitan citizenship unifies them in a higher, cosmic law transcending geopolitical borders. He gathers the blacks of the diaspora under the 'God of the Ethiopians,' or alternately the 'God of the *Blacks*,' claiming the 'God of Israel' as theirs.[45] They are a nation of newly chosen people, divinely elected for salvation. Walker has thus created a discursive and ideological hybrid. If it is a social contract for the black nation, it is also a religious covenant in which Walker outlines blacks' obligations to themselves, to other blacks, and to their God. The social contract here is subordinate; 'natural law' has validity only insofar that it is in accordance with God's law. Thus he tells blacks that freedom is their 'natural right,' but if they are set free, 'instead of returning thanks' to their masters, they should return thanks 'to the Holy Ghost, who is our rightful owner.'[46] Following this logic, the secular 'right of revolution' cannot be a self-sufficient rationale for black rebellion. Walker must tie it to God's prophecy for his people.

To achieve these ends, Walker places liberational violence in this covenant; moreover, he warns that those who disobey this commandment will be divinely punished. Writing of an incident where a black slave woman rescued a man whom slave rebels had tried to kill, he argues that '*humanity, kindness* and the *fear of the Lord*, does not consist in protecting *devils* ... Are they not the Lord's enemies? Ought they not to be destroyed? Any person who will save such wretches from destruction, is fighting against the Lord, and will receive his just recompense.'[47] Significantly, Walker tosses the rebellion into a swirl of revolutionary activity, in the United States and elsewhere, past and future, sacred and secular – the collapsing of time and space essential for the event to carry eschatological significance. In the pages before, he refers to 'Hayti' as 'the glory of the blacks and terror of tyrants';[48] in the pages after, he calculates the black population in some Southern states to consider the feasibility of full-scale black rebellion. He decides that if blacks 'be well equipt for war,'[49] victory would be probable, and cautions against fear: 'when that hour arrives, and you move, be not afraid or dismayed; for be you assured that Jesus Christ the King of heaven and of earth who is the God of justice and of armies, will surely go before you.'[50] Walker has declared a holy war. The grand tautology underlying Walker's justification for violence in the *Appeal* is evident here: you must rise up because God commands it, and when you rise up, you will know it is his command. He closes his work declaring that whites will be humbled, quoting from Revelation and the Declaration in rapid succession, bringing natural and divine law within close ideological and syntactical proximity of one another, as King will do later.

This is not all he and King have in common rhetorically and ideologically. Walker attempts to unite blacks of the diaspora in cause, anticipating King's 'world house,' and does so under the banner of Christianity, a religious chauvinism King shares. We also see that Christianity and revolution were not wholly antonymic in either's rendering of prophecy. The historical imaginary represented by the unfulfilled promise of the Revolutionary War (the egalitarian nation) and the religious imaginary represented by the unfulfilled promise of black deliverance (the promised land) are corollaries as secular and sacred visions of utopia. They are also corollaries practically, as utopias whose realization involved violent means. Most importantly, King was partial to the jeremiad, turning to it for rhetorical and moral force throughout his civil rights campaign. Most famously, in his 1963 'I Have a Dream' speech he recalls the 'magnificent words' of the 'Declaration of Independence,' cautioning that 'there will be neither rest nor tranquility in America until the Negro is granted his citizenship rights. The whirlwinds of revolt will continue to shake the foundations of our nation.'[51] King puts the nation on notice: continuing discrimination will unleash uncontrollable forces. He then asks blacks not 'to degenerate into physical violence' but to use 'soul force' to make themselves felt,[52] a retreat that nearly undermines the 'inevitably' of violence that gives the first statement its power. His anti-war speech 'Why' also includes a jeremiad: 'And don't let anybody make you think that God chose America as his divine, messianic force to be a sort of policeman of the whole world. God has a way of standing before the nations with judgment, and it seems that I can hear God saying to America, "You're too arrogant! And if you don't change your ways, I will rise up and break the backbone of your power, and I'll place it in the hands of a nation that doesn't even know my name. Be still and know that I'm God."'⁵³

King's repeated references to revolutions that have threatened the social order – nationalist revolutions, anti-imperial uprisings, social revolt, and even God's wrath – create rhetorical tensions in his speeches as the violent images these references raise clash with the non-violent idealism King intends to convey. These tensions become threatening themselves, but to King's own philosophy, threatening to reveal the conflicted political impulses lying beneath the (seemingly) undisturbed linguistic surfaces. Recall that King says he may hear his Lord promising to 'break the backbone' of U.S. power in a speech in which he is attempting to galvanize sentiment against violence and war. Certainly, the exaltation of divine violence, a ritual expression in black prophecy, challenges the purity of his pacifist message.

Black Liberation and the Problem of the Gospel

Of course, King did not rely upon the Old Testament God as a model for pacifist practice. For that purpose, King employed the 'suffering servant' as he had done to great effect during the civil rights movement: 'Jesus Christ means taking up the cross. Before the crown we wear, there is the cross that we must bear. Let us bear it – bear it for truth, bear it for justice, and bear it for peace ...'⁵⁴ Asking blacks to 'take up the cross' once more is another way King endeavours to create a continuum between participating in the two causes. But he was asking them to carry it for a cause that many did not yet consider their own at a time when some in the Black Power movement had begun to critique King for clinging to an image of Jesus that ostensibly provided blacks with a detrimental model of suffering, servility, and passivity. King's redeployment of familiar imagery and language in this entreaty can be interpreted as an effort to control the meaning of Christ for his followers as they entered into this new political arena, and as the struggle over the meaning of Christ in black theology and politics took on renewed urgency.

The long history of debates in black communities surrounding Christ as symbol of pacifism is at its core an expression of the ongoing debates about the form black politics should assume. That point is perhaps best exemplified by the revolutionary jeremiad penned by the Presbyterian minister, Northern abolitionist, and former slave Henry Highland Garnet, who was also a great admirer of Walker. In 1843 Garnet delivered 'An Address to the Slaves of the United States of America'[55] before an abolitionist convention in Buffalo, New York, in the form of a resolution delegates would consider for adoption and circulation. In Garnet's words, the 'Address' was rejected because it was too 'war-like, and encouraged insurrection.'[56] Warlike it was. After suggesting that obedient slaves who submitted to their own 'DEGRADATION' were 'SINFUL IN THE EXTREME,' Garnet issues an unmistakable bat-tle cry: 'Brethren, arise, arise! Strike for your lives and liberties. Now is the day and the hour. Let every slave throughout the land do this and the days of slavery are numbered ... *Rather die freemen than live to be slaves.* Remember that you are FOUR MILLIONS!'[57] Garnet omitted the insurrectionary call in the revised version he published within his 1848 edition of Walker's *Appeal*, advising against 'revolution with the sword': 'Your numbers are too small, and moreover the rising spirit of the age, and the spirit of the gospel, are opposed to war and blood-shed ... and remember that you are three millions.'[58] His voice here sounds as diminished as his revised numbers. Had he truly begun to read the Gospels in such a radically different manner? In 1872 Garnet would switch again, vocally supporting the Cuban Revolution because the insurgents vowed to abolish slavery.

The theologian Elmer Martens has claimed that accepting a pacifist interpretation of scripture requires 'coming to terms with' the inten-tions of the 'violent, wrathful deity' of the Hebrew Bible. Converse-ly, for many black Americans, as Garnet's reversals demonstrate, an acceptance of Christianity has required grappling with the implica-tions of a non-violent Christ. Black studies scholar Lawrence Levine theorizes that a preference for the heroes of the Hebrew Bible led black slaves to reimagine Christ as a warrior in the manner of the Yahweh of the Exodus Psalms.[59] But the need for a warrior figure could also entail choosing the Christ of the Apocalypse over Christ of the Gospels, as this spiritual illustrates:

De lightnin' and de flashin' ...
Jesus set poor sinners free.
I can't stand the fire.[60]

It is evident why the fact of slavery rendered it nearly impossible for many black Americans to embrace a pacifist legacy of Christ uncritically, especially as slaveholders held up that ideal to coerce slaves' submission to bondage. They referred to biblical passages such as Peter's counsel to slaves under Roman dominion: 'Slaves, accept the authority of your masters with all deference, not only those who are kind and gentle but also those who are harsh ... Christ also suffered for you, leaving you an example' (Pet 2:23). Some slaves indeed accepted non-resistance as behavioural code, one black Southern church going so far as to censure slaves who ran away.

Recognizing the dangers of biblical literalism in relation to slavery, Walker, Garnet, and other black abolitionists made unmasking non-resistance as a ruse of 'slaveholding Christianity' part of their anti-slavery programs. Still, literalism was at work within abolitionist circles, guiding many who had accepted a *non-violent* Christ as their ethical model for social action. Black Christian revolutionaries had to confront the consternation of fellow Christian abolitionists – followers of William Lloyd Garrison particularly – who were armed with the same scripture King would wield some 120 years later in his anti-war speeches: 'love your enemies.' The influence of Garrisonians, including Frederick Douglass, at the Buffalo Convention where Garnet presented his resolution contributed to its defeat. Eleven years earlier, Garrison in fact grieved over the Southampton Revolt, which had left approximately sixty whites dead: 'For ourselves, we are horror-struck at the late tidings ... We have warned our countrymen of the danger of persisting in their unrighteous conduct. We have preached to the slaves the pacifist precepts of Jesus Christ.'[61] Its leader, the slave preacher Nathaniel Turner, had the 'other' Christ in mind: he believed he had been chosen to usher in the Day of Judgment.[62]

As I have mentioned, many in the Black Power movement who agreed with King's stance on the war disagreed with non-violence as an ethical rationale for it. The rejection of King's incarnation of Jesus as the same 'white' Jesus who had been used to domesticate slaves and who had left blacks a legacy of servile passivity was one way detractors expressed their dissatisfaction with his politics and strategies. They felt it was politically and *psychologically* necessary to develop an iconography and a theology to complement their philosophical turn. Notably, in the years immediately following King's death, the theologian James Cone published two books outlining a 'black theology of liberation' altering how large numbers of African Americans would conceptualize Christianity. Cone argued that King had failed to 'meet the needs' of a changing black community who had grown weary of being told their suffering was noble.[63] 'What we need,' he writes, 'is the divine love as expressed in Black Power, which is the power of black people to destroy their oppressors ... Unless God is participating in this holy activity, we must reject his love.'[64] Accordingly, 'soul force,' as King called the power of non-violent love, could not match the ruling class's psychological and physical arsenals. The pressure of such oppositional visions of black Christianity might go much of the way in explaining why King's appeal to anti-war Christian pacifism failed to capture the political imagination of his followers during his lifetime. Still, King and Cone were both operating within the Afro-Protestant prophetic tradition in recognizable ways. Cone's liberation theology, descended more directly from Walker's and Garnet's revolutionary Christianity, is simply the prophetic tradition's radical extreme.

Another answer why King's appeal to Christian pacifism failed may lie in this shared cultural inheritance. Critics have noted that King's jeremiads became increasingly apocalyptic as his disillusionment with the United States intensified and as the violence raging around him continued unabated. Psychoanalytically speaking, the essence of the black jeremiad is religious sublimation: a prohibited instinct for liberational violence against the oppressor is expressed through vivid religious fantasies that safely hand the nasty work of retribution to God. This psychic process will redistribute the thoughts, but not wholly extinguish them. The larger tradition's emphasis on deliverance with its apocalyptic reveries is itself sublimation. Any impulse to harm is repressed, displaced, but finds an acceptable, even healthy, 'economy' in spectacularly violent imaginings of end times. Under the 'wrong' circumstances, however, the repressed instincts could re-emerge with a frightening amount of force, requiring ever more psychic exertion to keep them from appearing.[65] Those who resisted King's call to convert to pacifism might have felt (instinctively) that his philosophy was too obviously repressive as they were deciding how to respond to the same violent world King was living in. Finally, it can simply be argued that black prophecy was never intended to yield pacifism, and that King, a 'preacher by calling,' was attempting to fill a received cultural formation with new, but ultimately unsuitable, political content. After all, the prophetic tradition hinges upon the belief that a violent means *will* bring about a peaceful ends. When crafted into a rhetoric used to justify war, this very belief is what King, transformed into a peacemaker by calling, would spend the last years of his life advocating against.

NOTES

1 Martin Luther King, 'A Time to Break Silence,' 4 April 1967, Riverside Baptist Church, in *A Testament of Hope: The Essential Writings of Martin Luther King, Jr.*, ed. James Melvin Washington (San Francisco: Harper and Row, 1986), 232.
2 Ibid.
3 Simon Hall, 'The Response of the Moderate Wing of the Civil Rights Movement to the War in Vietnam,' *The Historical Journal* 46, no. 3 (2003): 639.
4 Wallace Terry, *Bloods: An Oral History of the Vietnam War by Black Veterans* (New York: Ballantine Books 1984), xiv.
5 King, 'A Time.'
6 Martin Luther King, 'Why I Am Opposed to the War,' 30 April 1967, Riverside Baptist Church, http://www.lib.berkeley.edu/MRC/pacificaviet/ riversidetranscript.html (accessed 16 October 2009). Pacifica mistakenly names Riverside Church as the location for the speech.
7 Although influenced by other secular and religious philosophies, ultimately King felt that they had strengthened his pacifist interpretation of Christianity.
8 See Hall, 'The Response.'
9 Cornel West, *Prophesy Deliverance! An Afro-American Revolutionary Christianity* (Louisville, KY: John Knox Press, 2002), 111–2.
10 Ibid., 112.
11 Dwight Hopkins, 'Slave Theology in the "Invisible Institution,"' in *African American Religious Thought: An Anthology*, ed. Cornel West and Eddie S. Glaude Jr (Louisville, KY: Westminster John Knox Press, 2003), 790.
12 Thomas Wentworth Higginson, *Army Life in a Black Regiment and Other Writings* (New York: Penguin, 1997), 156.
13 *The New Oxford Annotated Bible: New Standard Revised Version*, ed. Michael D. Coogan (New York: Oxford University Press, 2001), 790.
14 King, 'Why I Am Opposed.'
15 Martin Luther King, 'A Christmas Sermon on Peace,' 24 December 1967, Riverside Baptist Church, in *A Testament of Hope*, 253.
16 Ibid.
17 Ibid.
18 King, 'Why I Am Opposed.'
19 This and all subsequent scriptural quotations are from the New Standard Revised Version of the *Holy Bible*.
20 See Shane White and Graham White, *The Sounds of Slavery: Discovering African American History through Songs, Sermons and Speech* (Boston: Beacon Press, 2005), 61.

21 Richard S. Hess, 'War in the Bible: An Overview,' in War in the Bible and Terrorism in the Twenty-First Century, ed. Richard S. Hess and Elmer A. Martens (Winona Lake, IN: Eisenbrauns, 2008), 19.

22 Ibid., 25–31.

23 Harold Bloom, Jesus and Yahweh: The Names Divine (New York: Riverhead Books, 2005), 59.

24 W.E.B. Du Bois, The Souls of Black Folk: Essays and Sketches (Chicago: A. C. McClurg & Co., 1903), 201.

25 Higginson, Army Life, 152.

26 Ibid.

27 Higginson, Army Life, 20.

28 See Hall, 'The Response,' 674–7.

29 Floyd McKissick, 'CORE Endorses Black Power,' in Let Nobody Turn Us Around: Voices of Resistance, Reform and Renewal: An African American Anthology, ed. Manning Marable and Leith Mullings (New York: Rowman and Littlefield, 2003), 460.

30 Martin Luther King, 'The Current Crisis in Race Relations,' in A Testament of Hope, 86.

31 Martin Luther King, Where Do We Go from Here: Chaos or Community? (New York: Beacon Press, 1967), 57.

32 Ibid., 179.

33 King, 'A Time.'

34 King, 'Why I Am Opposed.'

35 Ibid.

36 'Ain't Gonna Let Nobody Turn Me 'Round,' in Let Nobody Turn Us Around, ed. M. Marable and L. Mullings, 397.

37 King, Where Do We Go, 175.

38 Thomas Jefferson, Writings (New York: The Library of America, 1984), 289.

39 Quoted in Theophus H. Smith, Conjuring Culture: Biblical Formations of Black America (New York: Oxford University Press, 1994), 94.

40 Theologians tend to derive this interpretation from the Apostle Paul's quotation of God's admonitions that 'Vengeance is mine.' See Romans 12:19–21.

41 David Walker, Appeal to the Coloured Citizens of the World, ed. Sean Wilentz (New York: Hill and Wang, 1995).

42 Ibid. Walker included an unnumbered introductory note in which he makes this comment.

43 Ibid., 43.

44 Ibid., 75.

45 Ibid., introductory note; 'God of the Blacks,' 18.

46 Ibid., 71.

47 Ibid., 25.
48 Ibid., 21.
49 Ibid., 63.
50 Ibid., 11–12.
51 King, 'I Have a Dream,' 28 August 1963, Washington, DC, in *A Testament of Hope*, 218.
52 Ibid.
53 King, 'Why I Am Opposed.'
54 Ibid.
55 Henry Highland Garnet, 'An Address to the Slaves of the United States,' Buffalo, New York, 21 August 1843. http://www.pbs.org/wgbh/aia/part4/4h2937t.html (accessed 15 October 2009).
56 *Walker's Appeal, With a Brief Sketch of His Life by Henry Highland Garnet; and Also Garnet's Address to the Slaves of the United States of America*, ed. Henry Highland Garnet (New York: J.H. Tobitt, 1848), 90.
57 Ibid.
58 Ibid., 96.
59 Lawrence Levine, *Black Culture, Black Consciousness: Afro American Folk Thought from Slavery to Freedom* (New York: Oxford University Press, 1977), 43.
60 Higginson, *Army Life*, 156.
61 Quoted in Thomas Gray and Nat Turner, *The Confessions of Nat Turner*, ed. Kenneth S. Greenberg (Boston: Bedford Books, 1996), 71.
62 See Gray and Turner, *Confessions*.
63 James H. Cone, *A Black Theology of Liberation* (New York: Orbis, 1989), 37.
64 Ibid., 70.
65 See Sigmund Freud, 'Repression,' in *The Freud Reader*, ed. Peter Gay (New York: Norton, 1989), 568–71.

8 Exchange of Sacrifices: Symbolizing an Unpopular War in Post-Soviet Russia

SERGUEI ALEX. OUSHAKINE

Russia does not pay us much – in money or in glory
But we are Russia's only soldiers.
Hence we must hold out, until the very death.
Forward! Forward! Forward!

Trofim, a popular singer

Introduction

The Chechen war became one of the most vivid representations of the political and social chaos that followed the collapse of the Soviet Union. To a large degree, the war was an unexpected outcome of the fight for independence that had started in Chechnya in the early 1990s. At the time, Boris Yeltsin's government was capable of neither negotiating with the pro-independence forces in Chechnya nor suppressing them. Apparently misinformed by his advisors about the possibility of defeating heavily armed Chechen rebels, in December 1994 Yeltsin began a military campaign aimed at 'restoring the constitutional order' in Chechnya (see figure 8.1).

Since then, the war has gone through a series of stages. A comprehensive ceasefire achieved in August of 1996 was followed in 1999 by a new period of a large-scale fighting. After 2001 the military component of the war was gradually scaled down: massive fights were replaced by episodic armed conflicts between isolated groups of Chechen fighters and professional troops staged by the Russian government in the region.

The war exposed the least attractive features of the new Russian state:

ВЫБИРАЙ
сердцем

8.1 A bullet-ridden poster from the 1996 presidential election campaign. The line on the poster reads, 'Choose with your heart.' Vladimir Bykov, a Chechen war veteran who took this picture in June 1996 in Serjen-Yurt, Chechnya, provided his own title: *Our beloved president*. Courtesy of the photographer.

its cruelty, its indifference, and its lack of responsibility. War is never an organized event, and the history of every generation of war veterans is always one of trauma, confusion, and disillusionment. Yet the Chechen war, like the Korean and Vietnam wars in the United States, added to these veterans' traumatic biographies a profound feeling of being betrayed – by the Russian state, by the military leadership, by the general public. Decidedly unpopular among Russia's citizens, the war nonetheless caused little opposition. Yet, unlike other mass-scale military operations conducted by the Soviet government, for instance, in Afghanistan, the Chechen war from the very beginning was marked by legal, political, ideological, and moral ambiguity. As a result, the task of framing the Chechen war in a language understandable for a larger audience was left to the soldiers drafted to participate in the unpopular war.

Unlike Soviet veterans of previous wars, whose post-war legal status had been determined by special laws, participants in the Chechen war had no legal framework that could outline or even clarify their postwar status, rights, and entitlements. Technically speaking, the war in Chechnya has never been officially classified as a war. From the legal point of view this military campaign was a limited 'anti-terrorist operation' in the North Caucasus. Correspondingly, there were no war veterans produced by the conflict. Chechen war veterans were officially classified as 'participants in combat activities' and were not eligible for the statewide subsidies or assistance available to veterans of previous wars and military conflicts.

Given the uncertainty with which the Chechen war was presented in the Russian media, it is perhaps understandable that very few servicemen used the war as a ground for substantive criticism of the state's military policy. Unlike mandatory drafted soldiers, senior officers had more freedom in expressing their opinions, but even they exercised this freedom very rarely. Some officers approached the war as an opportunity, making some money on the side by selling arms and soldiers; few resigned quietly. The majority of Russia's higher officers preferred to follow orders silently, ignoring the increasing number of the dead and injured civilians and soldiers. There was no equivalent of Vietnam Veterans against the War in Russia. Nor was there anything comparable to the investigations through which American veterans ('winter soldiers') challenged the U.S. military and civic authorities in 1971.[1] A possible anti-war stance as a way to create a *post*-war identity was replaced by a different symbolic framework: demobilized soldiers increasingly couched their appeals for public recognition and monetary assistance in the language of exchange. At times, this uneasy attempt to establish an economic equivalent of patriotic values produced unexpected results: veterans' search for recognition of their financial and social entitlements implicitly pushed the state to define the war in Chechnya in legal and political terms.

Using interviews with veterans of the Chechen war and war-related materials that I collected during my fieldwork in Barnaul (Altai region, Siberia) during 2001–3 and later visits in 2004–5, in this essay I want to explore how military experience and identity are constructed and represented in veterans' post-war life. More specifically, I am interested in understanding those rhetorical moves and tropes that allowed Chechen war veterans to frame their war past in terms of business exchanges with the state. War activity emerged here, I shall argue, as a peculiar form of entrepreneurship, with suffering being a main commodity transacted between Chechen veterans and the state.

'Article 0' of the Constitution

In January 2005, a regional court of the Orel province in central Russia overturned the previous decision of a lower court that had obliged the Ministry of Defence to provide a pension and financial compensation to Gennadi Uminskii, a retired ensign. In 1996 he was severely wounded while performing contracted military service for the Ministry of Defence in Chechnya. As the new court decision concluded, 'war conditions' made it impossible to determine 'the real agent of harm.' Therefore, there was 'no ground for any claim about the state's responsibility for injuries and disabilities incurred.'[2]

As a contract serviceman, Uminskii had participated in a particularly bloody battle when Grozny, Chechnya's capital, was stormed by federal troops in August 1996. On 6 August 1996, with his platoon positioned outside Grozny, Uminskii (with 202 other servicemen) was ordered to unblock several checkpoints in the city's downtown and to rescue several journalists as well as a general captured by the rebels. As soon as the platoon entered the city, the soldiers were encircled. Most of them were killed on the spot, yet fifty managed to survive, hiding in a ruined building nearby. Despite the rebels' repeated demands that they surrender, the soldiers continued to fight back, turning the building into a defence ground. On 10 August 1996, however, the besieged soldiers were startled by a radio news report: their commanders had announced an official mourning service to commemorate the annihilated platoon. As the soldiers learned later, the regiment's bureaucracy had even issued official 'funeral letters' (*pokhoronki*) to inform the soldiers' relatives about their deaths. Although all the besieged soldiers were seriously wounded, not all of them were killed. Some managed to stay in the building for several weeks until a ceasefire between Russia and Chechnya, signed on 31 August 1996, effectively stopped the first Chechen war (December 1994–August 1996) and put an end to their defence post's blockade.[3]

Having survived the siege, Uminskii spent the next year in hospitals, recovering from concussion and shell shock. He was released in 1998 with a diagnosis that allows for very limited employment under medical supervision.[4] Uminskii's attempts to secure a pension from the Ministry of Defence failed. As he learned, his original contract with the ministry had been voided due to his 'prolonged absence.' Moreover, his military division was disbanded, and in the local office of the Ministry of Defence in Orel, his hometown, he was informed that the person listed under his name was still 'missing in action.'[5]

Uminskii's case is a good example of the legal and political uncertainty that has been associated with the Chechen war. *Krasnaia Zvezda* (Red star), the official newspaper of the Ministry of Defence, bitterly pointed out that it was not just the ministry that should be held responsible. Taken aback by the fact that the ministry was being sued for compensation, the paper insisted that it was 'the duty of the whole state to take care of the people who defended its territorial integrity.'[6] This deflection of responsibility through splitting the ministry from the 'whole state' is revealing. Indeed, the Chechen war has been first of all a political event, not a military one. Memoirs and interviews of Russian soldiers and generals replay this theme even more strongly. As officers claim, the army was used as a tool in a political game, used irresponsibly and unjustifiably to carry out a humanitarian and military disaster. A commandant of the Russian troops in Chechnya, for instance, complained to a popular magazine in 1996: 'The army, the interior troops, the police never do anything because of their own desire or will. They follow orders … It is a shame, it is a pity … that nobody has any idea what our army, our people, our guys are dying for.'[7]

In 2002, in the midst of the second stage of the Chechen war (1999–), the situation was not that different. By that time the question 'What are our guys dying for?' was toned down, and the army switched from relying on largely untrained conscripts to using contracted volunteers, reservists, and professionally trained military. However, this move changed relatively little; new forms of state-organized violence revealed the same lack of basic organization. In January 2001 a provincial newspaper reported on a group of 350 policemen who were to leave the Altai region for a three-month assignment in Chechnya.[8] The report included an appeal made by the Chamber of Local Entrepreneurs to the broader business community. Describing the poor equipment of the Altai policemen, the chamber asked for contributions: 'The Federal [government] provides for the troops while in Chechnya, but it is up to the troops themselves to take care of their personal equipment and gear. [Our policemen] have neither modern helmets, nor bulletproof vests, nor portable radio sets. And without our help – they never will ... We ask you for your help in equipping our guys so that they could at least remotely resemble the technical level of the [Chechen] fighters [boeviki].'[9] A week later, the newspaper listed some contributions: sheet metal and welding machines from a metal company, five sacks of spaghetti from an individual, a three-month supply of cookies and bottled water from a businessman, first aid sets from a hospital, portable wood-burning ovens from a factory, cash from companies and private citizens – all 'for those who go to Chechnya.'[10]

This commodification through which the war becomes a part of the public discourse is crucial for sustaining the war itself. Devoid of political context, the war emerged as a story of individual and collective sacrifices, as an everyday practice of perseverance that radically transformed people's lives. Commodities here are the symbols of an imagined community that is shaped by a shared understanding of everyday survival. As if epitomizing the essence of this depoliticized approach to the war, a local newspaper headlined its report about Altai soldiers in the North Caucasus: 'Chechnya: The everyday [byt], work, life, and death.'[11] A veteran of the Chechen war makes a similar point in his recollection: 'Some people like to say – it is not possible to forget this service [in Chechnya] ... Of course it is possible. At least, it is possible in my case. For me it all became like a dream now; a very distant night dream. Actually, I do have dreams about Chechnya. Not about fights, though. Just daily life there: mud up to my knee; lice. I brought an undershirt from there. My buddies left their signatures on it. But I dropped it into mud, so it turned out that I brought home some Chechen soil' (see figure 8.2).[12]

Through distant dreams or soiled shirts, such displacement of the war memory helps to encapsulate traumatic experience. Bitter irony

8.2 From a series on Chechnya by Vladimir Bykov, the veteran photographer: 'The Dreaming Soldier,' Chechnya, 1996. Courtesy of the photographer.

makes it easier to keep a sane distance. It also provides some form of rationalization, as in this military joke told by a veteran:

– What does Article 0 of the Constitution say?
– Is there such an article at all?
– Yes, there is. It says that the officer must suffer![13]

Yet this forgetting and distancing – ironic or desperate – does very little to change the lives of veterans and victims after the war. Unwilling to frame the Chechen war in legal terms (as opposed to the politicized rhetoric), the state provided no recognizable juridical language through which survivors could frame their claims and complaints under existing law. The general impasse in defining the legal status of the war's participants and victims produced two main outcomes. First, the government's persistent unwillingness to address issues of financial and political responsibility for the consequences of the ongoing war was exacerbated by the courts' inclination to rationalize and institutionalize the situation of ambiguity even further. Second, the war's participants and refugees, suffering from physical and psychological injuries, reacted to the lack of any substantive support with bitterness and anger. Veterans in their reactions often expressed a clear recognition of their extreme alienation from the state along with a sense of profound dependency on the state's welfare policy.

When the Orel court dismissed – because of the 'unlocatability' of proof – 'any possibility for compensation of disabilities incurred by the combatants during their participation in military operations in the Chechen republic,'[14] frustrated veterans complained: 'We are actually being told that we should demand compensation from [the Chechen leaders] Maskhadov and Basaev. It appears that protecting the Motherland is just citizens' own private business [*chastnoe delo grazhdan*].'[15] In turn, human rights activists quickly pointed out that the Orel regional court had finally acknowledged a practice that had been pursued by the Ministry of Defence for years: claims for compensation filed by refugees affected by the war in Chechnya were consistently undermined by the ministry's demand for proof that the federal army had indeed caused harm. As one activist put it, 'It might take fifty years or so to make the state recognize its own responsibility. It was just the same with compensation for survivors of the Nazi camps.'[16]

Yet, as Uminskii's case demonstrates, the state's disengagement could not be limited to issues of material compensation. Also, such a withdrawal resulted in a serious crisis of recognition: without the ideological and legal support of the state, the soldier's military experience could easily mutate into an act of banditry. To put it differently, the state's retreat from performing a necessary symbolic work stripped its subjects of categories of perception and rituals of recognition that were used to legitimize the experience through which these subjects were constituted in the first place. What kinds of symbolic practices were available to veterans in this case? How did they communicate their experience to the broader audience – without established narrative scripts and reliable legal frameworks?

Veterans' dependence on public acknowledgment of their military past significantly determines the forms of their self-presentation. Recognition requires a dialogue, however limited it might be. Hence, practices and metaphors of exchange became crucial in veterans' attempts to evoke signs of social respect. Following Georg Simmel, I call this symbolic strategy 'exchange of sacrifices.'[17] Closely weaving together loss and gain, judgment and emotion, interaction and interconnection, exchange of sacrifices is a dialogical event through which distinctive values are simultaneously represented and recognized. Sheet metal, sacks of spaghetti, supplies of cookies, or cash enter this exchange, trying if not to balance, then at least to acknowledge, the value of soldiers' lives. Delineating a community of loss, the exchange of these sacrifices points to a seemingly shared cultural assumption about the universality of 'Article 0' of the Constitution: the officer must suffer.

Benefits of War

In my conversations with veterans, I was always surprised by their persistent reluctance to discuss the goals of the war in Chechnya: my questions were usually dismissed as irrelevant. At best, veterans would simply justify the status quo by saying that there must have been 'some reason.' Critical opinions were few, and in their attempts to frame relations with the state in terms of business exchange, veterans continued the same old strategy of depoliticizing the war that has been performed by the state for more than a decade.

In displacing these *whys*, however, the veterans of the Chechen war were not original. Samuel Hynes in his historical study of soldiers' narratives has traced the same tendency: soldiers of different wars and different generations have usually preferred to leave these *whys* in the shadow of their descriptions of combat experience. Regardless of the type and timing, war memories seem to follow the same plotline: with some predictable variations, the descriptions of mud, lice, cold, or heat radically overshadow the infrequent questioning of political rationales that determined these wars in the first place.[18] However, as Hynes insists, 'the soldier assumes – *must* assume – that if he did ask that question, if he were allowed to ask it, there would be a rational answer, that what he is doing and suffering makes sense to someone farther up in the chain of command.'[19] What happens, though, when no reasonable explanation can justify one's experience of horror?

When I asked Kirill P., a Chechen war veteran, to describe his perception of people's attitude to veterans, he told me about one incident. The Altai regional government issued free transportation passes for the veterans of the Chechen war. Using such a pass, Kirill once boarded a tram, where he was confronted by a female ticket officer. With a big magnifying lens, she closely examined Kirill's pass, deemed it fake, and demanded that Kirill leave the tram. The veteran refused, despite the officer's threat to call the police. As if dismissing the importance of the story, Kirill finished his description with a phrase: 'Those who know us, they realize very well that we have already paid our Motherland in full.' This instantaneous translation of a failed monetary transaction into a metaphor of exchange and sacrifice was the most characteristic feature of veterans' commentaries. Many sincerely believed that the state had not delivered its part of the deal. As one veteran put it, 'the state has not settled the account [with us].'

Ironically, by building their post-war narratives around descriptions of literal or metaphorical payments, veterans endowed the notions of money and debt with a strong moral connotation. The theme of compensation, benefits, privileges, and money emerged alongside the theme of patriotic duty. Sometimes both themes complemented each other, and economic benefits were presented as a logical sign of respect and recognition. Sometimes the two themes contradicted and undermined each other, construed as two totally incommensurable ways of acknowledging veterans' war past.[20] What seemed to be constant in both cases was the assumed understanding that the state was ultimately responsible not only for veterans' post-war economic dislocation but also for the crisis of their state-oriented identity. Complaining about the disengaged state, Nikolai F., a Chechen war veteran, framed this idea in the following way:

We realize what kind of policy it is. As if a puppy is thrown into a river, and if the puppy manages to get to the surface, it means that it is worthy of living; if not, so be it ... We do not like to see the state performing this sort of policy toward us ... If the state managed to turn us, civil people, young guys, into *boeviki*, well, not quite that, let's say, into warriors, into people who know how to fight, then the state should think hard about the way it can turn us back into civilians [see figure 8.3].

Veterans' attempts to attach a monetary value to their war experience to a large extent stems from a particular form of governmentality that the Russian state introduced in the beginning of the Chechen war. At the end of 1994, the Ministry of Defence doubled the base salary for contract officers and tripled the per diem allowances to servicemen deployed in Chechnya. As a result, a soldier's 'combat payments,' as they are usually called, could easily come up to one thousand dollars a month, roughly six times more than an average salary in the country at the time. Normally deployed for up to six months, servicemen often returned from Chechnya with a substantial amount of cash, at least in theory.[21]

Combat payments significantly modified veterans' assumptions about an exchange of sacrifices: the payments set a clear financial benchmark, a certain level of economic expectations below which veterans did not want to sink. Against the sign of personal financial success epitomized by combat payments, low-income jobs available in the Altai region were not even considered as the starting point of a potential career. Veterans dismissed them out of hand even as a temporary occupation. As Vitalii, one of my informants, explained, 'Yes, job banks have vacancies; they say there are seven thousand positions available today. But, excuse me, a guy who went through all that [war experience], he just would never even think about this job, this "occupation" for 600 rubles [$20] a month. He would never think about it. Because he knows his own price.'

The quick conversion of salary into personal worth is instructive. Sacrifice, to recall Simmel, 'is not only the condition of specific values, but the condition of value as such ... it is not only the price to be paid for particular established values, but the price through which alone values can be established.'[22] Hence, one's war experience, one's potential sacrifice of his life, was used as the ultimate measurement for other social relations. Interactions, in short, were construed as exchanges. But as in any exchange, this particular desire to gain something else in return for what has been given up brought with it a double-sided conflict. As Vitalii's comment demonstrates, the search for an appropriate equivalent to mediate between one's sacrifice and its external recogni-

8.3 ' ... if the puppy manages to get to the surface, it means that it is worthy of living': Russian soldiers with puppies in Chechnya, 1996. Vladimir Bykov, the photographer, called this photo *Puppies*. Courtesy of the photographer.

tion requires an ability to negotiate between different moral accounts. In other words, different 'regimes of value,' without which exchange would not be possible, are based on potentially conflicting expectations of this exchange; they also produce dissimilar interests associated with similar values.[23] For Vitalii and many other veterans, competing regimes of value did not represent different points of view about social exchange; rather, these differences were construed as attempts to justify *failed* exchanges – that is, to justify exchanges that devalued the high price originally paid by veterans.

The comment also demonstrates how military identity is resuscitated in the post-war situation: entitlement to a better salary is justified not by better professional skills but by one's experience of war. Significantly, in his attempt to convert the military past into a post-war value, Vitalii failed to find any stable or even positive representation. Heavily rooted in the operation of negation ('would *never even* think'), his rhetorical strategy indexes rather than describes the starting and final points of the argument. Neither the formative war experience ('who went through *all that*') nor one's own worthiness ('price') provided a positive explanation.

Such a discursive paralysis, such an untranslatability of the war experience often determined the veterans' tendency to self-enclosure: their social interactions were often limited to a narrow circle of those who needed no explanation of what 'all that' might have meant. Practically every conversation that I had with ex-soldiers would eventually evolve into a discussion about friendship ties and military bonds formed by the combat experience. Some of them framed it in terms of nostalgia. 'It is not a nostalgia for blood or death that hangs freely around there,' as Aleksei T., a veteran of the first Chechen war, emphasized. 'It is a nostalgia for relations, for situations when people would die for each other; where the collective was one perfect wholeness' (see figure 8.4).

The appeal to an idealized community tested by blood and death is a standard response to one's own dislocation. Studies of American soldiers who participated in the Iraq War similarly indicated that it was 'solidarity with one's comrades,' the bond of trust developed in the field, that motivated the soldiers most. The following quotation from an interview with an American soldier in Iraq could be easily paralleled by similar examples from interviews with Chechen war veterans: 'Everybody just did what we had to do. It was just looking out for one another. We weren't fighting for anybody else but ourselves. We weren't

8.4 '... the war collective was one perfect wholeness': a group of Russian soldiers in Chechnya. The tank hatch in the middle says 'Tanya I love you.' Chechnya, 1996. From a series on Chechnya by Vladimir Bykov. Courtesy of the photographer.

fighting for some higher-up who is somebody; we were just fighting for each other.'[24] It was exactly this bonding component that was missing from the post-war lives of Chechen war veterans.

The trope of combat brotherhood had an additional meaning in the history of Russia, too. Memorialization of the Second World War, which accelerated in the Soviet Union in the 1960s, capitalized on the symbolic possibilities that the notion of war-tested solidarity provided. Back then, in the wake of Khrushchev's Thaw, the melodramatic tone of war films and the intimate intonation of the so-called war lieutenants' prose helped to extricate the victory in the Second World War from the messy problem of the Stalinist legacy.[25] In post-Soviet Russia, the intimate discourse of military friendship helped again to move one's attention away from political aspects of the war, from the unimaginable and unjustifiable number of casualties and refugees, from (often) incompetent military leadership. Also, it was used as a justification for social withdrawal and self-isolation. War was construed as an emotional experience that radically set veterans apart, making their biographies almost incomprehensible to others.

Minding Their Own Business

Veterans often interpret their unsuccessful attempts to integrate themselves into the community of civilians as a consequence of a prejudice against them on the part of those who did not have the same (war) past.[26] The imposed or imagined experience of non-integration, in other words, was reframed as veterans' enforced marginalization. Admitting the zero-level opportunity available to them, in their discussions my informants referred to *bezyskhodnost'* (despair) – a feeling of being interminably captured, literally, 'a situation without exit' – as a main source of their own criminality. Deeply aware of their negative public image, very few veterans tried to defend crimes committed by their brothers in arms. But almost every ex-soldier I talked to was strongly compelled to explain the origin of this situation, as in this quotation from my interview with a veteran: 'We are told all the time: "Sorry we do not have any job vacancies." In fact, they just do not want to hire us. But for how long could a man wander about, with no job, with no money? ... He won't beg. He'd rather pick up a stem [*stvol*, a gun].'[27] References to their own special sensitivity and psychological imbalance were used by veterans if not to justify, then at least to downplay outbursts of violent behaviour.

In this context, veterans' solidarity rooted in the shared experience of war was perceived not only as a source of individual and group identity but also as an effective preventative tool. Nikolai F., a leader of the Union of Chechen War Veterans, which brings ex-soldiers together, passionately described the essence of this precautionary solidarity in an interview. As he put it, the main goal of the union 'is to bring everyone together and to prevent once and forever our guys from any further fighting. Because they still wage their wars here. Some are in criminal gangs, some by themselves. If we let it go in this direction ... many lives would have a very pitiful end. Even today many of our guys are behind prison bars, convicted of anything from armed robbery to murders. This is our tragedy.'

A combination of this military solidarity with a perceived (or experienced) rejection by the outside world resulted in a peculiar striving for self-enclosure. Used as a navigation tool in veterans' life after demobilization, war identity and war experience were projected onto business relations in the form of an idealized military fraternity. The solution to a permanent conflict between potential employers and ex-servicemen was found in the idea of a homogenized environment: a community of war veterans minding their own business. Within this business and symbolic context, the veterans' idea about enterprises for 'veterans only' seemed to be a plausible solution for an extended crisis.[28] I quote an excerpt from my conversation with two veterans, Vladimir V. and Grigorii B. Both were participants of the first Chechen war and are actively involved in the veteran movement in the region. Explaining the socio-economic reasoning behind organizing enterprises for veterans, they said:

> *Vladimir V.*: We are trying to raise the economic activity [of the veterans], and it would be desirable if the power structures [authorities] would help us in doing this, because it is much easier for veterans to work with other veterans. Look, an average chief manager of a factory would never hire a veteran because he is afraid of him. But I would hire him right away. And there is a simple reason for this. If a veteran is my employee, I could pull very different levers to punish him when he confuses which shore to swim to, so to speak ... I would have a moral right to reprimand him. Unlike this chief manager, who most likely is a civilian, with no army experience whatsoever, with no moral right to reprimand ...

> *Grigorii B.*: It is simple. Nobody knows us better than we ourselves. We

need only half a word to understand each other. And usually, we don't let each other down, that's our upbringing. And when we do let people down, it is not our fault. If we organize our own working environment, it could help us to avoid situations when a boss would kick a veteran around ... We are trying to pick guys in such a way that in the end there would be a single wholeness. It is not a secret that our brother takes things too close to his heart. If someone on a street gives him a wrong look, he would 'define' this person without saying a word.[29] And in principle, he has a moral right to this, even though it is wrong from a legal point of view.

These remarks reveal the clear impossibility of military economics to produce a necessary social effect. Creating a special working environment for young men cannot be justified by the logic of market competition. Instead, the possibility of social self-enclosure – the production of a special niche – was constructed through a discourse on morality. It was not the short-term effectiveness of veterans' professional skills that mattered; what counted instead was the long-term preventative social effect that the enclosed environment could deliver.

This image of an enclosed working community brings back utopian fantasies of self-sustained and self-policing phalansteries. Yet what is striking about this particular attempt to create a business environment through military bonds is the underlying belief in the incommensurability of military and civilian experiences. The scope of exchange of sacrifices between the two worlds becomes extremely limited here, producing two parallel domains of value circulation. Veterans' perception of their war experience implies a peculiar regime of non-coverage that could recognize once and for all the inconvertibility of the values around which their community was built.

As the relationship between the veterans' 'moral right' and the civilians' 'legal point of view' spelled out by Grigorii B. demonstrates, this dissimilarity of 'war-related' and 'civil' values was also a hierarchy. Perhaps even more important was the discursive gesture by which this contradiction deepened. The supremacy of illegal-yet-moral right was defended by references to one's performance of his civic duty. Military service was construed as superior to legal equality. What is crucial for understanding veterans' post-war identity is the fact that their appeals to (illegal) moral right had no content apart from patriotic experience. It was precisely the *origin* of this right that the formality of the law failed to recognize or purposefully ignored.

'What if there is a war tomorrow?'

The veterans' rhetoric of a post-combat economy, with their emphasis on completing the exchanges started between officers and the state, created a discursive position outside the potentially charged political framings of the Chechen war. Similar to the language of legality, analysed by Jean and John Comaroff the language of exchange indicated a point of entry into the field of interaction with the state by suggesting a (somewhat) non-confrontational way of articulating one's social claims and entitlements.[30] The limits of this war-as-a-business approach, however, became very clear when the state refused to recognize its debts to soldiers – that is, when soldiers' claims to being paid back were simply dismissed as irrelevant or inappropriate. Moreover, effective as it might be in settling financial disputes, the language of the post-combat economy failed to evoke signs of social respect, crucial in the post-Soviet situation where the personal and the economic tend to be tightly intertwined.

The social impasse produced by metaphors of war-as-a-business pushed veterans to activate a different symbolic strategy in which militarized economics was complemented or overshadowed by patriotic values. In the following quotation from my interview with Viktor Z., the financial persistently echoed and emphasized the patriotic. Our conversation was about the goal of the Chechen war. Without my prompting, Viktor immediately started talking about combat payments: 'Some people think it is all because of money. But the amount of money that we get there cannot justify the fighting … True, it is hard to survive without money. But you know there is a line that I often recall: "Not for bucks or rubles did our guys fall here, but in order to be able again to call you, Russia, the Great Rus' [*Rus' velikaia*]." Average conscripts like us, we all had in our subconscious that we were doing it really for Russia. But I have no idea what the big shots thought about this.'

It is important to see how the initial split, bucks versus death for the Great Rus', was amplified by yet another form of differentiation: average soldiers versus big shots. Eventually these two juxtapositions would be reassembled and reconnected in a different configuration: 'Big shots with bucks' would oppose the community of rank-and-file soldiers who 'have paid to the Motherland' with blood and life, as another Chechen war veteran put it. Exhibiting a tendency towards self-enclosure, this splitting once again justified social exclusions/ inclusions, this time on moral grounds.

Sometimes, this striving for a close (and closed) community of shared values and experience would take veterans in unexpected directions. In several discussions, I was told that it was prison – or rather, the *zona*, a prison camp – that Chechen war veterans saw as the ultimate moral antidote to the lack of public respect and recognition. It was exactly in this social milieu, as Vladimir V. put it, that 'veterans are appreciated accordingly.' 'It is a paradox, but somehow in the zones it is valued a lot that someone has defended his Motherland. Not in school, but in the zone! ... [in the zones] they managed to preserve the patriotism that the civilians almost completely lost. We should set this as our benchmark.'

In this implicit vindication of criminality through patriotism, the seemingly sudden juxtaposition of schools and prisons is jarring only at first. The two institutions, being perhaps the most vivid metonymies of the state, logically point to a third one that remained unmentioned: the army. The implied triangulation usefully outlines the closed circuit of a symbolic economy within which these institutions – along with prisoners of war – are involved and within which patriotism is actively promulgated. Respect for defenders of the motherland is associated with enclosed institutions of state power.

Significantly, attachment to one's country is construed here in terms of one's ability to endure traumatic hardship and the ordeals that this country offers. The hardship of the war experience not only becomes fundamentally formative and life defining but also untranslatable. In their interviews, songs, diaries, and memoirs, veterans again and again point to the profound absence of any symbolic equivalent that could render their experience meaningful for outsiders. For instance, recently published notes from a war journal kept by the soldier Aleksandr Zhembrovskii in Chechnya are preceded by the following epigraph: 'We found the most loyal friends here. People who have not been here, who never took a risk, would never understand us. Only mother, father, brother, and friend who went through Chechnya or Afghanistan, would understand us.'[31] The experience and memory of war are used as a symbolic shield and a last refuge from the outsiders. As an Afghan war veteran put it in a response to an interviewer, 'Just leave [the war] alone. It's ours!'[32]

This perception of an individual or group experience as incomprehensible to others – this adamant insistence on a hermeneutical enclosure of sorts – could be interpreted as yet another version of idealized collectivity. The sociosymbolic cartography of binaries (civil versus military, military versus education, education versus camps) helped to structure, classify, and homogenize the experience and representations of the Chechen war. This cartography isolated units (mother, brother, friend, big shot). It created connections among them. It rationalized social interactions (bucks, blood) or rediscovered forgotten continuities. It also shifted the discursive production from forms of exchange to notions of identity and recognition.

In the remark quoted earlier, the spontaneous juxtaposition of the patriotically inclined zones versus unpatriotic schools was not merely a rhetorical or structural opposition. Continuing a long-established tradition to appeal to the educational importance of the combat experience, local schools often ask Chechen war veterans to take part in various patriotic events. Traditionally, this participation amounts to veterans' public talks and informal conversations with students. What distinguished the veterans' union in that respect was a ramified system of so-called military-patriotic clubs that veterans started creating in Barnaul after the first Chechen war. The initial motivation for creating these clubs, as I was told by Kirill P., the leader of the 'patriotic division' of the Union of the veterans of the Chechen war, had to do with ex-soldiers' conscious attempt to 'pull kids from basements, to distract them from alcohol, drugs, and crime.' By and large, the ordering and normalizing effect of this education was associated with the incorporation of a militarized structure of conduct. All cadets, as the members of the clubs are called, are expected to memorize and recite on request the actual Rules of Army Conduct. All cadets know their respective place in the hierarchy, determined by a respective rank. They also participate in staged combats, sport competitions, and boot camps in the nearby Altai Mountains.

Fantasizing, the twenty-four-year-old Kirill also told me about his two biggest dreams. Getting his hands on enough Kalashnikovs was one of them. The veteran described how these guns could be arranged nicely on a special ladder-like stand, how an armed cadet would be put on guard next to it; how cadets would get busy with cleaning and assembling guns, each with a specially assigned number. Acting as an important sign of group belonging, the Kalashnikov was invested with some educational capacity as well. 'When they handle these weapons, they become more responsible: it *is* a gun after all! This way, they take themselves more seriously, too.'

Interested in understanding the specifics of the 'patriotic' part in the 'military-patriotic' name of clubs, I tried to get some explanations from Kirill. His initial answer was quite formal: 'The task is to love our

Motherland.' I pressed further, asking him to elaborate. 'The Mother-land, as I understand it, is about one's own home, mother, relatives. What if something happens? Who is going to defend us? If you are a real man, you could just pick up an automatic gun, and would go to protect.' The explanation quickly changed into a discussion about the legacy of the Chechen and Afghan wars. 'We are not trying to impress upon cadets any specific view about Afghanistan or Chechnya. We just teach them how not to be afraid of the situation that we are in … It is not easy. But who has an easy life today? And what if there is a war tomorrow?'

This structural dominance of the logic of siege is emblematic of the Chechen war veteran movement in general. The impact of the war experience on ex-soldiers is obvious. What is unexpected, however, is the shift in emphasis in the process of reclaiming this experience *after* the war. As mentioned earlier, the war past was rarely turned into a starting point for an anti-war or war-preventing activity in the present, as was common in official Soviet pro-peace propaganda. Instead, it was the idea of being ready for a possible war, the perception of the region in danger that brought people together and organized them in their post-war life. It was in the process of this shift, as the quotation indicates, that the task of loving the motherland was straightforwardly and unproblematically equated with the training of how not to be afraid of the current situation.

Conclusion

In this essay, I have tried to show that the absence of a recognizable and legitimate framework for representing the unpopular war created a particular discursive and identificatory crisis for ex-soldiers. In many cases, their demobilization also meant a lack of social status. Veterans responded to this crisis by presenting publicly their war experience in Chechnya as a particular form of business in which sacrifice and suf-fering should be compensated or, at least, recognized by the state. This discursive move bracketed off the questionable nature of the unpopu-lar war and the veterans' own role in it.

Simultaneously, as if mirroring the disengaged state, veterans dis-covered solutions to their problems in various forms of departure from the public sphere. As a result, regimented social and symbolic settings – phalansteries, boot camps, zones – were envisioned as emotionally charged places where exchanges were completed and sacrifices did not remain unnoticed. In a reversed form, these militarized metaphors and practices of enclosed but understanding military brotherhood provided striking illustrations of veterans' own notion of exitlessness: a lack of entry into the world of the civilians experienced by the veterans was transformed into fantasies of a militarized community of brothers in arms who walled themselves off from the outsiders.

NOTES

This chapter is drawn from research presented in my study *The Patriotism of Despair: Nation, War, and Loss in Russia* (Ithaca, NY: Cornell University Press 2009). It has been substantially reworked for inclusion in this volume, but I wish to thank Cornell University Press for its permission to reuse parts of my earlier work.

1 Richard Stacewicz, *Winter Soldiers: An Oral History of the Vietnam Veterans against the War* (New York: Twayne Publishers, 1995), 188–252.
2 Yaroslav Zorin, 'Veteranu Chechenskoi voiny posovetovali sudit'sia s Basaevym i Maskhadovym,' *Gazeta*, 12 January 2005.
3 Sergei Zhdakaev, 'Veteran chechenskoi voiny putaetsia vzuskat' uscherb s Basaeva i Maskhadova,' *Izvestia*, 13 January 2005; Valentina Ostroushko, 'Basaev gotov platit',' *Novye Izvestia*, 18 January 2005.
4 Dmitrii Smetanin, 'Neob'avlennaya voina,' *Severnyi Kavkaz*, 26 January 2005.
5 Zhdakaev, 'Veteran chechenskoi voiny putaetsia.'
6 Vladimir Mokhov, 'Realii. V sud vyzyvaetsia … Basaev,' *Krasnaya Zvezda*, 15 January 2005.
7 See a collection of materials in *Medved'* 14 (1996): 53–4; see also Vitalii Noskov, 'Liubite nas, poka my zhivy' (Novosibirsk: RIF-Novosibirsk, 2001).
8 In 2001 regular troops in Chechnya were replaced officially by professional divisions of the Ministry of the Interior. Chechnya was divided into eighteen temporary zones that have been policed on a rotating basis by professional officers brought from all over the country. See 'Otriad osobogo naznacheniia,' *Altaiskaia pravda*, 24 January 2001.
9 *Boevik* is routinely used in Russian in regard to Chechen rebels. Russian soldiers also use this word to describe themselves. The word has a common root with the word *boi* (combat) and is sometimes translated as 'fighter,' 'hit man,' or 'assassin.' Unlike a hit man or assassin, *boevik* also implies belonging to an organized group beyond state control or even opposed to the state. There is a certain similarity to the mafia, but the *boevik's* professional iden-

tity, unlike the mafioso's, is solely defined by the production of violence.

10 Namedni, 'Peredaite tem, kto poedet v Chechniu,' *Altaiskaia Pravda*, 31 January 2001.

11 Sergei Kochevnikov, 'Chechnia: byt, rabota, zhizn, smert',' *Svobodnyi kurs*, 4 May 2000, 16.

12 Konstantin Somov, 'Dmitrii Kappes: Boi po pravilam,' *Altaiskaia Pravda*, 28 April 2001.

13 Aleksandr Agalkov, 'Khozhdenie za tri goroda,' in *My byli na etikh voinakh*, ed. Ya. Gordin and V. Grigoriev (St Petersburg: Zvezda, 2003), 210.

14 Zorin, 'Veteranu Chechenskoi voiny.'

15 Zhdakaev, 'Veteran chechenskoi voiny putaetsia.'

16 Valentina Sunlianskaia, 'Otpravliat' postradavshikh v Chechne za kompensatsiei k Basaevu – obychnaia praktika v Rossii.' *IA REGNUM*. Electronic document, http://www.regnum.ru/news/389145.html (accessed 9 November 2009).

17 Georg Simmel, *The Philosophy of Money*, trans. T. Bottomore and D. Frisby (New York: Routledge, 1978).

18 Catherine Merridale, *Ivan's War: Life and Death in the Red Army, 1939–1945* (New York: Picador, 2006), traces these descriptions of daily life during the Second World War in her interviews with Russian veterans. For similar recollections of the participants of the Afghan and Chechen wars, see, respectively, Svetlana Alexievich, *Zinky Boys: Soviet Voices from a Forgotten War*, trans. J. and Robin Whitby (London: Chatto & Windus, 1992); and Valerii Gorban, 'Dnevnik ofitsera OMONa,' in *My byli na etikh voinakh*, ed. Gordin and Grigoriev.

19 Samuel Hynes, *The Soldiers' Tale: Bearing Witness to Modern War* (New York: Allen Lane, 1997), 12.

20 I.M. Dynin, *Posle Afganistana: 'Afgantsy' v pis'makh, dokumentakh, svidetel'stvakh ochevidtsev* (Moscow: Profizdat, 1990), 59–130, provides a set of examples suggesting that the trope of duty/debt became a central part of the public rhetoric in the late 1980s, after the Soviet withdrawal from Afghanistan.

21 See Aleksei Zakharov, 'Voennaya sluzhba: napravlen v Chechiu – poluchi kompensatsiiu,' *Parlamentskaia gazeta*, 20 September 2000; Julia Mikhailova, 'Snachala zabyli o mertvukh, teper' – o zhivykh,' *Izvestia*, 17 November 1995; 'Syn pogib v Chechne, a chto zhe gosudarstvo?' *Na strazhe Rodiny*, 9 September 1997.

22 Simmel, *Philosophy of Money*, 84–5.

23 See Arjun Appadurai, 'Introduction: Commodities and the Politics of Value,' in *The Social Life of Things: Commodities in Cultural Perspective*, ed.

Arjun Appadurai (Cambridge: Cambridge University Press, 1986), 57; David Graeber, *Toward an Anthropological Theory of Value: The False Coin of Our Dream* (New York: Palgrave, 2001), 30–3.

24 As quoted in Leonard Wong et al., *Why They Fight: Combat Motivation in the Iraq War* (Carlisle Barracks, PA: Strategic Studies Institute, U.S. Army War College, 2003), 12.

25 The term 'lieutenants' prose' is used to describe novels about the Great Patriotic War written by low-ranking officers with war experience. These attempts to look at the war from 'below' drastically contrasted with the official glorifying canon of the perception of the war. For a discussion, see Lev Gudkov, *Negativnaia identichnost,' Stat'i 1997–2002* (Moscow: NLO, 2004), 20–58.

26 For a similar attitude among South African ex-combatants, see Jacklyn Cock, '"Guards and Guns": Towards Privatized Militarism in Post-Apartheid South Africa,' *Journal of Southern African Studies* 31 (2005): 796–7.

27 After their demobilization, many ex-soldiers join various quasi-military institutions, private as well as public. Following the war in Afghanistan, mass culture also links veterans with late-Soviet and post-Soviet Mafia.

28 Cock, 'Guards and Guns,' indicates a similar trend in her study of South African ex-combatants: 87 per cent of interviewed ex-soldiers strongly believe that the government must establish a job creation program that would be aimed specifically at them.

29 The veteran used the verb *opredeliat'*, which usually means 'to define.' Here the verb is used in its less common meaning – 'to determine the limits,' 'to size up,' but also 'to confine.'

30 Jean Comaroff and John L. Comaroff, 'Reflections on Liberalism, Postculturalism, and ID-ology: Citizenship and Difference in South Africa,' *Social Identities* 9 (2003): 457.

31 Aleksandr Zhembrovsky, 'Iz boevogo zhurnala,' in *My byli na etikh voinakh*, ed. Gordin and Grigoriev, 235.

32 As quoted in Alexievich, *Zinky Boys*, 14. On the impossibility of the secondhand comprehension of war, see Hynes, *The Soldier's Tale*, 1–2; for an opposite view, see James Tatum, *The Mourner's Song: War and Remembrance from the Iliad to Vietnam* (Chicago: University of Chicago Press, 2004), ch. 6.

9 Identity and the Representation of War in Ancient Rome

JAMES T. CHLUP

In ancient Rome the historian's reputation rested on his ability to balance the narrative of events at Rome (*domi*) and those elsewhere (*militae*).[1] Of the latter wars were particularly worthy of narration. They necessitated the writing down of Roman history with a special focus on short but intense wars of Rome's early period in which she fought for survival against other Italian city states (ca 750–300 BCE); wars fought over several years or decades against rival nations as she established and expanded her empire; and civil wars.

While the omnipresence of war in Roman culture is readily acknowledged in the critical literature, war's *representation* has not yet been studied in a systematic way.[2] The study of war in Roman historical narrative, for instance, has hitherto been limited to the examination of history's narrative intricacies (such as speeches, battle descriptions, focalization). Most contemporary Classical scholarship glosses over the representational aspects of war, particularly over the attitudes towards war evinced from the author and his reader. In light of this explanatory insufficiency, this chapter aims to begin to move the critical discussion of Roman historical narrative forward. Its first part delineates the importance of war in Roman historical narrative. Two authors – Sallust and Livy – are used to demonstrate the persistence and utility of war as a historical subject. As the chief participants in the maturation of the genre in the first century BCE, they established the conventions for the representation of war in their exploration of Roman identity. That is, war played a role in the evolving discourse of Roman identity, on how the Romans perceived themselves, which almost always centred on their professed military potency. As the German classicist Karl-Joachim Hölkescamp writes, 'remembrance of things past – Roman style –

revolved around the great figures who invariably enhanced Roman power in a seemingly endless series of wars that the "nation in the toga" (Virgil *Aeneid* 1.282) underwent in the course of its history.'[3] The Romans defined themselves by their perceived moral excellence (*virtus*), and war provided the Roman elite with a platform to demonstrate their *virtus*. The consulship, the highest elected office of the Republic, was in effect a military position that required the leading of an army. To be perceived as an effective politician one had to demonstrate *virtus*, and the best way to do this was to run a successful military campaign. Roman historical narrative was written by and for the Roman elite in order to encourage exactly such activity.

The second part of this chapter explores the representation of war in two historical texts pertaining to the Jewish War (66–70 CE): Josephus's *Jewish War* written in the 70s to 80s CE) and the Arch of Titus (erected in the early 80s CE in Rome). Josephus initially fought as a Jewish soldier against the Romans but then worked and wrote to advance their cause. His work thus allows for both the Roman and the non-Roman perspective. As a former enemy combatant, Josephus affords the Romans external validation of the beliefs regarding their military potency and the identity that they derive from the war. Josephus's close (re)alignment with Roman thinking about war is brought into sharper focus when his work is considered alongside the Arch of Titus, a monument that commemorates the Roman victory in the Jewish War. The Jewish War is therefore unique in that it allows one to explore Roman warfare as both a historical and an architectural text, the consistent messages of which demonstrate a unity in how Romans and non-Romans thought about Rome as a nation defined by war, and her inevitable success therein.

Approaches to War in Roman Historical Narrative

In writing about war, Roman historians followed in the footsteps of the Greeks, who had long been fascinated with the subject. Thucydides's account of the wars between Athens and Sparta (431–404 BCE) was especially influential for all subsequent Greek and Roman historians writing on war.[4] Roman historians were eager to write about wars because it saved their narratives from being tedious outlines of political events – names of consuls, lists of laws passed, prodigies, unusual natural phenomena, notable criminal trials, famous Romans' obituaries, and so forth.[5]

Sallust's *Bellum Iugurthinum* (probably written in the 40s BCE) describes a regional war in North Africa in the late second century BCE against the Numidian regent Jugurtha.[6] Sallust's text can provide insight into how Roman historians thought about war. Of special interest in this regard is that his work shows how a single conflict could be – or *ought* to be – the subject of a Roman historical text. Sallust describes the war as 'long, sanguinary and of varying fortune.' He notes that it was 'the beginning of a struggle which threw everything, human and divine, into confusion, and rose to such a pitch of frenzy that civil discord ended in war and the devastation of Italy.'[7] Here Sallust incorporates into Roman historical writing a feature originally introduced by Thucydides: the magnification of the subject.[8] What initially appears to be a regional difficulty for the Romans is imagined to have serious political consequences. A war could cross from *militae* to *domi*. Wars are represented as connected and not as isolated events, one frequently leading directly into or serving as the cause of another. It is for this reason that understanding a war requires knowledge of events and wars before and after. This then makes a monograph that concentrates only on one war appear incomplete. It also complicates war's narration.[9] Sallust demonstrates this when at the end of the *Bellum Iugurthinum*, the Jugurthine War (111–105 BCE), he refers to difficulties in southern France, to which the Romans now direct their attention, but which Sallust does not narrate. The Jugurthine War thereby is reimagined by the historian as a prequel to another war, not as a conflict to be studied in its own right. The conflicts are connected through the presence of Marius, who brought the former war to a successful conclusion and in whom the Romans placed their hopes in the latter conflict. The historian and the reader are thus prompted to think even further ahead, aware of the eventual civil war when Marius and Sulla (a general who plays a supporting role in the final stages of the war) battle for control over Rome.[10]

At the time Sallust wrote the *Bellum Iugurthinum*, Rome had experienced a century of near-constant internecine fighting. This was a result of the Romans' moral decline, and Sallust believed that it was evident to his own generation. This decline was expressed in his concept of *metus hostilis* (fear of the enemy).[11] After the destruction of Carthage in 146 BCE the Romans had no enemy against whom to fight, or were prepared to fight, so they turned against themselves. By his narrative framing of events in this way, Sallust reveals how the Romans saw war as a positive cultural process, one which through its waging, preparation, or reflective analysis enabled them to exhibit their *virtus*.

If Sallust believes that war illustrates the positive aspects of Roman identity, then it might seem odd that in the *Bellum Iugurthinum* he narrates the beginning of the deviation from *virtus*. He may have felt he had to explain fully the problem before the solution could be understood, envisioning his successors writing the history of earlier periods (i.e., pre-146 BCE), revealing explicitly the ascendancy of Roman moral excellence through her military success. The Romans therefore would have a narrative that would facilitate engagement with their past *virtus*, and therefore arrest – or maybe even begin to reverse – the political depravity that he perceived as epidemic in the late first century BCE.

Narrating Rome's entire history in his *Ab Vrbe Condita* (From the foundation of the city, written from the 20s BCE to 10s CE), Livy works to reconnect the Romans with their glorious past so that his text reveals the emergence of Roman identity. Livy was not able to focus exclusively on one conflict at a time. Instead he moved between different theatres of war; sometimes the victory in one conflict was followed immediately by the commencement of the next war. He consistently demonstrates that the Romans of the early and middle Republic (the extant text ends in the 160s BCE) enjoy repeated military victories thanks to their steadfast determination to adhere to the positive aspects of their *virtus*. Livy also explores the consequences for those who deviate from or oppose the *virtus* (e.g., Coriolanus and Appius Claudius the Decemvir), postures which bring them crushing military defeat.[12]

Since Livy could not focus upon a single conflict as, for example, Caesar[13] does in his commentaries or as Sallust does in his monographs, it is not possible to define his history as easily in terms of war. However, he divided his 142 books (of which only thirty-five survive) into units of five or ten books, with a war or closely connected series of wars the focus of each unit. Books six to fifteen, for example, cover the Samnite Wars (343–290 BCE); books sixteen to twenty, the First Punic War (264–241 BCE); books twenty-one to thirty, the Second Punic War (218–201 BCE). War thus enables the historian to arrange, and his reader to navigate, the *long durée* of Roman history more easily. *Virtus* as a binding element of Roman identity serves as a ground for consistent positive portrayal of Romans. The Roman victory and the reiteration of the aspects of the Roman collective character that brought about that victory punctuate the narrative; they mark the end of one section and the beginning of the next.

By representing war, Livy can illustrate the specifics of Roman identity, particularly in his narration of the Second Punic (Hannibalic) War. This can be seen in the following passage in which Livy explains that

In a preface to just a section of my work I am allowed to declare that which most historians have made at the beginning of their entire work: I am going to provide an account of the most momentous war ever fought [*bellum maxime omnium memorabile quae unquam gesta sint*]. This is the war the Carthaginians, led by Hannibal, waged against the Roman people. For no other states or peoples that have come into conflict had greater resources than these two nations, nor had the combatants themselves ever been stronger or more powerful than they were at that time [*neque validiores opibus ullae inter se civitates gentesque contulerunt arma neque his ipsis tantum unquam virium aut roboris fuit*].[14]

Livy does not preface every war this way, which reveals his belief in the pre-eminence of the Hannibalic War. In the quoted passage, he argues that this conflict must be seen as two distinct wars, one fought by 'states' (*civitates*) and one fought by 'peoples' (*gentes*), reinforced by the compound verb *contulerunt*. Rome's darkest hour exemplifies that which made her the world's greatest nation. Yet even in defeat or its expectation, Rome's path to victory is assured. Responding to news of their defeat at the Battle of Cannae, for instance, the Romans immediately refocus their efforts on rebuilding their forces.[15] Reading about Romans on the verge of defeat, then rebuilding, and in due course winning the war through their collective *virtus* validates the Roman pride that Livy unashamedly proclaims in his preface.

Understanding why the enemy loses enhances an audience's appreciation of Roman victory. Livy therefore provides glimpses of the enemy's perspective, in this case the Carthaginian one, including instances where Carthaginians imagine the Romans as *hostes*.[16] This shift in perspective appears strongest in the description of the thoughts and actions of Hannibal, where the historian explores his antagonist's development as a military and political leader.[17] Hannibal's speeches to his troops early in the campaign, for example, demonstrate his intellectual ability in a way that encourages the reader to compare Hannibal favourably to the Romans against whom he fights. These enemy perspectives are dispersed sufficiently in order not to detract from the patriotic Roman narrative. It is also noteworthy that Livy was not concerned only with narrating war top-down, that is, with focusing on Hannibal's perspective. Livy frequently includes scenes that represent the experiences of soldiers, both Roman and non-Roman, such as the response of the Carthaginian soldiers to Hannibal's arrival, which allows Livy to represent a complex, multilayered picture of war.[18] Non-Roman perspectives always have implications for those of the Romans themselves, since the experiences of their opponents foreshadow success or the possibility of danger for Rome. Hannibal's successes and defeat, for instance, foreshadow Scipio Africanus's future – and possibly the future of Rome herself.[19]

Livy goes even further in blurring the boundary between Romans and Carthaginians. When the latter revisit the site of the Battle of Cannae, the historian observes that the battlefield was 'a shocking sight even to enemies [etiam hostibus spectandam stragem insistunt].'[20] That is, Carthaginians gazing upon the battlefield as victors elicit a similar response to Livy's (Roman) reader, which reveals that differences of nationality and time are bridged by the shared response to defeat.[21] Carthaginian unease at their victory implies that they are unworthy of it. If the Hannibalic War represents a battle for control over an identity centred on military victory, Cannae represents the Carthaginians about to lay claim to that identity, as if it were a spoil of war, but here they instead relinquish it. 'You know how to conquer, Hannibal; you do not know how to use victory,' Maharbal warns Hannibal immediately following Cannae.[22] The description of the Roman soldier who, having lost the use of his arms, assaults an enemy soldier by biting off his nose and ears, is a powerful symbol of the Roman reluctance to be portrayed as losers in war. The reader is encouraged to realign himself with the Romans inside the text, and by working through subsequent chapters in which the Romans quickly redoubled their war effort, he participates in, and therefore derives a (much time delayed) benefit from, the reaffirmation of Roman identity.

Roman and Jewish Identity in the Jewish War

In Josephus's *Jewish War* and the Arch of Titus, the Flavian imperial dynasty, which ruled the Roman Empire between 69 and 96 CE, manipulated Roman memory of the Jewish War, thereby encouraging Romans to infer that this was a final conflict that would confirm the permanence of Rome's identity as master of the civilized world. The construction of the Temple of Peace in the early 70s CE by Vespasian, the first Flavian emperor, suggests that war was now part of Rome's past since the Flavians had won the peace. In other words, the Flavian (re)definition of Roman identity required that the Flavians place themselves at the fulcrum where Rome's resplendent past of military potency was balanced by her glorious present and future peace.

Josephus's Jewish War[23]

In Josephus's Greek version of the *Jewish War* (written in the 70s and 80s CE), revised on the basis of the original Aramaic version, the author's primary audience was not Romans, but Jews, and he sought to explain to his readers why the Jews lost to the Romans.[24] Josephus follows the argument of Polybius, a Greek historian who witnessed the Roman conquest of Greece in the mid-first century BCE, and whose goal was to explain to the Greeks why the Romans deserved to rule the world.[25] Whereas Polybius understands that the Greeks would influence Roman identity, and that engagement with Roman identity would provide a platform on which Greek identity could be rediscovered (as would eventually occur in the Second Sophistic in the second century CE), Josephus does not envisage the same position of privilege for the Jewish intellectual elite, of whom he perceived himself to be a member.

Josephus in the *Jewish War* is clearly influenced by the way Sallust and Livy represent Roman identity through war. As a Jewish historian (or a Roman-Jewish historian), Josephus pushes or blurs boundaries of national identity, in order to avoid being labelled as a mere adherent to the conventions laid down by Sallust and Livy. By focusing on one war, for example, Josephus initially appears to follow Sallust. But Josephus's narrative is much longer than Sallust's. Josephus thoroughly explores the causes (*aitia*) of the war in the manner of Thucydides, devoting the first two books to dissecting the complex events in Palestine from Pompey's conquest in 63 BCE to the outbreak of the war in 66 CE. Josephus's writing can be seen as the next step in the evolution of history writing in the Graeco-Roman world, since he consciously calls attention to himself as a hybrid author, someone who combines aspects of Greek, Roman, and Jewish historical thinking. The Jewish aspect of his historical consciousness comes from his holistic point of view; he looks for the origins of the Jewish War not in an event that immediately caused its eruption, but rather sees the war as having its origins in the very beginning of the Roman-Jewish relationship. Josephus also magnifies the war as does Thucydides, Sallust, and Livy, asserting confidently his belief that 'the war of the Jews against the Romans was the greatest of our time; greater too, perhaps, than any recorded struggle between cities or nations [*poleis he ethnon*].'[26] While the magnification of war is a Thucydidean feature, Josephus is in this instance appropriating Thucydides through Livy: the phrase 'cities or nations' appears to be borrowed from Livy's 'states or peoples.' Josephus imagines that the war he narrates is the greatest, since the direct consequence of it is the destruction of Jerusalem, which is a defining element of Jewish identity. For Livy, the Hannibalic War heralds the permanent ascent of Roman over Punic identity, but not necessarily the destruction of Carthage. For Josephus, only one city (*polis*), either Jerusalem or Rome, will remain the capital of the world, and thus imprint (or restore) its identity on Palestine and the empire, and thereby either preserve or delete the identity of the Jewish race (*ethnon*).

Sallust's Jugurtha and Livy's Hannibal are initially described in positive terms in order to emphasize their worthiness as enemies of Rome. Their defeats reaffirm Roman military pride in the fact that such formidable enemies can be conquered. Josephus does not blur the boundaries between Romans and their enemies in the manner of Livy. He instead constructs barriers between Romans and their enemies through his exceptionally negative representation of the Zealots. Writing several centuries after the Roman victory over Hannibal, and with Carthage herself no longer in existence, Livy could blur boundaries between Romans and their enemy, the Carthaginians, without endangering Roman identity. In contrast, Josephus writes only one decade after the Jewish War and is possibly still sensitive to his past association with the Zealot cause. His erection of a clear barrier between Romans and Zealots reveals firmly his desire to be identified with the former in the present instead of with the latter in the past. We can therefore use Livy and Josephus to demonstrate the temporal aspect of the representation of identity through war in historical narrative, whereby the greater the temporal distance between the historian (and the reader) and the events, the more licence the historian has.

Josephus's contempt for the Zealots is noticeable by his use of several derogatory terms to describe them. For example, the term that occurs most often is *oi lestai* ('thieves'); the Penguin edition translation by G.A. Williamson frequently renders this as 'insurgents,' and very occasionally 'terrorists.'[27] Josephus invites side-by-side comparison between the Romans and Zealots, in which the magnanimous behaviour of the former compares very favourably to the violence instigated by the latter. Receiving the surrender of Gishala, for example, Titus, the second Flavian emperor, displays kindness towards the defeated citizens, while shortly afterwards the historian records the Zealots' infiltration of Jerusalem, where they eliminate those they perceive as a threat.[28] Josephus's assault appears strongest in his description of the effects of the prolonged privation in Jerusalem during the siege: whole families die, and the streets are lined with the dead.[29] Josephus mentions the sight and smell of the rotting corpses,[30] and characterizes it as so powerful that it hinders the advance of the Romans when they gain access to the city.[31] The ignominiousness of the rebels' failure is conveyed in the vivid account of the mother who eats her own child.[32] Whereas in Livy the threatened ascent of Carthaginian over Roman identity is abnegated by Carthaginian pity for the Romans, Josephus very effectively undermines Jewish identity near the beginning of his work by noting the sharp differences of opinion between different Jewish communities. This reinforces the historian's division of Jewish society into four groups, of which the Zealots are the political activist element of Jewish identity, but not, as they themselves insinuate, the religious element, which Josephus appears to ascribe to the Essenes, the authors of the Dead Sea Scrolls.[33]

Josephus is an extradiegetic narrator as he directs his criticism against the rebels through his narration of events *and* his own voice inside the text.[34] An example of the latter appears in his impassioned speech to the Zealots at Jerusalem:[35]

> Fortune, indeed, had from all quarters passed over to [the Romans], and G-d who went the round of nations, bringing to each in turn the rod of empire [*ten archen*], now rested over Italy. There was, in fact, an established law, as supreme among the strongest as among men, 'Yield to the stronger' and 'The mastery is for those most skilled in weapons.' That was why their forefathers, men who in soul and body, indeed and in resources as well, were by far their superiors, had acquiesced to the Romans – a thing intolerable to them, had they not known that G-d was on the Romans' side.[36]

This passage reflects Josephus's thoughts on the mutability of fortune (*tuche*), which finds its origins in Sallust. The historian argues that G-d is currently with the Romans, and therefore it is appropriate to yield to them, just as the Jews yielded to the Romans earlier.[37] Summarizing the entire Jewish history as contained in the Hebrew Bible, from Exodus to 2 Kings, which includes both victories over, and setbacks against, various enemies, Josephus provides a 'highly tendentious recounting of biblical history,'[38] warning the rebels of what will happen. Basing his argument on historical and religious realities, he undermines the religious authority to which the rebels hitherto laid claimed. The inability of the Zealots to understand Josephus's speech weakens their Jewish identity, which prepares them for defeat by Titus. That Roman victory means Jewish defeat should not be an unfamiliar concept to Josephus's audiences, since the Hebrew Bible itself appears to foreshadow Roman rule in Daniel's prophecy at 11:1–12:4.[39] Josephus expects both his listeners inside the text and his readers to make the connection.[40]

Given its role in Jewish identity, Josephus's description of post-destruction Jerusalem is an important passage: 'All of the rest of the wall encompassing the city was so completely levelled to the ground as to leave future visitors to the spot no ground for believing that it had ever been inhabited. Such was the end to which the stupidity of revolutionaries brought Jerusalem, that splendid city of worldwide reputation.' This passage seems unique in that it calls for the viewer and reader to understand the significance of a place by gazing upon an empty space.[41] 'Future visitors' could include Romans, Jews, and possibly others coming here to gaze at the place where Jerusalem once stood. The second sentence exonerates the Romans and assigns fault to the Zealots. The final clause magnifies the error of the latter, their stupidity (*anoias*) bringing down a famous (*lampra*) city. Josephus brings his argument full circle, that is, the greatest war ever fought has the greatest consequence: the destruction of a universal city (implied by the phrase 'splendid city of worldwide reputation'). Thus, Romans and Jews use the same topical focal point to experience a shared history that reinforces their respective identities as defined by the war they fought against each other: Romans as winners, Jews as losers. But Josephus focuses on Jewish defeat, making it appear self-imposed, since the destruction follows not an act of Roman conquest but Zealot error.

A reader of Josephus infers Roman victory in the *Jewish War* through the persistent affirmation of the positivist Roman world view constructed around the (exceptionally) favourable presentation of the Roman general Titus.[42] Josephus describes Titus's military and political potency in powerful terms: 'master of both war and the world [*kai tou polemou kai tes oikoumenes despoten*].'[43] Titus is portrayed as a divine agent when he raises his hands to the sky and calls upon the singular god (*to theon*) to witness that the difficulties in Jerusalem are not his doing.[44] Josephus represents Titus as praying to the Hebrew G-d, as whose agent he is consequently serving. The author foreshows this in the narrative of events at Gishala, where the inhabitants proclaim Titus their 'benefactor and liberator,'[45] and ask him to punish the Zealot 'insurgents.' Titus is thus cast as the protector of Jewish identity, an identity from which the Zealots are rhetorically excluded by the Jews themselves. Invited to negotiate by the rebel leaders, Titus's words reveal his magnanimity in the expectation of victory, while he simultaneously chastises the Jews for their errors,[46] and accuses them of using Roman benevolence (*philanthropia*) as a reason for rebelling against them.[47] Josephus creates a positive platform for Titus to make such a remark, and for the reading of the speech as a whole, when he prefaces Titus's words by noting the general's 'innate humanity' (*philanthropon*), and his desire to save the city. Josephus therefore works diligently to advance his positive representation of Titus.

Titus does not forget his responsibilities to his soldiers, despite their disregarding his orders not to sack the Temple. He has the names read out of soldiers who performed extraordinary deeds, praises them, and places golden crowns on their heads.[48] This passage is important given Josephus's (probably deliberate) omission of Titus's speech to his soldiers (*adlocutio*) before the final assault on the city, which presumably contained Titus's orders to spare the Temple. The soldiers' disregard of this order would reflect very badly on the general. Titus therefore rewards his army for what they have done (secured Roman victory) without explicitly condoning the way that they did it. Finally, Titus's sacrifice of thanksgiving is a public spectacle witnessed both by the Roman victors for whose benefit it is undertaken as well as by the Jewish survivors,[49] reminding the latter that they have just lost the participation in the rituals of the Temple. Titus therefore initiates the redefinition of Jerusalem as a Roman space in advance of the rebuilding of the city.[50]

Titus's later return to Jerusalem enables the historian to synchronize his negative presentation of the Zealots and his positive impression of Titus: 'The grievous desolation that met his eyes with the splendour of the city that was, and calling to mind the mighty structures in ruins now but once so beautiful, he was pained by the city's destruction ... [he] cursed and cursed again those who had instigated the revolt and caused this retribution to fall on the city: so clear did he make it that he would never have wished the terrible punishment that had been inflicted to serve as proof of his prowess.'[51] Titus's response is the one to be expected from a Jewish spectator, since he appears to understand what the city represents for Jewish identity. The general's sorrow at seeing the ruins of the city confirms his concern for the city and the lack of similar concern displayed by the Zealots. By recalling the former 'splendour of the city' and its 'mighty structures,' Titus, at this moment marking the termination both of the Jewish War and of the history of the Jews as defined by Jerusalem, is validated as the best person to preserve Jewish identity. In addition to the representation of this moment in Josephus's history, its memory is also preserved in the Arch of Titus.

The Arch of Titus

Ancient historical narrative is enhanced when read alongside the physical structures that defined the *urbs Roma*.[52] Several kinds of structures served to convey messages about Roman war: temples, memorial columns, and arches are the most common examples.[53] In the case of Josephus's *Jewish War*, his narrative acquires additional significance when read alongside the Arch of Titus, one of the monuments to the Roman conquest of Jerusalem.[54] Erected in the early 80s CE, when the conflict was still in current memory, and as a permanent structure, the Arch serves to keep the story of the war alive, particularly the Roman victory as its most important part of it.

The Arch was not a stand-alone monument; it was part of the ambitious Flavian (re)definition of Rome.[55] Viewed from the Palatine, the home of Rome's elite, it is framed by the Flavian Amphitheatre (see figure 9.1). Paid for by the spoils of the Jewish War, the Arch reaffirms Rome's identity as a nation continuously successful in warfare. The sounds emanating from the amphitheatre during games would have supplied an additional aural element to the Romans' experience of the Arch.

In the heart of Rome, several arches were erected to perpetuate significant Roman victories: the Arch of Augustus, which commemorated the victory over Cleopatra, and the Arch of Septimius Severus, which commemorated victory over the Parthians. The surfeit of victory monuments ensured that Romans (and visitors to the city) were continuously bombarded with images of Roman military potency. One can ruminate on the effect of these monuments on different groups. For those who would become soldiers, for instance, these monuments educated them in the belief that they were building upon Rome's past military successes. They were possibly encouraged to imagine the commemoration of their own victories in some future monument. A foreign visitor, on the other hand, had the inevitability of Roman victory powerfully impressed upon him, and if his nation existed outside Roman control he would come to the inevitable conclusion that resisting Rome was a futile exercise.

In a city where space was very limited, especially in the central area around the Palatine Hill, the placement of the Arch of Titus reveals

9.1 Arch of Titus (lower foreground) and Flavian Amphitheatre (background) viewed from the Palatine Hill. Photograph by author.

the Flavians' desire to stress the significance of the Jewish War as the definitive conflict in Roman history. Placed near the terminus of the traditional triumphal route, the triumph of Titus becomes the definitive triumph, imposing its message on all future victory processions that would pass by – or through – the Arch.[56] As Paul Spilsbury observes, 'Vespasian and his sons needed to convince the Roman people of the legitimacy of their claim to imperial power. The Jewish revolt provided them with some of the political capital they needed. By exaggerating the magnitude of the war they were able to highlight their own glorious victory.'[57] But to exaggerate the war's magnitude they needed to find a ready audience; the construction of the Arch near the Forum provided them with such an audience.

Appreciation of the Arch's formal features can be simplified by paying close attention to two of its elements: the inscription on the front and the reliefs contained on the inside as one walks through. The inscription (see figure 9.2) translates as: 'The Senate and People of Rome to the Divine Titus Vespasian Augustus, son of the Divine Vespasian.' This inscription connects the Arch to Titus and Vespasian, but it does not explain *why* it was built.[58] It draws the viewer closer in the search for elaboration. *Senatus populusque Romanus* is a stock phrase referring to the Republican era (pre-30 BCE), but it also links the Arch to that period since that was when Palestine was added to the empire (in 63 BCE, under Pompey). Thus, just as they did on their coinage, the Flavians retroactively claim *Iudea capta* (Judaea is conquered) and not *Iudea subiecta* (Judaea is suppressed).[59]

The Roman arch is an interactive monument: the viewer is meant to walk through it, reading the story on the inside. The relief on the left (see figure 9.3) displays the spoils of the Temple – menorah, trumpets, and a table – being carried. They possibly represent the Jewish God Himself, defeated by a (divine) Roman.[60] The relief on the right (see figure 9.4) displays the triumph of Titus.[61] The reliefs assign different identities to each cultural group. The Jews are the defeated and the spoils represent the consequences of their defeat; the Romans are the victors. The triumph indicates that the logical conclusion to a war involving Romans is the commemoration of their victory. The spoils represent Jerusalem and the triumph indicates Rome, and by shifting one's gaze from left to right, the viewer travels instantaneously from Jerusalem to Rome. The arch shifts the 'centre' from the former to the latter.[62] The viewer occupies the role of co-narrator, participating in the realignment of the world.

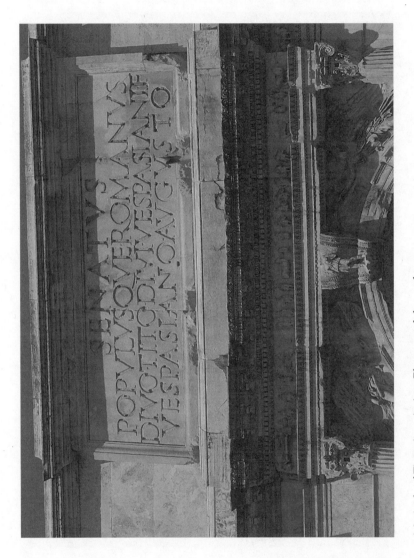

9.2 Arch of Titus, inscription. Photograph by author.

9.3 Arch of Titus, relief on the left: the carrying of the spoils of the Temple. Photograph by author.

9.4 Arch of Titus, relief on the right: triumph of Titus. Photograph by author.

While the Arch is a monument to Roman victory, it is not necessarily a monument to Jewish defeat, since it does not explicitly denigrate Jewish identity.[63] Jewish captives are not depicted being beheaded, as are Dacian fighters on Trajan's Column, for instance. In fact, the strongest representation of Roman domination appears on the Arch relief, where the River Jordan appears as a Roman prisoner or guest. The great victory in this war, therefore, is not over the Jews, but over Palestine herself. The absence of any clear submission of Jews to Romans allows the Arch to be interpreted as the continuation of Jewish identity through the representation of the Temple spoils. This provides a visual point of reference for the Jews of Rome and allows them direct access to elements of their religion that were once considerably more distant. In other words, either it helps Rome's Jews connect directly with their identity, or it facilitates the emergence of a new Jewish identity – one that exists in a Roman context. The Arch constitutes a (Roman) replacement for the Jerusalem Temple, enabling the Romans to bring the Jewish world into alignment with Rome. Being Jewish now means being Roman-Jewish, a process of cultural synthesis initiated through the Jewish War.[64] To recall a point made above, the placement of the Arch in the centre of Rome suggests its role in the construction of the new Flavian Rome, and therefore it also conveys the importance of the new Roman Jews in the Flavian Roman world order.

This Flavian position of incorporating Jewish identity rather than denigrating it in the Arch of Titus may explain a particular historical problem. Neither Vespasian nor Titus added the title *Iudaicus* to their name, a permanent identifier of their status as conquerors of the Jews. Vespasian and Titus could claim military victory over the Jews through the Arch and Josephus's *Jewish War*, but a silent vituperation of Jewish identity – which is what an ethic nomenclature such as *Iudaicus* was in part meant to convey – seemed to both men unnecessary and counterproductive.[65] In other words, these texts of the Jewish War were sufficient to define the conflict as one that demonstrated conclusively the primacy of Roman over Jewish identity and therefore the inevitability of the latter (re)defining itself within the context of the former. Moreover, as permanent entities, their messages would remain, while the deaths of Vespasian and Titus (the former died in 79, the latter very prematurely in 81 CE) would remove any message conveyed by the name *Iudaicus*. Without the Arch, Rome's Jews post-Titus would find themselves in an unenviable position of being without a positive mnemonic focal point with which to identify themselves.

Conclusion

The historical and architectural texts discussed in this chapter demonstrate the persistence of war in ancient Rome, and the importance of war representation to convey Roman national identity. Rome's historians and political leaders present a common front in defining Rome by her (perceived continuous) successful military action. Despite the vastness of geography and time, and the very large number of wars fought against a very diverse range of opponents, the identity that the Romans continued to draw from war remained constant. Josephus's narrative is of unique importance because it demonstrates that even a non-Roman writing for non-Romans comes to the same conclusion as a patriotic Roman historian such as Livy. That Romans and their (former) opponents arrive at the same conclusion constitutes a powerful validation of the Romans' identity and the world empire they constructed around it.

The prevalence of war in – and *as* – Roman historical narrative may be attributed to audience expectations. The readers of Sallust, Livy, and Josephus – Rome's intellectual elite in the first two centuries CE – preferred to read about war because it was their only remaining direct connection to Rome's past. With the exception of Trajan's Parthian campaign of 113–116 CE, the great Roman wars had already been fought and won; the infinite temporal and spatial boundaries of the Roman Empire as promised by Virgil's Jupiter (*Aeneid* 1.278–9) had been secured. Rome was at peace (for the most part), and the chance to lead a military campaign was confined to the emperor or members of his circle. Reading about war, therefore, enabled elite Romans to engage with and to participate in the continuing construction of Roman identity.

NOTES

1 E.g., Livy: *The Rise of Rome*, trans. T.J. Luce (Oxford: Oxford University Press, 1998), Preface §9: 'my wish is that each reader will pay the closest attention to the following: how men lived, what their moral principles were, under what leaders, and by what measures at home and abroad our empire was won and extended [*domi militaeque et partum et auctum imperium sit*].'

2 The recent volume *The Representation of War in Ancient Rome*, ed. Sheila Dil-

lon and Katherine Welch (Cambridge: Cambridge University Press, 2006), contains only one chapter on historical narrative: Jonathan P. Roth, 'Siege Narrative in Livy: Representation and Reality,' 49–67.

3 Karl-Joachim Hölkeskamp, 'History and Collective Memory in the Middle Republic,' in *A Companion to the Roman Republic*, ed. Nathan Rosenstein and Robert Morstein-Marx (Oxford: Wiley Blackwell Publishers, 2006), 480–1.

4 Tim Rood, 'The Development of the War Monograph,' in *A Companion to Greek and Roman Historiography*, ed. John Marincola (Oxford: Wiley Blackwell Publishers, 2007), 147–58.

5 See Christina S. Kraus, *Livy: Ab Vrbe Condita VI* (Cambridge: Cambridge University Press, 1994), 9–17.

6 See Christina S. Kraus and A.J. Woodman, *Latin Historians* (Oxford: Oxford University Press, 1997), 21–30 in the first instance; also Ronald Syme, *Sallust* (Berkeley: University of California Press, 1964), 138–77.

7 *Sallust*, trans. John C. Rolfe (Cambridge, MA: Harvard University Press Loeb Classical Library, 1971), 5.1–2.

8 See John Marincola, *Authority and Tradition in Ancient Historiography* (Cambridge: Cambridge University Press, 1997), 34–43.

9 David S. Levene, 'Sallust's *Jugurtha*: a historical fragment?,' *Journal of Roman Studies* 82 (1992): 53–70.

10 *Sallust* 114.1–4.

11 Boris Dunsch, 'Variationen des *metus-hostilis*-Gedankens bei Sallust (Cat. 10; Iug. 41; Hist. 1, fr. 11 und 12 M.)', *Grazer Beiträge* 25 (2006): 201–7, with additional bibliography.

12 *Livy: The Rise of Rome*, Coriolanus: 2.33–5; Appius Claudius: 3.44–9. Coriolanus led an army against Rome after going into exile. Appius Claudius refused to resign his special powers after the conclusion of his assignment, which was to establish a Roman legal code.

13 I have deliberated omitted this author – Caesar – due to the (very complicated) question of his presence in his text. See John Henderson, *Fighting for Rome* (Cambridge: Cambridge University Press, 1998) 37–69; Andrew M. Riggsby, *Caesar in Gaul and Rome: War in Words* (Austin: University of Texas Press, 2006); William W. Batstone and Cynthia Damon, *Caesar's Civil War* (Oxford: Oxford University Press, 2006).

14 *Livy: Hannibal's War*, trans. John Yardley (Oxford: Oxford University Press, 2006), 21.1. See P.G. Walsh, *Livy: Book XXI* (London: University Tutorial Press, 1973), 121.

15 *Livy: Hannibal's War*, 22.53–61.

16 E.g., ibid., 22.4, 22.16, 28.12.

17 James T. Chlup, '*Maior et clarior victoria*: Hannibal and Tarentum in Livy,' *Classical World* 103 (2009): 1–24.

18 *Livy: Hannibal's War*, 21.4. Philip Sabin, 'The Face of Roman Battle,' *Journal of Roman Studies* 90 (2000): 1–17, explores the soldiers' perspective.

19 Scipio and his family came under attack from political opponents (led by the famous Cato the Elder), accused, amongst other things, of accepting bribes from Antiochus of Syria. Andreola Rossi, 'Parallel Lives: Hannibal and Scipio in Livy's Third Decade,' *Transactions of the American Philological Association* 134 (2004): 359–81.

20 *Livy: Hannibal's War*, 22.51.

21 On internal and external audiences, see Jane D. Chaplin, *Livy's Exemplary History* (Oxford: Oxford University Press, 2000), 50–72.

22 *Livy: Hannibal's War*, 22.51.

23 The bibliography on Josephus is vast: see in the first instance Honora Chapman, 'Josephus,' in *The Cambridge Companion to the Roman Historians*, ed. Andrew Feldherr (Cambridge: Cambridge University Press, 2009), 319–31.

24 Josephus's (lost) Aramaic version was a very different text. See Tessa Rajak, *Josephus* (London: Duckworth Press, 1983), 175; and Gottfried Mader, *Josephus and the Politics of Historiography: Apologetic and Impression Management in the Bellum Judaicum* (Leiden: Brill Academic, 2000), 153n6. On Josephus's audience, see Steve Mason, 'Of Audience and Meaning: Reading Josephus' *Bellum Judaicum* in the Context of a Flavian Audience,' in *Josephus and Jewish History in Flavian Rome and Beyond*, ed. Joseph Sievers and Gaia Lembi (Leiden: Brill Academic, 2005), 71–100.

25 See Craig B. Champion, *Cultural Politics and Polybius's Histories* (Berkeley: University of California Press, 2004).

26 1.1. All translations (modified) are from G.A. Williamson, trans., *Josephus: The Jewish War* (London: Penguin Books, 1970).

27 Ibid., 4.138; 6.129.

28 Ibid., 4.104–207.

29 Ibid., 5.512–5.

30 Ibid., 6.1–3.

31 Ibid., 6.431.

32 Ibid., 6.201–13.

33 *Josephus: The Jewish War*, 2.119–61. See Geza Vermes and Martin Goodman, *The Essenes according to the Classical Sources* (Sheffield, UK: University of Sheffield Press, 1989); Jonathan Campbell, *Deciphering the Dead Sea Scrolls* (Oxford: Blackwell Publishers, 2002); Geza Vermes, *The Dead Sea Scrolls: Qumran in Perspective* (London: SCM Press, 1994).

34 On ancient historians' self-presentation, see John Marincola, *Authority and Tradition*, 205–16.

35 *Josephus: The Jewish War*, 5.361–420.

36 Ibid., 5.367–9.

37 Ibid., 5.376–419.

38 See Paul Spilsbury, 'Flavius Josephus on the Rise and Fall of the Roman Empire,' *Journal of Theological Studies* (2003): 10–15.

39 Esp. Daniel 11:30. The *kittim* (enemies of the Hebrew G-d) in the Hebrew text appears as *Romaioi* in the Septuagint and *Romani* in the Vulgate. That the Romans are *kittim* is suggested by other texts. See Shani Berrin, 'Pesher Nahum, Psalms of Solomon and Pompey,' in *Reworking the Bible: Apocryphal and Related Texts at Qumran*, ed. Esther G. Chazon, Devorah Dimat, and Ruth A. Clements (Leiden: Brill Academic, 2005), 65–84.

40 Steve Mason, 'Josephus, Daniel, and the Flavian House,' in *Josephus and the History of the Greco-Roman Period: Essays in Memory of Morton Smith*, ed. Fausto Parente and Joseph Sievers (Leiden: Brill Academic, 1994), 161–91; Spilsbury, 'Flavius Josephus,' 15–20.

41 *Josephus: The Jewish War*, 7.3–4. On Josephus and spectacle, see Honora Howell Chapman, 'What Josephus Sees: The Temple of Peace and the Jerusalem Temple as Spectacle in Text and Art,' *Phoenix* 63 (2009): 107–30.

42 Zwi Yavetz, 'Reflections on Titus and Josephus,' *Greek, Roman, and Byzantine Studies* 16 (1975): 411–32; B. Jones, 'The Reckless Titus,' in *Studies in Latin Literature and Roman History VI*, ed. Carl Deroux (Brussels: Latomus Publishers, 1992), 408–20; G.M. Paul, 'The Presentation of Titus in the *Jewish War* of Josephus: Two Aspects,' *Phoenix* 47 (1993): 56–66.

43 *Josephus: The Jewish War*, 5.88.

44 Ibid., 5.519.

45 Ibid., 4.113–114.

46 Ibid., 6.325–350.

47 Ibid., 6.333; cf. 344–7.

48 Ibid., 7.5; 13–15.

49 Ibid., 7.16.

50 Yaron Z. Eliav, *God's Mountain: The Temple Mount in Time, Place, and Memory* (Baltimore: Johns Hopkins University Press, 2005), 83–124, discusses the Roman Jerusalem that arose after 70 CE.

51 *Josephus: The Jewish War*, 7.112–13.

52 Livy, *Preface* §10: 'what especially makes the study of history wholesome and useful is this, that you behold the lessons of every kind of experience set forth as on a splendid memorial [*in inlustri … monumento*].' See John Moles, 'Livy's Preface,' *Proceedings of the Cambridge Philological Society* 39

(1993): 153–5; Mary Jaeger, *Livy's Written Rome* (Ann Arbor: University of Michigan Press, 1997), 1–18; T.P. Wiseman, 'Monuments and the Roman Annalists,' in *Past Perspectives: Studies in Greek and Roman Historical Writing,* ed. Ian S. Moxon et al. (Cambridge: Cambridge University Press, 1986), 87–100.

53 On arches, see Sandro De Maria, *Gli Archi Onorari di Roma e dell'Italia Romana* (Rome: L'Erma Publishers, 1988); Fred S. Kleiner, 'The Study of Roman Triumphal and Honorary Arches 50 Years after Kähler,' *Journal of Roman Archaeology* 2 (1989): 195–206.

54 See Fergus Millar, 'Last year in Jerusalem: Monuments of the Jewish War in Rome,' in *Flavius Josephus and Flavian Rome*, ed. John Edmondson, Steve Mason, and James B. Rives (Oxford: Oxford University Press, 2005), 101–28. Benjamin Issac, 'Roman Victory Displayed: Symbols, Allegories, Personifications?' in *The Sculptural Environment of the Roman Near East: Reflections on Culture, Ideology, and Power*, ed. Yaron Z. Eliav, Elise A. Friedland, and Sharon Herbert (Leuven: Peeters Publishers, 2008), 575–604, delineates the challenges of interpreting Roman victory monuments. See also Tonio Hölscher, 'Images of War in Greece and Rome: Between Military Practice, Public Memory, and Cultural Symbolism,' *Journal of Roman Studies* 93 (2003): 1–17, with additional bibliography.

55 Robin Darwall-Smith, *Emperors and Architecture: A Study of Flavian Rome* (Brussels: Latomus Publishers, 1996). On the Arch of Titus, see Michael Pfanner, *Der Titusbogen* (Mainz: Philipp von Zabern, 1983); R. Ross Holloway, 'Some Reflections on the Arch of Titus,' *Acta Classica* 56 (1987): 183–91; Fred S. Kleiner, 'The Arches of Vespasian in Rome,' *Mitteilungen des Deutschen Archäologischen Instituts* 97 (1990): 127–36.

56 On the Roman triumph, see Mary Beard, *The Roman Triumph* (Cambridge, MA: Harvard Belknap Press, 2007), esp. 143–86 on its representation.

57 Spilsbury, 'Flavius Josephus,' 3.

58 On the inscription, see Pfanner, *Der Titusbogen*, 15–16.

59 Harold Mattingly and Edward A. Sydenham, *The Roman Imperial Coinage Volume II: Vespasian to Hadrian* (London: Spink Publishers, 1968), 73–4, 127, 131, and Plate 2.29.

60 Pfanner, *Der Titusbogen*, 50–5 and 71–6. See Leon Yarden, *The Spoils of Jerusalem on the Arch of Titus: A Reinvestigation* (Stockholm: Swedish School at Rome, 1991), 29–32, on Titus's acquisition of the menorah. See Jodi Magness, 'The Arch of Titus and the Fate of the God of Israel,' *Journal of Jewish Studies* 59 (2008): 201–17, on the temple relics representing the Hebrew G-d.

61 Pfanner, *Der Titusbogen*, 44–50 and 65–71.

62 Isaac, 'Roman Victory Displayed,' 604: 'any Roman citizen who saw a coin or a large sculpture showing a scene would be looking at very familiar imagery and, even if only three figures were depicted, he or she would imagine the rest.'

63 I acknowledge that my argument in this paragraph offers a very different interpretation than most ancient and contemporary Jewish viewpoints on the Arch of Titus. But my basic argument in this section holds – that the Arch plays a role in (re)defining Judaism in(to) a Roman (con)text. In fact, the Arch played a role in Jewish identity in the twentieth century. The menorah on the Arch was taken for the symbol of the State of Israel; and on the day of the State's declaration, Rome's Jews are said to have gathered at the Arch and walked through it in reverse as a symbolic restoration of the Temple.

64 On Rome's Jews, see David Noy, *Foreigners at Rome* (Cardiff: Classical Press of Wales, 2000), 255–67, with additional bibliography.

65 Barbara Levick, *Vespasian* (London: Routledge Publishers, 1999), 71; Fred S. Kleiner, 'The Arches of Vespasian in Rome,' *Mitteilungen des Deutschen Archaeologischen Instituts* 97 (1990): 127.

Aftermaths

The redrawing of state borders, the dissolution of empires, and the emergence of new states; the decline of some political and social groups and the rise of others; the depopulation of whole regions and economic collapse; the adjustment of legal systems and attempts at international cooperation in preventing future wars – these are only a few of war's many aftermaths. Historians, political scientists, philosophers, sociologists, psychologists, environmentalists, and scholars representing a number of other academic fields have written thousands of volumes on the dramatic changes wars bring to geopolitical and political arrangements as well as to different countries' ideological, legal, demographic, social, moral, and environmental orders. All of these are intricately related to culture and the works of art that, ideally, come to be understood by their creators as humanity's last hope in the face of the social and spiritual upheavals war brings.

Since this collection's goal is to demonstrate that in theorizing war representations a crucial contribution is made by disciplines such as historiography, literature and film studies, art history, and, more generally, by interdisciplinary research conducted within the framework of cultural studies, the last section of the present collection focuses specifically on examinations of war's cultural aftermaths. Although almost all chapters in this collection are in one way or another concerned with war's impact on culture (and with war's embeddedness in culture), the three essays grouped in this section expressly explore the complex relations between war and art forms that either appear in response to military conflict or else become exploited by politically or commercially minded groups.

In her essay 'The Battle of Stalingrad in Soviet Films' (chapter 10), Elena Baraban examines how one of the most decisive battles in the Second World War was represented in Soviet feature films. Baraban explores the formation of the Soviet Stalingrad myth of the Red Army's heroic self-sacrifice, valour, and endurance, which, having first appeared in wartime propaganda, was further reinforced in films of the four post-war decades. Exploited as a topic of great ideological import, the Battle of Stalingrad was used by the Soviet party-state to promote various political agendas, including the symbolic appropriation of victory in the war by the country's Communist leadership, Cold War criticisms of the United States and Great Britain, and the promotion of nationalist ideas about Soviet moral superiority in comparison to the West. At the same time, Baraban demonstrates the historicity of war memory not only by tracing political uses of representations of the Second World War in Russia but also by examining the ways in which these representations of the war were able to address some of the Russians' individual and collective emotional needs when commemorating it. This ability of war representations to fulfil the social and ethical function of making sense of the war-ravaged world explains why fragments of the Soviet Stalingrad mythology remain popular even today, twenty years after the dissolution of the totalitarian state and its state-controlled art.

Related to Baraban's investigation of a national imagining of war is David Lubin's essay 'Monsters in America: The First World War and the Cultural Production of Horror,' which examines the impact of war representations on the American nation during and after the First World War. Through his analysis of wartime propaganda posters, post-war lithographs, literature of the Lost Generation, and horror films, Lubin uncovers how war shapes narrative story elements and creates a specific narrative gaze, inextricably linked to the trope of the 'monster.' The latter encapsulates the experience of this war for those who had never experienced it first-hand. Lubin argues that images of 'monsters' captured the war's horrors mimetically or symbolically in four overlapping phases: *anticipation, projection, alienation,* and *commercialization*. 'Monsters,' he concludes, evolved in the American popular imagination from manifestations of anxiety about war's horrors, to projections of moral outrage at a brutal enemy, and finally into symbols of alienation later commercially exploited by Hollywood.

Baraban and Lubin both demonstrate the significance of historicizing the processes of imagining war in different art forms. They thereby emphasize the need to compare representations of war created during the time of a particular military conflict with those emerging in war's aftermath. Their essays also demonstrate the potential of a comparative analysis to advance discussions of how the same military events come to be represented differently by 'the victors and the vanquished.' At the same time, via its analysis of mass culture's many capitalizations on war experiences in America, Lubin's work relates to the last chapter in this section, that by the art historian Simon Baker. In his essay '"Ruins: The Ruin of Ruins" – Photography in the "Red Zone" and the Aftermath of the Great War,' Baker examines a series of photographs from devastated areas of post-war France to demonstrate how these images expressed the sensibilities typical of European modernism, a new aesthetic language that was greatly influenced by the First World War.

The photographs of the ruined city of Reims by the architect Pierre Antony-Thouret form the centrepiece of Baker's broadly associative meditation on the aesthetic and psychological dimensions of sacred spaces hollowed out by war. Baker's analysis is informed by H.P. Lovecraft's and Sigmund Freud's views of the nature and functioning of the uncanny. Through his analysis of the images of Reims' ruins, Baker uncovers aspects of psychological ruination (alienation, trauma) that hit individuals and communities harder than places. Physical devastation captured by these images becomes a powerful metaphor for war. Moreover, as Baker's analysis demonstrates, it in fact serves to inspire novel and psychologically intricate forms of creative production.

An analytical concern shared by all three chapters of this section involves the relationship between artworks in different media capable of expressing individual and collective psychological traumas of war. These works can serve to domesticate the uncanny and reify the traumatic through their reiteration and commercialization of once-powerful images. At the same time, however, they can also stimulate diverse and artistically subtle explorations of the human psyche in the aftermath of war, allowing for expressions of pain sometimes capable of transforming individuals and societies alike. The research presented here demonstrates that, regardless of how traumatized societies remember war, war creates a decisive turning point in culture. The juxtaposition of the three contributions that make up this section reveals how war can disrupt familiar cultural and aesthetic categories, and how in its wake artists begin looking for new ways of adequately accounting for its aftermaths. This section's essays also show how art, unconstrained by temporal, spatial, and national (as well as nationalistic) boundaries, can become a rich resource for individuals attempting post-war reconciliation with the world. As they appear here, the essays by Baraban,

Lubin, and Baker also assist in sharpening perceptions of what happens when conventional art forms fall victim to the ideological dictates of the state, a co-optation which can destroy (or severely reduce) the possibility of deepening our understanding of human nature in the aftermath of war. In their consideration of the psychological, political, and social underpinnings of specific narrative techniques and images, all three contributions gesture towards the concerns that have also inspired other parts of this project. In particular, there is an interplay of ideas between this section's essays and those of the volume's other essays that are preoccupied with gaps and omissions, the repressed and suppressed, as well as with images resulting from one's struggle for words, and with words, that mask confusion and inarticulacy.

10 The Battle of Stalingrad in Soviet Films

ELENA V. BARABAN

Commemorating the Battle of Stalingrad

The Battle of Stalingrad claimed the lives of more than one million people. In September–October 1942 a newly arrived Soviet private had little chance of living longer than twenty-four hours on the battlefield. In January 1943 German soldiers died by the hundreds every hour. The scope of events, their military, political, and ideological significance as well as their emotional intensity – the struggle of the Russians to achieve the unthinkable in the first part of the battle and the struggle of the Germans 'to cope with the unthinkable'[1] in its second part – account for the unending flow of stories about Stalingrad. Turned into a symbol of the Second World War,[2] Stalingrad has inspired thousands of memoirs, scholarly studies, and popular narratives.

During the first part of the battle – from 17 July to 19 November 1942 – the Soviet Union was on the brink of catastrophe. Surrender at Stalingrad would have sliced the country into two parts, with Caspian oil in Hitler's hands, Moscow under a renewed attack, and Japan primed to invade the Far East. The ferocious fighting inside the Don Bend and then between the Don River and the Volga in July and August resulted in the retreat of Soviet troops to the city. On 23–4 August alone German air raids killed forty thousand civilians and pulverized about 90 per cent of Stalingrad's buildings. By 13 September the Sixty-second Army was isolated on the right bank of the Volga River from the rest of the Russian forces and had to defend a narrow band of the riverbank until 18 November, with the struggle raging for each pile of rubble and the front line sometimes drawn between floors of the same building. With 90 per cent of the city in German hands, the Soviet defeat seemed imminent. Yet even at the time when the Volga was about to succumb to ice and resupplies for the city's defenders had stopped,[3] Stalingrad held on.[4] The second part of the battle, from the start of the Soviet offensive on 19 November 1942 to the final surrender of the Sixth Army on 2 February 1943, turned into a nightmare for the encircled German troops. For the Soviet Union, the victory at Stalingrad meant a turning point in the war and aroused a genuine feeling of national pride. For the Germans, in turn, the dramatic reversal of their fortunes on the Volga signified the 'most traumatic event of the war,' 'a mind-paralyzing calamity to a nation that believed it was the master race.'[5]

The density and scale of events complicates the task of telling a story about this battle. A particular narrative's perspective depends on the author's position vis-à-vis the narrated events, such as the narrative's ideological stance, purpose, and audience as well as many other factors. Additionally, as even a cursory look at various representations of Stalingrad demonstrates, all of the above factors and, consequently, a resulting narrative are conditioned by 'collective memory'[6] about the war, a culturally specific tradition of its commemoration. In consideration of such cultural construction of memory about the war, it is worthwhile to raise the question why, for instance, both many Soviet and most German popular narratives about Stalingrad focus on the *second* part of the battle.

On the German side, post-war memoirs, novels, and films about Stalingrad markedly avoid panoramic depictions[7] of the battle and focus instead on the experience of individual German officers and soldiers, with particular attention to the second part of the fateful siege. Such narratives, one may speculate, fit the paradigm of representing the German wartime suffering, a strategy that creates a counterpoint to narratives of German guilt, with both kinds of stories constituting the so-called working through the war traumas. While offering gripping scenes of the forsaken army's agony or of the subsequent suffering of German prisoners of war,[8] such accounts of the battle avoid discussing what brought their protagonists to the bank of the Volga River[9] in the first place, thus eschewing depictions that would implicate the German Army in war crimes against both the Slavic and non-Slavic populations of the Soviet Union. Created from the point of view of the vanquished, such representations also silence the German exuberance about a close-at-hand victory on the Volga in July–October 1942[10] and instead depict the Sixth Army in November 1942–January 1943 as victims of the ruthless Bolsheviks, the treacherous Nazi command, or the harsh Russian winter.[11]

By contrast, the emphasis of Soviet narratives on the second part of the battle forms part of the Soviet heroic discourse of the war, which even today is used by Russians as a point of reference in the process of re-evaluating the Soviet past.[12] As Helena Goscilo writes in this volume, 'officially and personally,' Russians 'bond in viewing the Second World War as the single unadulterated moment of heroic self-sacrifice in their history.'[13] By sidestepping depictions of the Red Army's retreat to the shores of the Volga, Soviet narratives about Stalingrad commonly preclude questions of why, despite the authorities' pre-war declarations regarding the country's military might, most of the European part of the Soviet Union was quickly surrendered in 1941, and why the country suffered so many casualties. Nor do these narratives ever make clear that Soviet losses at Stalingrad exceeded those by Axis powers; that Red Army soldiers, often ill-equipped in the first months of the battle and lacking necessary training, went through unprecedented trials; and that Stalingrad civilians suffered immensely.[14] An examination of such highlights and lacunae in Soviet representations of the battle can shed light on the process of constructing the Soviet Stalingrad myth as well as on the overall formation of collective memory about the war. Such memory may be understood as a cultural resource available for individuals and groups of people trying to cope with various psychological, social, economic, or political aftermaths of the war. Conceptualized as decisive for the war's outcome already in the summer 1942, the Battle of Stalingrad had a tremendous impact on shaping personal and collective memories about the war. The victory at Stalingrad was widely used by Soviet authorities to boost the population's morale and to improve the country's international reputation. In addition, this victory and its official uses for propaganda purposes accelerated the process of individual acceptance of the state-promoted rhetoric of Soviet wartime valour.[15]

Drawing on the idea of memory's historicity,[16] this chapter examines Soviet feature films about the Battle of Stalingrad as contributing to the Russians' Stalingrad mythology and, more generally, the discourse of wartime heroic self-sacrifice. With its audience counting millions of viewers, film became a very important site for the construction of memory about the war,[17] for generating 'a pool of ideas' and providing 'cognitive and rhetorical frameworks for interpreting the past' by individuals and groups of people.[18] Following the victory at Stalingrad, during a film-makers' conference in July 1943, which decided the aesthetics of Soviet war films for years to come, the Chair of the Cinematography Committee Ivan Bol'shakov expressed a feeling of pride for the nation that during the Great Patriotic War[19] had accomplished the unthinkable and thus decided 'the fate of the mankind.' He called on Soviet film-makers to create artworks that would be worthy of such a nation and its people's 'heroic struggle for the honour and independence' of the Soviet Motherland.[20]

Bol'shakov's emphasis on collective experience, on the Soviet citizens' 'greatness,' 'spiritual beauty and nobleness,' their 'limitless love and devotion' to the Soviet Motherland and the Bolshevik Party,[21] as well as on the global significance of the Soviet war effort suggests purposeful construction of the audience's historical consciousness in the tradition of Stalinist nationalism. However, even when the triumphalism of Stalin-era interpretations of the Great Patriotic War was questioned during and after the de-Stalinization of the 1950s and 1960s, the idea of Russians' self-sacrificial heroism during the war still remained popular and was reiterated time and again in Soviet artworks. Instead of interpreting the durability of the Soviet discourse about the war in terms of the party-state's manipulation of individual and group responses to the war through essentially bad art,[22] this chapter will take a closer look at the political, social, and psychological contexts that shaped and sustained this discourse throughout the years.

This study is inspired by recent scholarship that has uncovered attempts by survivors of the war and their children to make personal use of state narratives in order to cope with their own or their family's painful memories of the conflict, and so as to find meaning in wartime tragedy.[23] In light of this scholarship, Soviet war films may be viewed as collectively produced narratives that, albeit closely monitored by the party-state, were nonetheless markedly subjective on each level of their production and reception. Film, as an art form, translates for millions of viewers confusing and contradictory individual and collective experiences of the war into a coherent story. Even if it does not accommodate one's personal war experience, it still provides illusions of familiarity and plausibility of the depicted events that are indispensable in the process of making sense of the war. It is beside the point to accuse a particular film of misrepresenting reality.[24] In the famous dictum by Walt Whitman, 'the real war will never get in the books.' For combatants or witnesses who saw only fragments of the whole or followed the events on the battlefield from a distance, any war narrative would be inaccurate. Film does 'violence' to war's 'raw experience' already when it 'restores' a more or less comprehensible picture of the events, let alone when it becomes part of a Soviet practice of imposing a 'proper' look at the past. Also important is the fact that film suggests the language for describing war experience, including that of the dead and the traumatized, inarticulate, or even semi-literate combatants whose 'actual' perceptions of the war could not be accessed or, in case of those suffering from post-traumatic war disorder, could be (mis)interpreted only by psychologists. Film also helps those whose relatives and friends never returned from the war to come to terms with their personal loss if only by means of creating an illusion of knowing what might have happened to their family members and possibly an explanation of why they died. Film thus contributes to war signification regardless of how accurate or complete it may be. In highlighting and in simultaneously bracketing out some facets of the war experience, film responds to and at the same time produces certain emotional needs in its audience. A film's emotional register can prevent the viewer from identifying with the main characters while at the same time making it possible to imagine being in combat. Alternatively, a film may invite the viewer to experience the battle in tragic terms and identify with the protagonists; or else it may evoke feelings of proud belonging to a collective, or, vice versa, of being marginalized by one's social group. Given Russia's catastrophic experience of the Second World War, the emotional complexity of its artworks about this war must be examined in no less detail than these works' ideology, since they constitute society's continuous attempts to make sense of the war, to address its wartime and post-war traumas.

Besides several documentaries,[25] between 1943 and 1989 Soviet film studios produced seven feature films about Stalingrad: 1) *Dni i nochi* (*Days and Nights*, 1945) directed by Alexander Stolper; 2) *Velikii perelom* (*The Great Turning Point*, 1945) by Fridrikh Ermler; 3) *Stalingradskaia bitva* (*The Battle of Stalingrad*, 1949) by Vladimir Petrov; 4) *Soldaty* (*Soldiers*, 1956). by Alexander Ivanov; 5) *Vozmezdie* (*The Retribution*, 1967) by Alexander Stolper[26]; 6) *Goriachii sneg* (*The Burning Snow*, 1972) by Gavriil Egiazarov; and 7) *Stalingrad* (1989) by Yuri Ozerov. Each of these films can be located within a particular period of Soviet political history: Stalinism, the Cold War, the de-Stalinization of the 1950s and 1960s, a return to more conservative politics in the 1970s, and, finally, liberalization of the Soviet society during perestroika. These changes in politics required a number of narrative adjustments in each subsequent film about Stalingrad but did not destroy the overall approach to representing the battle in terms of Soviet heroic self-sacrifice and stoicism.

What follows examines how each of the above-mentioned films relates to Stalingrad mythology, what aspects of the battle are depicted, in what way valour is personified, what elements of the proposed depiction remained unchanged throughout the years, and what was renegotiated or added in comparison with the previous versions of the events.

A Need for a Stalingrad Myth

The creators of the first feature film about Stalingrad were under special pressure to produce an emotionally moving and, at the same time, ideologically 'correct' account of the battle. Based on the 1944 novel of the same title and the script by the writer and war correspondent Konstantin Simonov, Stolper's *Days and Nights* is a cinematic diary; it follows Captain Saburov's battalion for two months as it defends a narrow stretch of Stalingrad's ruins. The film depicts the soldiers' daily routine, their camaraderie, and a romance between Captain Saburov and the nurse Ania.

The film was a failure. During the discussion of the filmed material by the Film Studios Artistic Council renowned directors such as Vsevolod Pudovkin and Ivan Pyriev criticized its excessively theatrical positioning of a machine gun, unrealistically clean uniforms and helmets that bore no traces of the enemy's bullets, and also poorly shot scenes of destruction with the demolished buildings looking 'too theatrical,' 'too pleasant.'[27] Excessive frontal lighting contributed to depicting Stalingrad as unbelievably quiet, destroying 'the atmosphere of combat' that, in combination with the actor Soloviev's unjustifiably low-key performance as Captain Saburov, 'cooled' the viewer's perception and made the audience follow the events at Stalingrad with detachment.[28] Even after the changes, the film was criticized for its weak dramaturgy,[29] its static images and characters, as well as the lack of chemistry between Saburov and Ania.[30]

Notably, in the discussion of *Days and Nights* the aestheticization of war scenes was considered a flaw precisely because it interfered with portraying the heroism of Stalingrad's defenders. Those who criticized the film, however, disagreed about what was meant by 'heroic struggle' and about the details that could best convey soldiers' valour. For Pyriev, who fought in the First World War, the film's depiction of combat was impossibly easy: 'Here people walk freely, without helmets, as if they were taking a stroll. They begin their attack having taken only one machine gun and one grenade. Maybe it is humiliating to show our people crawling but they did crawl!'[31] Inherent in Pyriev's critique is the belief that by introducing more verisimilitude into combat scenes, Stolper would better succeed in promoting the idea that only true heroes could face the challenge of fighting at Stalingrad. Other members of the Artistic Council, however, argued that Simonov failed to represent Stalingrad's heroic struggle because he had doggedly followed the events on the Volga without reconceptualizing them sufficiently artistically. The composer Tikhon Khrennikov, for instance, called the filmed material 'mediocre' and complained that the film that 'was to spearhead our understanding about … Stalingrad' had failed 'to move' anyone. Moreover, while perhaps offering the 'the truth of a photo,' the film had nothing to do with art. In Khrennikov's words, 'the understanding of Stalingrad by people who hadn't been in combat' was 'more interesting' than the one shown in the film whose script had been written by a witness of the events.[32]

The point that is of special interest here is that a witness's account might be considered as having *little* representational value for people (Khrennikov clearly believed he spoke on behalf of the millions of Soviet viewers) who expect a depiction suited to their preconceptions of what the Battle of Stalingrad must have been like. At stake here is the *correct* portrayal of the battle, with correctness understood not as accuracy but as an emotionally and politically befitting way of representing grand military events. Offering little suspense and very few elements of adventure or action, *Days and Nights* provided an unacceptably tepid depiction of the war's decisive battle.

In response to such criticisms, Simonov said that his 'laconic' and 'austere' representation of the war was truthful, that a sense of the narrative's 'dry' factuality and the impression of 'the quiet' Stalingrad as well as Soloviev's detached performance of Captain Saburov even in the scenes when Saburov's comrades die one after another were all *intended*.[33] Nonetheless, the verdict of the Artistic Council was that although the film was ideologically acceptable (and, therefore, could be released), it offered 'nothing new in the art of cinematography' and was 'saved' only 'by its topic.'[34] The film's ideological acceptability did not mean, of course, that it was ideologically (or otherwise) successful. The Artistic Council's judgment of *Days and Nights* clearly signalled a need for a myth as an 'adequate' way of representing the Red Army's exploits on the Volga.[35]

Understanding the Big Picture: Stalin-Era Epics of Stalingrad

When Simonov defended his film script, he explained that he had not attempted a depiction of the Battle of Stalingrad 'in all its immensity,' for the epic defence of the city took place 'in two hundred different locations.'[36] He wished *Days and Nights* were not the *first* film about the battle.[37] He thus implied that had there already existed an epic account of the Battle of Stalingrad, it could have provided the context necessary for justifying the existence of a case study such as *Days and Nights*. An 'epic' depiction of the battle was also needed in view of the Soviet cinema's post-war tasks. When, following the victory at Stalingrad, it became clear that Russia would eventually win the war, the Soviet film industry began preparing films that could be shown both domestically and abroad.[38] *Days and Nights* was considered unsuitable for international distribution: the film showed the 'everyday life' of the Russian troops but did not reflect 'the immensity of events' and could not 'explain to international audiences what took place in Stalingrad.'[39] In view of this film's inadequacy, the next two films about Stalingrad – Fridrikh Ermler's *The Great Turning Point* and Vladimir Petrov's *The Battle of Stalingrad* – both attempted to provide panoramic depictions of the events, which, among other things, enabled an emphasis on the battle's international significance.

The Great Turning Point shows the battle from the point of view of Soviet generals, who, supposedly, have an understanding of the 'big picture.' As the historian Denise Youngblood observes, most of the film 'features [General] Muravev poring over maps and talking to other generals.'[40] Criticizing the film's weak dramaturgy, Youngblood notes that 'only about twenty minutes out of more than one hundred show any aspect of the titanic struggle on the field' and that on the screen 'time passes through numerous close-ups of clocks and watches.'[41] Although this description is overall accurate, it must be noted nonetheless that the film's creators did not intend to produce a Hollywood-style thriller. Like many other Soviet films about the war from the Stalin era, *The Great Turning Point* was not in fact intended to be entertainment. Its task was to explain the Soviet military strategy that led to a victory and turned the tide of the war. The numerous shots of maps, clocks, and watches in this film were meant to intensify the narrative's documentary thrust.[42] Given the feeling of suspense generated over the course of half a year internationally and domestically and the absence of a mass-oriented overview of the battle (newspaper and radio reports that, by nature of their media, were too brief and focused on most recent events, could not fulfil this task), *The Great Turning Point* was a timely approach to representing the Battle of Stalingrad.[43]

Produced in the battle's aftermath, Ermler's film suggests detached contemplation rather than giving the impression of the immediacy of events. One of the film's most emotional episodes[44] depicts how a dying Soviet soldier reconnects the phone cable. The scene is documentary: it captures a heroic deed by a nineteen-year-old sergeant named Matvei Putilov which took place in October 1942 and was widely publicized during and after the war and probably well-known to the film's audience. In the film, Putilov's heroic exploit is ascribed to Minutka, General Muraviev's driver. The rendering and the framing of this heroic exploit contribute to understanding the battle as a collective effort that subsumed individuality and required a self-sacrificial subjugation of one's personal interests for the sake of the higher common cause. The melancholy violin in the scene's soundtrack makes the close-ups of the dead soldier especially sombre. But an abrupt cut from this scene to the next one containing absolutely no response to or commentary on the soldier's death changes the sequence's emotional register and produces an impression that the soldier's self-sacrifice is a typical occurrence in Stalingrad. In fact, the abrupt cutting between the film's many different scenes focusing on a variety of characters precludes a more detailed psychological rendering of any of the film's heroes.

Following the end of the war, the victory over Nazi Germany was increasingly rationalized as won thanks to the leadership by the Communist Party and Stalin himself. In the context of the post-war glorification of Stalin and the party, *The Great Turning Point*, in which the battle's actual topography and the names of both Russian and German military commanders were changed and Stalin was not represented at all, became inadequate. Petrov's two-part *The Battle of Stalingrad*, which featured commanders' real names and emphasized Stalin's leadership in the war, became one of the most vivid examples of Stalin's cult-of-personality films. Executed in the genre of fictionalized documentary (*khudozhestvenno-dokumental'nyi fil'm*),[45] which, in comparison to Ermler's film, further underscored the idea of 'objective' representation of the battle, *The Battle of Stalingrad* contributed to solidifying the myth of unparalleled heroism of the Stalingrad defenders. Tellingly, when selecting the documentary footage to be included into the film, Petrov thought that the 'German footage was not interesting because it showed prisoners of war and burnt villages':[46] in other words, the portrayal of the war experience was deemed insufficiently heroic. Petrov, furthermore, had to shorten or cut out scenes in which Stalin mentioned Soviet commanders' 'difficulties' and also the scenes showing the German advance. The Germans were not to be depicted 'at the peak of their glory' and, instead, were to be shown 'at the point of their destruction.' Petrov was also to ensure that Paulus did not look excessively tragic, as Hitler's victim who 'envisioned the catastrophe even before Russian generals saw the German destruction coming.'[47] Such requirements in depicting the Germans helped creating additional emphasis on the Red Army's exploits and the Soviet command's brilliant leadership.

An emphasis on the events' historical significance in the films by Ermler and Petrov also befitted the emerging Cold War discourse.[48] Both *The Great Turning Point* and *The Battle of Stalingrad* include criticisms of the former allies, whose leaders are depicted as betraying the idea of the second front in Europe, as sparing their nations from serious involvement in the fight against the Nazis, and thus as prolonging the war and making the Soviet Union bleed to death.[49] In *The Battle of Stalingrad*, when Churchill announces there will not be second front in Europe in 1942, Stalin says that the Red Army will of course stop the German advance but the responsibility for additional Soviet casualties will rest with those who broke their previously given 'solemn promises' regarding the second front in Europe. Especially dismissive are remarks about the British military efforts in North Africa, which, instead of distracting German divisions from the Eastern Front, in fact resulted in the transfer of troops from North Africa to Stalingrad.[50] Such rendering of the Great Alliance underscores the Soviet Cold War notion that the Soviet Union practically single-handedly defeated Nazi Germany. Along with other disparaging depictions of the former Soviet allies, the scene in which Stalin exposes Britain's military campaign as self-serving, as proving the British wish 'to arrive first in the Balkans,' points to the post-war division of Europe into spheres of influence and to the Cold War status of the Soviet Union as a superpower. Depicted as being performed not only in the name of Russia but also in the name of the humankind, Soviet self-sacrificial heroism in the Battle of Stalingrad is thus intended to justify Soviet post-war territorial and political claims.

It is important in this regard that in *The Battle of Stalingrad* Roosevelt is made to envision that 'mankind will be in great trouble if anyone starts a conflict between the United States and Russia.' While this claim suggests the United States and Russia are equal as partners and as rivals, a different scene that focuses on Stalin reinforces the belief in the Soviet Union's military and moral superiority in comparison to the morally feeble, cowardly, and self-serving West. Stalin in Petrov's film implicitly connects Hitler and Russia's 'new adversary' and emphatically asserts the country's new status: 'the Soviet ability to resist the German bandits is not smaller and is perhaps even greater than the ability of Nazi Germany – or of any other aggressive state – to reach global superiority.' The shot that opens this scene shows the Kremlin Spasskaya Tower with the clock indicating it is past midnight, thus emphasizing Stalin's dedication to work and also serving as a metaphor for Soviet watchfulness, the country's preparedness for a new military challenge. In light of this Cold War twist on representing Stalingrad, the film's combat scenes featuring masses of soldiers and mountains of military equipment were not only meant to capture the battle's magnitude but were also intended to remind the viewer of the Soviet Union's new superpower status. This idea is further reinforced by the film's ostentatious closing scene, which shows thousands of soldiers greeting their commanders to the accompanying soundtrack of the Soviet national anthem performed by a mighty choir, with the anthem's lyrics underscoring the ultimate triumph of socialist values. Instead of the country having been bled white by the war, the viewer is given a spectacle of the nation empowered by its ordeals.

Representing Stalingrad after Stalin

Following Stalin's death in 1953, the tenor of Soviet films about Stalingrad changed. They presented the Battle of Stalingrad without fanfare in case studies that focused on an individual's war experience. Unlike Stalin-era films with their upbeat or solemn intonation and spirited characters, Ivanov's *Soldiers* (1956), Stolper's *Retribution* (1967), and Egiazarov's *The Burning Snow* (1972) depict soldiers and officers as ordinary people with their own weaknesses, insecurities, and fears. The main characters in these films are low-ranking officers in charge of a company or a battalion and generals who command a division or an army, who may question their own and their country's war experience and may also feel melancholy, lonely, misunderstood, or even betrayed by their fellow combatants or family members. Instead of painting a rosy picture of the unshakeable unity among and between soldiers and officers, these three films criticize those commanders who treated their troops as cannon fodder.

Such departures from the style of Stalin-era narratives about the war caused controversy during the films' production. Opposition to the previously established image of the Red Army and its heroic struggle against Nazi invaders was especially strong during the production of *Soldiers*,[51] released only three years after Stalin's death. The film's military consultants, including Marshal Andrei Eremenko, who was commander of the Stalingrad Front, advised that the film-makers should abbreviate the scenes of the Red Army's retreat in July-August 1942, convey how concerned soldiers were about the retreat and how the commanders did their best in order to stop it, as well as make clear that elsewhere the Red Army continued its heroic struggle.[52] He also recommended introducing an episode that would capture the unparalleled gallantry and endurance of the city's defenders.[53] In Eremenko's view, it was disrespectful of the army to show how during the retreat soldiers tied poultry to the barrels of artillery guns, dried their underwear on gun barrels, and how (lacking horses and harness) transport soldiers rode on cows and tied their puttees to the cows' horns to steer the animals. Even if such things indeed took place, they were deemed 'not typical' and, therefore, were not to be represented.[54]

But even though in the film's final editing practically all of these recommendations were addressed, *Soldiers* still differed dramatically from Stalin-era representations of the war. It was a typical film of the liberalization of Soviet society under Nikita Khrushchev, which allowed artists to focus on humanist issues and on ordinary persons' highly subjective interpretations of events.[55] This change is evident, for example, in the *Soldiers'* use of voice-over. Whereas *The Battle of Stalingrad* features the voice-over that belongs to Yuri Levitan, a legendary radio announcer famous for his daily Soviet government's wartime reports who was instantly associated by the viewer with the official interpretation of the events, in Ivanov's *Soldiers* the voice-over belongs to the protagonist Lieutenant Kerzhentsev (actor Vsevolod Safonov), who reflects upon the events of the past approximately ten years after the war. Kerzhentsev's soft-voiced commentary intensifies the impression the whole narrative presents a deeply personal view of the battle.

In *Soldiers, The Retribution,* and *The Burning Snow* wartime heroism is not presented as practically natural for any Soviet citizen; instead it becomes an issue of the individual's dignity and of the hero's tragic awareness of the necessity to 'do the job.' This representational shift is especially striking in rendering high-ranking officers associated in the preceding films with a more detached perception of combat. In

Stolper's *The Retribution*, for example, one of the main characters is General Fedor Fedorovich Serpilin, a division commander whose perspective of the 'big picture,' or, to be more precise, of what is 'big' in the picture, exemplifies a dramatic departure from the Stalin-era mythology of Stalingrad. Instead of describing Stalingrad as the great internationally important turning point in the war, Serpilin limits himself to a modest discussion of his own division's military efforts. One episode shows the general – who comes to Moscow for his wife's funeral – sharing a meagre meal with a teenaged neighbour in his communal apartment. The boy, who has obviously followed the government's reports of the events at Stalingrad, is excited about the opportunity to talk with someone who has just returned from the place where 'the fate of the war' is being decided. However, his expectations of a tale about a grand battle are not fulfilled, as Serpilin tells him of how one battalion in his division recaptured a hill. When asked about the name as well as the strategic and symbolic significance of this hill, Serpilin quietly explains it is just an ordinary hill. Anatolii Papanov's brilliant low-key performance of Serpilin underscores the idea that real valour has little to do with youthful postures, loud voices, brisk movements, agitated gestures, and unwavering optimism.

It is also important that this judgment of the battle is given to the most tragic of the film's main characters. Unlike commanders from Stalin-era films, who had impeccable reputations, General Serpilin is a Gulag survivor. Denounced as 'an enemy of the people' by a fellow officer in the 1930s, he served a term in Siberia and was rehabilitated only with the start of the war. The physical scars Gulag left in his body are exacerbated by a psychological trauma: while Serpilin was in a labour camp, his beloved adopted son publicly renounced him, which, in turn, brought Serpilin's wife to an early death. While being a true patriot, Serpilin (and other characters of very different social backgrounds and political beliefs) has no use for the rhetoric of patriotism suggested by the state. The episodes capturing the war's horror[56] and people's personal tragedies additionally characterize *The Retribution* as subverting Stalin-era representations of Stalingrad and as befitting ideas of the Thaw period,[57] even though it was released three years after Khrushchev was ousted from power. *The Retribution* is but one example of how hard it is to define the end of the Thaw and the beginning of the Brezhnev era,[58] conventionally described by scholars as a rollback of Soviet society's de-Stalinization.

Based on Yuri Bondarev's 1969 eponymous novel written in the tradition of the so-called lieutenant's prose,[59] Egiazarov's film *The Burning Snow* tells the story of a two-day-long battle that took place during the Soviet offensive in November 1942, when Field Marshal von Manstein's tanks[60] attempted to break through to the encircled Sixth Army. The narrative focuses on an anti-tank artillery battalion that after ferocious fighting is reduced to only seven survivors. The battalion's fate is so tragic that the army commander, General Bessonov, comes to the surviving heroes to thank them personally for their valour and distribute military awards[61] with the words that explicitly indicate the inadequacy of these awards as signs of recognition of the battalion's exploits: 'That's all I can give you.' The general's gratitude for the soldiers' heroism, which goes beyond the call of duty and is represented as being deeply personal, intensifies the impression that the war was extremely hard and that therefore those who bore the brunt of combat couldn't be thanked enough by those who followed the fighting from a distance. Such representation, while perhaps tempting a scholar to interpret the film as continuing the humanist traditions of the Thaw,[62] in fact echoes the commemoration of the war under Brezhnev, when Soviet citizens' younger generations were educated about their eternal personal indebtedness to those who fought in the war and thus ensured their freedom and happiness. In this sense, General Bessonov's sadness about the inadequacy of his thanks to the surviving heroes emotionally evokes Soviet public rituals honouring the war's veterans in the 1970s and 1980s.

Like many films of the Thaw period and dozens films from the 1970s and 1980s, *The Burning Snow* is an attempt at a psychologically complex depiction of the war.[63] Here, the Battle of Stalingrad marks a turning point in the characters' psyches. The film's protagonists, two lieutenants torn by rivalry over their respective roles in the battalion and over their feelings of love towards the nurse Tania, are transformed during the battle. The formerly ambitious Lieutenant Drozdovskii is deranged by this bitter victory. He walks away from the battle's other survivors to mourn Tania's death. Lieutenant Kuznetsov is also traumatized: when soldiers, according to tradition, put their new awards into a bowl filled with vodka, he refuses to drink first. For him there is nothing to celebrate. Both protagonists' responses to the battle's outcome relate to the survivors' traumatic guilt at the realization that someone else died in order to allow them to live. This feeling of guilt once again evokes Brezhnev-era commemorations of the war with their emphasis on people's individual and collective indebtedness to war victims and the imperative to be worthy of their memory and their heroic self-sacrifice. The social importance of memory about the war is additionally communicated to the viewer through the series of famous and almost instantly recognizable wartime photos opening and closing the film. Capturing the war's iconic milestones (the Nazi invasion, the bombings of Soviet cities, the defence of Sevastopol, the Battle of Stalingrad, the placing of the Red Flag over the Reichstag in Berlin, the soldiers' return home, etc.), these photos frame *The Burning Snow* as a typical part of a larger war narrative that is well known to the audience.

Given this familiarity with the war narrative that by the end of the Soviet period had lost some of its original appeal through constant reiteration, it would seem that a new panoramic depiction of the Battle of Stalingrad could only be justified if it offered a decisively new approach to its representation. But the process of the aesthetic, emotional, and ideological crisis of the Soviet war discourse is nowhere more evident than in Yuri Ozerov's[64] two-part *Stalingrad* (1989). Created during perestroika, this last Soviet film about the battle attempted to address the historical imbalances and omissions of the preceding narratives.[65] Ozerov's film depicts all relevant Russian and German historical figures and includes in the narrative's subplots stories about the sons of the Communist leaders (Stalin, Khrushchev, and Ibárruri).[66] Conceptually and aesthetically, however, the film by Ozerov, which unlike Stolper's *Days and Nights* did not face a special challenge of being the first Soviet film about the battle, has contributed nothing new to the existing discourse. Underscoring Stalingrad's special status as the symbol of Soviet victory in the war, the aerial shots in the beginning and at the end of the film capture the famous Mamaev Hill memorial erected by sculptor Evgenii Vuchetich in 1963–7.[67] The centrepiece of this memorial is the huge statue of Mother Russia flourishing her sword high above her head in a patriotic call to defend the country. With her dress and posture evoking Nike of Samothrace, Vuchetich's sculpture reminds the viewer of the nation's military, political, and moral triumphs promoted earlier by Stalin-era films about the Battle of Stalingrad.[68] The shots of the war memorial in Volgograd and monotonous aerial shots of the columns of tanks that look like matchboxes and infantry that look like ants suggest an emotional distance from the depicted events rather than inviting the viewer to identify with the film's characters.

The framing of this narrative by symbols of Soviet victory – the images of maps, watches, and clocks, which deal with precision and evoke the notion of historical accuracy; the film's droning soundtrack of trumpets associated with depictions of military events – are unimaginative repetitions of techniques used in many other Soviet war films. In comparison to *Soldiers, The Retribution,* and *The Burning Snow,* which – each in its own way – personalized the victory at Stalingrad for the viewer, Ozerov's film shows Soviet heroic discourse of the war as wearing out through incantation.

Because of its political context, Soviet films about the war have been readily interpreted in terms of their compliance with or resistance to state-imposed propaganda. But a more careful study of the films about the Battle of Stalingrad reveals that approaching Soviet cinema with an ideological yardstick does not always produce the most sensitive reading of these cinematic texts that are 'at one and the same time artistic, thematic, formulaic, commercial, and political.'[69] Moreover, it cannot explain why twenty years after the fall of the Soviet Union old Soviet representations of the battle continue to be meaningful for Russians. The politically and pragmatically informed variations of the Stalingrad myth have apparently been less important for Russians' collective memory of the war than an opportunity to furnish a reiteration of the overall tale of the wartime individual and of collective endurance and self-sacrifice. Curiously enough, one of the popular video clips[70] about the battle posted on YouTube is a 2009 fast-paced re-editing of Petrov's film. The anonymous video clip's creator got rid of Aram Khachaturian's solemn symphonic music typical in Stalin-era slow-paced didactic films. The new soundtrack is the deeply lyrical song 'Na vsiu ostavshuiusia zhizn' ...' ('For the rest of our lives ...'), which originally was the title song of the four-part 1975 TV film of the same title by Petr Fomenko. In comparison to its performance in the film, a faster and musically inferior arrangement of this poignant song[71] by the contemporary group Grazhdanskaia oborona (Civil defence) is more casual and perhaps better suits the purposes of shortening the emotional distance suggested in both Petrov's and Fomenko's films. This in turn may be viewed as a sign of a further interiorization of the Soviet heroic discourse of the war. This post-Soviet personalization of the habitual discourse through fragmenting and rearranging the previous versions of the events evokes the readiness of Soviet individuals to (re)formulate their personal experience of the war in terms of the state-promoted ideas of heroism.[72] These ideas served the purpose of bracketing out the war survivors' most traumatizing memories of the horror, inhumanity, guilt, shame, and other feelings that would get in the way of the individuals' transition to post-war life. In turn, the survival and enduring popularity of different representations of the Battle of Stalingrad even from a distant past points to the endurance of psychological traumas inflicted on Russian society by the war, as well as by the inadequate process of working through these traumas suppressed and put to political use during the Soviet period. Present-day invocations of the fragments of the war's old representations, however, may also point to the Russians' inability to deal with the disintegration of the Soviet Union and to reassess the nation's past.[73] In this sense, contemporary tales of the war's traumatic aftermaths become a symbolic substitute for representing the aftermath of the disappearance of the Soviet state.

NOTES

I gratefully acknowledge the financial help from the Social Sciences and Humanities Research Council of Canada, which facilitated the gathering of the archival material for this chapter. I also wish to thank Serguei Oushakine, Rodney Symington, Jochen Hellbeck, and my co-editors for their comments on earlier versions of this essay.

1 William Craig, *Enemy at the Gates: The Battle for Stalingrad* (New York: Reader's Digest Press, 1973), xiv.
2 At least in Germany and Russia.
3 At that time soldiers of 138th Rifle Division had on average thirty rounds for each rifle and sub-machine gun and a daily ration of less than fifty grams of dried bread. Antony Beevor, *Stalingrad: The Fateful Siege, 1942–1943* (London: Penguin Books, 1998), 216.
4 Many German popular accounts of the battle emphasize the poor preparedness of the German troops. See, for example, Heinrich Gerlach, *Die verratene Armee. Der Stalingrad-Roman* (Augsburg: Bechtermünz-Verlag, 2000); and Jens Ebert, ed., *Feldpostbriefe aus Stalingrad* (Göttingen: Wallstein-Verlag, 2003).
5 Craig, *Enemy at the Gates*, xiv.
6 Maurice Halbwachs, *On Collective Memory*, ed. and trans. Lewis A. Coser (Chicago: University of Chicago Press, 1992).
7 On the refusal to discuss the war experience in post-war Germany, see George L. Mosse, 'Two World Wars and the Myth of the War Experience,' in *Journal of Contemporary History* 21 (1986): 491–513, esp. 497–8.
8 On the Stalingrad myth in Germany, see, for example, Joseph B. Perry, 'The Madonna of Stalingrad: Mastering the (Christmas) Past and West German

National Identity after World War II,' in *Radical History Review* 83 (2002): 7–27.

9 Cf. Norbert Frei, 'Stalingrad' im Gedächtnis der (West-) Deutschen ('"Stalingrad" in the (Western) Germans' memory'), in *Stalingrad Erinnern: Stalingrad im Deutschen und im Russischen Gedächtnis*, ed. Peter Jahn (Berlin: Ch. Links Verlag, 2003), 8–15.

10 On German propaganda about a near victory at Stalingrad, see Jay W. Baird, 'The Myth of Stalingrad,' *Journal of Contemporary History* 4, no. 3 (1969): 187–191.

11 See, for example, Géza Radványi's *The Doctor from Stalingrad* (1958) and Frank Wisbar's *Dogs, Do You Want to Live Forever?* (1958). Joseph Vilsmaier's *Stalingrad* (1993), although it omits the earlier decades' rhetoric of the Germans' mission 'to save Europe from the Asiatic Hordes,' still avoids the issue of the German troops' atrocities on the Eastern Front. The film's main characters arrive in Stalingrad from sunny Italy and are depicted as essentially different from the German soldiers they encounter on the Eastern front, who look as if they had been dehumanized by Russia. On the Germans' 'race war' in Russia, see Omer Bartov, *Hitler's Army* (New York: Oxford University Press, 1992), 12–106; and Beevor, *Stalingrad*, 57–9, 177–9.

12 On collective or 'cultural' memory as a form of cultural capital, see Andreas Huyssen, *Twilight Memories: Marking Time in a Culture of Amnesia* (New York: Routledge, 1995), 1–13.

13 See the article by Goscilo in this volume.

14 Catherine Merridale, *Ivan's War: The Red Army 1939–1945* (London: Faber and Faber, 2005), 148–56.

15 On propaganda uses of the battle, see Jochen Hellbeck, '"The Diaries of Fritzes and the Letters of Gretchens": Personal Writings from the German–Soviet War and Their Readers,' *Kritika: Explorations in Russian and Eurasian History* 10, no. 3 (2009): 571–606.

16 On memory as an object of historical knowledge and the relations between history and memory as well as between individual and collective memory, see Paul Ricœur, *Memory, History, Forgetting*, trans. Kathleen Blamey and David Pellauer (Chicago: University of Chicago Press, 2006), esp. 93–132.

17 Between 1941 and 1991 Soviet film studios released more than five hundred feature films about the war, a very impressive number for an industry that yearly produced far fewer films than Hollywood.

18 Halbwachs, *On Collective Memory*, 43, 51–3.

19 As the Russians traditionally refer to the part of the Second World War during which the Soviet Union fought against Nazi Germany.

20 RGALI, f. 2456 (Komitet po delam kinematografii pri SNK SSSR. Sekretar-

iat.), op. 1, d. 839. Stenogramma soveshchaniia kinodramaturgov, pisatelei i kinorezhisserov, sozvannoe Komitetom po delam kinematografii pri SNK SSSR 14–15–16 iulia 1943 goda. 243 ff. 1943: 7.

21 Ibid., 8.

22 Such is, for example, the argument in Nina Tumarkin, *The Living and the Dead: The Rise and Fall of the Cult of World War II in Russia* (New York: Basic Books, 1994).

23 See, for example, Lisa Kirschenbaum, *The Legacy of the Siege of Leningrad, 1941–1995: Myth, Memories, and Monuments* (New York: Cambridge University Press, 2006). On the clichéd language of the Soviet veteran's recollections about the war, see the chapter 'Russia at War,' in Catherine Merridale, *Night of Stone: Death and Memory in Russia* (London: Granta Books, 2000), 211–41.

24 The notion of 'an authentic war film' is criticized in Jay Winter, 'Film and the Matrix of Memory,' *The American Historical Review* 106, no. 3 (2001): 857–64.

25 Released on 10 March 1943, the first film about the Battle of Stalingrad was Leonid Varlamov's documentary based on footage prepared by five different cinematographers and with text written by Vasilii Grossman.

26 The film was based on Konstantin Simonov's novel *Soldatami ne rozhdaiutsia* (No one is born a soldier, 1964).

27 RGALI (Russian State Archive of Literature and Fine Arts), f. 2456, op. 1, d. 954, ff. 3–4.

28 Ibid.

29 Ibid., 24.

30 Ibid., 25.

31 Ibid.

32 RGALI, f. 2456, op. 1, d. 954, ff. 37–8.

33 Ibid., 29.

34 Ibid., 8–9.

35 RGALI, f. 2456, op. 1, d. 954, ff. 11–2.

36 Ibid., 27.

37 RGALI, f. 2456, op. 1, d. 954, ff. 26.

38 The first post-war exports of Soviet films were occasionally done at the expense of the domestic market with fewer copies circulating within the Soviet Union and more copies made for distribution abroad. See RGASPI, f. 17. op. 125. d. 291. 193 ff. January 1944–March 1945. ff. 168–173.

39 RGALI, f. 2456, op. 1, d. 954, ff. 20–22.

40 Denise J. Youngblood, *Russian War Films: On the Cinema Front, 1914–2005* (Lawrence: Kansas University Press, 2006), 85.

41 Ibid.
42 On Soviet art's obsession with fact, see Elizabeth Astrid Papazian, *Manu-facturing Truth: The Documentary Moment in Early Soviet Culture* (DeKalb: Northern Illinois University Press, 2009).
43 The film was awarded the Grand Prix at the first Cannes International Film Festival in 1946.
44 Youngblood describes this scene only as 'purportedly based on fact.' Youngblood, *Russian War Films*, 86.
45 In 1947 the Council of Ministers of the USSR commissioned several films about the destruction of the German troops in 1943–4: 1) at Stalingrad; 2) in the Crimea; and 3) at Leningrad. The protagonists in these films were to be Party leaders and military commanders; the locations of the great battles, historical dates, etc., were to be *documentary*. At the same time, 'artistic development of characters' was expected, for these films were to become 'an artistic chronicle of the Great Patriotic War,' the chronicle created for 'generations that in fifty or one hundred years, thanks to these films, would see the era of the battles of our military commanders under Stalin's genius leadership for Stalingrad, the Crimea, and Leningrad.' See RGALI, f. 2456, op. 1, d. 1324, ff. 3–4.
46 RGALI, f. 2453, op. 2, d. 167, ff. 16 reverse.
47 Ibid., 10–12.
48 In the West, as Youngblood points out, the 'great and improbable victory' at Stalingrad became 'a victim of cold war politics. As far as the West was concerned, it might never have happened. The invasion of Normandy in June 1944 became the centerpiece in the Anglo-American mythologization of the war in Europe, whether on- or off-screen.' See Denise Youngblood, '*Enemy at the Gates* as a "Soviet" War Film,' in *Repicturing the Second World War: Representations in Film and Television*, ed. Michael Paris (New York: Palgrave Macmillan, 2007), 148–61, esp. 148.
49 Other critical depictions of the allies include, for example, the film *Semnadtsatyi transatlanticheskii* (*The Seventeenth Transatlantic*, 1971), directed by Vladimir Dovgan', and Alexander Kott's eight-episode film *Konvoi PQ-17* (*The Convoy PQ-17*, 2004). Both films tell of the most tragic allied convoy to Murmansk (Russia). Abandoned by its British escort midway in July 1942 and bombed by the Nazis, it lost 75 per cent of its cargo vessels.
50 Petrov's film spares Roosevelt similar reproaches and even makes him a mouthpiece for similar criticisms of the British. Roosevelt died before the start of the Cold War and was regarded as much friendlier to the USSR than his successor, Harry Truman.
51 Based on Victor Nekrasov's novel *In the Trenches of Stalingrad* (1946).

52 TsGALI St Petersburg (Central State Archive of Literature and Fine Arts in St Petersburg), f. 257, op.17, d. 1176, ff. 281–282; TsGALI St Petersburg, f. 257, op.17, d. 1215, ff. 59.

53 TsGALI St Petersburg, f. 257, op.17, d. 1215, ff. 60.

54 TsGALI St Petersburg, f. 257, op.17, d. 1215, ff. 45–6.

55 See more on Thaw films in Birgit Beumers, *A History of Russian Cinema* (Oxford and New York: Berg, 2009), 112–46.

56 In one scene in the film the voice-over describes the horrors Soviet military doctors see at the site of a Soviet prisoner of war camp located on territory controlled by the encircled Sixth Army. Having not been fed for weeks, many Soviet prisoners of war walked out of the barracks to the camp's fence in order to freeze to death. In order to reach those still alive in the barracks the medics had to walk on the corpses.

57 This film is criticized by Youngblood as a 'typical' example of 'big, loud war films' from the Brezhnev era. *Russian War Films*, 145.

58 See more in Beumers, *A History of Russian Cinema*, 112.

59 'Lieutenant prose' refers to a tide of mostly autobiographical novels by war veterans who were low-ranking officers during the war. These novels began to appear in the late 1940s and formed a recognizable trend in the literature of the 1950s and 1960s.

60 Von Manstein was the overall commander of the Army Group Don. The real breakthrough effort was attempted by the panzer army led by Colonel General Hoth. However, in Soviet popular historiography and in cinema and literature about the battle of Stalingrad, the attempt to rescue the Sixth Army is associated with the name of von Manstein.

61 Normally, a soldier would have to wait for up to several weeks or even months for his award to arrive.

62 Youngblood describes this film as continuing Thaw-era traditions in the 'more conservative climate of the 1970s.' *Russian War Films*, 166–7.

63 Depictions of war as inflicting psychological traumas, which began to appear during the Thaw period, developed further in narratives of the 1970s and 1980s. See, for example, Leonid Bykov's *Aty-baty, shli soldaty* (*There the Soldiers Went*, 1976), Nikolai Gubenko's *Podranki* (*The Orphans*, 1977), Igor' Talankin's *Vremia otdykha s subboty do ponedel'nika* (*The Resting Time Is from Saturday to Monday*, 1984), and Elem Klimov's *Idi i smotri* (*Come and See*, 1985).

64 Ozerov became famous as the creator of the five-film war saga *Osvobozhdenie* (*The Liberation*, 1970).

65 Whereas *The Great Turning Point* did not mention the real names of Russian and German military commanders, *The Battle of Stalingrad* was a eulogy

to Stalin while omitting, for example, Marshal Georgii Zhukov's role in designing the Soviet counteroffensive, and the narratives of the 1950s and 70s avoided references to Soviet political and military leadership.

66 Dolorez Ibárruri was the General Secretary of the Spanish Communist Party from 1942 through 1960. Her only son Rubén Ibárruri was killed at Stalingrad while fighting in the Red Army.

67 See a detailed study on the construction of this memorial in Scott W. Palmer, 'How Memory Was Made: The Construction of the Memorial to the Heroes of the Battle of Stalingrad,' *Russian Review* 68, no. 3 (2009): 373–407.

68 It is ironic that this symbolic reminder of the country's empowerment resulting from its victory in the war is reiterated in the year when the Berlin Wall fell and the Soviet Union lost its superpower status.

69 Winter, 'Film and the Matrix of Memory,' 863.

70 With more than 8,300 views: http://www.youtube.com/watch?v=RPe2OPi Tlsw&feature=related (accessed 15 August 2010).

71 Fomenko wrote the song's lyrics.

72 In her memoirs of the Siege of Leningrad Lidiia Ginzburg discusses this interiorization of the state-suggested heroic discourse. See more in Emily Van Buskirk, 'Recovering the Past for the Future: Guilt, Memory, and Lidiia Ginzburg's *Notes of a Blockade Person,' Slavic Review* 69, no. 2 (2010): 281–306, esp. 281–2.

73 See more on the use of Soviet symbols by post-Soviet communities in Serguei Alex. Oushakine, *The Patriotism of Despair: Nation, War, and Loss in Russia* (Ithaca, NY: Cornell University Press, 2009).

11 Monsters in America: The First World War and the Cultural Production of Horror

DAVID M. LUBIN

Monsters Arise

Monsters, madmen, and ghouls have always stalked the American imagination. Between the Revolution and the Civil War, headless horsemen, murdering apes, killer sharks, giant white whales, pillaging barbarians, and other evil avatars inhabited the fiction of Washington Irving, Edgar Allen Poe, Nathaniel Hawthorne, and Herman Melville as well as the art of John Singleton Copley, Benjamin West, and Thomas Cole. After the Civil War, the presence of such grotesque and aberrant figures diminished. Beholden to evolutionary science, naturalism had little use for the supernatural. In the opening years of the twentieth century, the public's faith in technology, progress, and rational administration further pushed monsters and their ilk to the margins of literary and visual culture. Political cartoons sardonically likened corrupt officials to rodents and corporate trusts to hulking predators of the sea, but, despite their serious intentions, such renditions were jocular, not frightening.

With the advent of the First World War, however, monsters began to reappear in American art and literature. The war furnished Americans with their first significant external enemy in over a century. Previous clashes with Mexico (1846–8) and Spain (1898) had aroused far less fear and hatred in the United States than did the European bloodbath, which subjected the ancestral homelands of most Americans to extreme violence. Not even the Civil War (1861–5) spawned such loathing, for however strong their enmity, northerners and southerners hailed from shared cultural origins and could not, therefore, credibly imagine one another as inhuman incarnations of evil. Such was not the case in the

First World War, when Americans at large were encouraged to regard their distant opponents as creatures of an alien species: in effect, as monsters.

That was only the start. After the war, with millions of doughboys returning home wounded in body or spirit and tormented by recurring nightmares, and with the public's faith in progress painfully diminished, trauma, paranoia, disillusionment, and dissociation became prevalent mental and emotional conditions. These war-related states of mind provided a fertile seedbed for a new generation of monsters in America.

The re-emergence of monsters occurred in four overlapping phases. We might usefully characterize these as *anticipation, projection, alienation,* and *commercialization*. When war erupted in Europe in 1914, Americans feared being dragged into it. At that stage they had no obvious course of action or even a clearly defined enemy against which to direct their anxieties. As war fever mounted, they settled on imperial Germany as the target of their animus, and popular illustration obliged by depicting the Reich as an insatiable beast or ghoulish vampire deserving destruction. The third stage of monster-making occurred when Americans confronted their own signal failure to make the world safe for democracy.

Embittered and alienated, they split into rival factions and interest groups, viewing one another with heightened suspicion. Now, instead of demonizing Germans, Americans were more likely to do so to fellow Americans – and, indeed, to themselves. As the literature of the Lost Generation amply demonstrates, self-hatred and estrangement among returning veterans reached sizable proportions in the decade following the armistice. Eventually, though, monster-making lost its sting, metamorphosing into a profitable enterprise for film studios and pulp fiction magazines. What had originally been a means of expressing turbulent public emotions and waging ideological warfare became in the end a mode of containment through consumption.

In this essay, a monster is an artistic, literary, or cinematic representation of extreme evil. It operates within the realm of imagination. It is a tool or weapon wielded by the artistically creative members of a social group to advance claims against rival social groups by means of symbol and metaphor. Monsters signify aberration, abnormality, malformation. They and the societal formations they represent are made to seem not only repugnant, misshapen, and worthy of annihilation, but also to be self-evidently so. The word 'monster' comes from the Latin

term *monere*, to admonish, warn, or show; hence monsters are negative examples. Monsters themselves are not real, but real people and
real identity groups are sometimes *perceived* as monsters or, if not as
monsters per se, then as *monstrous*, a rhetorical label that serves political ends.

The cultural production of monsters during and after the First World
War was not exclusively American. Europeans, too, excelled in this
mode of representation. Cubism, surrealism, expressionism, and other
avant-garde movements introduced shocking new visual languages
attuned to war-ravaged sensibilities. Nonetheless, monsters arose in
America in a different way and for different reasons. While Europeans
beheld the war at close range, Americans looked on from a great distance, separated from the conflict by a buffer thousands of feet deep and
thousands of miles wide. Removed as well from their own tumultu-
ous Civil War by two generations, they no longer possessed first-hand
memory of war's destructiveness. As their country drifted inexorably
towards massive military conflict, Americans became increasingly subject to terror: if horror is repulsion at what one sees, terror is dread of
what one *might* see.

Similarly, after the war, Americans experienced nightmares of a different sort from those that roiled the sleep of their European counter-
parts. Here, again, the latter had borne the brunt of the war and seen
its depredations up close. Even after the war ended, its horror lingered
for Europeans, who were daily reminded of it by charred cities, obliterated landscapes, and the mangled bodies of wounded and disfigured veterans. In the United States, however, remnants of the war's
monstrosity were far less visible and therefore, perhaps, more readily
sublimated into other forms, other public and private manifestations
of dread, repugnance, repulsion, and despair. Before entering the war
and then while fighting it, Americans had 'monsterized' the enemy, but
once the fighting stopped, the fear that had been directed at faraway
enemies was rechannelled into concern over a new brace of monsters
that seemed to be springing up in their own backyard.

Red scares, race riots, hate rallies, lynch parties, monkey trials, the
literature of exile and alienation, and the rise of the Hollywood horror
film – these disparate phenomena, when taken together, suggest that
monsters flourished in a variety of related guises. The war, it seems,
inculcated a habit of seeing monsters that persisted long after the troops
came home.

An Era of Atrocities

In 1915 a series of atrocities abroad dismayed and confounded Americans. One outrage concerned the nation directly: the murder of 128 American citizens (out of a total of nearly 1,200 passengers who died) when a German submarine torpedoed the British ocean liner *Lusitania*. Only a few days later, Americans confronted more atrocity news with the publication of shocking excerpts from the official report of the Bryce Committee, a British tribunal charged with investigating war crime allegations against the German army of occupation in neutral Belgium. The third major abomination was the murder of a million or so Armenians by the Ottoman Turks, who were allies of the Germans.

The *New York Times* published no fewer than 145 stories that year on the Armenian massacres and many more about the violence of the Germans against the Belgians.[1] Yet these numerically superior atrocities did not disturb Americans nearly so much as did the sinking of the *Lusitania*, in which only a relatively small number of their compatriots perished. As an aphorism attributed to Stalin would have it, a single death (or, in this case, a handful) is a tragedy, but a million deaths only a statistic. Spurred on by the lucrative newsstand attention devoted three years earlier to the *Titanic* disaster, the American press laboured mightily to describe every aspect of the new catastrophe in grisly detail. Interventionists, eager to end America's neutrality, exploited the horror of the incident for all it was worth, relying on verbal and visual expression to characterize the German perpetrators as monsters. Former president Theodore Roosevelt compared their act of 'murder on the high seas' to wholesale poisoning of wells, shipping infected rags into an unsuspecting city, torturing prisoners, and turning captured women into enslaved concubines.[2]

One of the posters spawned by the attack shows a ghostly, wraithlike young mother sinking to the bottom of the sea with an infant cradled in her arms (1915; see figure 11.1). Bubbles rise from her lips, indicating she is not yet dead, and a fish floats by as an impassive onlooker. Dark and murky, grey, green, and brown, the oceanic depths surrounding the mother and child would have chilled viewers, who required no supplementary text to understand the picture's allusion to the sinking of the *Lusitania*. The poster needs only a single word spelled out in block letters, the imperative 'enlist,' to drive home its point: the Kaiser's minions, who are not depicted in the image, had slaughtered innocent American women and children and must never be allowed to

11.1   Fred Spear, *Enlist*, 1915. Library of Congress.

do so again. The artist's decision to leave the perpetrators of the crime entirely to the imagination probably intensified the poster's emotional effect on viewers.[3]

While it is true that far more British women and children died in the catastrophe than did Americans, the British counterpart poster, *Irishmen – Avenge 'The Lusitania'* (1915; see figure 11.2), which shows survivors clutching broken spars and paddling about on the surface of the sea, was less alarming than the American depiction. The British poster converts the calamity into spectacle, stolidly repeating the conventions of earlier shipwreck illustrations such as *The Sinking of the Titanic* by German artist Willy Stöwer (ca 1912). The American poster, unlike these counterexamples, zeroes in on the pathos of the dying mother and child and taps into the viewer's primordial terror of isolation and drowning, as well as dread of ominous, unseen danger.

The American comic strip artist and animation pioneer Winsor McCay seized on the same incident for the concluding sequence of his eleven-minute animated film *The Sinking of the Lusitania* (1918), which, because of a painstaking production, was not released until after America entered the war. McCay's rendering shows the mother and child descending down, down, down into a watery underworld. The movie ends with a sarcastic title card: 'The man who fired the shots was decorated by the Kaiser. And they tell us not to hate the Hun.'[4] Thus, in the animated film as well as in the enlistment poster, the perpetrators of the savage attack are not shown, but their monstrosity is clearly evoked. A propaganda film that also appeared in 1918, *The Kaiser, Beast of Berlin*, similarly treats the German sovereign, if not the nation under his command, as an ur-monster requiring nothing less than eradication.

One of the most vivid posters printed in the United States in the run-up to the declaration of war anthropomorphizes Germany as a snarling, drooling, wild-eyed gorilla wearing a Prussian helmet, wielding a cudgel marked *Kultur*, and clutching a half-naked white woman in his bloodstained arms (1916; see figure 11.3). He appears to have sprung across the ocean to plant his hairy paws on American soil. 'Destroy This Mad Brute,' the text admonishes in block letters, elaborating in smaller print: 'If this War is not fought to a finish in Europe, it will be on the soil of the United States.'[5]

Here we see evidence of a shift from the sensibility of the earlier enlistment poster, which alluded to the as-yet undeclared enemy without resorting to personification. Now, grotesque and menacing, the enemy to be dominates the visual field. With this depiction of Germany

11.2 'W.E.T.' [pseudonym for artist unknown], *Irishmen – Avenge* The Lusitania, 1915. Library of Congress.

as a wantonly destructive beast, a new phase in political representation had arrived. For reasons to be considered in the following section, the phase was short lived, and the Mad Brute poster did not spawn others of its ilk. Perhaps for that very reason, though, it remains one of the most frequently reproduced images of the First World War, conveying, as few other posters from the period do, the hatred and fear of Germany that simmered and boiled in American public discourse in the months leading up to the declaration of war.[6]

Monsters in Spiked Helmets

Soon after declaring war, Congress established a propaganda agency, euphemistically called the Committee on Public Information (CPI). The fine arts division of the CPI recruited hundreds of professional artists and illustrators to design posters meant to boost morale, inspire enlistment, promote the rationing of goods and products, and cajole Americans to buy war bonds.

Previously, non-governmental organizations had issued posters such as *Enlist* and *Destroy This Mad Brute* that allegorized Teutonic monstrosity, but once the United States entered the war, imagery of this incendiary nature became infrequent. We can only speculate as to why that was. Government and non-government agencies alike must have concluded that the best way to motivate enlistment was by providing positive images of American fighters. They may also have sensed that exaggerating the viciousness of the enemy could have a chilling effect on recruitment and morale while also needlessly offending millions of patriotic German American citizens. Most wartime posters were sunny and upbeat. They showed handsome young soldiers bearing arms but not using them. Or they featured the mothers and girlfriends left behind and the beautiful Red Cross nurses and YMCA hostesses that a recruit might dream of encountering. When the enemy did appear in recruitment and Liberty Bond posters, his potential for ferocity was typically downplayed.

Occasionally, though, posters did portray the enemy as a demonic figure. *Beat Back the Hun* (1918; see figure 11.4), for example, shows a cadaverously grey, zombie-like German soldier looming over the smouldering ruins of a church or abbey. His wolfish green eyes pulsate with supernatural malevolence. Blood slathers the tips of his fingers and drips from the edge of a bayonet that has probed the entrails of an unseen opponent (thus reversing the technique of *Enlist*, in which the

11.3 H.R. Hopps, *Destroy This Mad Brute*, 1916. Harry Ransom Humanities Research Center, The University of Texas at Austin.

monster, not its victim, remains hidden). All that separates the viewer from this glowering creature is a patch of oceanic water and the words stretched across it: 'Beat back the HUN with LIBERTY BONDS.'

While there is no shred of pathos in this horror image, pathos abounds in the graphically stunning *Remember Belgium* (1918; see figure 11.5). Composed in a vertical format, the poster silhouettes a pair of figures against a pea-green sky flecked with burning cinders. On the low horizon, a conflagration consumes a town. The silhouettes reveal a dance of opposition between a walrus-mustached, spike-helmeted German soldier and the young, prepubescent girl he drags behind him. Though her features are lost in shadow, her terror manifests itself in her gaping mouth and violently disarrayed tresses. The stock of the German's rifle protrudes between his legs with phallic assertion, while the child's free hand, reaching back in hopeless counterweight to his forward thrust, seems almost seared by the flames that devour her pillaged homeland.

Even though posters such as *Beat Back the Hun* and *Remember Belgium* were the exception rather than the rule, they may have had more long-term effect on the interior lives of Americans than any number of anodyne images of stalwart doughboys and plucky maidens, whose idealized forms, already familiar from turn-of-the-century art and illustration, were prevalent. Unlike those stock romantic figures, monsters had not previously been afforded such vividly coloured and massively distributed compositions. Their relative rarity in the visual culture of the time maximized their shock value, and this in turn assured their proliferation in the mass culture of the post-war era. Horror fiction became a mainstay of the new pulp magazine industry. *Weird Tales* began publication in 1923, the fantasist H.P. Lovecraft achieved acclaim as the new Poe, and Hollywood, as we will see in the final section, began to embrace the dramatic possibilities of haunted houses, mad scientists, severely disfigured villains, and other distorted progeny of the darker impulses. But before we examine how post-war culture, both high and low, conceived of monsters, let us first look at the monsters envisioned late in the war by one of America's most prominent artists, George Bellows.

The American Goya

A century before the Kaiser's army engulfed Belgium, Napoleon's overran Spain. The Spanish artist Francisco Goya expressed outrage at the military occupation of his homeland with a series of mordant etch-

11.4 Fred Strothmann, *Beat Back the Hun*, 1918. Library of Congress.

11.5 Ellsworth Young, *Remember Belgium*, 1918. Library of Congress.

ings that describe man's inhumanity to man. Known as *The Disasters of War* (ca 1810–20), the series details torture, murder, and execution, all committed in the name of righteousness, whether that of the invaders or the insurgents, who resort to methods as brutal as any devised by their assailants.

Goya's vision of hell on earth influenced America's leading urban realist painter and left-wing social satirist, George Bellows. As a pacifist, Bellows adamantly opposed America's entrance into the war. But once American forces were committed to the endeavour, he changed his stand and gave intervention his full support. In 1918 he completed a series of lithographs illustrating German war crimes in Belgium, as detailed in the sixty-one-page Bryce Committee report that the British had issued three years earlier.[7]

Taking depositions from hundreds of witnesses and examining diaries found on the bodies of dead or captured German soldiers, the Bryce Committee had concluded that the vast majority of atrocity charges levelled at the German army were well-founded. Almost from the start, however, controversy beset the committee, and to this day scholars debate the legitimacy of its claims.[8] Nonetheless, the report proved extremely effective in portraying the Germans as monsters. Published in thirty languages on 12 May 1915, five days after the sinking of the *Lusitania*, it grabbed headlines around the world.

At least seven of Bellows's war lithographs depict crimes outlined in Bryce. Works of technical finesse and formal beauty, with dynamic compositions and rich gradations of tone, they attract the eye but punish it for what it sees. One, *Belgian Farmyard*, depicts a dark outdoor setting wherein a bare-shouldered German soldier, pulling on his uniform, stands over the supine body of a young female whom he has raped and possibly murdered. In *The Last Victim*, three depraved German soldiers in a middle-class parlour stare hungrily at a distraught young woman who has entered the room to discover her mother, father, and brother sprawled dead or dying on the floor. The corresponding passage in the Bryce report states, 'At Herve some 50 men escaping from the burning houses were seized, taken outside the town and shot. At Melen, a hamlet west of Herve, 40 men were shot. In one household alone the father and mother ... were shot, the daughter died after being repeatedly outraged, and the son was wounded.'[9]

These are among the more reportorial of Bellows's war lithographs. Others in the series seem downright phantasmagoric. *Bacchanal*, for example, depicts German soldiers guzzling wine in the open space of a village while guards bring in a young mother whose hands are bound. Two small, naked children have been impaled on bayonets and are being waved in the air, but no one takes notice, as though this were a common, everyday occurrence. According to one of Bryce's witnesses, a drunken German soldier in the town of Malines 'drove his bayonet with both hands into [a] child's stomach, lifting the child into the air on his bayonet and carrying it away on his bayonet, he and his comrades still singing.'[10] Here Bellows, displaying the art-historical knowledge expected of any artist of his era, has invoked themes familiar from Old Master paintings – the massacre of the innocents and the callous indifference of soldiers who torture holy martyrs – but updated the costumes and setting.

Another lithograph, ironically entitled Gott Strafe England – a wartime slogan meaning 'May God punish England' – shows German soldiers nailing captured British soldiers to doors made of rough wooden planks while a crowd looks on and jeers. In The Cigarette, a solitary soldier seated in the shadows on the right side of the image scowls while smoking (1918; see figure 11.6). On the left, the corpse of a man sags in a window frame, beside a broken shutter. In the center, incandescently lit, a naked woman writhes in agony and shame. Her left arm, drenched in blood, extends high above her head, a bayonet driven through the palm to fasten her to the wall. A gash where one of her breasts should be indicates that the smoker has sundered it from her body.

Bellows exhibited these lithographs in New York in November 1918, just as the war was ending, and some were reproduced in popular magazines.[11] But mostly during the eighteen months of America's participation in the war, the public was 'protected' from horrific images of the conflict, including those that demonized the enemy. A strict system of censorship made sure of this. The Espionage Act of 1917, passed in June, criminalized the publication or sale of any writing or visual representation that could be construed as aiding the enemy. The government thus brought a case against the left-wing anti-war periodical The Masses for publishing cartoons that lampooned warmongers and profiteers.[12] Terrifying or repellant pictures of Germans were also liable to prosecution. Additional legislation, the Sedition Act of 1918, further restricted the circulation of literature and imagery that officials deemed disloyal, unpatriotic, or unduly disturbing.[13]

Such laws, together with the drumbeat of public opinion, which insisted on a tenor of cheery optimism regarding 'our boys' and their benevolent doings 'over there,' ensured that most Americans remained

11.6 George Bellows, *The Cigarette*, 1918. Library of Congress.

ignorant of the physical and psychic damaged wreaked on – or by – members of the American Expeditionary Forces. They had almost no way of knowing about the horrors of war on the field of battle, inasmuch as reporting from the front was tightly restricted, battlefield photography was controlled by the War Office, and soldiers' letters home were stripped by censors of first-hand accounts deemed demoralizing or objectionable. Americans did encounter in newspapers and war poetry, such as that of the popular Canadian author Robert Service, sad tales about grievously wounded soldiers.[14] But these accounts usually came wrapped in thick patriotic padding, emphasizing noble self-sacrifice while steering clear of anger, bitterness, and disgust, either on the part of the soldiers themselves or those who cared for them.

Thus, the now-conventional notion of the First World War as an interminable bloodbath, a Grand Guignol of mutual mass destruction, did not take shape in the United States until some years after the war ended. The depressing imagery of shrapnel-shredded bodies, limbs torn asunder, dead men impaled on barbed wire, wounded men shrieking in agony, begging to be put out of their misery, and rats gnawing on gangrenous legs – all this came later.

Aliens at Home

Entering the war in its last stages and shielded by their government from knowing the full extent of its horrors, Americans were late in coming to a realization of how truly ugly and awful the conflict had been. Various reasons caused this belated reappraisal. Censorship, for example, had ended with the armistice, and previously suppressed information and images could now circulate freely. Although dictates of taste still kept the more violent imagery out of the visual field, some of it inevitably filtered into the public realm. Another way awareness was raised is simply that many of the soldiers and sailors who had gone off to Europe full of idealistic hopes came back to their hometowns alienated, angry, and benumbed. It would have been hard not to notice the change or wonder what torments had caused it.

Some veterans were so badly disfigured or disabled by their wounds that strangers found it difficult to look at them without revulsion, a reaction that was painfully obvious to those whose aberrant appearance had caused it. A military surgeon remarked, 'it's the poor devils without noses and jaws, the unfortunate of the trenches who come back without the faces of men, that form the most depressing part of the work. Their wives may love them ... but there's something about a man with his face gone that hurts the eyes ... You see, the race is only human, and people who look as some of those creatures look haven't much of a chance.'[15]

After the war, a rising tide of novels, plays, movies, memoirs, and drawings from members of the Lost Generation shocked and repelled middle-class readers. Meanwhile, the squabbling in Versailles over the terms of peace, the continuing revolution in Russia, the street revolts in Berlin, and the riots, political assassinations, and bloody reprisals throughout Central and Eastern Europe troubled Americans, not only because they feared having to embark on another foreign war but also because they worried that the unleashing of new demons abroad would lead to dire consequences at home. The so-called Red Scares of 1919–21 were the most prominent but far from the only manifestation of this culture-wide dread.

In the United States, as in every other nation that saw the return of millions of war-weary fighters, homecoming required painful adjustments for those who had gone away as well as those who had stayed behind. Although the war ended in November 1918, it was six months to a year, or longer, before Johnny came marching or limping home. For the most part, combat veterans were notoriously circumspect about what they had seen and faced while overseas. Returning doughboys were expected to be chipper and glad, ready to 'play ball' again with the world they had temporarily forsaken and that now, in some ways, threatened to forsake them. As reported by a gunnery sergeant who served in the Army of Occupation, 'Much was done in Germany to infuse in the men the zeal that was theirs upon entering the service. Baseball, football, track, and etc. But the men seemed indifferent, and I believed then that the zest for such things was sapped out of them by the war.'[16]

Another returning serviceman noted, 'Before the war I was an innocent, ignorant child, while now I feel that I could easily go insane by permitting my mind to recall and dwell upon the horrors of my experience.'[17] Explaining the emotional struggles of repatriation, a Marine colonel reported: 'I was getting more restless and more nervous every day ... then it dawned on me that it didn't matter where I was ... I began waking up at night, shuddering, from dreams of the rain and the cold and the mud. In nightmares, the rats in the trenches kept jumping on me. Champillon, Les Mares Farm, the Bois de Belleau, St. Mihiel, the Argonne – I was living them all over again all the time.'[18] Another Marine stated, 'I know how we all cried to get back to the States ... but now that we are here, I must admit for myself at least that I am lost and somehow strangely lonesome.'[19]

Ernest Hemingway caught the mood of this estrangement in his short story 'Soldier's Home' (1925). 'By the time Krebs returned to his home town in Oklahoma,' writes Hemingway, 'the greeting of heroes was over. He came back much too late. The men from the town who had been drafted had all been welcomed elaborately on their return. There had been a great deal of hysteria. Now the reaction had set in.' Public desire not to know what had really happened at the battlefront heightened the inability of the veterans to give an honest account of the trauma they had experienced. At first, Krebs 'did not want to talk about the war at all. Later he felt the need to talk but no one wanted to hear about it.' When Krebs's mother, anguished by his lack of warmth, asks him point-blank, 'Don't you love your mother, dear boy?' he at first answers truthfully, 'No ... I don't love anybody,' but then recants under the pressure of her tears.[20]

The homecoming of millions of mildly to severely disaffected soldiers created aliens, as it were, on both sides: veterans like Krebs, whose emotions had been cauterized, and civilians who lacked comprehension or empathy for what the veterans had been through. The horrors of the Civil War had also been great, maybe even greater, than those to which Americans were subjected during the First World War. But because that earlier war was contested on American soil, its civilian population was bound to be more understanding of the soldiers' ordeal, more connected to the veterans emotionally, than was the civilian population during and after the 1917–18 war. The sorrows and alienation attendant on homecoming were thus perhaps more pronounced in America this time around.

Modernist Monsters

Modernist writers such as Ernest Hemingway, e.e. cummings, and John Dos Passos set out to disturb the emotional complacency of readers by shattering traditional modes of narrative address. In Hemingway's 1929 best-selling novel, *A Farewell to Arms*, for example, the narrator deploys simple, repetitive language to recount the night he and his Italian comrades were caught in an Austrian bombardment:

> There was a great splashing and I saw the star-shells go up and burst and float whitely and rockets going up and heard the bombs, all this in

a moment, and then I heard ... some one saying 'Mama Mia! Oh, mama Mia!' ... It was Passini and when I touched him he screamed. His legs were toward me and I saw in the dark and the light that they were both smashed above the knee. One leg was gone and the other was held by tendons and part of the trouser and the stump twitched and jerked as though it were not connected.[21]

This was – and still is – strong stuff, shocking because of its immediacy, but also because we are made to witness disfiguration. A normal, healthy body is transformed into something hideous and grotesque. The bombardment creates a monster, but not an enemy monster. This makes him, in a sense, all the more frightening, because the reader identifies with him, or at least with the narrator-comrade who describes his agony; it is not so easy to wall him off as a vile and unredeemable Other.

Besides providing American readers with their first truly graphic depictions of battlefield agony and violence, authors such as Hemingway and the German novelist Erich Maria Remarque raised important questions about the difficult re-entry of the soldiers into the peacetime economy. 'What do they expect from us when a time comes in which there is no more war?' Remarque's soldier-narrator demands in *All Quiet on the Western Front* (1929), an anti-war novel that appeared in twenty-five languages within eighteen months of its original publication in Germany and was the best-selling novel in America in 1929. Its protagonist, Paul Bäumer, observes that 'For years our occupation has been killing – that was the first experience we had. Our knowledge of life is limited to death. What will happen afterwards? And what can possibly become of us?'[22]

Such questions beset every homeland to which the veterans returned. What was to be done with the millions of men who had been taught to overlook lifelong inhibitions against violence and killing? What monsters had they themselves become, and how could they be reabsorbed into peacetime society without radically disrupting it? Would they arrogantly expect to reclaim their old jobs? Would they poison the small-town values they had abandoned, corrupting the innocence of those who had stayed behind? The returning fighters instilled some degree of fear in those who had remained at home, but they in turn feared those fellow citizens, who seemed incapable of grasping what it meant to face the terror of the trenches. Veterans' lodges became places of refuge and commiseration, where former soldiers sought to recreate the male camaraderie and knowing sympathy that was now absent from their lives. In some sense, each group was strange and potentially monstrous in the eyes of the other.

World Out of Whack

The general anxiety both in the United States and abroad about reintegrating men of war into peacetime society was powerfully, if indirectly, expressed in the small tale of terror that inaugurated German expressionist cinema, *The Cabinet of Dr Caligari* (1919). Though not the first horror film in motion picture history, it was the most influential; it was to the genre of fantasy-horror what *Birth of a Nation* was to historical melodrama. In his magisterial *Rise of the American Film* (1939), Lewis Jacobs recalls that *Caligari* was 'the most widely discussed film of the time' and quotes a 1921 trade publication that states 'It is a matter of record that no picture, not even *The Birth of a Nation*, ever created quite as much comment, argument and speculation in one month's time as did *The Cabinet of Dr Caligari*.'[23]

Caligari explores the theme of destruction by proxy. An innocent but suggestive youth becomes a killer at the behest of an authority figure, Dr Caligari, who hypnotizes him into committing violence. The writers of the original screenplay, two embittered veterans of the German army, conceived their story as a parable that lays blame for the disastrous war at the feet of the political leaders who had authorized it. Notoriously, the film's producer subverted this radical theme by adding a denouement in which the mad scientist, Caligari, proves to be a benign figure after all; the character who has been narrating the saga of the doctor's nefarious designs turns out to be an inmate in an insane asylum run by the good doctor.[24]

The film thrilled and frightened audiences worldwide. In the United States, where it was released in 1921, critics praised it for its weirdly eccentric set design, dazzling pace of action, and thematic exploration of moral relativity in a world destabilized by violence on command. Blurring the line between sanity and insanity and depicting a writhing, seething, expressionistic universe, the film, as one of its American admirers averred, 'constitutes a valuable offset to the American tendency to oversureness of intellectual values.'[25]

Not all Americans welcomed *Caligari* so enthusiastically. In Hollywood, a crowd of nearly two thousand angry protesters, many of them wounded or disabled members of the local chapter of the American Legion, staged a demonstration against the film, which they termed

'Hun propaganda.'[26] Most probably, they objected on protectionist grounds, for *Caligari* was clearly spearheading a challenge by foreign film-makers to the United States' domination of the international market. Even more galling, the country leading the attack was the recently reviled enemy.

But surely the boycotters were responding as well to the modernist alienation and moral incertitude for which critics back east, such as the anonymous reviewer cited above, had so lavishly praised it. In attacking the film before its West Coast premier, the protesters were taking part in a larger national movement to reject foreign, Jewish, modernist, and relativist points of view.

In boycotting *Caligari*, that is, Hollywood's American Legion members resisted not only this one motion picture and the foreign competition that produced it. They were also, it seems, attempting to protect themselves from a whole ensemble of adversaries, both foreign and domestic, whom they believed threatened the safety and sanctity of American conservative traditions. Although the Red Scare of the late teens had petered out by 1921, xenophobia remained an active force throughout the United States. Americans had long feared an influx of foreign-born anarchists, communists, and labour agitators, but those earlier anxieties, rife since the late nineteenth century, were magnified by the war and the revolutionary uprisings that followed in its wake.

Even the many race riots and racially motivated lynch-mob killings that swept the United States in the early post-war years can, in part, be seen as a cultural by-product of the war. African American war veterans had hoped that their military courage in the American Expeditionary Forces would prove to white Americans that they deserved equality and respect. When this desired change in public perception failed to materialize, many black Americans felt betrayed by leaders, both white and black, who had promised otherwise. Paired with concern on the part of whites about disruption of the racial and economic status quo, such frustrations exploded in interracial violence.

African-American soldiers who had won medals in France for hand-to-hand combat with the enemy were, on their return, mocked in the white press as blood-thirsty thugs innately predisposed towards violence. Some onlookers worried that these black veterans represented a greater threat to civil society now than they had been before leaving for overseas, precisely because they had been trained to kill. Pre-emptive measures, especially in the South, took the form of humiliation, intimidation, and outright pre-emptive violence.[27]

Other aspects of the post-war experience frightened Americans. A deadly influenza epidemic – thought to have been transmitted by infected soldiers returning from abroad – consumed millions of lives. In 1924 the horrifying Leopold and Loeb case centred on a pair of young homosexual Jewish intellectuals who were convicted of murdering a child for the cold-blooded thrill they took in organizing his demise. The following year, the sensational Scopes 'monkey' trial not only subjected traditional biblical values to ridicule but also made it difficult for many Americans to avoid the distressing thought that they and their kind were descended from apes: that they, in fact, were the offspring of the 'mad brute' they had previously been encouraged to destroy. The common term for the post-war decade, the 'Roaring Twenties,' usually evokes its unprecedented social, cultural, and economic dynamism, but, to expand on the metaphor, we might note that some of this roar came as well from the period's many designated 'monsters.'

Monsters on Film

Millions of American soldiers and sailors sustained wounds during the war, but most of them recovered and were able to get on with their lives. Others, however, were less fortunate. Nearly a million (930,000) American veterans of the war applied to the United States government for disability benefits relating to permanent or long-term physical or psychological impairments that compromised their ability to earn a living.[28] Despite the reluctance of mainstream society to pay attention to the wartime disabled and adequately address their pleas and demands for jobs and rehabilitation, the unavoidable presence of these men within the population at large proved an embarrassment to claims of 'normalcy' (a term in wide use at the time) and prosperity. Their plight, largely ignored in official discourse, found symbolic expression in crime and horror melodramas produced in Hollywood. The twenties were the heyday of disability on film, or what disability studies scholar Martin Norden calls 'the cinema of isolation.'[29]

The two most important figures here were the film director Tod Browning, who specialized in movies about 'cripples' and 'freaks,' and the actor Lon Chaney, 'the Man of a Thousand Faces,' who, though able-bodied himself, played a wide assortment of armless, legless, or grotesquely disfigured heroes and villains, including the title characters of *The Hunchback of Notre Dame* (1923) and *The Phantom of the Opera* (1925). Chaney's repellent yet sympathetic monsters amplified, distorted, or embellished versions of the soldiers who had returned with conspicuous disabilities. In exploring the outer reaches of disability and impairment, he gave expression to the problematic emotions raised – or repressed – by the ongoing presence of maimed veterans in the new social order.

After Chaney's unexpected death in 1930, Browning (who subsequently directed the 1932 revenge tale *Freaks*, about a group of physically anomalous sideshow performers) reached the pinnacle of his career with the first horror tale of the sound era, *Dracula* (1931). Silent horror movies, among them *The Cabinet of Dr Caligari*, *The Hunchback of Notre Dame*, and *The Phantom of the Opera*, had certainly spooked audiences, but the addition of sound brought with it a new layer of creepiness, suspense, and outright terror that the earlier films lacked.

Like their silent predecessors, the horror films of the early thirties also connected metaphorically to the war. While today they are usually viewed by historians as either expressions of Depression-era despair or escapist holidays from it, they can equally well be viewed as delayed responses to the First World War. The decadent aristocrat Count Dracula, for example, hails from the Balkans, the very region that had initiated the global conflict that sucked dry the lifeblood of millions. In *Frankenstein* (1931), another deadly monster emerges from the benighted Old World. His creator, Dr Frankenstein, like Dr Caligari of the earlier film and the flawed political leadership *he* was originally intended to represent, embodies rational authority gone mad. In hubristic miscalculation, parallel to that of the arrogant European powers on the eve of the cataclysm, he sets loose a murdering giant, portrayed in this instance by Boris Karloff.

The title character of *The Mummy* (1932), again played by Karloff, is another reanimated corpse, this one swathed in bandages head to toe like the most severely burned victims of trench warfare. The vengeful character depicted in *The Invisible Man* (1933) is also covered in bandages. Once they are removed, it is impossible to see him – a common complaint of severely impaired veterans, who found themselves ignored by society or sequestered from it. In *Dr. Jekyll and Mr. Hyde* (1931), a peaceful, upstanding member of the community gives way to his evil inner self, a monster whom no one, not even the doctor himself, can control. *The White Zombie* (1932) conveys the emotional distress of finding a beloved family member (in this instance, a young wife) transformed into a cold and alien automaton. *King Kong* (1933) animates the 'mad brute' of the war poster and shows what happens when a raging beast with a predilection for white female flesh sets his hairy paws on American soil – all hell breaks loose, and it takes a squadron of First World War–vintage fighter planes to put him back in his place.

Although the literary sources for several of these titles originated in the nineteenth century, the films adapted from them had resonances specific to the times. These movies, we may reasonably surmise, reverberated for viewers as encoded reminders of the recent upheaval that had not yet faded from memory. They gave audio-visual substance to terrors that the war had awakened in Americans a decade and a half earlier and to traumatic memories and emotional dissonances that they had yet to put behind them. This was the first golden age of the horror film. Not until another war – specifically, the Cold War – would monsters parade so prolifically and poetically across cinema screens. (Still reeling from the previous war and its nightmarish conclusion, 1950s Japan contributed mightily to this international revival of monster movies.)

And yet it may be that the Hollywood horror films of the 1930s were not so much the culmination of the post–First World War age of monsters as an indicator that the war and its haunting could finally be laid to rest. By turning the cascading traumas of the war into formulaic allegories of dismemberment and disfiguration, violent death, premature burial, barbarous cruelty, innocence defiled, and murder on command, the monster movies of the early sound era made the unspeakable 'speakable' and normalized the abnormal. They commodified the sublime. Emotions that had been too great to bear or forget – hatred, dread, and grief on a world-historical scale – could now be downsized to the dimensions of mass entertainment. That which had defied representation could now be packaged conveniently within the tidy confines of generic horror.

Count Dracula and Dr Frankenstein were the paradigmatic evil figures of the First World War – one a bloodsucking European aristocrat and the other a mad scientist/misguided idealist who created a deadly giant and set him loose. But the Mummy may have been the true icon of the post-war period: a man disinterred from the past yet alienated from the present, neither dead nor alive, wrapped in layers of protective swaddling, insulated, isolated, and angry, a monster to others, if not also to himself.

Indeed, isolation was a dominant theme of the post-war era, and Americans in general sought insulation from the terrors rampant in the outer world. But as fascism, communism, and diseased capitalism reared their ugly heads and another battle of monsters loomed on the horizon, the citizens of the United States seemed to have little choice but to quake with fear or seek refuge in closed communities, religious zeal, and commercial forms of fantasy, delirium, and delusion.

NOTES

I wish to thank my research assistant Sarah Pirovitz, members of the Wake Forest University Social Science Research Seminar, the editors of this volume, and Jennifer C. Raab for their thoughtful readings and helpful suggestions.

1 *New York Times* figure given in Samantha Power, *'A Problem from Hell'*: *America and the Age of Genocide* (New York: Basic Books, 2002), 9.
2 Theodore Roosevelt, *Fear God and Take Your Own Part* (New York: George H. Doran, 1916), 352.
3 See Peter Paret, Beth Irwin Lewis, and Paul Paret, *Persuasive Images: Posters of War and Revolution from the Hoover Institution Archives* (Princeton, NJ: Princeton University Press, 1992), 26, which calls *Enlist* 'one of the best known American posters of the First World War.' See also Walton H. Rawls, *Wake Up America!* (New York: Abbeville Press, 1988), 81, which states that the artist's rendition was based on a widely circulated news item reporting that the corpse of a drowned mother had washed ashore with her drowned infant locked in her arms. On the 'damsel in distress' theme in First World War poster art, see Pearl James, 'Images of Feminity in American World War I Posters,' in *Picture This: World War I Posters and Visual Culture*, ed. P. James (Lincoln: University of Nebraska Press, 2010), 273–311; and Anne Classen Knutson's richly detailed dissertation 'Beasts, Brawn and Selling a War: American World War I Propaganda Posters 1917–1918' (PhD diss., University of Pittsburgh, 1997).
4 John Canemaker, *Winsor McCay* (New York: Abbeville Press, 1987), 149–56.
5 Even though the monster here is clearly identified as German, the poster also alludes to long-standing white fears of black uprising and recalls the infamous admonition of the European ivory trader Kurtz concerning African natives in Joseph Conrad's 1899 novella *Heart of Darkness*: 'Exterminate all the brutes!' See Conrad, *Heart of Darkness*, ed. Robert Kimbrough (New York: Norton, 1988), 51 – the 'brutes' passage appears in Section II.
6 So disturbing was the imagery of *Destroy This Mad Brute* that Nazi propaganda minister Joseph Goebbels reproduced it in an anti-American poster on the eve of the Second World War, with text asserting, 'When they

assaulted us 25 years ago, they wrote on their rotten slanderous poster: "Destroy this mad brute" — they meant the German people!!!' See Paret, Lewis, and Paret, *Persuasive Images*, 144–5.

7 *Report of the Committee on Alleged German Outrages appointed by His Britannic Majesty's Government and Presided Over by the Right Hon. Viscount Bryce* (London: H.M. Stationery Office, 1915). For Bellows's response to the Bryce report and Goya's influence on his war images, see Jane Myers and Linda Ayres, *George Bellows: The Artist and His Lithographs 1916–1924* (Fort Worth, TX: Amon Carter Museum, 1988), 62–4.

8 See Larry Zuckerman, *Rape of Belgium: The Untold Story of World War I* (New York: New York University Press, 2004).

9 Bryce Report, 10.

10 Bryce Report, 52.

11 Myers and Ayres, *George Bellows*, 131.

12 The cost of legal fees drove the magazine out of business before its case came to trial.

13 On the repression of dissent, see David M. Kennedy, *Over Here: The First World War and American Society* (New York: Oxford University Press, 1980), 75–88.

14 See, for example, Robert W. Service, *The Rhymes of a Red Cross Man* (New York: Barse & Hopkins, 1916).

15 Sir Arbuthnot Lane, Head Surgeon at the Cambridge Military Hospital, quoted in 'Want Public to Aid Disabled Soldiers,' *The New York Times*, 14 June 1918: 6.

16 Artillery First Sergeant Stephen J. Weston, as quoted in Edward A. Gutiérrez, 'Sherman Was Right': *The Experience of AEF Soldiers in the Great War* (PhD dissertation, Ohio State University, 2008), 168–9.

17 As quoted in Gutiérrez, 'Sherman Was Right,' 168 (Private First Class Garnett D. Claman).

18 Gutiérrez, 'Sherman Was Right,' 208 (Colonel Frederic M. Wise).

19 A 'buck leatherneck,' quoted in Dixon Wechter, *When Johnny Comes Marching Home* (Cambridge, MA: Riverside Press, 1944), 320, as found in Kennedy, *Over Here*, 217.

20 Ernest Hemingway, *In Our Time* (1925; New York: Scribner's Sons, 1970), 69, 76.

21 Ernest Hemingway, *A Farewell to Arms* (1929; New York: Scribner's Sons, 1957), 55.

22 Erich Maria Remarque, *All Quiet on the Western Front*, trans. B. Murdoch (1929; London: Vintage, 1996), 186.

23 Lewis Jacobs, *Rise of the American Film: A Critical History* (New York: Har-

court, Brace, 1939), 303; quotation from Willard Huntington Wright in *Photoplay* (Sept. 1921). On Caligari's history and international reception, see Mike Budd, ed., *'The Cabinet of Dr. Caligari': Texts, Contexts, Histories* (New Brunswick, NJ: Rutgers University Press, 1990). On *Caligari*'s metaphoric relationship to the war and political insanity, see Anton Kaes, *Shell Shock Cinema: Weimar Culture and the Wounds of the War* (Princeton, NJ: Princeton University Press, 2009), 45–86, parts of which also appear in 'The Cabinet of Dr. Caligari: Expressionism and Cinema,' in *Masterpieces of Modernist Cinema*, ed. Ted Perry (Bloomington: Indiana University Press, 2006), 41–59.

24 The first detailed account of the film's vexed production history is in Siegfried Kracauer, *From Caligari to Hitler: A Psychological History of the German Film* (Princeton, NJ: Princeton University Press, 1947), 61–76.

25 Unsigned review (March 1921) in *From Quasimodo to Scarlet O'Hara: A National Board of Review Anthology, 1920-1940*, ed. Stanley Hochman (New York: Frederick Ungar, 1982), 13.

26 The *Caligari* incident is described in David K. Skal, *Monster Show: A Cultural History of Horror*, rev. ed. (New York: Faber and Faber, 2001), 37–40. Upton Sinclair recreates it fictionally in the opening chapters of his 1922 novel *They Call Me Carpenter* (Chicago: Paine Book Co., 1922).

27 See Richard Slotkin, 'The Battle of Henry Johnson,' in *Lost Battalions: The Great War and the Crisis of American Nationality* (New York: Holt, 2004), 138–51.

28 Figure for disability benefit claims taken from K. Walter Hickel, 'Medicine, Bureaucracy, and Social Welfare: The Politics of Disability for American Veterans of World War I,' in *The New Disability History: American Perspectives*, ed. Paul K. Longmore and Lauri Umansky (New York: New York University Press, 2001), 238. See Wechter, *When Johnny Comes*, 385, for a lower estimate of permanent disabilities caused by the war.

29 Martin F. Norden, *Cinema of Isolation: A History of Physical Disability in the Movies* (New Brunswick, NJ: Rutgers University Press, 1994).

12 'Ruins: The Ruin of Ruins' –
Photography in the 'Red Zone' and the
Aftermath of the Great War

SIMON BAKER

The period between the conclusion of hostilities on the Western Front in 1918 and the start of the Second World War twenty years later is one within which several cultural trajectories comprising the subjects of this essay overlap: the reconstruction of the built environment in north-eastern France (the devastated areas known as the 'Red Zones'); the development and popularization of modernist and avant-garde photography in Europe; and the development and cultural assimilation of the work of Sigmund Freud, both in avant-garde literary and artistic circles and more widely in popular cultural forms such as 'pulp' fiction. These three very different sets of concerns, it will be argued, coincided and collided in France in the aftermath of the Great War in a very particular way. The character of this relationship will be explored here in relation to a series of photographs of the ruined city of Reims assembled *in* Reims by the architect Pierre Antony-Thouret. The implications of the representation of ruins – in visual (and related literary) forms – extend beyond the practicalities of recording destruction and reconstruction or of accepting the transience of cultural achievements. This raises the possibility of seeing time and memory themselves as in some sense ruined in the wake of such a devastating war.

Lovecraft and the Uncanny

H.P. Lovecraft's 1921 short story 'The Music of Erich Zann' concerns an unnamed, presumably French, city: one like Paris, perhaps, where street names change over time, playing tricks on the memory.[1] Although one of the less outlandish works by an author associated with extreme horror fiction (or 'weird fiction' as it is sometimes called), it is remarkable for the peculiar variant of the uncanny that Lovecraft sets out:

I have examined maps of the city with the greatest care yet have never again found the Rue d'Auseil ... I have delved deeply into all the antiquities of the place, and have personally explored every region, of whatever name, which could possibly answer to the street I knew. But despite all I have done, it remains a humiliating fact that I cannot find the house, the street, or even the locality, where ... I heard the music of Erich Zann. ... That I cannot find the place again is both singular and perplexing; for it was within a half-hour's walk of the university and was distinguished by peculiarities which could hardly have been forgotten by any one who had been there.[2]

The troubled narrator then concludes by admitting that he has, in fact, *'never* met a person who has seen the Rue d'Auseil.'

The impossible complex of geography and memory summarized here is underpinned in the story itself by the fact that the narrative unfolds over a period of weeks, so that the failure to recognize or rediscover the house, road, and neighbourhood where the protagonist lived during this time amplifies the strangeness of the tale. Complicating the Freudian idea of the uncanny as a 'class of the frightening which leads back to what is known of old and long familiar,' the story generates its effect from the fact that it is precisely that which should be most familiar (the home itself) that disappears.[3] This suggests a striking reversal of one of the episodes that Freud himself used to explain the uncanny: he recounts stumbling upon a street of brothels but leaves in such embarrassed haste that he repeatedly finds himself back in precisely the place he sought to escape.[4] But where, in crude psychoanalytic terms, Freud's 'bad luck' might suggest an unfulfilled wish (he doesn't know what he secretly desires), for Lovecraft's protagonist in 'The Music of Erich Zann' misrecognition constitutes a defence mechanism: a shattered mind refusing to return to a site of trauma. What happens in the house (with Erich Zann) both constitutes the central narrative and causes the peculiar loss of orientation that frames it. And as Hal Foster has emphasized (reaffirming the principles outlined by Jean Laplanche), in psychoanalytic terms at least, 'it always takes two traumas to make a trauma.'[5]

To ask what this failure of recognition means, then, is to open up two issues central to Lovecraft's fiction, and indeed to the nascent language of popular psychology with which it was concerned.[6] On the one hand, Lovecraft is an author who deals consistently with things becoming utterly and irrevocably unlike themselves, as in the classic tradition of supernatural horror: vampires, werewolves, Jekyll and Hyde, even

Maupassant's 'Horla.'[7] Lovecraft's protagonists, like latter-day victims of Ovidean metamorphoses, are mutilated, deformed, and consumed, until nothing human of them remains. And yet somehow they continue to exist, long enough, at least, to tell their tales.

On the other hand, and perhaps in this story Lovecraft was more conceptually original and outrageous, there are passages in his work that suggest visions and phenomena beyond human comprehension and outside the laws of nature. This idea is epitomized in terms of physics, for example, by the bizarre 1927 proto-science-fiction story 'The Colour Out of Space,' which presents readers with what the narrator describes as 'just a colour, but not any colour of our earth or heavens.'[8] But this imaginary sense of the unnatural (or perhaps it would be more accurate to say culturally alien) recurs most frequently in architectural terms, as Lovecraft puts it in 'certain *proportions* and *dimensions*' ('The Nameless City,' 1921), or in abandoned ruins, where 'all the rules of matter and perspective seemed upset' ('The Call of Cthulhu,' 1926).[9] Lovecraft talks of spaces at the edge of the world, beneath the earth, buried in deserts or frozen wastes, or on the remotest islands where (*almost* unbelievably) Euclidean laws cease to function.[10] His narrators recoil in horror from ruined sites where scale, proportion, perspective, and geometry are all somehow, indescribably, '*wrong*.'

While for Lovecraft the causes and processes of this absolute ruination and deterioration signal impossible passages of time, they are, nonetheless, drawn specifically into a much more immediate understanding of the psychology of trauma, memory, and recollection.[11] Many of his narrators go out of their way to tell us that they've been damaged by their experiences and aren't sure either what has happened to them, or what is happening to them as they speak: 'My conception of *time*, my ability to distinguish between consecutiveness and simultaneousness, seemed subtly disordered ... The War gave me the strange impression of remembering some of its far off consequences – as if I knew how it was coming out and could look *back* upon it in light of future information. All such quasi-memories were attended with much pain, and a feeling that some artificial psychological barrier was set against them.'[12]

Here, in *The Shadow out of Time*, a story set between 1908 and 1935 (and first published in 1934), it is precisely the Great War (of 1914–18) to which Lovecraft refers, an exceptionally specific historical context for a writer who made few direct references to current affairs. Its protagonist (inevitably, like so many others) also dreams of strange, abandoned architectural sites: immense towers without windows or stairs, monstrous dilapidated constructions with aberrant masonry, and 'countless miles strewn with age-blasted basaltic ruins.'[13]

Dead Houses and Red Zones

It is to the reality of a world in a comparable state, in the aftermath of the Great War (as the First World War was known at the time) that I wish to direct the complex of issues around ruination and recognition introduced so vividly in Lovecraft's work of the same period. Specifically, I wish to turn now to representations of a world rendered completely unrecognizable to its inhabitants and particularly to forms of habitation – to homes (both hometowns and houses) – that had, in every sense, become unfamiliar and 'unhomely.' This was a world blown to pieces, become utterly alien even to those best able to recognize it, a world rendered even stranger in its mediation by the obtuse and jarring conflations of the anatomical and environmental imagery used to describe it. Not only was the other-worldly language of 'moonscapes' used to refer to the most devastated battlefields (almost to the point where it has become a cliché), but in representations, forms, faces and spaces were ruined so utterly as to appear completely beyond either comprehension or repair.[14] Otto Dix's etchings for the phenomenal 1924 series *Der Krieg* (*The War*) together constitute one such example in which bodies and buildings are interchangeably derelict, ruined, and de-formed almost to the point of total abstraction.[15]

But before turning to the reality of wartime ruination, it may be useful to revisit an episode from its prehistory; not an account of the effects of conflict, it is true, but rather an attempt to explore the notion of alienation and recognition in appropriate theoretical terms.[16] In a now classic account of the relationship between ruination and the uncanny, exploring the idea of the 'unhomely house,' Anthony Vidler draws attention to the remarkable drawings of abandoned, shut-up, 'dead' houses made by Victor Hugo in Guernsey in the 1860s.[17] Against a literary backdrop drawn from Poe, Hugo's 'maison visionée,' or 'haunted house,' assumes a peculiar, anthropomorphic aspect: 'One could say,' Vidler quotes Hugo describing frameless windows, 'that the empty holes were two gouged out eyes.'[18] And elsewhere Hugo's account returns to issues of familiarity and recognition, the very issues that Vidler wishes to raise in relation to the Freudian uncanny. In fact, Vidler translates Hugo's term 'inquiétante' (usually rendered as 'disquieting' or 'disturbing') as though the writer had used precisely Freud's term in relation to his 1866 drawing: 'This house is uncanny at mid-day; what is it at midnight? Looking at it one looks at a secret … Sacred horror is in these stones. This shadow inhabiting these walled up rooms is more than a shadow, it is the unknown.'[19]

There is, however, something more than just 'the unknown' here, suggested cumulatively by Hugo's sinister pen and ink drawing and its accompanying text. This house is afflicted, set aside by local rumour and superstition about a long-distant crime; it is not only abandoned and ruined but also shunned. For Vidler, Hugo's house is 'haunted' not by a single event as such but by irrational (over)reactions to something rumoured to have happened in it, or to it. And Hugo completes this misidentification both visually and textually: his haunted house is, in graphic, black-and-white terms, annexed from the world of life, a representation of the terrible, but inevitable, distortions produced by the passage of time. It has ceased to resemble itself and become 'un-homely,' as Vidler observes, returning to Freud's well-known formulation: 'some languages in use today can only render the German expression "an *unheimlich* house" by "a *haunted* house."'[20]

In the aftermath of the Great War, in parts of north-eastern France but particularly the areas of utter devastation known as the 'Red Zones,' it was entirely possible for returning inhabitants to find themselves unable to find a house, street, or even town in which they had lived for years.[21] Arguably one of the most poignant Great War monuments (or perhaps it would be more accurate to say 'anti-monuments') is the ruined village of Craonne, one of a number of so-called heroic villages so utterly destroyed by shelling that it was left to moss-over completely with the new village rebuilt nearby.[22] Present-day visitors to the original site find only wooded parkland with a strangely uneven surface, which on closer inspection turns out to consist of the barely remnant skeletons of absent buildings: mossy foundations that imply the spectral trajectories of what once were walls.

The dramatic material effects of war at home (and *on* homes) epitomized by the absolute destruction of habitation that was visibly evident both during and after the conflict gave rise to a wealth of representational forms: a clear contrast, in many ways, to the absolute restriction of many kinds of images of physical damage to people.[23] There were always 'mutilated' churches even when mutilated bodies were kept hidden.[24] And the analogies between bodies and buildings (often, but not exclusively, sacred ones) offered then, as they still offer now, a most direct means of providing evidence of the horrific effects of military bombardment on civilian life.[25] The descriptive possibilities available within the discourse of destruction and devastation are evident in recent times, too, as when journalists were allowed into Gaza following the lifting of reporting restrictions after a series of sustained Israeli incursions. In a film for the Channel 4 news, broadcast in the United Kingdom on 21 January 2009, the journalist Jonathan Miller described the village of Juhor ad-Dik as having been 'wiped off the map' and compared the 'breathtaking' devastation (which the film crew's cameras 'could not hope' to capture) to the effects of the earthquakes and tsunamis on which he had also reported. Almost inevitably, the report focused for maximum impact on shattered pieces of mosque, just as during the Great War instances of damage to churches and cathedrals, both in language and representation, were employed specifically to support claims of wilful 'barbarism.' In another unpleasant parallel, in 2009 the United Nations drew attention to shelled schools in Gaza to point out that the Israeli army knew precisely where and what they were, just as the citizens of Reims (and France) were appalled in 1914 when their cathedral, a landmark identifiable even at a great distance from the city, was repeatedly shelled, and then firebombed, with the German army later claiming that the building had been put to some (inappropriate) military use (see figure 12.1).[26]

The city of Reims, and its environs, because of the symbolism attached to the cathedral and its position at the edge of the devastated 'Red Zone,' is the subject of some of the most dramatic representations of ruins during, but particularly after, the Great War.[27] There are small-scale examples such as *The Chemins-des-Dames, From Reims to Soissons*, a postcard booklet showing various degrees of destruction along a ridge that was, arguably, the most totally devastated space on the Western Front.[28] The village of Corbeny, for example, is 'represented' (if this is even the right word) by an impossibly mangled landscape of churned soil and debris, which almost entirely fills the picture plane.[29] And there was a broad range of memorial publications about the effects of shelling on the city and its cathedral, often sold specifically to raise money for their reconstruction. In one photograph from one such compilation produced by the 'friends of the cathedral,' *Reims Avant et Après les Bombardements*, the cathedral's postcard shop (in which the book itself would have been sold) is visible in a ruined building on a street corner.[30] Such publications and albums ranged from these small, cheap

12.1 Pierre Antony-Thouret, *Reims au Lendemain de la Guerre* (Paris: Budry, 1927), plate 127: 'The Fire – above, the start of the fire of 19th September 1914, below, about an hour later' (all caption translations are the author's own).

albums of postcards and photographs to well-illustrated books, right up to luxurious loose-leaf folios such as Pierre Antony-Thouret's *Reims au Lendemain de la Guerre*, which contains 127 large-format gravure plates (see figure 12.2).[31]

There were literary contributions too, meditations on the meaning of war and its effects framed as eulogies to the cathedral or the city. Sometimes the cathedral was addressed directly (and anthropomorphically) as 'our lady of Reims,' draped in black like a widow; sometimes it was evoked poetically in human terms.[32] *Nôtre-Dame de Reims* is a 1918 text by a (still-devout) local, Georges Bataille, and is the first work he is known to have published:

> When ... I returned to this city ... I had hoped, despite her wounds, to see in the cathedral once again a reflection of past glories and rejoicing. Now the cathedral was as majestic in her chipped or scorched lace of stone, but with closed doors and shattered bells she had ceased to give life ... And I thought that corpses themselves did not mirror death more than did a shattered church as vastly empty in its magnificence as Notre-Dame de Reims. Truth to tell a skeleton's rictus grimaced from the cracks torn in the formerly living stone, like on a human face.[33]

Bataille's anthropomorphic vision is unsettling, not least because, unlike Hugo's reference to 'dead' houses that actually resembled faces, it is difficult to see how the cathedral could 'grimace,' although the idea of the bones of the building exposed through flesh, what Bataille calls 'living stone,' better evokes religious rhetoric. What is obvious here, though, is the sense in which what is most important is that the iconic building can be identified and recognized for all that it represents (as an embodiment of resurrection), in spite of its material condition. This is the vital kernel of optimism within Bataille's text, which goes on, in rather purple prose, to describe the eventual rebirth of both the building and the French nation (in defence of which the war was fought).

Transience and Aftermath

The openly nationalistic and sentimental nature of the genre of wartime writing in which Bataille's uncharacteristic debut should be situated was not limited to France, however, as another unusual text by a much older contemporary, writing from the other side of the Western Front, makes clear. Freud's short wartime essay 'On Transience,' which offers

12.2 Pierre Antony-Thouret, *Reims*, plate 1: 'The Cathedral rising above ruined houses of the Place du Parvis, October 1918.'

a preview of his better-known *Mourning and Melancholia,* was written late in 1915 for a collection of essays published in Berlin entitled *Das Land Goethes (Goethe's Country).*[34] Freud begins with a summer walk through what he calls a 'smiling countryside' but is actually concerned with the process of dealing with the losses caused by war: 'not only the beauty of the countryside' but 'works of art which it met on its path.'[35] Freud's essay suggests a series of psychological stages in which such losses might result: first comes a shattering of pride and faith in reason; then a libidinous over-investment in 'love of one's country,' accompanied (or tempered) by anger at the perishable nature of what has been lost; then follows mourning and, finally, the potential for reconstruction. 'Once the mourning is over,' he says, 'it will be found that our high opinion of the riches of civilization has lost nothing from our discovery of their fragility.'[36]

This idea of a process (or cycle) of destruction and reconstruction is key to the specific ways in which both the cathedral of Reims, and the city itself, were represented in memorial publications in the years after the conflict. Although not strictly in accord with Freud's model, there is nonetheless a remarkable sense in which both the production of images and their rhetorical uses shift from propagandistic (even libidinous) nationalism *during* the war to more complex contemplative and reflexive forms in its aftermath, a phenomenon particularly evident in the case of the most emotive subjects.

During the war, for example, a statue known as the 'Smile of Reims' came to embody feelings about the value and fragility of the cathedral's cultural capital. It, along with the neighbouring statue of the saint who founded the cathedral, St Niçaise, were related in dramatic and corporeal terms to nationalist discourses on cultural violence (see figure 12.3). In the year 406, Niçaise, the cathedral's first bishop, tried to block the doorway to barbarian invaders and was decapitated (although according to legend the priest nevertheless continued reciting a psalm). The 'Smile of Reims' was also decapitated (and lost a wing and an arm) after an incendiary bomb caused scaffolding around the cathedral to collapse.[37] After the war, the face was painstakingly reconstructed from fragments and this in turn came to symbolize the rebirth of the cathedral, a process celebrated by a 'Smile of Reims' postage stamp as late as 1930.

During the war, then, the symbolic associations of decapitation and barbarism were well established, linking an ancient set of barbarian invaders from the north-east (the Huns) with their modern counter-

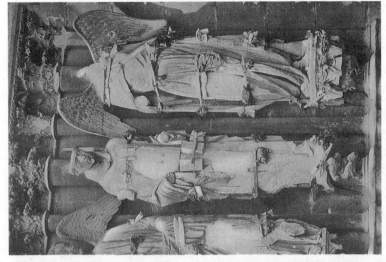

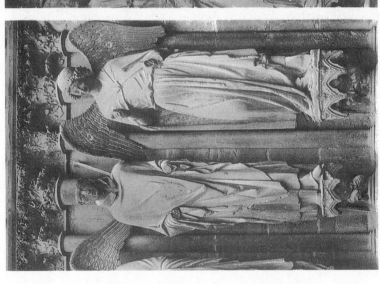

12.3 *Reims Avant et Après les Bombardements* (Reims: Amis de la Cathedrale, 1918): St Nicaise and the Angel called 'The Smile of Reims' – on the left, before the fire; on the right, after the fire.

parts, referred to as 'the hun,' or 'barbares' in French, and frequently depicted visually through the same conflation.[38] And beyond this, the potential propagandistic use value of the two iconic (headless) sculptures is confirmed by an episode described by Monseigneur Maurice Landrieux, the admittedly partisan author of *The Cathedral of Reims: The Story of a German Crime*. According to Landrieux, in 1915 a number of postcards were produced and circulated in which some imaginative post-production techniques, which appear similar to brûlage, had been used to suggest that the two statues had been almost completely destroyed when they were, in fact, still partially intact (see figure 12.4).[39] The actual nature of the damage eventually done (visible on the right-hand image in figure 12.3 from *Reims Avant et Après les Bombardements*) was actually of an altogether different nature and extent. What is more, the way the two statues were presented for comparison in the format of the book – 'before' and 'after' their damage – is typical of many similarly widely circulated representational forms: objects and buildings are shown whole, intact, healthy, and then 'mutilated' (in the emotive language of the time).[40]

Usually, however, the 'before' and 'after' format was used to address more immediate, more prosaic, concerns: with buildings especially, even one-time local landmarks, it was often impossible to determine what the pile of rubble in any particular photograph actually was. And there is a grim repetition of these heaps of debris in post-war tourist guides: chateaus, town halls, and churches all reduced to interchangeable piles of masonry and timber. Reading such a guide, one is confronted with a sobering series of municipal sights followed by captions such as 'now ruined,' 'completely destroyed,' 'disappeared,' and so on.[41] So in the aftermath of the war, and particularly in response to tourism in the battlefield areas, many guidebooks and souvenir publications relied on the 'before' and 'after' format. The intended effect is to account for, and reiterate, facts about the nature and extent of the devastation in a manageable way. But it also deals with the problematic issue of the relationship between the passage of time and the unfolding of traumatic events since the terms 'before' and 'after' presume relative temporal positions, evoking Freud's notion of transience.

The normative nature of these 'before' and 'after' layouts, and their status as a transparently manipulative convention, are underlined by the ways in which those seeking to critique post-war tourism, like the pacifist Ernst Friedrich, sought to lampoon the convention. In *Krieg dem Kriege* (*War on War*), for example, Friedrich deliberately captions pairs of

SPECIMENS OF "FAKED" PICTURE-POSTCARDS CIRCULATED IN 1915. THE STATUES
IN THE UPPER PHOTOGRAPH, PURPORTING TO BE FROM THE CENTRAL PORCH,
ARE ABSOLUTELY INTACT. THOSE IN THE LOWER PHOTOGRAPH, PURPORTING
TO REPRESENT THE CONDITION OF THE LEFT PORCH AFTER THE FIRE,
ARE QUITE WRONG. See Plates 23, 25, 26 (face p. 174)

12.4 Monseigneur Maurice Landrieux, *The Cathedral of Reims: The Story of a
German Crime*, trans. E. Williams (London: Kegan Paul & New York: E.P. Dutton,
1920), plate 95: 'Specimens of "Faked" picture-postcards circulated in 1915.'

photographs showing destroyed buildings 'before use' and 'after use,' emphasizing what he calls the 'destructive work of capitalism,' and elsewhere he describes a destroyed building as 'European Cultural Work.'[42]

Such acerbic responses to the perceived failure of captioning conventions to adequately frame images can also be seen in a broader cultural context, in the image-culture of avant-garde Europe in the 1920s and 30s. What Walter Benjamin characterized as the rising star of the caption (in 'The Work of Art in the Age of Its Technological Reproducibility') is linked, dialectically, to the much-quoted line in which Benjamin cites Brecht's claim that 'a photograph of the Krupp works or the AEG factory reveals next to nothing about these institutions.'[43] With his acerbic re-captioning of images representing the consequence of wartime violence on both bodies and buildings, Friedrich seems to have been influenced in equal parts by this emerging discourse of political image-use and by the visual politics of montage and manipulation exploited to best effect by the German Dadaists.[44]

In Paris, however, the French surrealists also had recourse to critique this same 'before' and 'after' format to suggest 'evidence' of the effects of violence on outward appearances; in a parodic sense, less straightforwardly political than Friedrich's but evidence, nonetheless, of the widespread currency of the rhetorical form. In the radical surrealist magazine *Le Surréalisme au Service de la Révolution*, a photograph of the infamous servants Christine and Lea Papin 'avant' (before they committed the crime of murdering their female employers) was placed immediately above a convincing photomontage of them 'après' (after their arrest), which preserved their relative positions, allowing viewers to read off the sisters' own lack of resemblance both to themselves and one another.[45] Jean-Paul Sartre offers a most sensitive reading of this pair of images in his short story *Erostratus*:

I have seen the photographs of two beautiful girls – those servants who killed and plundered their mistresses. I saw their photos *before* and *after*. *Before*, their faces poised like shy flowers above pique collars. They smelled of hygiene and appetizing honesty. A discreet curling iron had waved their hair exactly alike. And even more reassuring than their curled hair, their collars, and their look of being at the photographer's, was their resemblance as sisters ... *After*, their faces were resplendent as fire. They had the bare necks of prisoners about to be beheaded. Everywhere wrinkles, horrible wrinkles of fear and hatred, folds, holes in the flesh as though a beast with claws had walked over their faces ... Yet they did not resemble one another. Each, in her own way, bore the memory of the common crime.[46]

But the sense of a visible 'common crime' in the aftermath of the Great War was less tangible, harder to represent, and increasingly so as the war receded into the recent past. For the families of servicemen, war graves and official monuments were central to the recognition and realization of the impact of events, but for local French civilians, the stakes were somewhat different. Traumatized by a war of attrition that dragged the front line back and forth over their homes, driven away (in some cases, to live in caves) only to return to places that they couldn't recognize or find, theirs was a very different experience of aftermath. As Freud suggests in 'On Transience,' there may well have been ambivalence here too: confusing or collapsing conflicting feelings of anger at what had been destroyed; frustration at its fragility; and a willingness to begin the work of mourning.

Reims and Soissons in Ruins

Perhaps the most striking images of the aftermath of the Great War were produced by those most familiar with the places that had been destroyed, not always famous names, reporters dispatched from Paris, but local, professional photographers like Pierre Antony-Thouret in Reims and André Vergnol in nearby Soissons.[47] What is remarkable about the way that these men responded to, reimagined, and represented the places they knew best (particular, parochial, provincial spaces that had been subjected to the greatest imaginable upheavals) are the distortions and rhetorical devices that they employed in their work.

Antony-Thouret's publication, which took eight years to complete and is an important record of his practice as both photographer and collector/archivist, traces a path from mourning to reconstruction through the most eloquent and unexpected representational forms: photographs that, in every conceivable sense, surpass the aesthetic requirements of simply recording or documenting their topic. It is in a sense the contradictory, conflicted nature of the images that Antony-Thouret produced and assembled to represent his home city that complicates the usual relationship between familiarity and convention. He does, undeniably, engage with subject matter imbued with a straightforward (even predictable) level of pathos, like the archbishop and a priest staring down from atop a pile of rubble – presumably the collapsed roof – in the ruins of the interior of his own cathedral.[48] There is a mordant romanticism too, common both to those photographs that Antony-Thouret took himself and those that he collected to republish: the 'shock and awe' more readily associated with the paintings of Caspar David Friedrich, evident in a brilliant image of a bomb-blasted cemetery credited to a photographer called Loth.[49]

But even more striking is a frank, pragmatic form of modernism through which Antony-Thouret's creative contributions to the folio, begun immediately after the war but not published until 1926, seems to duplicate (and even predict) the most sophisticated avant-garde photographic practice of the time. The battered cathedral interior, bisected by deep shadow, is reframed according to the modish Bauhaus aesthetic of Làslò Moholy-Nagy, and elsewhere with what the Russian constructivist Alexander Rodchenko would later call a 'worm's-eye view' (see figure 12.5).[50] And we also find the vertiginous perspective and cropping now associated with the Parisian modernism of André Kertész and Germaine Krull in the 1930s. Indeed, the extent to which Antony-Thouret's view onto the town through the cathedral's blown-out rose window seems to pre-empt Kertész's later (and much better known) *Paris Clocktower* (1931) is quite remarkable (see figure 12.6).[51]

Antony-Thouret's responses to the city of Reims and its cathedral are as disorienting and confusing as the ways in which the appearances of these sites had altered: through the process of its transposition into representation the city becomes unlike itself, loses its own familiar resemblance (through photography, that most trustworthy of media) to the point that what is clearly the city of Reims in the twentieth century is impossible to resolve as such. Stranger still, though, are those places where Antony-Thouret undertakes alchemical aesthetic gambits, transforming twentieth-century municipal debris into antique ruins with double exposures and tissue-paper masking (see figures 12.7 and 12.8). At sea in history here, Antony-Thouret uses the technology upon which he relied to record and document, to reflect disbelief, dissociation, and even fantasy. He seems to have become, in a sense, like one of Lovecraft's unhinged protagonists, set loose from the familiarity and safety of his assumptions and preconceptions, adrift in time and space and yet still desperate to describe the terrifying extent of the alienation to which he has recently been subjected.

Nor was Antony-Thouret alone in this response to the architectural residue of war. André Vergnol, whose hometown of Soissons and its surrounding villages had also been completely reduced to rubble in many places, produced equally remarkable photographs, albeit for less luxurious editions. He fills the frame so that his local church seems to rest on a giant scree-slope, transforming the blasted-out, fractured

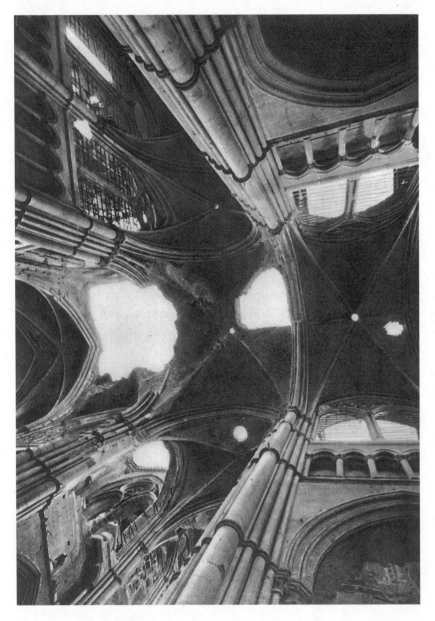

12.5 Pierre Antony-Thouret, *Reims*, plate 40: 'View of the crossing of the transept, January 1919.'

12.6 Pierre Antony-Thouret, *Reims*, plate 49: 'Rose-window of the south transept. View from the destroyed vault – visible below are the ruins of the Episcopal Palace.'

12.7 Pierre Antony-Thouret, *Reims*, plate 85: 'Ruins of houses on the Place Des Marchés at night.'

12.8 Pierre Antony-Thouret, *Reims*, plate 84: 'Ruins of houses on the Place Des Marchés, December 1918.'

building into something afflicted by an impossibly ancient dereliction. Vergnol, however, whose career in the Section Photographique of the French army kept him close to Soissons throughout the conflict, also recorded something remarkable in the aesthetic folklore of the Great War when in 1918 a warm spring led to an outbreak of foliage adorning ruins both ancient and modern with the trappings of a Piranesi fantasy.[52]

Time and Ruination

The partially natural, partially cultural, but entirely unexpected transcendent reach across the ages that we find in the treatment of sites of ruination in the work of Antony-Thouret and Vergnol is also evident at the heart of the poet Benjamin Péret's illustrated essay 'Ruins: the ruin of ruins', which he published in the luxurious surrealist magazine *Minotaure* in 1939.[53] Although there is no overt admission that the topic was intended to relate to the idea of post-war ruination, it is significant that the publication followed the twenty-year anniversary of the end of the Great War, a moment which saw a renewed interest in themes of destruction (and more importantly perhaps) reconstruction.[54]

Péret, however, who describes man as 'a phantom both for himself and the castle that his phantom haunts' and elsewhere as a hermit crab, is concerned not with progress and reconstruction but instead with the conceptual collapsing of human, environmental, and architectural forms, and in particular, those peculiar distortions produced by the ebb and flow of time. 'Ruins,' he says, 'are disowned by those for whom life is nothing more than a ruin, of which nothing remains but the memory of a glob of spittle.'[55] Concerned not only with the derelict traces of medieval history in 'castles whose mosses have consumed their battlements, whose armoured ghosts shake their collapsing rooms' (represented visually in the pages of *Minotaure* by stunning photographs of fragments of Hungarian castles), Péret describes a trans-historical state of conceptual ruination, from the depths of prehistory whose 'caverns are the fossils of the ruins of castles,' to 'revolting Versailles ... opposed to the ruins of the middle ages, like a waterfall to a power station.'[56] But it is the riddle of time in the most expanded sense, the deterioration of conceptual boundaries that collapses or conflates antiquity, modernity, and posterity entirely, that leads Péret to imagine the most spectacular ruins of all:

Perhaps one might find one day, when its memory has disappeared from the minds of men, a gigantic fossil of that unique animal, the Eiffel Tower ... perhaps also the Grange-Batalière will rise up through the Opera, flowing behind the scenes at the entrance lined with watercress, irises and hatching kingfishers. And passing alongside the flowing water, in search of a place to cross, seeing this ruin bristling with thorns and chirping birds, someone will remember that in the past, all this foolishness was for the luxuriously dressed dead, and say: What a beautiful spring, the Opera is blooming as never before![57]

Péret's text concludes with these lines, which offer a meditation on a ruined Paris of the future, as choked and overcome with foliage as the ruined villages and battlefields of the Great War: re-consumed by (and returned to) nature like the 'heroic' village of Craonne. And it is through a poetic, but nonetheless dialectical allusion to the opposition between nature and culture that Péret makes his point, illustrated with great sensitivity in the pages of *Minotaure* by Raoul Ubac, who produced shattered photographic 'fossils' of the very monuments that Péret describes. The notion of the Eiffel Tower as the prehistoric bones of some nineteenth-century organism, which in a sense it was, posits a future from which vantage point human civilization itself (and its delusions of progress) will have ceased to have meaning. This telescoping of time and memory, and its potentially ruinous consequences, brings to mind the conceptual horrors imagined by Lovecraft (impossible architectures and urban spaces). But in a more prosaic sense, Péret's imaginary vision of Paris reflects the way in which in the aftermath of the Great War, and on the eve of another, ruination may have come to seem an ever-present alternative state: a painfully disfigured mirror image in which Europe might recognize itself from time to time.

NOTES

1 For more on the politics of Parisian street name changes, see Maurice Agulhon, *Histoire Vagabonde I, Ethnologie et Politique dans la France Contemporaine* (Paris: Gallimard, 1988).
2 H.P. Lovecraft, 'The Music of Erich Zann,' in *H.P. Lovecraft Omnibus 3: The Haunter of the Dark and Other Tales*, ed. A. Derleth (London: Grafton, 1985), 335–45.

3 Sigmund Freud, 'The Uncanny,' in *Writings on Art and Literature* (Stanford: California University Press, 1997), 195.
4 Ibid., 213.
5 Hal Foster, *The Return of the Real* (Cambridge, MA: MIT Press, 1996), 29. Foster is citing Jean Laplanche, *New Foundations of Psychoanalysis*, trans. David Macey (London: Basil Blackwell, 1989), 88.
6 See H.P. Lovecraft, 'Supernatural Horror in Literature,' in *The H.P. Lovecraft Omnibus 2: Dagon and Other Macabre Tales*, ed. A. Derleth (London: Grafton, 1985), 423–512. See also perhaps the best critical essay on Lovecraft to date, Michel Houellebecq's *H.P. Lovecraft: Against The World, Against Life*, trans. D. Khazeni (London: Weidenfeld & Nicolson, 2006).
7 Guy de Maupassant, 'The Horla,' in *Selected Short Stories*, ed. and trans. R. Colet (London: Penguin, 1971), 313–44.
8 H.P. Lovecraft, 'The Colour Out of Space,' in *H.P. Lovecraft Omnibus 3*, 268.
9 H.P. Lovecraft, 'The Nameless City,' in *The H.P. Lovecraft Omnibus 2*, 130 (author's italics); H.P Lovecraft, 'The Call of Cthulhu,' in *H.P. Lovecraft Omnibus 3*, 95.
10 Elsewhere in the same passage of 'The Call of Cthulhu,' Lovecraft evokes the language of the contemporary art of his time: 'Without knowing what Futurism is like, Johansen [the protagonist] achieved something very close to it when he spoke of the city … the geometry of the dream-place he saw was abnormal, non-Euclidean, and loathesomely redolent of spheres and dimensions apart from ours.' Ibid., 93.
11 Lovecraft also, notably, imagined the dystopian flip side to the surrealist politics of the unconscious, positing dreams in many of his stories as conduits for very real and very dangerous 'outcomes': Lovecraft's dreamers find that they are subject to the visceral (rather than the intellectual/creative) effects of their dreamwork – see, for example, 'The Haunter of the Dark,' in *H.P. Lovecraft Omnibus 3*, 272–301.
12 H.P. Lovecraft, 'The Shadow Out of Time,' in *H.P. Lovecraft Omnibus 3*, 474.
13 Ibid., 523.
14 I refer here to the idea that the pockmarked battlefield landscapes of Belgium and the north of France were described as *resembling* the surface of the moon: the alternative sense of the two environments as inhospitable to human life is perhaps more interesting and opens up a different aspect of the analogy.
15 See particularly plate 22, 'Nocturnal Encounter with a Lunatic,' in which a figure with a blackened, grinning, but otherwise featureless face stands before a ruined townscape of shattered buildings; plate 23, 'Dead Man in the Mud,' in which a dead soldier seems to be absorbed by the ground;

or indeed plates 25, 'The Ruins of Langemark,' and 26, 'Dying Soldier,' in which first a face, and then immediately a village, are shown bomb damaged and cratered. For reproductions of the entire series, as well as critical essays on the subject, see Otto Dix, *'Der Krieg'* (*The War*), ed. Thomas Compère-Morel (Peronne & Milan: Historial de la Grande Guerre / 5 Continents Editions, 2003).

16 For more on the cultural history of ruination, see Michel Makarius, *Ruins*, trans. D. Radzinowicz (Paris: Flammarion, 2004).

17 Anthony Vidler, 'The Architecture of the Uncanny: The Unhomely Houses of the Romantic Sublime,' *Assemblage* 3 (July 1987), 8–10. Hugo's descriptions appear in his *Toilers of the Sea* (1866).

18 Ibid., 8.

19 Ibid., 10. Vidler cites only the original French text 'Les travailleurs de la mer' from Hugo's *Oeuvres complètes Roman III*, and so, presumably, translated the sections himself. I am grateful to Timothy Adès for assistance in exploring the possibilities for the translation of Hugo's text.

20 Ibid., 11.

21 For a full, detailed discussion of the classifications of devastation into blue, yellow, and red 'zones,' see Hugh Clout, *After the Ruins: Restoring the Countryside of Northern France after the Great War* (Exeter: University of Exeter Press, 1996), 19–58 (especially 24–5).

22 See Clout, *After the Ruins*, 287.

23 This essay is a small part of a much larger project concerning the great number and incredible variety of such images, particularly in and around Reims and Soissons.

24 This was true both during the conflict where publications drew upon the propaganda value of the 'barbaric' or 'blasphemous' actions of opposing forces (see, for example, the illustrated French publications *L'Art et Les Artistes* and *La Guerre Documenteé*, from 1914–18); and after the war too, in tourist publications such as the *Illustrated Michelin Guides to the Battlefields*, and more specific publications such as Monseigneur Maurice Landrieux's *The Cathedral of Reims: The Story of a German Crime*, trans. E. Williams (London: Kegan Paul; New York: E.P. Dutton, 1920).

25 In one striking example from a 1915 issue of *L'Art et les Artistes* subtitled *The Vandals in France*, a photograph shows a sculpture of Christ on the cross that had been blown to pieces to the extent that the only things left were the dismembered arms hanging from the crucifix. This image is captioned, significantly, *'un oeuvre Allemande,'* using the French term for a work of art as though it were some deliberate *assemblage,* or assisted ready-made. The propaganda value of such photographs is underlined

by the use that artists made of them, reinforcing their visceral undertones. The French artist Gustav Mossa, for example, specialized in replacing the alleged 'barbarians' in such contexts, producing watercolours in which the tiny German soldiers dance around and celebrate precisely this kind of attack on the body of Christ, which Mossa renders visceral and bloody, hanging dismembered on the cross.

26 See Landrieux, *The Cathedral of Reims*.
27 For comparative material on the area as a whole, see Frédérique Pilleboue et al., *Reconstructions en Picardie après 1918* (Paris: Editions de le Réunion des musées nationaux, 2000).
28 The exceptional status of the Chemin des Dames (literally, Ladies Way, named after a popular and panoramic route) is confirmed by the museum established there as a memorial to the Great War. The 'Caverne du Dragon' marks the network of caves under the Chemin de Dames in which the front line operated below ground at the same time as the conventional open-air battlefield on the ridge above.
29 *Reims à Soissons, Chemin Des Dames* (Reims: Baudet, 1918).
30 *Reims Avant & Après les Bombardements* (Reims: Amis de la Cathedrale, 1918).
31 Pierre Antony-Thouret, *Reims au Lendemain de la Guerre* (Paris: Budry, 1927).
32 See, for example, René Druart, *La Passion de Reims* (Reims: Imprimérie Cooperative, 1919).
33 Georges Bataille, 'Notre-Dame de Reims,' in Denis Hollier, *Against Architecture: The Writings of Georges Bataille*, trans. B. Wing (Cambridge, MA: MIT Press/October Books, 1995), 17.
34 Sigmund Freud, *Writings on Art and Literature*, 'editors notes,' 276.
35 Sigmund Freud, 'On Transience,' in *Writings on Art and Literature*, 176.
36 Ibid., 179.
37 Landrieux, *The Cathedral of Reims*, 174.
38 References to the Germans as 'Huns' (in association with alleged barbaric acts) were especially common. Gustav Mossa (mentioned above), for example, produced work that deliberately conflated imagery of modern German soldiers with previous invading forces including, notably, a crowd of miniature twentieth-century soldiers surrounding an enormous decapitated St Niçaise. See also the chapter by David M. Lubin in this volume.
39 Landrieux, *The Cathedral of Reims*, pl. 95 (brûlage is a post-production technique that involves burning areas of a negative prior to printing, resulting in a mottled, silvery effect).
40 In the folio compiled by Pierre Antony-Thouret, this format is extended

into the post-war period reversing the 'before' and 'after' to encompass ruination and reconstruction. Antony-Thouret's sensitivity to the theme of decapitation is further underlined in an unusual plate in which the photographer produces a joke through a carefully arranged pile of fragments of stone in which a severed crowned head (of a medieval French king) sits atop a stone inscribed with the date 21 January 1793, the date of the execution of Louis XVI during the French Revolution.

41 The Michelin Guides (although not the only examples of the genre) are most easily accessible as result of their continued facsimile reproduction. For a discussion of the philosophical ramifications of this practice, in relation to the practice of battlefield tourism after the Great War, see Simon Baker, 'Promotional Trip to Hell,' in *Jake and Dinos Chapman: Fucking Hell* (London: White Cube, 2008), 6–23.

42 Ernst Friedrich, *Krieg dem Kriege* (*War on War*) (Berlin: Freie Jugend, 1924): See also Karl Kraus's classic essay 'Promotional Trips to Hell,' in *In These Great Times*, ed. H. Zohn (Manchester: Carcanet, 1976), 89–93.

43 For the new, revised translation of this text (with its correct title) see Walter Benjamin, *The Work of Art in the Age of Its Technological Reproducibility and Other Writings*, ed. Michael Jennings et al. (Cambridge, MA: Belknap Press, Harvard, 2008), 19–55: For the Brecht quotation, see Walter Benjamin, 'Little History of Photography,' ibid., 293.

44 For more on Friedrich's place in relation to these rhetorical debates, see John Roberts, 'Photography after the photograph: Event, Archive and the non-symbolic,' *Oxford Art Journal* 32, no. 2 (2009): 1–18.

45 The images appeared originally in the *avant/après* format in *Le Surréalisme au Service de la Révolution* 5 (1933). For more on the repercussions of the case in art, film, and literature, see Rachel Edwards and Keith Reader, *The Papin Sisters* (Oxford: Oxford University Press, 2001).

46 Jean-Paul Sartre, 'Erostratus,' in *Intimacy and other stories*, trans. L. Alexander (London: Peter Nevill Ltd, 1951), 126.

47 Relatively little has been written on Vergnol, although many of his photographs were used at the time, and continue to be used in publications concerning the devastation in Soissons; see for example, Pilleboue et al., *Reconstructions en Picardie*.

48 See Pierre Antony-Thouret, *Reims*, plate 38, 'His Eminence the Cardinal Luçon and Monseigneur Neveu in the ruins.'

49 See, for example, Pierre Antony-Thouret, *Reims*, plate 123: 'The Cemetery in the Avenue de Laon, taken by Loth, 1919.'

50 I am thinking specifically here of Rodchenko's 1928 essay 'The Paths of Modern Photography,' in *Photography in the Modern Era: European Docu-*

ments and Critical Writings, 1913–1940, ed. Christopher Phillips (New York: Aperture Press/MMA, 1989), 256–63.

51 Like Antony-Thouret, Kertész took his photograph *Paris Clocktower* close-up to a focal point in the near ground, in this case the transparent face of a large clock, behind which the city appears below and at a distance. The Kertész work is reproduced in Pierre Borhan, *André Kertész: His Life and Work* (Boston: Bullfinch Press, 1994), 107.

52 It is unfortunate that, for logistical reasons, I have been unable to reproduce examples of Vergnol's work here although it will be the subject of a forthcoming publication. Examples of much of Vergnol's work are kept in the departmental archive of the Aisne region at Laon, with important material also housed at the Société Historique de la Ville de Soissons.

53 Benjamin Perét, 'Ruines: ruines des ruines,' in *Minotaure* (Paris: Albert Skira, 1939) , 12–13.

54 The popular magazine *L'Illustration*, for example, had a special issue on Reims and its cathedral, detailing the rebuilding work and celebrating the history of the city, while the more edgy magazine *Crapouillot* published special issues with alternative Great War themes.

55 All sections of Perét's text here are from my own translation, which will be published in a forthcoming issue of the online journal *Papers of Surrealism.*

56 Perét, 'Ruines.'

57 Ibid. (the Grange Batalière is a subterranean stream that runs beneath the Opéra Garnier in Paris).

Contributors

Simon Baker is the Curator of Photography and International Art at the Tate Modern in London, UK. He has written widely and curated exhibitions on subjects including surrealism, photography and contemporary art. His published works include *Undercover Surrealism: Georges Bataille and Documents* (2006), *Close-up: Proximity and Defamiliarisation in Art, Film and Photography* (2008); *Promotional Trips to Hell, Jake and Dinos Chapman: Fucking Hell* (2009); and 'Up Periscope!' (in *Exposed: Voyeurism, Surveillance and the Camera*, ed. S. Phillips, 2010).

Elena V. Baraban is Assistant Professor of Russian and Slavic Studies at the University of Manitoba. She is an expert on Russian twentieth-century literature and popular culture and is currently working on a SSHRC-funded research project on representations of the Second World War in Soviet and post-Soviet films. Her research is informed by theory of trauma, structuralism, and gender studies. Her publications on representations of war include the articles 'The Fate of a Man by Sergei Bondarchuk and the Soviet Cinema of Trauma' (*Slavic and East European Journal* 2007), 'The Family Circle: Representation of Kinship, Jews, and Prisoners of War in the Stalin-era Films about WWII' (*Ab Imperio* 2009), and 'The Return of Mother Russia: Representation of Women in Soviet Wartime Cinema' (*Aspasia* 2010). Elena Baraban is one of the three founding organizers of the University of Manitoba Research Cluster 'Representations of War.'

James T. Chlup is Assistant Professor of Ancient History in the Department of Classics at the University of Manitoba. His research interests include the Middle and Late Roman Republic, Roman historical narrative, Greek and Roman military manuals, and the Middle East under Rome. He has published articles on a range of ancient historical authors including Thucydides, Livy, and Plutarch. He is currently engaged in two major projects: a study of Marcus Licinius Crassus and the representation of Roman history in the Middle East in Arab nationalist historical discourses. He has travelled widely in the Middle East as part of his research, especially in Jordan, Syria, and Lebanon.

Lilie Chouliaraki is Professor of Media and Communications at the Department of Media and Communications, London School of Economics. She has published extensively on the mediation of suffering and death as a politics of pity, on historical transformations in humanitarian communication from a politics of pity to a politics of irony, and on the rise of technological self-mediation as therapeutic discourse. Her book publications include *Discourse in Late Modernity* (co-authored, 1999); *The Spectatorship of Suffering* (2006); *Self-Mediation* (ed., 2012) and *The Ironic Spectator* (to appear 2012). Her work has appeared in more than twenty articles in peer-reviewed journals, including *Media, Culture and Society, Television and New Media, Communication and Critical/ Cultural Studies, International Journal of Cultural Studies,* and *Discourse and Society.*

Helena Goscilo is Professor and Chair of the Slavic Department at The Ohio State University. Her work focuses primarily on contemporary Russian culture, gender, film, and graphics. Among her twenty-odd written or (co)edited volumes and special journal issues, the most recent include *Preserving Petersburg: History, Memory, Nostalgia* (co-ed. with Stephen M. Norris, 2008), *Cinepaternity: Fathers and Sons in Soviet and Post-Soviet Film* (co-ed. with Yana Hashamova, 2010), *Celebrity and Glamour in Contemporary Russia: Shocking Chic* (co-ed. with Vlad Strukov, 2010). Currently she is completing a volume on women in war (with Yana Hashamova) and a guest issue of *Studies in 20th and 21st Century Literature* on the mirror in Russian culture, as well as working on a collection of articles on cultural representations of Vladimir Putin.

Stephan Jaeger is Associate Professor of German Studies at the University of Manitoba. He has written extensively on the theory of representation in his monographs *Theory of Lyrical Expression* (2001) and *Performative Historiography in the Late-Eighteenth Century* (2011), as well in numerous articles on the narratology of history and on the representation of the Second World War in historiography and documentary film. He employs narratology as well as performative theories to discuss the aesthetic effects of historiographical writing, with a specific emphasis on war and its impact on representation and perspective in the late-eighteenth as well as in the late-twentieth and early-twenty-first centuries. He has also co-edited three books, among them a volume on the semiotics of war in literature, film, and the media (2006), and is one of three founding organizers of the University of Manitoba Research Cluster 'Representations of War.'

Jennifer C. James is Associate Professor of English and the director of the Africana Studies Program at The George Washington University. She is the author of the book *A Freedom Bought with Blood: African-American Literature of War, the Civil War–World War II* (2007), and an essay, 'Eco-melancholia: Slavery, Terror, War, and Black Ecological Imaginings,' in *Environmental Criticism for the 21st Century* (2011). Professor James has also published essays in *MELUS* and *The African American Review*. She is currently working on a project about African Americans and President Andrew Jackson.

David M. Lubin is the Charlotte C. Weber Professor of Art at Wake Forest University. He has published extensively on American art, society, and popular culture. His books include *Act of Portrayal: Eakins, Sargent, James* (1985), *Picturing a Nation: Art and Social Change in Nineteenth-Century America* (1994), *Titanic* (1999), and *Shooting Kennedy: JFK and the Culture of Images* (2003). The last of these titles won the Smithsonian American Art Museum's 2004 Charles Eldredge Prize for distinguished scholarship in American art. David Lubin's current research explores the intersection of art, war, and popular culture in United States history, with an emphasis on the decades surrounding the First World War.

Kate McLoughlin is Lecturer in English Literature at Birkbeck College, University of London. She is the author of *Authoring War: The Literary Representation of War from the* Iliad *to Iraq* (2011) and *Martha Gellhorn: The War Writer in the Field and in the Text* (2007), editor of *The Cambridge Companion to War Writing* (2009), and co-editor of *Tove Jansson Rediscovered* (2007) and *Memory, Mourning, Landscape: Interdisciplinary Essays* (2010). She is also the co-founder of WAR-Net, an international network for scholars working on war representation (http://www.bbk.ac.uk/english/our-research/war-net). Her first poetry collection, *This Is Just To*

Say / Las Meninas, was published by flipped eye in 2011. Her current projects are editing an essay collection on parties in modernist literature and writing her third monograph, on modernist aesthetics and the First World War.

Adam Muller is Associate Professor of English at the University of Manitoba. He specializes in literary theory, analytic philosophy (with special attention to ethics and the philosophy of history), and cultural studies. He is the editor of *Concepts of Culture: Art, Politics, and Society* (2006) and has published articles on diverse topics in *Jeunesse, Topia, New Literary History, Cultural Critique,* and *Textual Studies in Canada.* His current research focuses on the representation of war and atrocity in mass media and modern 'ideas museums.' He holds an adjunct appointment in the University of Manitoba's Arthur V. Mauro Centre for Peace and Justice Studies, and is a Research Associate with the University of Manitoba's Centre for Professional and Applied Ethics and Centre for Defence and Security Studies. He is one of the three founding organizers of the University of Manitoba Research Cluster 'Representations of War.'

Serguei Alex. Oushakine is Associate Professor in the Department of Slavic Languages and Literatures and Associated Faculty in the Department of Anthropology at Princeton University. He is the author of *The Patriotism of Despair: Nation, War, and Loss in Russia* (2009). He also co-edited *In Marx's Shadow: Knowledge, Power, and Intellectuals in Eastern Europe and Russia* (2010, with Costica Bradatan). His articles appear in *Public Culture, American Anthropologists, Cultural Anthropology, The Russian Review,* and other peer-review journals. He has edited three major volumes of essays in Russian, including a collection on trauma, and a collection on masculinity. His current interests include the ethnography of postcolonial discourses in the former Soviet republics.

Brad Prager is Associate Professor in the Department of German and Russian Studies and the Program in Film Studies at the University of Missouri. He is the author of two books: *Aesthetic Vision and German Romanticism: Writing Images* (2007) and *The Cinema of Werner Herzog: Aesthetic Ecstasy and Truth* (2007). He has also co-edited two volumes: *Visualizing the Holocaust: Documents, Aesthetics, Memory* (with David Bathrick and Michael D. Richardson, 2008) and *The Collapse of the Conventional: German Film and Its Politics at the Turn of the New Century* (with

Jaimey Fisher, 2010). He has published numerous articles in refereed journals such as *New German Critique, Forum on Modern Language Studies, Journal of Modern Jewish Studies, Modern Language Review, Journal of Germanic Studies,* and *Film Criticism,* as well as published a number of papers in edited collections.

Jay Murray Winter is the Charles J. Stille Professor of History at Yale University and a Fellow of the Royal Historical Society. He is the author or co-author of fourteen books including *The Great War and the British People* (1985), *The Experience of World War I* (1988), *Sites of Memory, Sites of Mourning: the Great War in European Cultural History* (1995), *Capital cities at war: Paris, London, Berlin: 1914–1919* (2 vols, with Jean-Louis Robert, 1997 and 2007), *Remembering War: The Great War between History and Memory in the Twentieth Century* (2006), and *Dreams of Peace and Freedom: Utopian Moments in the Twentieth Century* (2006). He has edited or co-edited sixteen essay collections, including *The Great War and the Twentieth Century* (with Geoffrey Parker and Mary Habeck, 2000) and *Power, Violence and Mass Death in Premodern and Modern Times* (with Hartmut Lehmann and Joseph Canning, 2003). He has published more than fifty chapters in edited books and more than thirty articles in refereed journals.

Index